Design, Specification and Verification
of Interactive Systems '95

Proceedings of the Eurographics Workshop
in Toulouse, France,
June 7–9, 1995

P. Palanque and
R. Bastide (eds.)

Eurographics

Springer Wien New York

Dr. Philippe Palanque
Dr. Rémi Bastide
LIS/Université Toulouse I
Toulouse Cedex, France

© 1995 Springer-Verlag/Wien

Typesetting: Camera ready by editors and authors

Graphic design: Ecke Bonk

Printed on acid-free and chlorine-free bleached paper

With 153 Figures

ISSN 0946-2767
ISBN-13:978-3-211-82739-0   e-ISBN-13:978-3-7091-9437-9
DOI: 10.1007/978-3-7091-9437-9

Preface

This book is the final outcome of the Eurographics Workshop on Design, Specification and Verification of Interactive Systems, that was held in Bonas, from June 7 to 9, 1995. This workshop was the second of its kind, following the successful first edition in Italy in 1994.

The goal of this ongoing series of meetings is to review the state of the art in the domain of tools, notations and methodologies supporting the design of Interactive Systems. This acknowledges the fact that making systems that are friendlier to the user makes the task ever harder to the designers of such systems, and that much research is still needed to provide the appropriate conceptual and practical tools.

The workshop was located in the Chateau de Bonas, in the distant countryside of Toulouse, France. This location has been selected to preserve the quiet and studious atmosphere that was established in the monastery of Santa Croce at Bocca di Magra for the first edition, and that was much enjoyed by the participants. The conversations initiated during the sessions often lasted till late at night, in the peaceful atmosphere of the Gers landscape.

Twenty-eight high quality papers have been submitted to the conference and seventeen of them were accepted for inclusion in the present book, after a thorough review by an international programme committee. This event brought together thirty-eight participants from North America and most of the European countries, as well as New Zealand. In order to favour discussions in working groups, only ten of the selected paper were presented orally during the workshop.

Each day of the workshop was started by an invited speaker, presenting high-level insights on the conference topics. The present book begins with an abstract of their presentations.

The presented papers were grouped into four broad topics, each one making up a chapter of this book: "User Side Modelling and Co-Modelling", "Requirements for Formal Specifications", "Prototyping, Generation and Evaluation". The remaining papers, not presented for lack of time, are grouped in a separate chapter called "Design and Verification".

A whole day of the workshop was devoted to the discussions in working groups. Four groups were set up: "Role of Verification", "The Challenge of Time", "User and Task Modelling", "Towards a Taxonomy for Interactive Graphics Systems". The results from these groups were presented in a plenary session, and they are summarised at the end of this book.

We would like to express our sincere gratitude to all the people and organisations that helped to make this event possible: Eurographics for their assistance in the organisation process; The Centre d'Etudes de la Navigation Aérienne (CENA) in Toulouse, which was our major sponsor, and also a partner in the organisation; The Université Toulouse I for its financial support and for the welcome lunch offered at the University; the members of the organisation committee, namely Stephane Chatty and Valérie Sengès, for their countless efforts; the programme committee members and external referees (both are listed hereafter) for the quality of their reviews, and the reporters for the working groups for their extra time and effort.

We wish all the best to the forthcoming 3rd Eurographics Workshop on Design, Specification and Verification of Interactive Systems, to be held in Namur, Belgium, in June 1996.

The chairs of DSV-IS'95
Rémi Bastide and Philippe Palanque

Contents

Prototyping, Generation and Evaluation

Design and Verification

Reports from Working Groups

Programme Committee

S.	Bagnara	University of Siena	*(Italy)*
R.	Bastide	LIS - University Toulouse 1	*(France)*
M.	Beaudouin-Lafon	LRI - Université de Paris Sud	*(France)*
J.	Coutaz	LGI-IMAG	*(France)*
D.	Duce	Rutherford Appleton Laboratory	*(U.K.)*
A.	Dix	University of Huddersfield	*(U.K.)*
G.	Faconti	CNUCE - C.N.R.	*(Italy)*
E.	Fiume	University of Toronto	*(Canada)*
J.	Foley	Georgia Tech, Atlanta	*(U.S.A)*
M.	Green	University of Alberta	*(Canada)*
M.	Harrison	University of York	*(U.K.)*
R.J.K.	Jacob	Tufts University	*(U.S.A.)*
P.	Palanque	LIS - University Toulouse 1	*(France)*
F.	Paternò	CNUCE - C.N.R.	*(Italy)*
A.	Sutcliffe	City University London	*(U.K.)*
P.	Sukaviriya	Georgia Tech, Atlanta	*(U.S.A.)*
M.	Tauber	University of Paderborn	*(Germany)*

External Referees

G.	Abowd	Georgia Tech	*(U.S.A.)*
D.	Carr	Univ. of Maryland and NASA	*(U.S.A.)*
S.	Chatty	CENA of Toulouse	*(France)*
M.F.	Costabile	University of Bari	*(Italy)*
D.J.	Duke	University of York	*(U.K.)*
K.	Goldman	Washington University	*(U.S.A.)*
I.	Herman	CWI	*(The Netherlands)*
C.W.	Johnson	University of Glasgow	*(U.K.)*
J.	Landay	Carnegie Mellon Univ	*(U.S.A.)*
B.	Myers	Carnegie Mellon University	*(U.S.A.)*
L.	Nigay	Universiy of Grenoble	*(France)*
D.R.	Olsen	Brigham Young University	*(U.S.A.)*
D.	Salber	University of Grenoble	*(France)*
P.	Szekely	USC/ISI	*(U.S.A.)*
G.	Reynolds	CWI	*(The Netherlands)*
C.	Rouff	NASA Goddard	*(U.S.A.)*
R.	Took	University of York	*(U.K.)*
J.C.	Torres	University of Granada	*(Spain)*
J.	Vanderdonckt	University of Namur	*(Belgium)*
C.	Wiecha	IBM T.J. Watson	*(U.S.A.)*

Interaction, Cognition and Visualization

D. A. Duce[1] and D. J. Duke[2]

[1] Rutherford Appleton Laboratory, Chilton, Didcot, Oxon OX11 0QX, United Kingdom.
[2] University of York, Heslington, York YO1 5DD, United Kingdom

Abstract. The Shorter Oxford English Dictionary defines the word 'visualize' as:

- to form a mental vision, image, picture of;
- to construct a visual image in the mind.

and 'visualization' as:

- the action, fact or power of visualizing: a picture formed by visualizing.

In the Oxford English Dictionary (1990) visualization is "... forming a mental picture of something not visible or present, or of an abstract thing ...".

This paper gives the background to the recent upsurge of interest in scientific visualization and describes some of the work to develop a framework for understanding visualization. Some consideration is given to issues of *truthfulness* in visualization both in the relationship between the data set and the display and the mapping from display to cognition. The paper describes some recent work in rule-based vizualization and the automatic generation of graphical presentations, and concludes with a brief discussion on recent work that may provide a theoretical basis for understanding the effectiveness and veracity of such approaches.

1 Introduction

The present day growth in Visualization in Scientific Computing dates from 1987 when an influential report on the subject was published [25]. This made a number of statements about the situation in the USA, which applied equally elsewhere.

1. The result of applying powerful supercomputers to scientific and engineering problems has been to generate "firehoses" of data with little thought and funding given to how the results can be interpreted.
2. The result of applying powerful computing and experimental equipment is to produce "warehouses" of data that are never looked at.

The report recommended an initiative on "Visualization in Scientific Computing". Although no such initiative ever took place, the result was an upsurge of interest around the world, and, in the USA, teams of 10 to 20 people have been set up in universities, research laboratories and companies for the purpose of advancing visualization.

Visualization of numerical data is not, however, a new activity starting in 1987, as Brian Collins' fascinating paper [9] shows. From the middle of the 17th century until the beginning of the 20th century, some of Europe's greatest scientists including Halley, Watt, Descartes, Lambert and von Humboldt all developed visual representations of numerical data. Tufte's books [36, 37] contain many examples. From the early 1960's such methods of data representation were used in areas such as chemical crystallography, biology and medicine. Hopgood [18] cites some early examples of the use of computer graphics in computation fluid dynamics (1962), terrain mapping (1963) and complex cartography (1964).

In the context of visualising discrete structures, the work of Feynman shows the power of visual representations to draw out the key aspects of complex problem spaces [39]. Recent work by Casner [8] is attempting to derive rules for generating visual representations in less esoteric application domains.

2   What is Visualization?

1637 Rene Descartes [9]

"Imagination or visualization, and in particular the use of diagrams, has a crucial part to play in scientific investigation".

1811 Alexander von Humboldt [9]

"Whatever relates to extent and quantity may be represented by geometrical figures. Statistical projects which speak to the senses without fatiguing the mind, possess the advantage of fixing the attention on a great number of important facts."

1987 McCormick et al. [25]

"Visualization is a method of computing. It transforms the symbolic into the geometric, enabling researchers to *observe* their simulations and computations. Visualization offers a method for seeing the unseen. It enriches the process of scientific discovery and fosters profound and unexpected insights. ... Richard Hamming observed many years ago that 'the purpose of [scientific] computing is insight, not numbers'. ... The goal of visualization is to leverage existing scientific methods by providing new scientific insight through visual methods."

1993 Rogowitz [28]

"Visualization is the process of mapping numerical values into perceptual dimensions."

It is interesting to note that three of these definitions refer explicitly to the role of perception (imagination, the senses, perceptual dimensions) in the use of visualisation. While this may seem obvious, there is as yet no systematic understanding of what constitutes a good visual representation in this respect. Tufte for example describes heuristics for good visual style, and offers some account of why particular examples are good, but can provide no underlying theory that supports sound generalisation from specific instances. Some confidence that such a theory is possible can be gained from work in a different domain, cinematography. There, Barnard and May [23] have shown that heuristics for 'filmic' cuts applied informally by editors over the last century can be justified in terms of a model of cognition, and through this, transferred to problems of human-computer interfaces. Initial steps towards such a theory for visualization are outlined in this paper.

Fred Brooks, in the abstract of his keynote address at the Visualization'93 conference [6] also notes the preeminent role of cognition, and brings in the second topic of this paper, that of veracity or truthfulness:

> Scientific Visualization is not yet a discipline. We have no general theory, much less one tied to the realities of human perception. We have few generalized recipes. At present we have a collection of ad hoc techniques and a collection of fine examples that show the power of computer graphics techniques to illuminate and convey scientific truth. The best of them also show power to compel the imagination and to delight the heart with their beauty. Understanding how to achieve illumination will require systematic exploration of *many different techniques*, and systematic evaluation of rules of thumb.
>
> The right visualization depends upon what question one is asking. I see us supplementing the present techniques, which proclaim *"See what I can see!"*, with visualization systems that program *"Let's see what I can see!"* and even, *"See what you can see in my data"*.
>
> A visualization is an experience, not an image, and modern graphics offers a sort of user-directed dynamic visualization that no medium has ever before offered. What is the potential of this new medium? How do we use it?
>
> A scientific visualization has to be designed, just as a book or paper does. ...
>
> Scientific visualization surpasses all other computer graphics in the pre-eminent obligation for *truthfulness* in what it conveys. Sadly, we have not always disentangled our art from show business, whose primary obligation is to please.

Robertson [27] pursues the idea that an 'observer can build a mental model, the visual attributes of which represent data attributes in a definable manner' and lists four questions that this raises:

1. What mental models most effectively carry various kinds of information?
2. Which definable and recognizable visual attributes of these models are most useful for conveying specific information either independently or in conjunction with other attributes?
3. How can we most effectively induce closer mental models in the mind of an observer?
4. How can we provide guidance on choosing appropriate models and their attributes to a human or automated display designer?

Robertson describes a methodology for choosing data representations (outlined later in this paper). In the discussion section he writes

The scope of interaction contributes the limiting factor in terms of the view generation rate and manipulation of the attribute tables ... The latter requires a better understanding of the perceptual and mental expectations associated with the use of the tools ... Interaction is clearly a key aspect of the interpretation process, just as in the real world, when an observer continually interacts through eye, head, hand and other movements.

In the remainder of this paper we look at the interplay between interaction, cognition and visualization.

3   Frameworks for Visualization

Bergeron [2] in his introduction to a panel session at Visualization '93 argues that the goals of visualization can be divided into three categories *descriptive visualization, analytical visualization* and *exploratory visualization*. Descriptive visualization is used when the phenomenon represented in the data is known, but the user needs to present a clear visual verification of this phenomenon (usually to others). Analytical visualization (directed search) is the process we follow when we know what we are looking for in the data; visualization helps to determine whether it is there. Exploratory visualization (undirected search) is necessary when we do not know what we are looking for; visualization may help us to understand the nature of the data by demonstrating patterns in that data. Bergeron argues that these goals share some subgoals (and, therefore, can share some tasks), but they may also have their own unique characteristics that demand unique facilities.

Springmeyer et al. have reported an experimental study of the process of analysing scientific data [34].

The GRASPARC project (University of Leeds, NAG Ltd and Quintek Ltd) has taken a problem solving point of view and has developed a framework in which existing numerical and visualization tools can be integrated [3]. The project developed a reference model for the mathematical modelling process, described in detail in [40]. The model is described in terms of two parallel structures, the *Investigator's Plane*, which holds the cognitive activities associated with problem solving, and a *Simulation Plane* which holds the states through which a simulation passes to a solution (see figure 1).

In this way, GRASPARC makes a high-level separation between system and user concerns. Its focus however is on the simulation plane which is divided into three layers:

1. the model layer in which the problem is expressed in some idealized form.
2. the continuum layer in which the problem is expressed as a functional specification, for example as a set of differential equations.
3. the discrete layer which contains a discretized formulation of the equations to be solved numerically.

Investigator's Plane

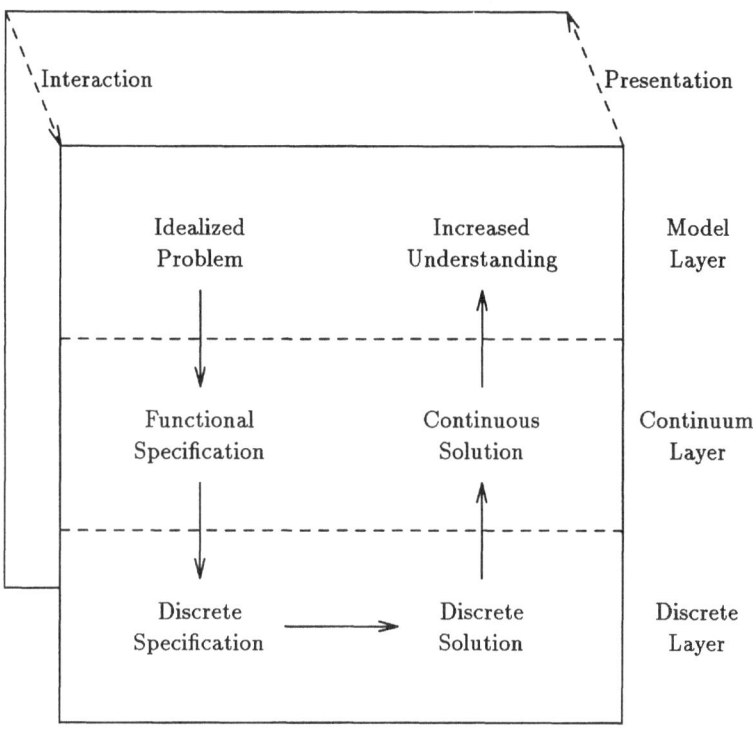

Fig. 1. GRASPARC reference model

Lower layers are invoked as necessary when a solution is not directly available in a higher layer.

There are tools for presentation and interaction between the layers. Presentation tools provide a representation (not necessarily visual) of what is occurring in the simulation plane and interaction tools provide the means for influencing the simulation.

GRASPARC models the search process by which a scientist investigates a problem in the discrete layer by a history tree. The computational process is considered as an ordered set of events in time, where an event might be points at which individual solutions can be output or at which the computation can be interrupted and a parameter changed before restarting. The scientist can manipulate the tree, by creating new branches, storing snapshots along a branch and restarting the computation from a particular snapshot. This approach is proving effective in a number of demonstrator applications [41].

Work by Upson et al [38] and Haber and McNabb [17] has established a model for data visualization that has underpinned many current visualization software systems. The model identifies three major transformations in the visualization process:

1. *Data enrichment*: interpolation of data.
2. *Mapping*: conversion of data into a geometric representation.
3. *Rendering*: assigning visual properties to the geometry (i.e. colour, texture) and creating an image.

In addition, there is often a filtering process before data enrichment to select the data of interest.

This decomposition is the basis of a number of visualization systems now in common usage, for example AVS [38], IRIS Explorer [15], IBM Data Explorer [22], apE [14], and Khoros [26]. They all have visual programming front ends which enable modules to be selected and wired together to form a dataflow network. A natural extension of this approach is to allow application code to be incorporated as a data source module, rather than simply reading data from a file. The term 'application builder' has been coined to describe such systems which accommodate both the computation and visualization.

Such application builders can act as simple problem solving environments but typically offer little or no support for the complex process that a scientist goes through in modelling some phenomenon. There is generally no support for data management and for backtracking in a simulation and restarting from an earlier point with some different parameters.

Brodlie [4] argues that the Upson, Haber and McNabb model can give a false view because it focuses on the data to be visualized. He argues that it is the *underlying field* from which the data have been sampled, rather than the data themselves, that is the real focus of interest. Visualization is about reconstructing the field from the data, and then displaying the field visually. He describes visualization as a two step process:

1. *Modelling*: construction of an empirical model from the data samples. This involves interpolation for exact data, and approximation otherwise.
2. *Viewing*: construction of a particular view from a model. This step will choose a particular technique for displaying the field, for example as a contour map or a surface view.

Brodlie argues that this gives a better separation than the Upson, Haber and McNabb model. The latter can be regarded more as an implementation model to support dataflow systems than a conceptual model to support the scientist or engineer.

Picking up on the remarks of Brooks quoted in section 2 and the structure of the frameworks described above, there are two ideas that come together. The first is the idea of 'truthfulness' between two models: the second is regarding visualization in terms of transformation between different kinds of information.

Barnard and his collaborators have provided a theoretical framework that can support an analysis of the issues involved in the use of advanced graphical interfaces called Interacting Cognitive Subsystems (ICS), described at the first DSV-IS workshop [1]. ICS is described by Barnard as part of a theoretical movement within cognitive psychology that represents the human information processing mechanism as a highly parallel organization with a modular structure; a collection of subsystems which operate on specific mental codes. ICS is comprehensive, encompassing all aspects of perception, cognition and emotion, as well as the control of action and bodily reactions. There are nine subsystems in ICS altogether, but for the present purposes, it is only necessary to mention three of these: visual, object and propositional. The visual subsystem is a sensory subsystem dealing with light, hue and brightness over visual space etc. The object subsystem is an abstract structural description of entities and relationships in the visual space, subjectively our 'visual imagery'. The propositional subsystem is a description of entities and relationships in semantic space, subjectively 'knowing that' for example some relationship exists, or some property holds.

Combining these concepts from Barnard's work with the ideas of truthfulness and transformation leads us to the framework illustrated in figure 2.

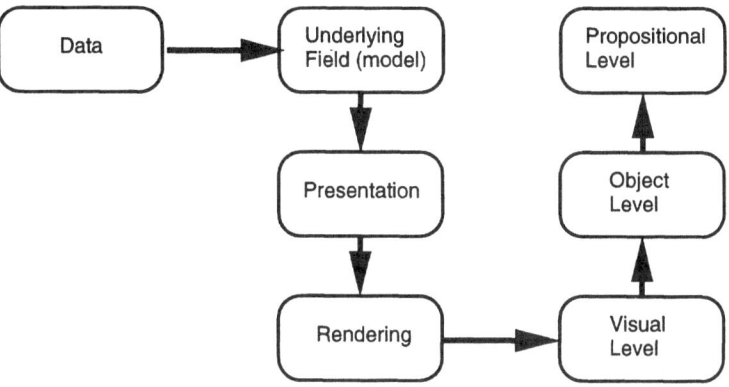

Fig. 2. An alternative reference model.

The point here is that visualization should provide truth-preserving mappings between the underlying field and the propositional level.

The next sections look at some recent work which impinges on the relationship between interaction, cognition and visualization. We will look at issues of truthfulness and effectiveness in visualization and will relate them to this reference model.

4 Modelling

Ken Brodlie in his lecture on Introduction to Advanced Visualization in the AGOCG Visualization Course for postgraduate students in the UK [5] gives the following example.

The table below gives the observed oxygen levels in flue gas, when 5kg of coal undergoes combustion in a furnace.

x (time in mins)	0	2	4	10	28	30	32
y (% of oxygen)	20.8	8.8	4.2	0.5	3.9	6.2	9.6

Figure 3 shows the raw data points plotted on a graph.

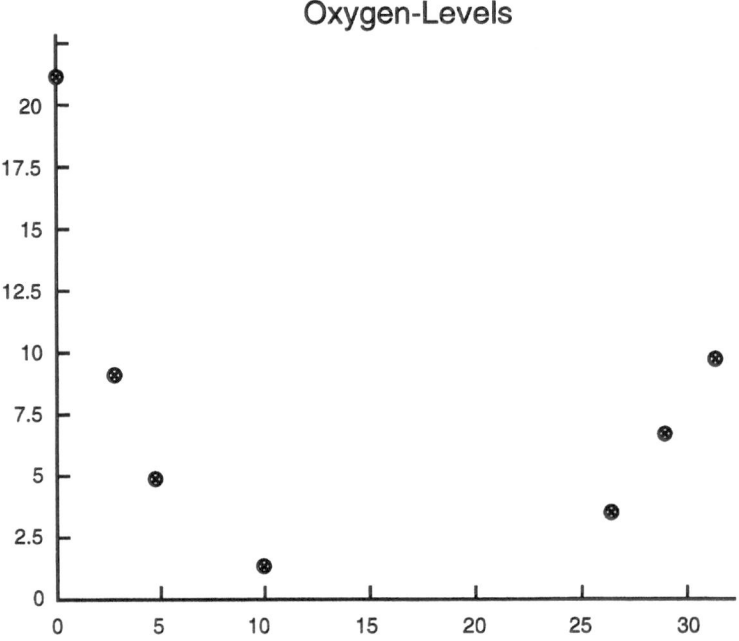

Fig. 3. Plotted data points.

However, the intermediate values are also of interest, so many users would leap for the nearest curve drawing routine and produce something like figure 4.

This may be pretty, but it is not exactly truthful as the oxygen level cannot fall below 0%! The following figure (figure 5) is more faithful and uses an interpolation/ curve drawing method that preserves the positivity of the data.

The point is that the data are samples from some underlying 'field' which we wish to understand. The first step is to create a best estimate of the underlying field, which involves interpolation and it is crucial that this takes into account the known properties (such as positivity) of the data.

This is an example of how numerical processing or data enrichment can lead to misrepresentation. What is important here is to identify the properties of the field and to guarantee that these properties are preserved under interpolation: that is, the model provides a truthful reflection of the underlying field. In terms of the framework in section 2, the issue here is the preservation of truthfulness

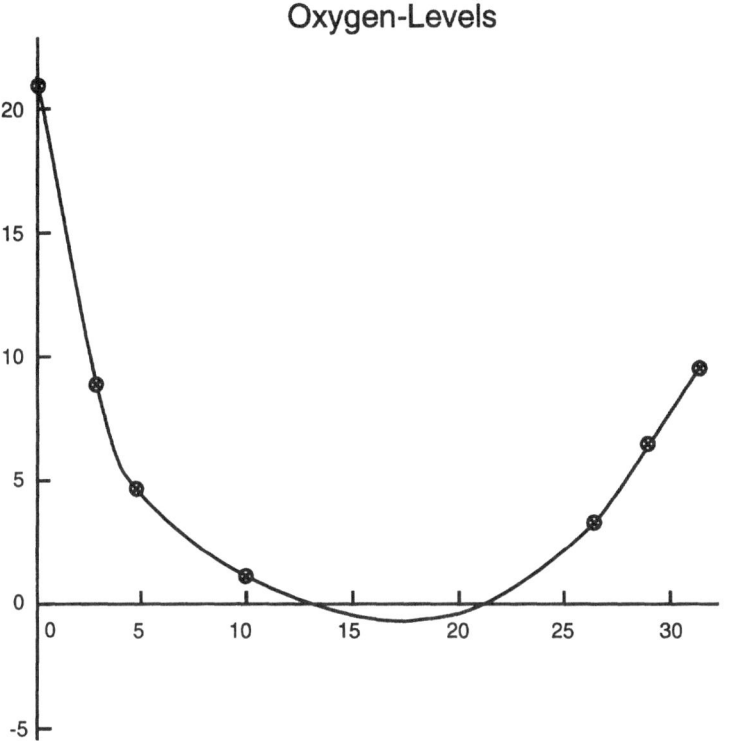

Fig. 4. Points plus curve.

in the extraction of the model of the underlying field from the data.

5 Viewing

At the viewing stage data are converted into a visual representation. The challenge is to develop comprehensive methodologies for choosing and generating display representations. To do so requires a systematic understanding of the tasks in which the representation is to be used, the characteristics of the data field (for example scalar, vector or tensor) and the appropriateness of particular techniques for particular tasks. A number of authors have described systems which automate this stage to some degree and a selection of them is described below.

5.1 Classification Schemes

Brodlie [4] has proposed a notation for describing the underlying field and an initial taxonomy of visualization techniques based on this notation. The latter was a preliminary exercise to show what is possible, this work is more interesting from the point of view of classifying the underlying field.

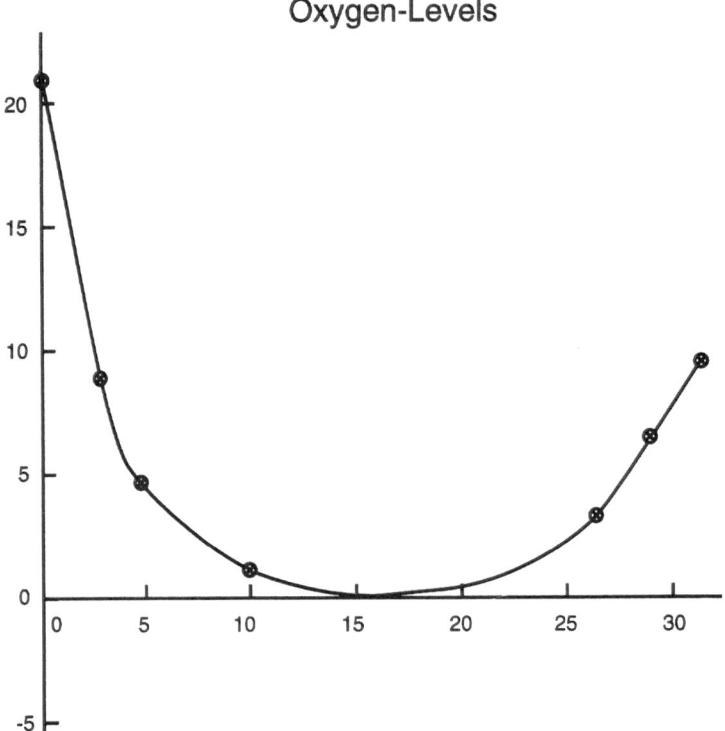

Fig. 5. A more thoughtful approximation.

The field is regarded as a function of many variables and is classified in terms of the dependent and independent variables. The scheme for classifying the dependent variable distinguishes *ordinal* (O) and *nominal* (N) types. An ordinal type has an associated ordering (for example the usual ordering on integers), the values of a nominal type are essentially names and have no associated ordering. The dimension of the dependent variable is also of interest and the common approach of scalar (S), vector (V) and tensor (T) field is followed. A second-order tensor of dimension 6 would be described as $O^{T_{6,6}}$ for example.

The independent variable can also be either ordinal or nominal. The dimension is attached as a suffix.

Following the mathematical notation for a function, $f(x)$, fields are described by the type of the dependent variable followed by the type of the independent variable in parentheses. Height over a 2D region, for example, would be written as $O^S(O_2)$. The notation is extended to classify views and visualization techniques. Visualization techniques are characterized by the field on which they operate and the view which results. A line graph, for example, has field $O^S(O_1)$ and view $O^S(O_1)$. A contourline plot has field $O^S(O_2)$ and view $O^S(O_1)$.

As Brodlie points out, the taxonomy of visualization techniques is a preliminary exercise. It makes no attempt to take into account the effectiveness, in terms of ease of building a mental model, of a particular technique for a particular purpose.

Approaches to classification based on different mathematical insights, for example fibre bundle theory, have appeared in the literature [7, 16, 35].

5.2 Colour

The aim of research in this area is to use knowledge of the rendering to visual level processing in the human observer in order to better understand how to design model to presentation and presentation to rendering transformations.

Many visualization tasks seek to create a faithful, isomorphic representation of the data. In an isomorphic mapping, a two-fold increase in the dynamic range of the data would be perceived as a two-fold increase in the intensity of the visual dimension. However, a two-fold increase in one perceptual dimension (e.g. brightness) may not appear to have the same perceived magnitude as a two-fold increase in another (e.g. height). Many visualization systems have a default colour map which paints the lowest value of a variable in blue and the highest in red, with a linear mapping of the data range onto a numerical red-green-blue representation of hue. The result is a colour scale which does not look like continuous variations in hue, but rather like bands of colour [19].

Levkowitz and Herman [19] discuss commonly used scales such as the linearized grey scale, rainbow scale, heated-object scale and magenta scales and a new linearized optimal colour scale. On one particular comparison concerning a medical image data task (detecting the existence of artificially superimposed lesions in brain slices) they still found that although their observers performed better with the new scale than with the heated object scale, the performance with a linearized grey scale was considerably better.

Margaret Livingstone at the Department of Neurobiology, Harvard Medical School has become a sought-after speaker at graphics and visualization conferences on visualization and perception and the relationship between knowledge of human vision derived from psychology and that derived from anatomical and physiological observations [21, 20].

5.3 Approaches to Methodology and Automation

The work discussed here exploits properties of the visual to object and object to propositional level mappings in order to choose appropriate models and presentations.

Robertson [27] has described a methodology for choosing data representations based on a natural scene paradigm. The idea is that humans are good at glancing at a scene and gaining an immediate appreciation of its 3D surface structure and the state of its covering. Real world surfaces exhibit two parameters over the same 2D spatial field: height and covering structure (e.g. undulating terrain covered by different kinds of forest). The surface covering structure can depend on different secondary parameters, its nature or type of material etc. (e.g. deciduous or conifer forest) and the condition of the material (e.g. overall growth condition). The latter might depend on tertiary parameters each of which can be indicated by aspects of colour and texture (e.g. the number of plants per unit area and the annual growth stage of each plant).

The approach proceeds by

1. characterizing the nature of the data to be displayed and the aim of the observer;
2. characterizing the capability of visual representations to convey information about the attributes of data;
3. choosing an appropriate representation (or set of representations) for the data by matching the interpretation aims to the representation capability.

Robertson's paper treats multiple scalar variables defined over a 2D field, but the methodology is not limited to this case.

Interpretation aims are described in terms of three attributes:

1. values at a point;
2. local distribution of values, such as gradients and features;
3. global distribution of values such as trends and structure.

An analyst looking at chemical reaction data, for example, might be interested in the correlation between (high) point values of one species with (maxima in) the local distribution in another.

Rogowitz, Treinish and colleagues [30, 31, 29] are working on an architecture for visualization that explicitly incorporates guidance based on principles of human perception, cognition and colour theory. The principles are incorporated in rules which the user can select. The rules are used to constrain the way in which data are mapped onto visual dimensions, based on higher level characteristics of the data. The motivation is to help to ensure that structure in the data is faithfuly represented in the image and that perceptual artifacts are not erroneously interpreted as data features.

The higher level characteristics of the data are described by an associated set of attributes, termed *metadata*. At the present state of the work, the set of attributes is open-ended and it is recognized that some attributes may be difficult to determine, for example where a data set is delivered by a computation process. The set of rules is also open-ended, though two types of rules are identified. Class I rules deal with the creation of a visualization which faithfuly represents the structure of the data (for example that equal steps in the magnitude of the data should produce equal changes in perceived magnitude). Another requirement might be to preserve the colour of an object or the size of an object independent of luminance. Class II rules intentionally transform the structure of the data to highlight features in the data to attract attention, scale dimensions to exaggerate details or segment into regions. The architecture also allows rules to be categorized by visualization task.

Rules are applied in the context of particular operations, for example choosing a colour map. The user is free to choose between rule-based and 'free-choice' styles of working. In the latter the user chooses a colour map directly. In the former, the system would suggest possible choices or make an initial selection based on application of the appropriate rule base.

Frits Post and colleagues at Delft University are also exploring the use of metadata to characterize features of potential interest in Computational Fluid Dynamics (CFD) datasets.

Senay and Ignatius [32] describe a knowledge-based system for visualization design, called Vista. Visualization knowledge is classified in five categories:

1. data characteristics;
2. visualization vocabulary;
3. primitive visualization techniques;
4. composition rules;
5. visual perception rules.

Data characteristics classification is based on the now familiar nominal/ ordinal, scalar/ vector/ tensor scheme, with additional attributes including units of measurement, coordinate system, scale etc.

The visualization vocabulary identifies the basic building blocks of visualization techniques. The most primitive building block in their approach is a *mark*, any graphical symbol visible on a display medium that can encode some useful information. Marks may be simple or compound. They recognize four types of simple marks: points, lines, areas and volumes. Compound marks are collections of simple marks that form a single perceptual unit. They identify three types of properties of marks: *positional, temporal* and *retinal*. Data content is encoded by varying these properties. Positional encoding shows the variation of the position of a mark, temporal encoding shows how the properties vary over time and retinal encoding is any variation in a mark that the retina can perceive besides position. Retinal properties include size, texture, orientation, shape and colour coordinates. They further classify marks depending on whether they represent simple or multiple data variables and single or multiple data points.

Primitive visualization techniques encode dependent and independent variables. The Vista system handles a range of visualization techniques in 1D, 2D and 3D, including bar plots, line plots, contour plots, surface diagrams and flow ribbons. The only temporal technique is animation and retinal techniques include texture, shape and colour. Vista's retinal techniques thus cover both the visual and object levels in the reference model of figure 2. One possible danger of conflating these activities in general is that shape and texture play a significant role in human perception of shape, as shown in some of the gestalt phenomena described in [1]. Interaction between colour and texture might lead to the perception of anomolous or emergent structures in the presentation.

Composition rules define the conditions under which visualization techniques can be combined to form composite techniques for displaying multivariate data. The composition techniques include composition by union (requires that marks belonging to each component must be at least partially distinguishable), composition by superimposition and composition by transparency.

The authors point out that 'Existing theories on visual perception offer valuable guidelines for effective visualization, but they are often limited in scope by the inherent complexity of the human visual system. In the absence of in-depth visual perception theories, visualization designers often must resort to heuristic rules developed through experience and experimentation.' Their system includes around 150 rules. Expressiveness rules identify the primitives capable of expressing a particular kind of information. Other rules deal with how to make the expression effective.

5.4 Visualization and Image Understanding

Visualization is primarily based on exploiting the human visual system to construct a mental model from a (static or dynamic) visual presentation. There is growing interest in using computer vision and image processing techniques to support the human in this task. A recent paper by Silver [33] describes a system being developed at Rutgers University to support visualization in computational fluid dynamics (CFD). The idea is to use imaging techniques to extract features of interest from the visualization and then track their evolution.

The use of computer vision techniques can be thought of as complementary to the visual level to object level transformation in ICS, and aims to augment the capabilities of the human analyst to recognize and track features.

5.5 BOZ

Casner has described an interesting system (called BOZ) for automating the design of graphical presentations [8]. He argues that the usefulness of a graphical presentation is a function of the task that the presentation will be used to support and hence graphic design should focus on designing efficient perceptual procedures to be performed by human users. He writes "The enabling step in the task-analytic approach is to capture the notion of a perceptual procedure performed by human users within the context of a graphic presentation using the same formal framework used to describe abstract computational processes, allowing design decisions to follow formal criteria."

BOZ uses five components:

1. A *logical task description language* is used to enumerate the individual problem-solving steps (called logical operators) that are required for a user to complete a task without the benefit of any information presentation.
2. A *perceptual operator substitution* component considers each operator in the logical task description looking for ways to substitute perceptual operators for logical operators, when the operators can be shown to produce the same output given the same input. In general several perceptual operators may qualify as substitutes for one logical operator, giving a set of possible perceptual procedures.

3. A *perceptual data structuring* component looks at the information manipulated by each logical operator and determines how information shared by several logical operators should be collected together to form complex graphical objects. This component determines the optimal grouping of distribution of information; it does not determine how the information is to be perceptually encoded.

4. A *perceptual operator selection* component chooses a single perceptual operator to substitute for a logical operator in a task description. Selection criteria include how efficiently and accurately the operator is likely to be performed by human users and the need to choose a complete set of perceptual operators that result in a set of graphical encodings that is consistent with the perceptual data structuring derived by the perceptual data structuring component.

5. A *rendering* component translates logical facts into graphical facts and displays them according to the design produced by BOZ.

Casner describes his system through an example.

> *Find a pair of connecting flights that travel from Pittsburgh to Mexico City. You are free to choose any intermediate city as long as the layover in that city is no more than 4 hours. Both flights that you choose must be available. The combined cost of the flights cannot exceed $500. Find an available seat on each flight.*

The task is expressed in the task description language. An extract gives a flavour of his approach.

```
(LOP determineDeparture(<flight> <DEPARTURE>)
     (ASK (Departure <flight> <DEPARTURE>)))
(LOP computeLayover(<departure> <arrival> <LAYOVER>
     (- <departure> <arrival> <LAYOVER>))
```

LOP denotes a logical operator. The lists (<flight> <DEPARTURE>) and (<departure> <arrival> <LAYOVER>) are the sets of arguments that the two operators receive as input. The ASK predicate states that a list of facts should be checked to see if the relation that follows can be shown to be true, namely, if there exists a fact expressing the departure time of the flight. The relation (- <departure> <arrival>) specifies that the predefined subtraction predicate is to be computed given the values of <departure> and <arrival> and the variable <LAYOVER> is to be instantiated with the result.

Logical facts describe relational information manipulated by a logical procedure, for example:

```
(destination flight117 hou)
(departure flight117 10.00)
(arrival flight117 12.50)
```

Perceptual operator substitution relies on two components: a *catalogue of perceptual operators* which describe the processing which occurs within the context of a graphic presentation and a *substitution algorithm* which considers each logical operator in a task description and searches for the perceptual operators which compute the same function.

Perceptual operators are organized into equivalence classes that can be shown to compute the same function over relational information. For example, the equivalence class which computes the subtraction relation includes the operators:

determine-horz-distance
determine-vert-distance
determine-height-difference
determine-width-difference

Each perceptual operator has an associated graphical representation object that is used to encode the information manipulated by the perceptual operator. The graphical representation object associated with the determine-height-difference operator, for example, is <rectangle>.

Perceptual operators are defined using the same notation as is used for logical operators. Substitution works by attempting to classify each LOP into the equivalence classes of POPs until either a matching class is found or the set is exhausted. In this example, the computeLayover LOP can be categorized into the subtraction class. One member of this class is determine-horz-distance. Since both operators compute the subtraction function and the arguments of the LOP can be mapped onto the POP, any graphic that represents departure and arrival times as objects positioned along a horizontal axis will allow the user to perform the determine-horz-distance operator and obtain the same answer as that produced by the computeLayover operator. This procedure gives a set of candidate POPs to replace a LOP. The selection of a particular candidate is determined by factors such as estimates of the relative performance, efficiency and accuracy of the perceptual operators (based on theory and experiment as available). The system then designs a graphical presentation around this choice.

In terms of our reference model, Casner's work looks at how relationships in the model can be presented in a way that supports object-level cognitive operations to interpret those relationships. In this way, the model supports the migration of human problem solving effort between the propositional and object levels.

6 Discussion

Visualization is a challenging area of interactive system design. Within the viewing system, two levels can be discerned. The first is concerned with the selection of an appropriate visualization technique for a particular task and data set. The selection of visualization techniques involves characterization of both data and task and matching these to a repertoire of known techniques, or possibly to some new technique. This requires a systematic understanding of the human visual and cognitive systems. In particular, Barnard and May [1] describe how visual presentations can also elicit a deeper response, drawing on latent human knowledge abilities at an implicational level. 'Sharp' shapes, for example, may be a useful tool for conveying 'threatening', 'dangerous' or 'interesting' features of a data field.

Having selected an appropriate visualization technique, there is then a second level of design to realize an effective and truthful visualization of a particular data set using that technique and for the analyst to interact with it in order to build a mental model of the data field. This calls for an understanding of the deployment of cognitive resources in the interaction.

Casner's paper described in section 5.5 hints at the benefits of capturing the perceptual procedure performed by human users within the context of a graphical presentation within the same formal framework as that used to describe abstract computational processes, enabling design decisions to follow formal criteria. Recent work in the Esprit BRA project, Amodeus 2, called syndetic modelling, promises to go much further in this regard [10, 13].

A syndetic model combines a formal expression of system behaviour with an approximate representation of cognitive resources to allow reasoning about the flow and utilization of information within the combined system. The approach has built on work using interactors to present formal models of computer agents [11, 12] and Barnard's Interacting Cognitive Subsystems (ICS) [1] model of human information processing. May, Scott and Barnard [24] have looked at mental representations of displays in the ICS framework. Duke has presented an application of syndetic modelling to reasoning about gestural interaction [10]. Such a framework presents a more general approach than that in Casner's work, and is ripe for application to visualization.

7 Conclusions

This short paper set out to show some of the challenges of visualization and the need for a close coupling between theory and practice in the design of visualization systems, in order to preserve properties in the structure of data sets across the visualization interface.

The systems described in some detail, rule-based visualization and BOZ are attempts at generative design of visualizations. The architectural ideas are interesting, but to be really effective there needs to be a well-developed and tractable theory of users and perception on which to ground them.

Finally, I am grateful to Julian Gallop at RAL for the following quotation.

The ideas are expressed in pictures
the pictures are explained in numbers

Clinging to the numbers
we fail to understand the pictures
clinging to the pictures

we fail to understand the ideas

Having understood the pictures
we can forget the numbers
having understood the ideas
we can forget the pictures

Wang Pi (226-249 A.D.) (*with a small alteration - he used "words" not "numbers"!*)

8 Acknowledgements

The initial idea for this paper came from an unpublished presentation given by the author at a workshop of the Amodeus-2 project, ESPRIT Basic Research Action 7040 funded by the Commission of the European Communities.

Information about the Amodeus-2 project, as well as many of the technical reports produced to date, is available electronically:
http://www.mrc-apu.cam.ac.uk/amodeus/amodeus.html
or
ftp://ftp.mrc-apu.cam.ac.uk/pub/amodeus

References

1. P. J. Barnard and J. May. Interactions with advanced graphical interfaces and the deployment of latent human knowledge. In *Eurographics Workshop on the Design, Specification and Verification of Interactive Systems*. Springer-Verlag, 1995. In press.

2. D. Bergeron. Visualization reference models (panel session position statement). In G. M Nielson and D. Bergeron, editors, *Proceedings of Visualization '93*. IEEE Computer Science Press, 1993.

3. K. Brodlie, L. Brankin, G. Banecki, A. Gay, A. Poon, and H. Wright. GRAS-PARC - a problem solving environment integrating computation and visualization. In G. M Nielson and D. Bergeron, editors, *Proceedings of Visualization '93*. IEEE Computer Science Press, 1993.

4. K. W. Brodlie. Models for scientific visualization. In *Animation and Scientific Visualisation*. British Computer Society, State of the Art Report, 1992.

5. K. W. Brodlie. Introduction to advanced visualization. In *Graphics and Visualization - Techniques and Tools*. Course organized by the Advisory Group on Computer Graphics, University of Leeds, 1993.

6. F. P. Brooks, Jr. A vision for visualization (keynote address). In G. M Nielson and D. Bergeron, editors, *Proceedings of Visualization '93*. IEEE Computer Science Press, 1993.

7. D. M. Butler and M. H. Pendley. A visualisation model based on the mathematics of fibre bundles. *Computers in Physics*, 3:45 – 51, 1989.

8. S. M. Casner. A task-analytic approach to the automated design of graphic presentations. *ACM Transactions on Graphics*, 10(3):111 – 151, 1991.

9. B. M. Collins. Data visualisation - has it all been seen before? In *Animation and Scientific Visualisation*. British Computer Society, State of the Art Report, 1992.

10. D. J. Duke. Reasoning about gestural interaction. *Computer Graphics Forum*, 14(3), 1995.

11. D. J. Duke and M. D. Harrison. Abstract interaction objects. *Computer Graphics Forum*, 12(3):C25 – C36, 1993.

12. D. J. Duke and M. D. Harrison. From formal models to formal methods. In *Proc. Intl. Workshop on Software Engineering and Human-Computer Interaction*. Lecture Notes in Computer Science, Volume 896, Springer-Verlag, 1995.

13. D.J. Duke, P.J. Barnard, D.A. Duce, and J. May. Systematic development of the human interface. In *APSEC'95: Second Asia-Pacific Software Engineering Conference*, 1995. Submitted.

14. D. S. Dyer. A dataflow toolkit for visualization. *IEEE Computer Graphics and Applications*, 10(4):60 – 69, 1990.

15. G. Edwards. Visualization - the second generation. *Image Processing*, 1992.

16. R. B. Haber, B. Lucas, and N. Collins. A data model for scientific visualization with provisions for regular and irregular grids. In *Proceedings of Visualization '91*, pages 298 – 305. IEEE Computer Science Press, 1991.

17. R. B. Haber and D. McNabb. Visualization idioms: A conceptual model for scientific visualisation systems. In Nielson G. M. and B Schriever, editors, *Visualisation in Scientific Computing*. IEEE Comp. Soc. Press, 1990.

18. F. R. A. Hopgood. Pioneering images. In *Graphics, Interaction and Visualization - The Challenge of the 1990's*. British Computer Society, State of the Art Report, 1992.

19. H. Levkowitz and G. T. Herman. Colour scales for image design. *IEEE Computer Graphics and Applications*, 12(1):72 – 80, 1990.

20. M. Livingstone. Art, illusion and the visual system. *Scientific American*, pages 68 – 75, January 1988.

21. M. Livingstone and D. Hubel. Segregation of form, color, movement, and depth: Anatomy, physiology and perception. *Science*, 240:740 – 749, 1988.

22. B. Lucas, G. D. Abram, N. S. Collins, D. A. Epstein, D. L. Gresh, and K. P. McAuliffe. An architecture for a scientific visualization system. In A. E. Kaufman and G. M. Nielson, editors, *Proceedings of Visualization '92*. IEEE Computer Science Press, 1992.

23. J. May and P. J. Barnard. Cinematography and interface design. In *Proceedings of INTERACT '95*, 1995.

24. J. May, S. Scott, and P. Barnard. Structuring displays a psychological guide. In *UM/WP31*. Amodeus project working paper, 1995.

25. B. H. McCormick, T. A. DeFanti, and M. D. Brown. Visualization in scientific computing. *Computer Graphics*, 21(6), 1987.

26. J. Rasure, D. Argior, T. Sauer, and C. Williams. A visual language and software development environment for image processing. *International Journal of Imaging Systems and Technology*, 1991.

27. P. K. Robertson. A methodology for choosing data representations. *IEEE Computer Graphics and Applications*, 11(3):56 – 69, 1991.

28. B. E. Rogowitz. The psychology of visualization (panel session position statement). In G. M Nielson and D. Bergeron, editors, *Proceedings of Visualization '93*. IEEE Computer Science Press, 1993.

29. B. E. Rogowitz, D. T. Ling, and W. A. Kellog. Task dependence, veridicality, and pre-attentive vision: Taking advantage of perceptually-rich computer environ-

ments. In *SPIE Vol. 1666 Human Vision, Visual Processing and Digital Display III*, 1992.

30. B. E. Rogowitz and L. A. Treinish. An architecture for rule-based visualization. In G. M Nielson and D. Bergeron, editors, *Proceedings of Visualization '93*. IEEE Computer Science Press, 1993.

31. B. E. Rogowitz and L. A. Treinish. Data structures and perceptual structures. In *SPIE Vol. 1913 Human Vision, Visual Processing and Digital Display IV*, 1993.

32. H. Senay and E. Ignatius. A knowledge-based system for visualization design. *IEEE Computer Graphics and Applications*, 14(6):36 – 47, 1994.

33. D. Silver. Object-oriented visualization. *IEEE Computer Graphics and Applications*, 15(3):54 – 62, 1994.

34. R. Springmeyer, M. M. Blattner, and N. L. Max. A characterization of the scientific data analysis process. In *Proceedings of Visualization '92*. IEEE Computer Science Press, 1992.

35. L. A. Treinish. Unifying principles of data management for scientific visualization. In *Animation and Scientific Visualisation*. British Computer Society, State of the Art Report, 1992.

36. E. R. Tufte. *The Visual Display of Quantitative Information*. Graphics Press, Cheshire CT, 1983.

37. E. R. Tufte. *Envisioning Information*. Graphics Press, Cheshire CT, ISBN 0-8186-8979-X, 1990.

38. C. Upson. The application visualisation system: A computational environment for scientific visualisation. *IEEE Computer Graphics and Applications*, July 1989.

39. M. Veltman. *Diagrammatica: The Path to Feynman Diagrams*. Volume 4 of Cambridge Lecture Notes in Physics, Cambridge University Press, 1995.

40. H. Wright, S. V. Pennington, and G. A. Banecki. Reference model for problem solving in a visual environment. In *Proceedings of Eurographics Workshop on Scientific Visualization*, 1993.

41. H. Wright, G. A. Stead, and K. W. Brodlie. Interactive exploration of chemical reaction mechanisms using novel visualization and integration techniques. In M. Gobel, H. Muller, and B. Urban, editors, *Proceedings of Visualization '93*. Springer-Verlag, Wien, 1995.

This article was processed using the LaTeX macro package with LLNCS style

Formal Specification Techniques for Interactive Systems

Extended Abstract

Marie-Claude Gaudel

LRI, URA 410 du CNRS
Université de Paris-Sud, Batiment 490
91405 Orsay, France

Abstract. This paper summarises a survey presentation on formal specification techniques and formal development methods. Currently, there is a significant amount of interest in the application of these methods to the specification, design, validation and verification of interactive systems (see for instance [9, 14] and several papers in these proceedings). This leads to the following questions: are general purpose techniques applicable? Is it better to design a specific formal approach for this kind of system?
After a brief survey of the main mature techniques, some examples of techniques specific to some application domains are discussed.

1 Introduction

Research in the area of formal specification techniques and formal development is very active. An exhaustive survey of these techniques would require a big volume. In such a paper it is impossible to describe all of them. Here, we will start by recalling what is a formal specification technique; then we will propose some classifications of these techniques, and we will locate the main "mature" techniques in these classifications and discuss their application domains. By a "mature" technique, we mean that there is a published documentation and there have been significant case studies.

The choice of a formal method must be guided by the kind of property which need to be expressed and proved. This point is briefly discussed. Moreover, the question arises of the design of a specialised method for interactive systems. The paper recall some examples of application domains for which such methods have been developed and discuss them.

2 Some Classifications of Formal Specification Techniques

Formal specification techniques for software are introduced in [8] as: "mathematically-based techniques, often supported by reasoning tools, that can offer a rigorous and effective way to model, design and analyse computer systems." Moreover, a formal development method provides a concept of refinement which makes it possible to pass from a given formal specification to another one which is closer to an implementation and to decide of the correction of such a step.

More precisely, a formal specification technique provides a *notation* for software specification with some *mathematical meaning*: with each specification is associated a mathematical entity. Moreover, there is a *formal deduction system* which makes it possible to perform some symbolic computations or proofs on a specification text. This formal system is consistent with the mathematical semantics, i.e. the properties which can be computed from a specification text are properties of its mathematical meaning.

The mathematical semantics describe the underlying concepts, the deduction system describes the mechanisms which can be used. A technique can be more or less *conceptual* or *deductive*: some techniques put emphasis on the conceptual aspects, for instance Z [23], some others on the deductive aspects, for instance VDM [17] or the specification languages associated with theorem provers such as EVES [7] or PVS [18]. Conceptual techniques turn out to be convenient for requirements analysis and understanding, while deductive techniques provide a better framework for validation and verification.

Another distinction can be made between *constructive* and *property-oriented* specifications: constructive techniques provide a "toolkit" of predefined specification components which can be combined to build a specification; property-oriented techniques provide a way of writing formulas for expressing the required properties. VDM, Z, CCS [20], CSP [15] are instances of constructive specifications; algebraic specification languages (ACT_ONE, LARCH, OBJ, PLUSS) [4, 12] and languages based on temporal logics [10] are examples of property-oriented techniques. It has been noticed that property-oriented techniques are more convenient to describe static aspects, while constructive techniques make the description of dynamic aspects easier; besides, constructive techniques may lead to implementation bias [17] more easily than property-oriented techniques.

Specification techniques can also be classified by the aspects of computing systems that they can describe: algebraic specifications are suited for the specification of abstract data types in an implementation independent way; VDM and Z address the specification of sequential, dynamic, state-based systems; Petri nets and languages based on process algebras make it possible to describe synchronized processes; statecharts are specialised in the description of real-time systems, etc. Several languages and methods provide a way of mixing some techniques, mainly in order to make it possible to address both data types and concurrency: examples are LOTOS [16], RSL [21], extensions of Petri nets [3]. It is necessary to mention that there is no mature formal development method which deals in a convenient way with quantitative aspects (performance, size); the problem is not the formal expression of such aspects (cf. timed Petri nets [6]), but the way they can be propagated and verified during the development.

A formal specification can be *executable*; it might be useful for prototyping, but it might be prejudiciable to abstraction. The execution mechanism is a special case of a formal system. Executability is not a fundamental aspect of formal specifications. In [13], executability is considered as an advandage, the statecharts technique being presented as "sufficiently formal to yield direct implementation". Other authors mention the use of formal specifications as "non executable prototype", i.e. as model of the future system. In [5], where a case study in algebraic specification is presented, it was found that it was better to ignore executability, at least in the first stage of the specification activity.

3 What is the "Best" Formal Specification Techniques?

Independently from the fact it is formal or not, the choice of a specification technique must take into account numerous criteria. Some are related to the context: the characteristics of the system to be developed, the development process followed by the project, the development team background, the client and regulator backgrounds, the availability of experts and tools, etc. Besides, some other criteria are intrinsic, such as the expressive power of the technique, its understandability, the easiness to write and debug specifications, its conciseness or its structuring facilities. All these points are developed and discussed in numerous software engineering textbooks.

However, some additional criteria arise in the case of formal specifications. Some are obvious: the semantic domains of the used formal techniques must correspond to the aspects of the system which must be formally specified; the underlying logics must provide a way to prove the properties which must be verified.

The use of plural expressions in the above sentence is important. It may be the case that several formalisms are required for some systems. It is a normal practice in other areas of engineering for the design of complex devices. The quest for an universal formalism is a frequent tendency in computer science, may be for historical reasons. However, this quest can lead to monsters, and it is probably useful to mention the so-called "Turing pitfall" which is defined in [19] as : "the formalism is easy to understand; everything is expressible; everything is difficult to express"!

An example of the use of different formal specification techniques for a case study is reported and discussed in [2].

Coming back to the choice of some formal specification techniques, the first questions to consider are:

- what must be described? The answer leads to the identification of some adequate semantic domains.

- what must be proved? The answer leads to some characterisation of the relevant logics.

Another more general question is how the formal specification will be used. As it is reported in various reports [8, 22], in practice formal methods are used in different ways. Often, they are used very *informally*, as an expression means, the underlying formal semantics being essential for the clarification of the requirements. In such cases, conceptual methods, as defined in section 1 are sufficient. In some other cases, they are used for certification purposes, and the possibility to perform formal proofs both on the specification and during the development is crucial. In such cases, deductive development methods are necessary.

A quick look at the published litterature on the specification and design of interactive systems shows that almost all the techniques mentioned in this paper have been experimented and used, with a clear emphasis on methods allowing the description on concurrency (which is not surprising). Therefore, it seems that general formal specification techniques are usable for interactive systems. An open question is whether it would be better to develop specialised techniques for this class of system. The answer is not clear. It is interesting to look at other domains where such techniques have been successful. It is the topic of the next section.

4 Specialised Techniques: some examples

Compilers are the most famous example of a class of system for which specialised formal specification techniques exist [1]. It is interesting to analyse the reasons why it has been feasible and successful.

A first point is that there is a general consensus on the way a compiler is organised. There exists a generic structure, roughly the decomposition into a lexical analyser, a syntactical analyser, and a code generator. These components are respectively specified by regular expressions, context-free grammars, and attributed grammars. It is likely that the consensus on the structure comes from the existence and good compatibility of these three formal specification techniques. New languages and new compilers are defined with these notions as bases.

Another point is that compilers deal with languages. There is a theory of formal languages which has led to very solid concepts, namely finite automata, stack automata and then LR parsers and their variants. For these aspects, the semantic domains and the corresponding computation mechanisms are completely delimited and established.

However, it is interesting to notice that the code generation is not actually formally specified: attribute grammars are just a convenient way for *programming* code generators. Generally, there is no formal definition of the actual object code. This part of a compiler description expresses how and when to put pieces of object code together, just as a program express the computation of a value. However, there is a huge amount of knowledge available, since the problem has been studied for more than 40 years. Thus, it is problably the case that a true formal approach is not very important there: people know what to do and how to do it.

Other domains where actual specialised formal specification techniques have been developed are very focused and there exist few publications on them (for instance a specification language for embedded flight command systems in a french company). These domain are very narrow, much more than the class of interactive systems.

Another approach is to specialise an existing method by means of a library dedicated to some application domain: it is well known that an important part of the work of requirement analysis is devoted to the understanding of the environment of the future system and its description. It means that the specifications of applications in the same domain contain a significant portion of very similar descriptions. On this ground, some developments of generic library of formal specification modules have been realised: a successful project for the software systems of a family of oscilloscope within Tektroniks is reported in [11].

Such an approach could be interesting for interactive systems or some subclasses of them.

Acknowledgement

I thank Michel Beaudouin-Lafon for some useful discussions during the preparation of this talk.

References

1. Aho A., Sethi R., Ullmann J., Compilers, Addison-Wesley, 1986.

2. Arnold A., Gaudel M-C., Marre B., An Experiment on the Validation of a Specification by Heterogeneous Formal Means : the Transit Node, March 1995.

3. Palanque Ph., Bastide R., Spécifications Formelles pour l'ingiénirie des interfaces homme-machine, Technique et Science Informatique, vol. 14, n° 4, pp. 473-500, 1995.

4. Bidoit M., Kreowski H.-J., Lescanne P., Orejas F., Sannella D. (editors), Algebraic System Specification and Development: a survey and annotated bibliography, LNCS n° 501, Springer Verlag, 1991.

5. Bidoit M., Gaudel M.-C., Mauboussin A., How to make algebraic specifications more understandable ? An experiment with the PLUSS specification language, Science of Computer Programming, Vol. 12, n°1, June 1989, pp. 1-38.

6. Chretienne P., Timed Petri Nets, Journal of Systems and Software, vol. 6, 1986.

7. Craigen D., Kromodimoeljo S., Meisels I., Pase B & Saaltink M., EVES: an overview, LNCS n° 551, Springer Verlag, 1991, pp. 389-405.

8. Craigen D., Gerhart S., Ralston T., On the use of formal methods in industry -- an authoritative assessment of the efficacy, utility, and applicability of formal methods to systems design and engineering by the analysis of real industrial cases, Report to the US National Institute of Standards and Technology, March 1993.

9. Dix A. J., Formal Methods for Interactive Systems, Computers and People, Academic Press, London, 1991.

10. Emerson E.A., Temporal and Modal Logic, in Handbook of Theoretical Computer Science, vol.B, Van Leeuwen J. editor, Elsevier, 1990.

11. Garlan D. and Delisle, N. "Formal Specifications as Reusable Framework", VDM'90, LNCS n° 428, Springer Verlag, 1990, pp. 150-163.

12. Gaudel M-C., Algebraic Specifications, Chapter 22 of Software Engineer's Reference Book, John McDermid ed., Butterworths, 1991.

13. Harel D., Statecharts : a visual formalism for complex systems, Science of Computer Programming, Vol.8, n°3, June1987, pp. 231-274.

14. Harrison M., Thimbleby H., (editors), Formal Methods in Human-Computer Interaction, Cambridge University Press, 1990.

15. Hoare C.A.R., Communicating Sequential Processes, Prentice Hall International, 1985.

16. ISO, LOTOS, IS-8807, 1989.

17. Jones, C.B. Systematic Software Development using VDM, 2nd edition, Prentice Hall, 1990.

18. Lincoln P. & Rushby J., A Formally Verified Algorithm for Interactive Consistency under a Hybrid Fault Model, IEEE 23th International Symposium on Fault-Tolerant Computing (FTCS), 1993, pp. 402-411.

19. Maibaum T., Taking more of the Soft out of Software Engineering, IEEE International Workshop on Software Specification and Design (IWSSD 93], 1993, pp. 2-7.

20. Milner R., A Calculus of Communicating Systems, LNCS n° 92, Springer Verlag, 1980.

21. Neilsen M., Havelund K., Wagner K. & George C., The RAISE Language, Method and Tools, Formal Aspects of Computing, vol 1, n° 1, 1989, pp. 85-114.

22. Rushby J., Formal Methods and the Certification of Critical Systems, SRI-CSL-93-07 report, Nov. 1993, 308 pages.

23. Spivey J.M., The Z notation : a reference manual, Prentice Hall International, 2nd edition, 1992.

Interacting With Information

Dan R. Olsen Jr.
Computer Science Department
Brigham Young University
olsen@cs.byu.edu

1. Introduction

In a workshop on formal specifications it is important to look carefully at the purpose of those specifications and to challenge some of their assumptions . This is not to discount the value of a formal approach but rather to expand the range of ideas that should be considered. This paper is not so much a report of research as it is an informal challenge to the community and a sketch of a potential direction of research.

1.1. The role of specifications

There are two major functions for a specification. The first is to capture the essence of a design so that human designers and users can agree that it represents the desired system behavior. This is the social aspect of a specification where it is used as a communication vehicle as well as a process discipline in creating good designs. Even formal proofs are merely social mechanisms for persuading ourselves and others that certain desired properties are true about the design. One of the key aspects of such a specification is to model the user interface at a higher or more appropriate level so that it can be more clearly understood that has been designed and/or implemented.

The second purpose for the specification is to form a basis for algorithmic manipulation of the design. A primary goal of many specification models is to support compilation of a specification into a working implementation. Additional algorithmic uses are to provide a basis for automatic analysis of the design and to support additional features such as contextual help or error detection.

1.2. The Abstraction tradeoff

One of the keys to creating higher level models of the user interface problem is the use of abstraction to suppress implementation details. The cost of a design can be measured in terms of the number of decisions that designers must make in creating a design. Such costs include the time required to consider and make decisions, the cost of communicating and justifying those decisions to others and the time required to understand decisions made previously by ones self or others. By abstracting the design problem to a higher level, one can reduce the number of decisions required to create a design of a given complexity.

Frequently, however, the abstraction process implies a loss of control. Decisions made by the system and therefore masked by the specification are no longer under the direct control of the designer. This loss of control, however, is frequently not important. Automobiles with automatic transmissions give the driver less control over the vehicle. The result is slightly worse gas mileage and slightly less power under certain conditions and almost no control over the RPMs of the engine. For a large number of drivers, however, they are interested in where and how fast the car is going and do not care what the engine is actually doing. The car is a tool, not an end in itself. The automatic transmission simplifies the use of this tool for its real goal which is getting from here to there.

The abstraction process, need not automatically produce inefficiencies or degradations into a system. In the early days of computing there were major discussions over the relative efficiencies of programs written in languages like Pascal as oppose to assembly language. In moving to a higher level language programmer lost control over where data was located, what instructions were selected and how registers were allocated. The point, however, that won out is that nobody cares about how well you allocate registers. What they care about is the features of the software, its usability and its reliability. These goals were simplified by higher level languages at the loss of control over irrelevant low level issues. In fact it can be clearly shown that on today's RISC processors with their complex interrelationships between instruction sequencing and memory caching, a good compiler will consistently outperform a programmer on any significant piece of code.

In the early days of user interface design and in the early discussions on User Interface Management Systems, there was a great deal of effort expended on designer control of the sequence of input events. Many systems were designed around the sequencing and control of the event stream. In today's user interfaces very little of the user interface design involves control of events. A majority of this effort is delegated to the widget tool set provided on the host system. User interface designers routinely accept sub-optimal input event performance so as to reuse the dialog fragments built into the underlying tool set. The reason for this is that in most cases functionality and visual presentation have far more to do with usability than careful tuning of the input events.

The point of this discussion is that in searching for specification models for user interface design we must focus on abstractions which mirror what people actually do rather than on how the program must be implemented. Issues such as event dispatching and state transitions are the assembly language of user interfaces. Users never sit down at a workstation with the goal of generating event sequences. The almost always intend create, understand or manipulate some information artifact.

It is our assertion that interaction is about the visual manipulation of information. Frequently that information is an abstract representation of a process or other design artifact but vast majority of the interface is about information. Based on this assumption our specifications, abstractions and models must be designed with the goal of facilitating information manipulation.

2. Two hurdles restricting UI development

Before proceeding with our model of how information-based interfaces can be designed, we first need to consider two difficulties that face anyone attempting to build a computer-based information solution. The first is the challenge of creating an abstract model of the problem and the second is the closed world assumption of most user interface solutions.

2.1. Creating of abstract models

Many programmers spend large parts of their day working with a particular workstation and its systems and tools. Despite their skills and their desire, most of the routine work that they do is rarely automated, even though they know how. A primary reason for this is an underlying assumption of most computer science. This assumption is that for every problem which has a computable solution an abstract model of that problem must first be constructed. In fact object-oriented design is geared exclusively to the creation of such abstract models of the world. The step from recognizing an automatable process in the everyday routine of a job, to the creation of a computable model for that process is a formidable one which even programmers rarely cross. One of the major challenges is that all possible contingencies must be considered in the design because any contingency not considered will cause major problems later. If facing this problem is formidable for programmers it is impossible for the rest of the world.

2.2. Closed world assumption

A second problem is that almost all user interfaces define a fixed model for information which cannot be extended or varied. Almost every property sheet, dialog box or data model schema has exactly N fields which the user can manipulate, no more and no less. Unfortunately the world in which we live is not clean nor as crisply defined. One of the problems is that our focus on formal models, languages and processes has lead to solutions which are far more rigid and inflexible than the world in which we live. When measured on the scale of the real world rather than the software world, even C++ is a very formal system.

3. An approach to UI Development

The work in our lab is focused on two basic concepts. The first is a somewhat different view of bottom-up software engineering and the second is a process of specialization from general tools.

As knowledge workers we live in a world of information artifacts which arrive and leave in various forms. When those artifacts and the processes that they are part of become routine and repetitive, we create a system for handling them which will expedite their use. When such repetitive processes are general enough to warrant the work, someone will program a system which alleviates the tedium and controls the mistakes. Unfortunately our tools and methods for software design do not flow up naturally from these routine artifacts. Instead they flow down from abstract models. One of our research goals is to reverse this so that repetitive information artifacts and processes can be readily converted into computer-based solutions without the burden of first creating an all encompassing abstract model.

The most popular tools for workstations are general tools which can handle broad categories of information artifacts. Virtually every workstation has a word processor and some drawing package. A large number of workstations also have a spreadsheet and some mail package. These applications are popular because of the huge range of information problems to which they can be applied. Our approach is to create new applications by specializing such general applications to a particular task rather than creating such an application out of whole cloth. To illustrate our approach, some examples are in order.

4.   Examples

4.1.   Simple forms
On my desk is a registration form for the Interact '95 conference. In a very real way this is a user interface to the conference's information system. This form was created using a very simple process of outlining the information they would need and enumerating any choices for which there are a small number of possibilities. Having done this, someone with visual design skills put a pretty face on the whole thing. This whole task was probably accomplished in some drawing or layout tool which is easily learned by any office worker. Having used such a general tool, this form now becomes a very restricted and specialized interface to Interact's registration process. Unfortunately the general tool used to created this form probably does not support specializing and restricting this particular form so that only the appropriate parts of the form can be changed or edited.

Of particular interest on this Interact registration form is a sticky note attached to the front which says "Check mailed on May 5, 95". This sticky note is part of a completely different information process from the one that Interact designed. This process involves myself, my secretary and the university travel office. This too is a routine process which could and should be automated. It is not automated, however, because it must embed in it the information processes of all of the conferences and meetings that I or any other faculty member might want to attend. If either our office travel process or the Interact registration process is computerized, their closed world assumptions would prevent them from interoperating with the other system.

4.2.   Computing forms
Our university research office publishes a budget form which must be used for all research proposals sent out from the university. Since I use this form a lot and it has some computation that I regularly get wrong, I have implemented the form as a spreadsheet. The process took about an hour and the resulting output looks enough like the original form that the research office is willing to accept it. This spreadsheet has been distributed to many of my faculty colleagues who also must work with the research office. By using a very general application such as a

spreadsheet a very specialized application is quickly created. Unfortunately the development process stops here. This spreadsheet is now a very specialized application in it own right but it cannot be distributed as such. Over 95% of the functionality of Excel is unneeded for this application but it cannot be removed. The general tool is quite effective but the specialization facility is not available.

This form is also a good illustration of our process for creating such specializations. Having created this budget spreadsheet I can fill it out for a particular proposal, print it and submit it to the research office. (I completely despair of them taking the electronic form via e-mail.) The next time I need to submit a proposal I retrieve this spreadsheet, modify the various numbers and fields to create a new proposal. At this point I have two example artifacts of a general process. It is then algorithmically possible to compare these two artifacts to determine what aspects are constant and which are variable. The constant portions become my new "application" and the variable portions become the information that drives this new application. By a compilation process using the semantics of the general tool and these two artifacts, a new special purpose application is easily created. This new application is derived directly from actual practice.

4.3.   The Closed World Assumption

Our travel office also has a form which I have implemented as a spreadsheet. This form calculates lodging and meal costs given the number of days that I will be gone. It is quite a simple application and I am the only user. However, when this particular spreadsheet was saved from the last time that I used it, at the top of the sheet is a note in a blank cell which says "Call Yasmine with travel number at x8-2342". This, like the sticky note on the Interact form, is part of a separate process that exists outside of this form involving my secretary and myself. Also in the field for the account number it reads "use my 6-xxxxx account". This is obviously not a valid account number. (My secretary keeps track of my account numbers). Because this travel application is embedded in a more general spreadsheet model, these notes and imprecise information are all possible. Such possibilities makes the whole system more usable to me as an information worker. Embedding such an application in the general spreadsheet model prevents creating a closed world.

4.4.   Picture models for applications

Spreadsheets and forms are not the only basis from which specialized applications can be built. Figure 1 shows a picture of a genealogical application. This application has been specialized from a general drawing editor which supports graphical constraints. This application supports many more affordances than the forms based applications normally used in genealogy. It is relatively simple, for example, to rearrange family structures using this drawing metaphor by simply drawing the lines between different people. The same specialization operations can be applied to such picture editors as were used with spreadsheets, thus creating a very different class of applications.

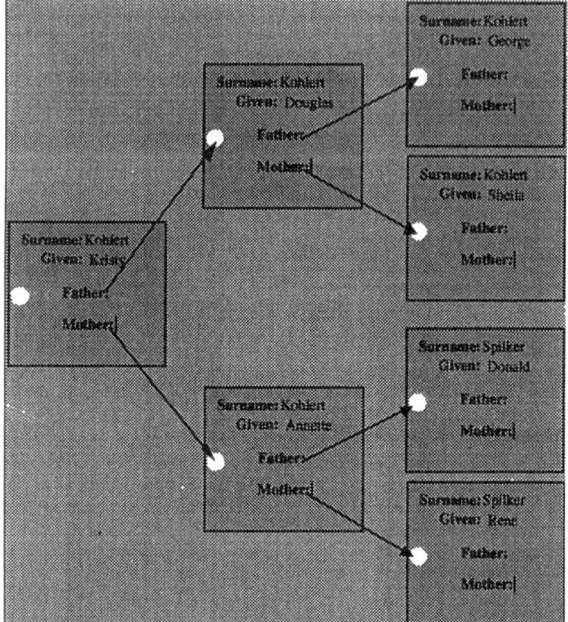

Figure 1.

Just as the spreadsheet has a language for expressing relationships between cells which create the application semantics. The picture editor, also has a language of relationships. Instead of rows and columns these relationships are geometric. Examples are shown in Figure 2.

```
Father ( !O ) =
        !L = Contains(!O,text,"Father:")
        !C = RightOf(!L,circle)
        !F = ConnectedTo(!C,arrow)
        return !F
Mother ( !O ) =
        !L = Contains(!O,text,"Mother:")
        !C = RightOf(!L,circle)
        !F = ConnectedTo(!C,arrow)
        return !F
```

Figure 2.

5.   Research Potential

There are a variety of issues which this user interface design approach presents. The first is the application of compiler optimization technology to the specialized applications. When the budget form is specialized, large portions of the spreadsheet become fixed. The constant folding optimization can precompute any function at compile time whose arguments are all constants. This produces a new constant which can then propagate to other functions which use it. This means that large amounts of line art, text and font information can be precompiled into a more compact form. Even the spreadsheet formulas can thus be optimized. Using dead code elimination, large numbers of functions and other code required for general spreadsheets can be discarded, thus producing a very small economical application.

Information applications which can be distributed across the World Wide Web are of great interest. Assuming the existence of general tools such as spreadsheets as viewers, these specialized applications can be sent in their original uncompiled form. Such applications also have well known semantics which can alleviate many of the security concerns in WWW-distributed code.

The process of generating specializations from artifacts is a challenge. Simple difference comparisons are one form of generalization from examples. These will not work, however, in the presence of variable amounts of information such as lists or sets. Detection of inductive relationships is a possibility. As was shown in the travel application, over specialization may reintroduce the closed world assumption and eliminate desired features from the general tool. Techniques for "unspecializing" applications created in this way are required.

The question of interoperation between applications is an important one. If the Interact registration form and our office travel procedures were both developed in the same general tool, can the fact that these special applications are embedded in a more general information model allow them to interoperate more effectively.

It is important to note that although general tools such as spreadsheets and drawing tools were used as examples from which specialized applications are built. They themselves are not sufficient. Most such tools do not have the specialization technology required to make them truely effective for this purpose. Most of them support data models which are not sufficiently rich for a broad class of applications. These examples only serve as demonstrated starting points for tools yet to be created.

6.   Summary

The point of all of this is that user interface specifications must be able to work upwards from actual practice rather than only downwards from abstract models. Abstract models are still a helpful and useful tool for design but they must not be the only tool. The second point is that interface design can be fruitfully embedded in a general model of information manipulation from which specific applications can be derived.

The approach described above meets many of the requirements specified for good specification models. By working up from actual practice it is very clear to users what is being accomplished. There is a deficiency in this regard, however, in that it is not always clear from a set of examples what the shape of the resulting set of solutions really is. Because this approach embeds design in the known semantics of a general tool many algorithmic manipulations of the design are possible. Also by embedding the design in the context of the general tool all of the low level details of how to process events and perform display updates are encapsulated in the design of the general tool and then reused in its specialization. This vastly reduces the number of detailed decisions that designers must consider.

A User Interface Evaluation Mapping Physical User Actions to Task-Driven Formal Specifications

Fabio Paterno'[1], Maria Sabrina Sciacchitano[1], Jonas Lowgren[2]

[1] CNUCE - CNR - Pisa - Italy

[2] Dept of Computer and Information Science - Linköping University - Sweden

Abstract. This paper describes the first results of a work which aims to join two different levels in order to evaluate user interfaces. The two levels are task specification and user physical actions. To achieve this goal we pass through an intermediate level: the formal specification of the system considered. The approach entails building an interactor-based LOTOS formal specification of the system starting from task specification. Then a tool, which we have developed, gathers information from both low and high abstraction levels and evaluates the user interactions. The behaviour and results of this tool are shown. We also present how the tool has been applied to Map, a real application used for presenting maps.

Keywords: User Physical Actions, Formal Specification, Tasks Analysis, User Interface Evaluation.

1 Introduction

The usability of user interfaces can be evaluated in several ways. There are methods involving users (*experimental techniques*), and methods applicable during the design phase (*predictive methods*). The former deal with real data observed from real users accomplishing real tasks. The latter are theory-based (such as GOMS or CCT [10]), and rely on abstract models, which are often based on an explicit hierarchical decomposition of user tasks.

Here we present a proposal aimed at linking these two types of methods. Our purpose is to analyze logs of actual interactions between the user and the system. Such logs typically contain records of all the user's physical actions. However, the actions cannot be interpreted in a context-free way. They need to be related to the tasks that the user performs (or intends to perform). Our work represents an exploration of a possible way to realize this relation. We use a formal approach, which provides a number of additional benefits (precise specifications, ability to prove certain properties, etc).

In order to link user actions and tasks together, we use an intermediate level, the user interface formal specification level. To achieve our goal, we are building a tool which takes information about the user tasks, the architecture of the user interface system and logs of user actions, then evaluates the information and returns comments on the design of the user interface. We preferred to use a formal specification language because it provides a well-defined semantic which gives an unambiguous description of user interface functionalities and better reasoning about the system being tested. We chose LOTOS [1] as a precise notation because it allows operators to define temporal ordering among processes. In addition, automatic tools [6] are available to evaluate the syntactic and semantic correctness of specifications, to build the finite state machine corresponding to a LOTOS formal specification, and to verify properties of the specification expressed in Action-based Temporal Logic.

This paper is organized as follows: first we compare our approach with other similar ones, and then we build an interactor-based specification of the system considered. Next we describe our tool and how it allows us to link different levels of information about the system. Finally, we also present a case-study to demonstrate our tool working on a pratical example.

2 Related works

Several techniques have been used to evaluate usability.

In [17] the authors use the LOTOS formal specification to verify properties of the Matis user interface expressed in ACTL, by applying automatic tools; but they do not consider user logs. We followed the same approach to write the formal specification but we use a different method to evaluate the user interface.

In [11] Löwgren and Nordqvist also describe a tool called KRI/AG to evaluate user interface designs produced in a UIMS. They show how design knowledge, general guidelines as well as toolkit-specific style guides, can be applied. However they admit that much of the design knowledge can only be applied by taking into account real user interactions. This is possible by using user logs.

In [3] the authors use Neimo, a multimodal Wizard of Oz platform to record logs of user actions. They need Neimo to supplement missing system functions. Similarly to our approach they define a conceptual task, record data corresponding to user physical actions and analyse the recorded data to find differences between conceptual and real tasks, and to derive usability problems from these differences.

Likewise in [18], Siochi and Ehrich analyse user logs to find repeated sequences of user actions which may indicate problems with the user interface. To do this they define an automatic method based on detecting of MRPs (Maximal Repeating Patterns).

The principal difference is that we use the formal specification to obtain the finite state machine of the user interface being tested as well as the user logs (see Fig. 1). We could study logs directly but, in order to get further information about the effects of user actions, e.g. which tasks are achievable on the basis of already performed user actions, we preferred to analyze the formal specification starting from user logs. In our approach the formal specification is obtained in a task-driven way. This means that user tasks are directly mapped onto architectural components (interactors) which describe the implementation.

In [7] the authors compared abstract traces with user logs by using neural networks. Our approach differs because we consider the LOTOS specification which implicitly defines the set of all the possible traces, and our tool also provides quantitative data organized in a task-structured way.

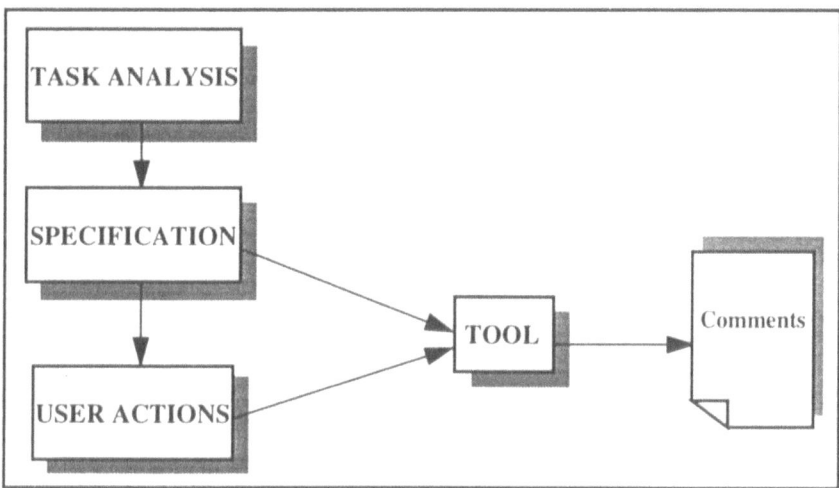

Fig. 1. The overall architecture of the tool.

3 Writing a LOTOS interactors-based formal specification

This section briefly introduces the interactor model we used, and then we illustrate the application we chose as an example and the identified tasks from its task analysis. First the tasks are graphically represented in a tree-like form and this information is then used to structure the specification of the interactor-based architecture.

3.1 The Interactor model

The interactor concept [16, 5, 2] is useful for structuring architectural specifications of Interactive Systems. We use the CNUCE model (for details see [16, 14]). In this model, an interactor can be seen as a black box (see Fig. 2) communicating with the user and application by channels called gates, of which there are six different types. Interactor behaviour can be described by using the basic LOTOS specification language.

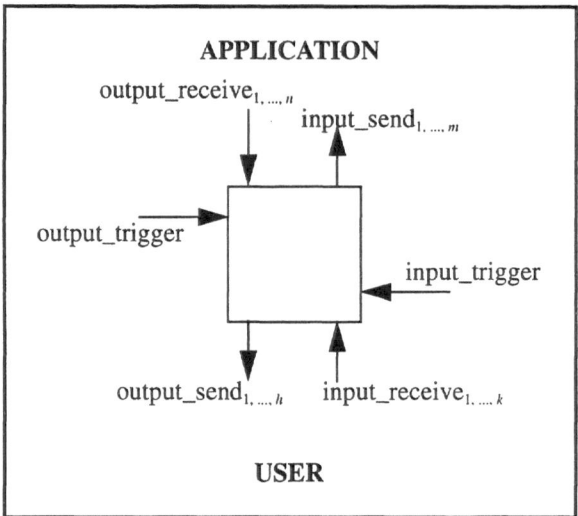

Fig. 2. Basic model of interactor.

On the user side we have two types of gates, *input_receive* and *output_send*, while on the application sides we have the *output_receive* and *input_send* types of gates. The user performs actions using the *input_receive* gate and receives system feedback through the *output_send* gate. *Input_send* is used in order to send the information generated by user actions to the application and the *output_receive* gate permits the application to send information about changes in the appearance of the user interface. The other two types of gates (*input_trigger* and *output_trigger*) indicate when information from the user side has to be sent to the application and vice versa.

It is also possible to have interactors with a different number of gates, both greater and smaller:

Interactors with only input components: these mostly interact with user. They only have the *input_receive*, *input_trigger*, *input_send* and *output_send* types of gates.

Interactors with only output components: these mostly interact with application.

For *interactors without triggers*, the information from the user is sent immediately to the application and vice versa.

Interactors can be connected to each other. This means that whenever we say *application side* we mean either the functional core or another interactor at a higher level. Similarly, whenever we say *user side*, we mean either the real user or an interactor at a lower level of abstraction. When we compose interactors we use five specific kinds of composition [14].

Two aspects of the interactor model have to be highlighted for the goals of the work presented here: one aspect is that events associated with task performance are of *input_send* type because it is by this type of event that it is possible to modify the state of the application; the other important aspect is that the model defines a temporal ordering among events (for example after an event of *input_receive* type there is an event of *output_send* type which provides the related feedback or after an event of *input_trigger* type there is always an event of *input_send* type) and these temporal ordering are useful when we know what are the user-generated events and we want to identify the next events which occur in the architecture of the interactive system.

3.2 The Map application

Fig. 3 shows the appearance of the application we chose to evaluate. Map is a tool for presenting maps of Sweden, and runs in a Windows environment.

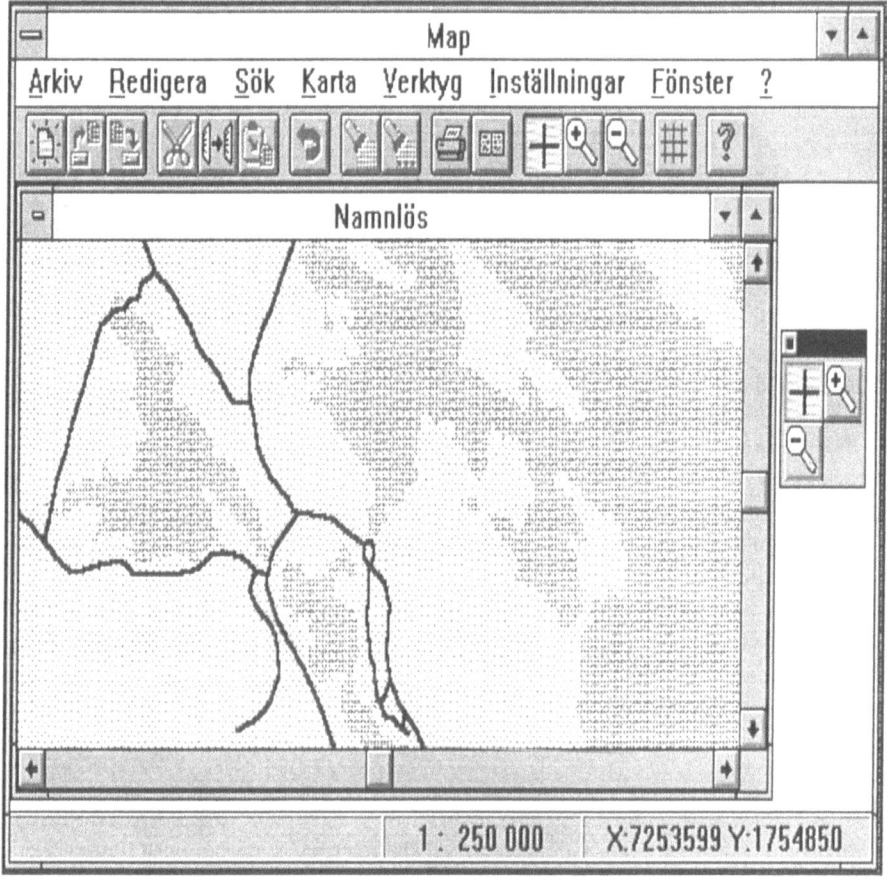

Fig. 3. The user interface of Map.

The Map user interface is divided into:

- a menubar: there are eight pulldown menus. Since the application is not completely developed, some menu items cannot be activated;
- a toolbar: sixteen tools are available as shortcuts to speed up the choice of main functions. Again, some buttons are not active;

- a main window: when the application starts this window is empty, afterwards it shows one or more maps.

Through the *Arkiv* (File) menu a new map can be created. Choosing this item a new map of Sweden appears in the main window. At the beginning the map is empty, which means that only the Swedish borders appear. More than one map can be shown at the same time. Afterwards it is possible to add and to remove elements which were previously defined as lakes, cities, airports and so on by using the *Karta* (Map) menu. The *Verktyg* (Tools) menu as well as the three buttons in the main window allow one to zoom on the map. The *Sok* (Search) menu is not active, while the *Redigera* (Edit) menu can only copy maps but not cut or paste them. The *Installningar* (Set Up) menu sets zoom parameters, the *Fonster* (Windows) menu changes what can be seen in the window (for example, since more than one map can be shown on the screen at the same time, using the *Fonster* menu it is possible to place the windows containing the visualized maps side by side) and the *?* menu provides help in using the application.

3.3 The task specification of Map

We show part of the task specification we derived by studying the Map application in Fig. 4. This figure also indicates the temporal order of task performance. For brevity, we decided to focus only on the *Locate & assess* task, which locates a place and assesses whether it has certain properties. For example, the user could be looking for a place to build a new airport. The features that the place has to satisfy could be: to be large enough, to be in a flat area, to be close to either motorways or main roads, and so on. The user thus needs to visualize the area he/she would build the airport (zooming and changing the appearance of the windows), visualize the most important elements which he/she is interested in (such as main roads, mountains, already existing airports and other significant elements), and then assess whether that place is suitable for building a new airport.

The assessment is mainly up to the user, but the system provides support, for example by means of a function for calculating the distance between two points on the map.

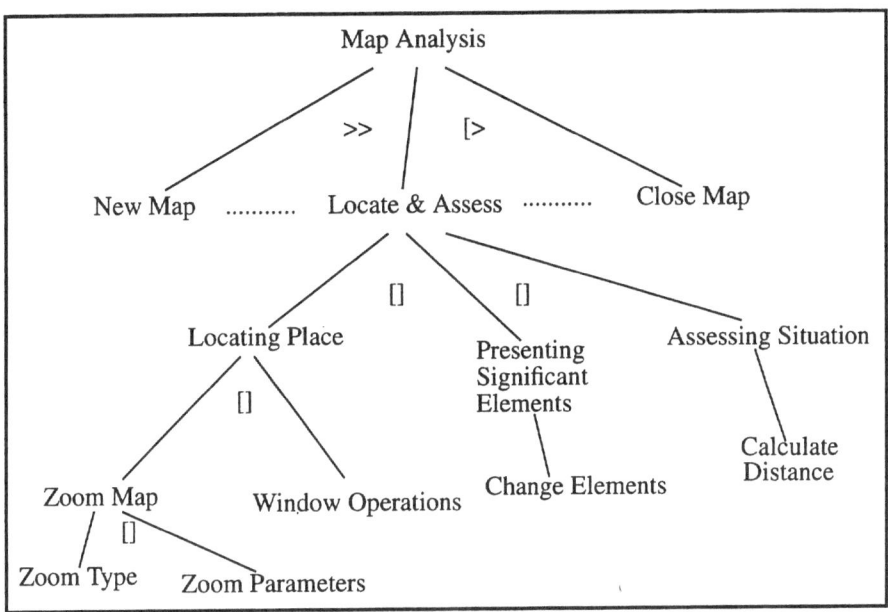

Fig. 4. The abstract *Locate & Assess* task.

The symbols in Fig. 4 mean: the >> operator indicates an enabling. If a task T1 is in enabling with a task T2 (T1 >> T2), the T2 task is executable only after T1 has been realized. The [] operator indicates a choice. Once a task has been chosen, then no other tasks can be executed until the chosen task is finished (i.e. all actions of these tasks are locked). The [> operator indicates a disabling. If a task T1 is in disabling with a task T2 (T1 [> T2), the T1 task is executable only as long as T2 does not start. When this happens, T1 is interrupted.

The architectural description of the abstract *Locate & assess* task using the interactors model is shown in Fig. 5. There is one interactor for each identified subtask and one more interactor called *View*. View activates the *Elements* and *Close* interactors (activation is graphically represented by gray arrows) when it receives the *open_map* event from the Functional Core, which happens when the Functional Core receives the *new_map* event from the *New* interactor. Both the *Distances* and *Windows* interactors and the Functional Core send information to *View* (*selected_dist*, *selected_wind* and *elem_map* events, respectively), which uses it to change the appearance of the map. *Zoom_Com* sends the type of zoom selected to View, while the *Parameters* interactor sends information about set up parameters (e.g. the scale of zoom). *View* will use this information when the *click_for_zoom* event occurs.

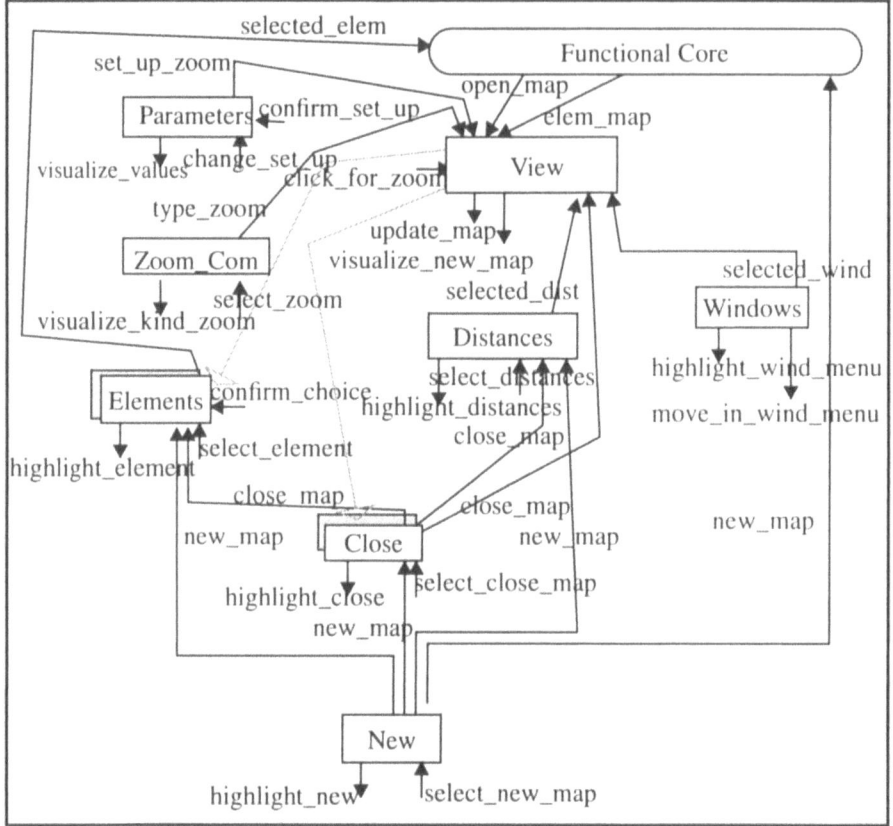

Fig. 5. An architectural description of the example considered.

4 Architecture of the tool

4.1 Inputs

As mentioned above, our tool (its name is *TASM* - Tasks, Actions, Specification Mapping) works on three different abstraction levels (see Fig. 6).

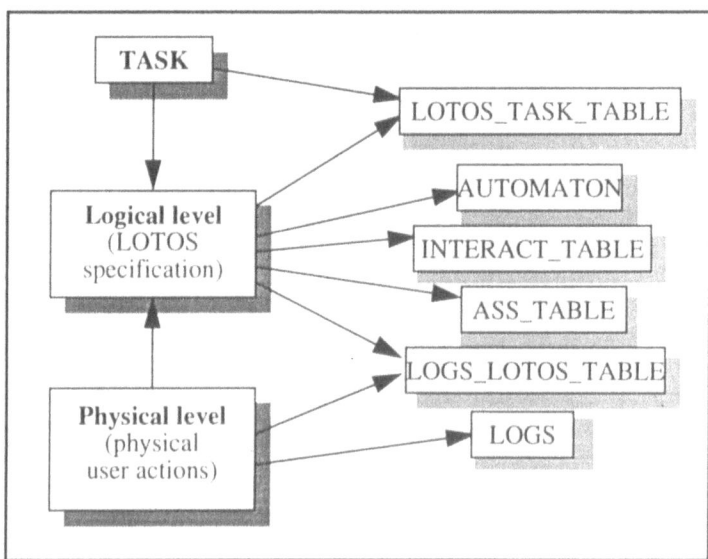

Fig. 6. Abstraction levels and data structures.

The lowest level is the user physical actions level. At this level we collect recordings of user actions using Win-Runner [13].

The next level is the LOTOS formal specification of the software component of the Interactive Systems to evaluate, structured according to the interactor model. The formal specification of the user interface which is being tested is used as an input for our tool. We use it to generate the corresponding automaton by MAUTO [4]. The third level is the task specification which is used to drive the modelling of the software specification.

4.2 Associating Physical and Architectural levels

To connect information on the first level with information on the second level, we use a table that we call LOGS_LOTOS_TABLE. Each user action is associated with one or more LOTOS events of the formal specification of the user interface (several user physical actions can also be associated with the same LOTOS event).

For example, suppose that we have a window with which it is possible to enter some values. They are sent to the application by clicking on a confirm button. Every action performed by the user is recorded by Win-Runner using its own format. For example, when the user clicks, Win-Runner writes button_press ("OK") in the logs file. Let us suppose that the behaviour of this button is described by an input interactor whose gates are move_on_OK_button as *input_receive* type of event and press_OK_button as *input_trigger* type of event. Then button_press ("OK") is associated in the LOGS_LOTOS_TABLE with move_on_OK_button and press_OK_button. In this way we move from physical to logical actions.

Because logs only include user actions and do not indicate system feedback, in the

LOGS_LOTOS_TABLE a user physical action can only be associated with the corresponding *input_send* and *input_trigger* types of event (which are the only types of events related to user actions) of the formal specification, and not with other types of event. This implies that we do not have information about the behaviour of the system being considered, particularly about internal events (i.e. synchronization events between different interactors and between interactors and the application part which is independent of the user interface). For example, let us divide the *Change Element* task shown in Fig. 4 into two subtasks, *Select Element* and *Unselect Element* (see Fig. 7). The two user logs corresponding to the two actions with which the user changes the visualized elements will be called *select_log* and *unselect_log*.

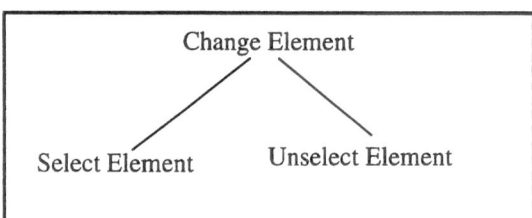

Fig. 7. *Change Element* task decomposition.

Fig. 8 shows the architectural interactor-based description derived from the Change Element task decomposition. We have three interactors, two of them receive the select and unselect actions and the third interactor sends the choices to the View interactor. In the LOGS_LOTOS_TABLE will be the associations indicating the possible sequences of events: select_log/select and unselect_log/unselect, but no information will be supplied about when the internal events (choice, reject, confirm_choice, change_view) and the output events (highlight, unhighlight) are performed.

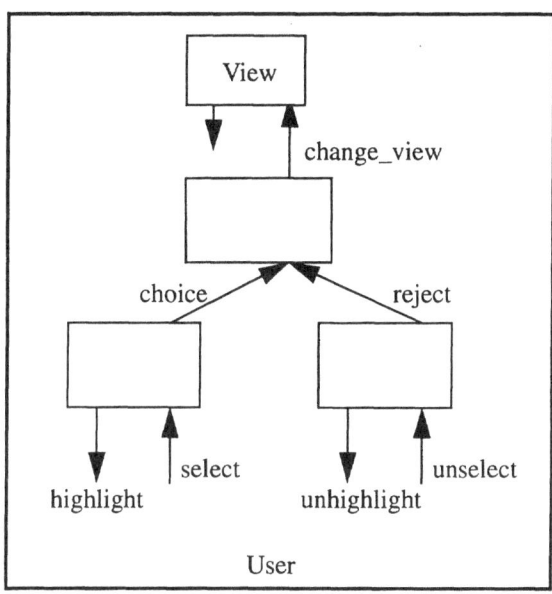

Fig. 8. The architectural interactors-based description of the *Change Element* task.

For this reason we need another table at the LOTOS formal specification events level (logical level), the INTERACT_TABLE. This is a table which associates events of the interactor-based specification. The associated events are those which occur immediately after the event considered.

Thus, for each input event on the user side (*input_receive* or *input_trigger*) we will have an association with the corresponding input event on the application side (*input_send*) and/or with the output event on the user side (*output_send*).

In order to make these associations, we identified some rules. In Fig. 9 (where the numbers mean the temporal sequence of events) some of these rules are identified considering two different cases: single interactor (rules 1, 2 and 3) and interactor composition (rule 4).

Rule 1: *input of single interactor with trigger*

If we have either an Input or a general kind of interactor, the INTERACTOR_TABLE associates the *input_receive* type of event with the corresponding *output_send* (which is the corresponding feedback) and the *input_trigger* type of event with the corresponding *input_send*;

Rule 2: *input of single interactor without trigger*

If we have an interactor without trigger events, the INTERACTOR_TABLE associates the *input_receive* type of event with both the corresponding *output_send* and *input_send* types of events;

Rule 3: *output of single interactor*

The INTERACT_TABLE associates the *output_trigger* type of event with the corresponding *output_send* type of event;

Rule 4: *composition of interactors*

If an interactor is composed with two or more other interactors, the INTERACTOR_TABLE associates the events in different way, depending on the kind of composition. For brevity, the association rules for every kind of composition are not explained here.

Considering the previous example (Fig. 8), in the INTERACT_TABLE we will have the following associations: select/highlight/choice, unselect/unhighlight/reject (rule 2), choice and reject/change_view (rule 4).

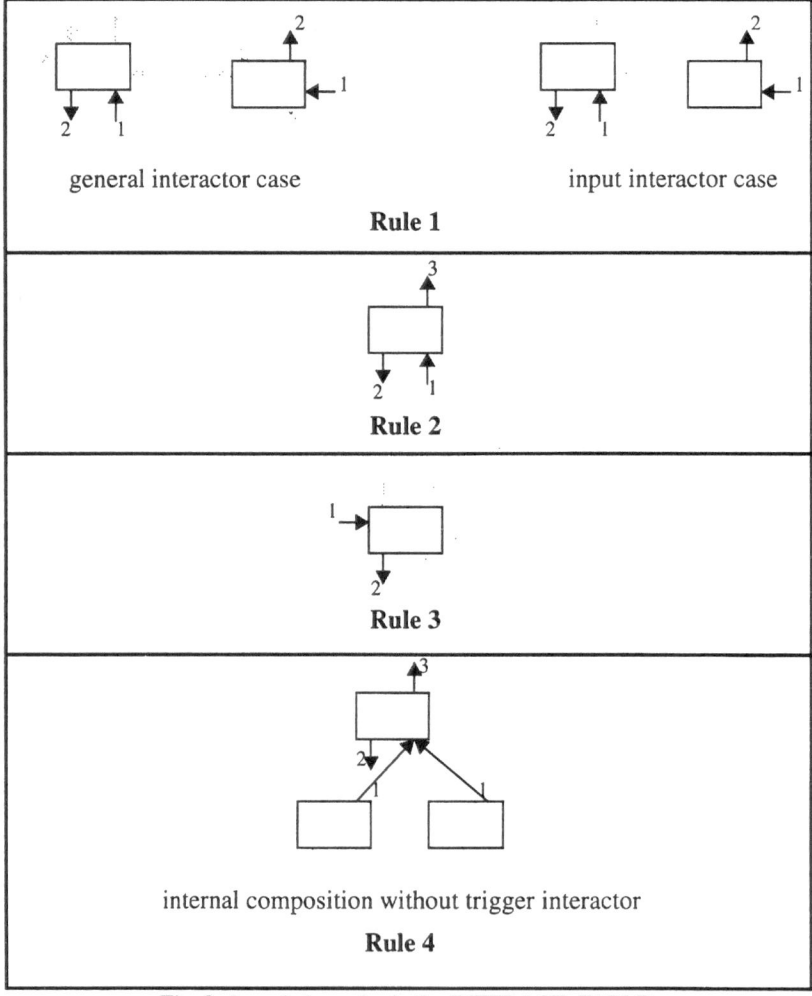

general interactor case   input interactor case

Rule 1

Rule 2

Rule 3

internal composition without trigger interactor

Rule 4

Fig. 9. Association rules in the INTERACT_TABLE.

4.3 Associating Task and Architectural levels

To link the user and the LOTOS levels with the tasks level we use another table, called LOTOS_TASK_TABLE.

This table associates each task with the corresponding LOTOS event needed in order to complete its performance. We can associate the name of the task with the *input_send* type of event which realizes it. Each interactor can be associated with a basic task and the composition of several interactors can be associated with abstract tasks. The type of event characterizing the task execution is the *input_send* of the corresponding interactor. If the *input_send* is known, the corresponding LOTOS events on the user side of an interactor can be derived with the INTERACT_TABLE and, using the LOGS_LOTOS_TABLE, the corresponding user action could be found.

However, with this method, we can only derive a subset of all possible actions performed by the user to execute a task. In fact, we only find the user action which determines the *input_send* event which realizes the task. If we consider a without trigger interactor, the previous reasoning works, because we identify the *input_receive* type of event we are interested in. In the case of an input interactor, we find the user action corresponding to the *input_trigger* type of event, but we lose information about the *input_receive* of the same interactor. We cannot derive this information from the INTERACT_TABLE (which associates *input_receive/output_send* and *input_trigger/input_send*, but not *input_receive/input_trigger* which belong to the same interactor). The LOTOS_TASK_TABLE thus provides, for each task, not only the *input_send* which realizes it, but also both *input_receive* and *input_trigger* types of events which are needed beforehand in order to perform it.

Returning to the previous example, the LOTOS events which carry out the *Select Element* and *Unselect Element* basic tasks are *choice* and *reject* respectively, while the LOTOS event which carries out the abstract *Change Element* task is *change_view*. The LOTOS_TASK_TABLE contains the following associations: *Select Element/select,choice, Unselect Element/unselect,reject, Change Element/change_view.*

It is important to know all the events needed to perform a task to be able to identify user errors.

In summary, the LOGS_LOTOS_TABLE and LOTOS_TASK_TABLE allow us to connect information from the LOTOS level with information from the immediately lower (logs level) and upper (task level) respectively. It is thus possible to pass from information on the lowest level (user physical action level) to information on the highest level (tasks level).

5 Results of the tool and their organization

Fig. 10 shows how the evaluation is performed.

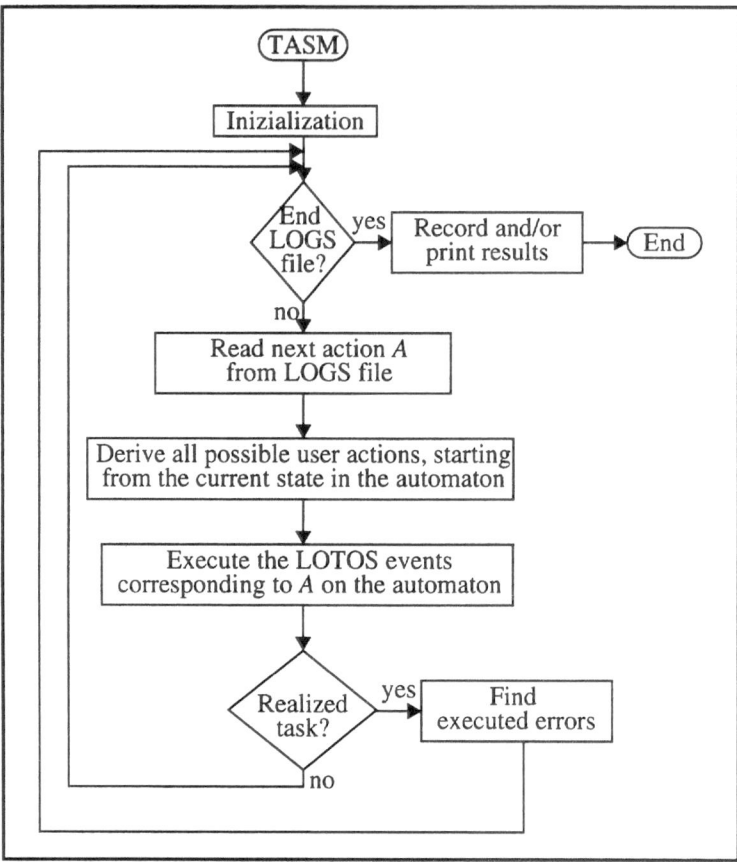

Fig. 10. The algorithm describing the tool behaviour.

Afterwards an inizialization phase, we have to read the next user action in the logs file. If the file finished, we pass to record and/or print the results, otherwise we consider the next user action. Before to evaluate it we derive all possible actions, starting from the current state in the automaton. Afterwards, we execute on the automaton the LOTOS events corresponding to the read action. If a task is realized, we find the errors executed by the user. Both if a task is realized or not, we return to read the next user action.

The tool returns some useful results for identifying user interface problems. We show the results of our tool in the next subsection. Afterwards we discuss how different information can be derived using the same data but organized in different ways.

5.1 Results

The information obtained from the tool mainly concerns how well users perform their tasks or, to be more exact, how well the user interface supports users in executing tasks.

Given a session log, the first information the test returns is what actions are strictly needed in order to perform a task. This result is useful for comparing these actions with those executed by the user carrying out the task, to find out and analyze the differences.

The tool also indicates how many times each individual task has been performed. In our context, task means not only abstract tasks (such as the *Locate & Assess* task shown above), but also simpler tasks corresponding to single user actions (such as the *Zoom Type* subtasks). It is important that the results show how an abstract task is decomposed into subtasks. In fact, when an abstract task is performed, it is not always true that each subtask is executed too. For example, a user can perform the *Zoom Map* abstract task without setting the zoom parameters, which means that the *Zoom Parameters* subtask is not executed. Thus, for each individual execution of an abstract task the tool returns a report which indicates how many times its subtasks have been performed. By recursive application, we find the number of executions of the most simple subtasks.

In addition, the tool also indicates how many actions a task has executed. Again, the test returns the number of actions that the user performed in order to execute the simplest task.

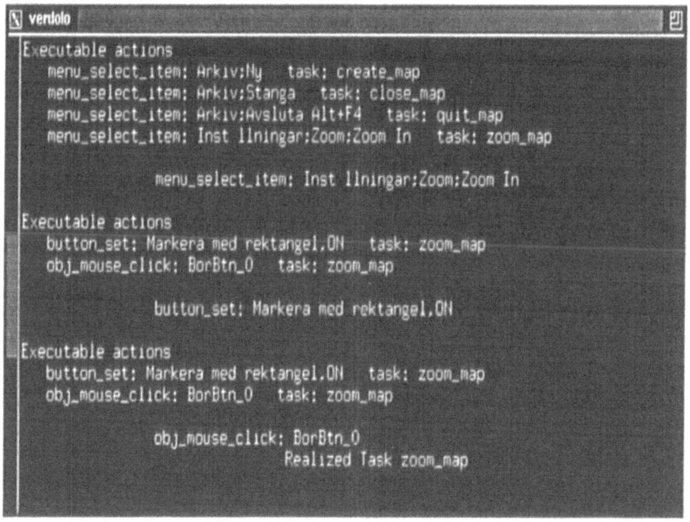

Fig. 11. Extract of the results obtained by applying the tool to Map.

However, one important result is to derive which actions, and then which tasks, are executables starting from a particular point in the logs. This is why we need the automaton of the formal specification of the user interface being tested. The automaton describes the general behaviour of the system (i.e. which actions are executables starting from which), while the user logs are only a part of the general behaviour (i.e. a set of actions identifying a path on the automaton). Fig. 11 shows an extract of the results obtained by applying the tool to the Map application. We can see the executable actions in a particular point of the user interaction. The figure supplies which actions the user can execute in that point of the interaction. Afterwards it shows which of these actions was executed and it also shows the name of the realized task (if any).

The tool exploits this result to obtain information on errors performed by the user. We can define errors as actions that are not needed to perform the current user task. They can be divided into minimal, recoverable and unrecoverable errors. If a minimal error occurs afterwards it is possible to perform an action useful to perform the current task, that is, a minimal error does not prevent the user from executing the current task. After a recoverable error some actions are needed before the execution of the current task can continue. An error is unrecoverable if it does not allow the user to perform the current task in the current session. Having the LOTOS_TASK_TABLE we can discover which tasks the current action belongs to, and by studying the actions' temporal order we can understand how the actions belonging to different tasks evolve. One problem is that we do not know which the current task is since it has not been completed. In fact, the same action can be part of different abstract tasks. This implies that user errors can only be studied after the task has been carried out. If we know which task has been completed and we study the evolution of the user actions we can ascertain whether a user error occurred, and also its type.

This information enables us to derive conclusions about how easy the user can perform his/her tasks and to find ways both to simplify and improve the user's work.

For example, by studying the automaton, the tool returns all possible actions that are executable starting from a certain state. We can consider only those actions needed in order to perform a particular task. Afterwards, by analyzing the user logs, we can understand the user's preferences when executing a particular task, and examine the application to see how well it supports the user's needs.

5.2 Organization of the Report

The information supplied by applying the test to a user interface can be organized in two different ways. The first way is to respect the tasks' temporal order, which means that results about the task executed first are the first to be shown. Respecting this order is very useful in order to analyze not only which tasks are executed by the user and how, but also in what order. Studying the tasks' temporal order makes it possible to reach better conclusions about user intentions and needs. For example, it is useful to notice that a user always performs a particular task before another one. If this behaviour is repeated a substantial number of times, then we can understand that a macro which carries out the two tasks is needed.

Another way is to supply the information ordered by task, which means that results about the same task are shown all together. In this case the temporal information is lost, but it is possible to establish whether the user's performance of a certain task improves over time. This is useful in order to decide whether the user's knowledge increases or not using the system.

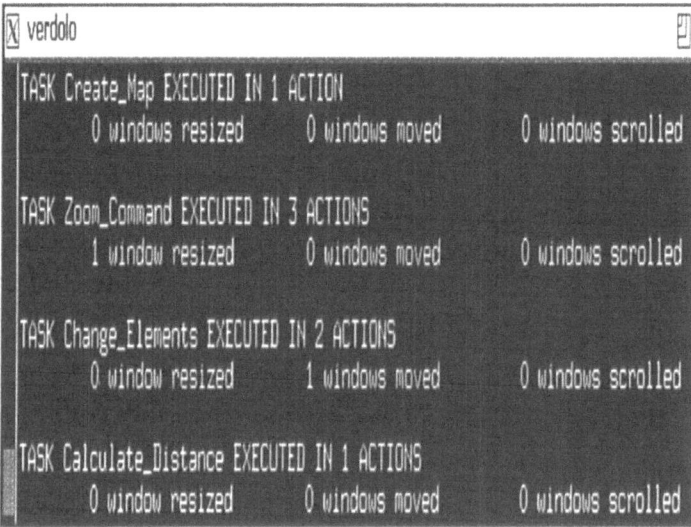

Fig. 12. Results ordered respecting the tasks' temporal order.

5.3 Evaluation of the Map application

We applied the first prototype of the tool on a user log session, in order to evaluate the Map application. We found that the *Window Operations* task had never been performed. With respect to the realized tasks the tool returned the following results (see Fig. 12): the user performed the *New Map* task; then she did some operations on the map, mainly concerning with the *Zoom Type* and *Change Elements* tasks; at the end she closed the map (*Close Map* task).

Studying what actions are strictly needed in order to perform a task and what actions the real user performed, we were able to understand that the user has no problems in using the application, in fact, she executed very few "wrong" actions, i.e. actions which were not needed to realize the current task. Obviously this information is not very meaningful if we do not know the application knowledge of the user, but, through some interviews we can know, for example, for how long the user has been using the application and decide how easy it is to learn to use.

By studying the number of times the tasks were executed and the number of actions performed in order to carry them out, we also realized that the *Change Elements* task is not well supported by the application. In fact, the user performed this task a considerable number of times (19 times, 12 of which were in succession). For each execution of the task she needs to select an item in the *Karta (Map)* menu. A popup window appears and she can select the elements (lakes, cities, roads and so on) she wants to present and unselect the elements she wants to hide. The task is completed when she clicks on the *OK* button of the window. Comparing the task length and its frequency we realized that this task needs shortcuts. In this way the user could just click on the button corresponding to the element type of interest. The elements of that type would be shown immediately, without the user having to confirm her choices. We can even go into more detail. In fact, we saw that some elements are chosen more often than others (for example the 8th element was selected/unselected 9 times, while the 7th element only 2 times), so it might be useful to have shortcuts at least for the more frequently used elements.

Conclusions

In this paper we have presented an approach which allows designers of user interfaces to evaluate user-generated interactions. Logs of events are analysed by means of a task-driven formal specification of the system considered. Results of the tool which we are developing allow designers to have information related to task-performance and user errors.

The current version of the tool is only a prototype. We are improving the user interface evaluation considering also the tasks the user wants to perform but he/she does not complete. In fact, since the tool only considers the realized tasks, if the user tries to perform a task and he/she is not able to carry out it, the tool does not consider this task. For avoiding to miss this information, we plan to introduce (as input for the tool) the sequence of all tasks the user wanted to perform (even if he/she did not complete it).

This work represents one of the first attempts to use formal specifications in tools for usability evaluation. The development of the formal specification can be one additional cost with respect to discounted evaluation methods but it allows designers to obtain more reliable and systematic results. Moreover the formal specification can give useful support in the development phase other than in the evaluation phase.

References

1. Bolognesi, T., Brinskma, E.: Introduction to the ISO Specification Language LOTOS. Computer Networks and ISDN Systems, vol. 14, pp. 25-59 (1989).

2. Coutaz, J.,: PAC, An Object-Oriented Model for Dialog Design. In Proceedings Interact'87. H.Bullinger and B.Shackel eds., North Holland, pp.431-436.

3. Coutaz, J., Salber, D., Balbo, S.: Towards Automatic Evaluation of Multimodal User Interfaces. Amodeus Project Document SM/WP32 (December 1993).

4. Vergamini, D.: AUTO/MAUTO User Manual, version 2.3. Draft CERICS (January 1992).

5. Duke, D., Harrison, M.: Abstract Interaction Objects. Computer Graphics Forum 12 (3), pp. 25-36 (1993).

6. Van Eijk, P.: The Lotosphere Integrated Tool Environment. Proceedings 4th International Conference on Formal Description Techniques (FORTE '91), Sydney, pp. 473-476, (November 1991).

7. Finley, J., Harrison, M.: Pattern Recognition and Interaction Models. HCI INTERACT '90, pp. 149-154 (1990).

8. Foley, J., Kim, W.C., Kovacevic, S., Murray, K.: Defining Interfaces at a High Level of Abstraction. IEEE Software, pp. 25-32 (January 1989).

9. Hartson, H.R., Siochi, A., Hix, D.: The UAN: A User-Oriented Representation for Direct Manipulation Interface Designs. Transactions on Information Systems, vol. 8, num. 3, pp. 181-203 (July 1990).

10. Kieras, D., Polson, P.G.: An Approach to the Formal Analysis of User Complexity. International Journal of Man-Machine Studies 22, pp. 365-394 (1985).

11. Lowgren, J., Nordqvist, T.: Knowledge-Based Evaluation as Design Support for Graphical User Interfaces. CHI May 3-7, pp. 181-188 (1992).

12. Madelaine, E., De Simone, R.: FC: Reference Manual, version 1.1. Esprit Basic Research Action CONCUR2 (July 1993).

13. Mercury Interactive Corporation: XRunner/WinRunner, Automated Software Testing Systems, technical overview, version 1.0. (1993).

14. Paterno', F.: A Theory of User-Interaction Objects. Journal of Visual Languages and Computing, vol. 5, num. 3, pp. 227-249.

15. Paterno', F.: A Methodology for a Task-Driven Modelling of Interactive System. Amodeus Project Document SM/WP7 (1994).

16. Paterno', F., Faconti, G.: On the LOTOS Use to Describe Graphical Interaction. HCI '92: People and Computers VII, pp. 155-173 (1992).

17. Paterno', F., Mezzanotte, M.: Analysing Matis by Interactor and ACTL. Amodeus Project Document SM/WP36 (September 1994).

18. Siochi, A.C., Ehrich, R.W.,: Computer Analysis of User Interfaces Based on Repetition in Transcripts of User Sessions. ACM Transactions on Information Systems, vol. 9 num. 4, pp. 309-335 (October 1991).

Interaction and Task Requirements

D.J. Duke and M.D. Harrison

Dept. of Computer Science, University of York, Heslington, York, YO1 5DD, U.K.
Email: {duke,mdh}@minster.york.ac.uk

Abstract. Novel interaction techniques required for particular work domains or user communities may interfere with the functional or task-oriented requirements that a system is intended to support. This paper suggests that potential conflicts between these two types of requirements can be identified early in the design process through the use of appropriate specification techniques. Here 'appropriate' means both that the structures used to express the specification must be able to represent perceivable elements of the system, and that the process through which the specification is constructed must allow for multi-disciplinary insight into the design problem. This paper explores the relationship between a specification and user requirements in the early stages of the design process of a multi-modal user interface.

1 Introduction

The design of an interactive software system is potentially a multi-disciplinary exercise spanning computer science, cognitive psychology and social models of work situations. There is no point in building a system that is functionally correct or efficient if it doesn't support users' tasks or if users cannot employ the interface to understand how the system will achieve task objectives. Likewise, the design of an effective interface cannot ignore constraints imposed by performance requirements, or software quality criteria such as maintainability. As software systems make increasing use of sophisticated interface technologies such as multi-modal input or gesture [4], it is becoming increasingly important to understand how these disparate perspectives can be brought to bear on the design problem early in the life cycle. This paper focuses on one design representation, a formal software specification, and examines its various roles within the development of an interactionally rich system.

Our approach is to take a design problem, inspired by an existing system, and to explore a design process structured around the use of formal methods. This in itself is not unusual. There are several books containing case studies in the use of formal methods [13, 15]. Our contribution is to address the problem of building an interface using multi-modal technology. Many of the issues here are human rather than functional, apparently a domain where cognitive and user models may have more value than formal specification techniques. However, experience with formal models of interactive systems suggests that they can provide valuable insight into design problems [7]. One of the aims of this paper is to obtain a first impression of when and how other relevant insights, for example from psychological and sociological analyses, might build on or relate to a formal model of the software system. We do not intend, in this context, to discuss or argue about the use of formal methods in software development. Several excellent papers, for example [12] and [2], have already described many of the 'myths' about formal methods, for example that formal methods are difficult for designers to use, or that they are expensive in industrial contexts.

The paper is organised around the initial phases of design, between requirements and system specification. Space precludes charting a complete development of an interactional system, and instead we focus on some specific issues in the development of a multi-modal interface to a flight information system. Section 2 describes domain assumptions and requirements that might underlie such a system. Building on a formal requirements model, Section 3 examines how the functionality of the system might be provided to potential users. Points at which multi-disciplinary analyses might contribute are identified, and alternative design options are captured as extensions to the core system model. Section 4 then looks at the interaction languages that will be supported. This is the level at which this paper stops, though the same techniques can be used to assess the interaction devices that will connect the interface structures with the user. The concluding section describes notations and techniques that might assist in structuring multi-disciplinary integration. Appendices contain: (A) an informal description of the system that we use as our design example, (B) an introduction to the interactor notations, and (C) a glossary of the mathematical notation used in the paper.

2 Domain Assumptions

For systems of any significant scale or cost, systematic development usually begins with a statement of requirements, an analysis of the domain. For a system that is designed to replace or augment some existing part of an enterprise, systems analysis may involve examining a wide range of change options and assessing the impact of each. Regardless of the steps involved, the net effect is that few commercial or public sector systems enter a design or specification phase without the existence of substantial documentation setting out system requirements and relevant information about user tasks and the work domain.

For systems that employ sophisticated interaction technology, structured design processes are not the norm. Applications such as AV media spaces [7] or gestural interfaces [4] are largely the product of research groups engaged in exploratory design. The development of the system is driven or motivated by technological innovation, and there may be no specific user community or work domain in mind. MATIS, the system that we are using as the case study for this paper, is a case in point. The current implementation was designed as a platform for testing and evaluating mechanisms for implementing integration of multi-modal data streams [20]. It does not support any specific set of domain requirements. So for the purpose of this paper we will assume some basic requirements that are consistent with the implementation.

MATIS stands for 'Multi-modal Air Travel Information System'. It allows a user to plan a multi-stage journey by querying a database containing flight information. The innovative part of MATIS is the means that the user can employ to enter queries. Apart from using keyboard and mouse to enter values into an on-screen form, information can also be conveyed through spoken natural language. Further, use of modalities can be sequential, alternate, or synergic [3], with the latter option illustrating the fusion of separate data streams. In synergetic interaction, the user employs speech and gesture, saying for example "Show me flights from *this* city to Boston" while using the mouse to indicate *which* city is the origin. Thus data provided via the speech stream contains deictic references that are resolved by input along a second stream.

Two kinds of domain constraint are relevant. Since MATIS is an interface to an existing database, the existence of that database and its query facilities may place constraints on possible implementations or at least may predispose an implementor towards a particular system architecture. The database also constitutes the functional core, the facilities of which are to be made available to the user through the interface. For this reason the database forms a good starting point for the application of formal description techniques. In this paper we view components of an interactive system as *interactors* [6], entities with an internal state, actions that update the state, and a presentation through which certain actions and state components can be invoked and perceived. The formalism used in this paper is based on modal action logic (MAL), with deontic operators used to define when an action is permissible or obligatory [23]. A summary of the notation appears in Appendix C. Other case studies include [5] and [8].

The database is viewed as a set of records, where each record is a function from attributes to an [optional] value. Queries are simply records where the value of some attributes is unknown. By allowing 'nil' valued attributes, we can define a partial order over records which will be used to define the result of a query.

type	attr	- attribute names for database records
type	value	- data values
type	record = attr → [value]	- a record maps attributes to values

Two global definitions are introduced; null represents the empty record, while matches defines a partial order whose least element is the empty record. Axiom 1 states that every attribute of null has value 'nil'; axiom 2 defines that one record (R) matches another (S) if S agrees with every non-nil value in R.

null	: record	- empty (null) record
_ matches _	: record ↔ record	- consistency between records

axioms

1   $\forall a : attr \bullet null(a) = nil$

2   $\forall R, S : record \bullet R \text{ matches } S \Leftrightarrow \forall a : attr \bullet R(a) \neq nil \Rightarrow S(a) = R(a)$

The actual database is defined as an interactor, albeit a rather trivial one containing a single state component that is not perceivable. One axiom is introduced to assert that there is no redundant information in the set of records.

interactor database

attributes

      records : $\mathbb{P}$ record   - the database is a set of records

axioms

1    $\forall\, R, S : \text{records} \bullet R \text{ matches } S \Leftrightarrow R = S$

The function of the system then is to 'reveal' the database to users in a way that takes account of work domain requirements. A short, and by no means exhaustive, list of *Domain Requirements* is given below.

DR.1   The system should allow the user to interleave the construction of multiple queries.

DR.2   It should be possible to obtain the result of one query independent from other pending queries.

These also are stated precisely in the form of an interactor, although now some parts of the state *are* intended to be perceived by users. As yet we have made no commitment to any interface technology, we simply define that certain structures are perceivable by decorating them with the symbol 'any'. In time these will be replaced by more specific modalities such as vision, sound, or gesture. Within the axioms of an interactor, the components of an attribute 'x' perceived via modality 'm' is denoted by the term $\boxed{\text{m}}$.

interactor system

      database   - include the database

attributes

      current : $\mathbb{P}$ qid   - queries in use

$\boxed{\text{any}}$ queries : qid $\rightarrow$ record   - queries being constructed

$\boxed{\text{any}}$ results : qid $\rightarrow \mathbb{P}$ record   - available results

actions

$\boxed{\text{any}}$ create   - create a new query

$\boxed{\text{any}}$ search : qid   - search the database

      update : qid $\times$ attr $\times$ value   - update a field on a query

Axiom 1 defines the effect of creating a new query; it becomes current and the new query is assigned the value 'null', i.e. the empty record. Although both queries and results are marked as perceivable, not all queries/results need (or can) be perceivable at once. Axioms 2 and 3 require that if the presentation of either a query or result is part of the overall system presentation, then that query/result must be current. Other axioms may be introduced later to account for the visibility of structures within particular interface metaphors.

axioms

1   queries $= C \wedge$ current $= Q$

$$\Rightarrow [\text{create}] \ \exists \, \text{new} : \text{qid} \bullet \left(\begin{array}{l} \text{new} \notin C \wedge \text{current} = C \cup \{\text{new}\} \\ \text{queries} = C \oplus \{\text{new} \mapsto \text{null}\} \end{array} \right)$$

2      $\forall \, q : \text{qid} \bullet \boxed{\text{queries}(q)} \ \text{in} \ \boxed{\text{system}} \Rightarrow q \in \text{current}$

3      $\forall \, q : \text{qid} \bullet \boxed{\text{results}(q)} \ \text{in} \ \boxed{\text{system}} \Rightarrow q \in \text{current}$

The result of the search action is given by axiom 4; the result of the search is made to conform to the set of records that match the corresponding query. However, it is only permissible to institute a search if the query is one that currently exists. This constraint is represented using a deontic 'permission' operator in axiom 5 (see [23]). Axiom 6 states that the create operation is always available in the presentation. The effect of the update action is given by axiom 7, which, by axiom 8, can only be applied to a current query. Axiom 9 indicates that initially no query identifiers are in use:

4      $[\text{search}(q)] \ \text{results}(q) = \{r : \text{records} \mid \text{queries}(q) \ \text{matches} \ r\}$

5      $\mathbf{per}(\text{search}(q)) \Rightarrow q \in \text{current}$

6      $\boxed{\text{create}} \ \text{in} \ \boxed{\text{system}}$

7      $\text{current} = X \Rightarrow [\text{update}(q, a, d)] \ \text{current} = C \oplus \{q \mapsto (C(q) \oplus \{a \mapsto d\})\}$

8      $\mathbf{per}(\text{update}(q, a, d)) \Rightarrow q \in \text{current}$

9      $[] \ \text{current} = \varnothing$

Apart from its role as a precise expression of requirements, a specification also acts as a 'forcing function', encouraging developers to consider issues or aspects of the requirements that might otherwise be overlooked until a later stage of the software life cycle. For example, the ability to identify percepts encourages the developer to consider what parts of the state should be perceivable, and under what conditions. Of course, other representations of an interface, not necessarily mathematically based, support similar forms of introspection. Where formal models are unique is in allowing properties about the behaviour of the system to be discharged through proof. This can serve two roles. It can demonstrate that a requirement is satisfied by a design (verification), or it can be used to gain assurance that the design is what the user(s) expect (validation). The latter can be accomplished by identifying properties that are a consequence of the specification, and posing these as questions to end users, i.e. "would you expect the system to do *this*?".

One such property that can be established with respect to the first system model described above is that initially the presentation of the system contains no results. A formal proof of this property uses the following inference rule ([A]-I) for modal actions:

$$\frac{P \vdash Q}{[A] \, P \vdash [A] \, Q}$$

The proof itself is set out below in a style based on that used by Lemmon [17]; it is also similar to the approach adopted by Gries [11] and Jones [14]. In words, the result is that from the axioms of the system model it can be shown that initially there does not exist any query-id 'q' such that the presentation of the result of q is part of the system presentation.

$$\text{system} \vdash [] \neg \exists q : \text{qid} \bullet \boxed{\text{results(q)}} \text{ in } \boxed{\text{system}}$$

1	[] current $= \varnothing$	[Ass]
2	$\forall q : \text{qid} \bullet \boxed{\text{results(q)}}$ in $\boxed{\text{system}} \Rightarrow q \in \text{current}$	[Ass]
3	current $= \varnothing \vdash \neg \exists q : \text{qid} \bullet \boxed{\text{results(q)}}$ in $\boxed{\text{system}}$	

    3.1 $\boxed{\text{results(a)}}$ in $\boxed{\text{system}} \Rightarrow a \in \text{current}$ [$\forall$-E(1,a)]

    3.2 $\forall x : T \bullet \neg x \in \varnothing[T]$ [set theory]

    3.3 $\neg a \in \varnothing$ [$\forall$-E(3.2,a)]

    3.4   current $= \varnothing$ [Ass]

    3.5 $\neg a \in \text{current}$ [=(3.3,3.4)]

    3.6 $\neg \boxed{\text{results(a)}}$ in $\boxed{\text{system}}$ [MTT(3.5,3.1)]

    3.7 $\forall q : \text{qid} \bullet \neg \boxed{\text{results(a)}}$ in $\boxed{\text{system}}$ [$\forall$-I(3.6)]

    3.8 $\neg \exists q : \text{qid} \bullet \boxed{\text{results(a)}}$ in $\boxed{\text{system}}$ [de Morgan(3.7)]

4   $[] \neg \exists q : \text{qid} \bullet \boxed{\text{results(q)}}$ in $\boxed{\text{system}}$ [[A]-I(1,3)]

The requirements described by the 'system' interactor define a potentially large design space containing implementations quite different from the existing system. At one level of development we might for example conflate query and request forms. In this model the system could interactively update the solution set shown on the display as the user adds or removes constraints on a flight. An interesting question is whether such a design decision can be taken purely at the level of functional specification, or whether such an option might be ruled out by human factors of the interface needed to support it. Either way, software engineering criteria might rule out the option on the grounds of efficiency.

3   Supporting Users' Goals

An abstract specification like the one defined in the previous section sets out *what* a system is required to do but provides few clues about *how* an implementation should achieve the desired behaviour. The aim of separating requirements from implementations is to give the implementor as much freedom as possible to design an implementation that satisfies the specification.

In the case of an interactive system, the choice of how a user interacts with an artefact in order to achieve some goal must take into account factors from the work domain and cognitive behaviour. Interaction should be designed to support users activities. In the case of MATIS, that activity is to plan a multi-flight trip, and to continue developing the system we should consider the role of the three system actions in supporting this activity. Two *Design Questions* that might be relevant at this point are:

DQ.1   which agent [user or system] should initiate the actions?
DQ.1.1   if the system is required to initiate an action, when should it do so?

The answers to these may have a profound influence on the design of the system. There are for example three quite different *options* for distributing the initiative for the actions between user and system. Here and later in the paper, options that relate to the question **DQ.1** are numbered **OPT.1.1 ... OPT.1.n**.

OPT.1.1   The system creates a query initially. The user edits the query, and once satisfied, tells the system to search the database. Once a result has been produced, a new query form is created; the previous form cannot be reused.
OPT.1.2   As above, but now the system does not create a new query once a result has been produced. Instead, the user can re-edit the query and by re-submitting it to the database, update the result. It is up to the user to create new query forms.
OPT.1.3   The user is responsible for creating and editing queries. However, after each update action the system immediately uses the query to produce a result from the database. It is up to the user to remove queries once they are of no further use.

Other variations on these themes can be imagined Each option imposes new requirements on the existing model of the system, which can be expressed concisely as further axioms. The numbers on the left match axioms against the option numbers above. Note that '[] P' means that 'P' is true initially.

1      $current = C \Rightarrow$ [search] $current = C - \{new\}$
1,2   [] **obl**$(system, create)$
3   [user, update(q, n, d)] **obl**$(system, search(q))$

Other issues follow from this discussion. If queries are being used to iteratively search the database then it may be sensible to combine the presentation of the query template and result set into a single structure. A second issue concerns deletion of queries and results. No mention was made of this in the requirements of the previous section, but the fact that option (1) allows queries to be used only once may prompt the question of what should happen to queries (and results) once they are not needed. In practice the resolution of these issues should involve negotiation between the client and the developer, though taking into account criteria from both user and system viewpoints. For example, the third option requires a database search after every edit operation. The cost of this in terms of system efficiency may be prohibitive. In such cases, a design rationale framework such as QOC [18] may be valuable in highlighting the trade-offs involved in choosing between competing options. Figure 1 shows a fragment relevant to the options that we have just discussed. Criteria for choosing between these options are given on the right, with a solid line indicating that a criterion supports an option and a dashed line indicating that a criterion argues against an option. In reality the fragment in the figure may be conflating issues such as whether to have separate query/request and the decision as to which party has the initiative for searching the database.

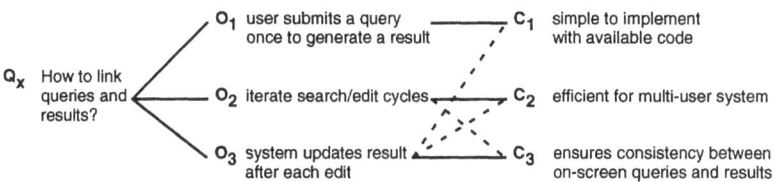

Fig. 1. QOC representation of goal-based issues.

Let us assume that the outcome of the discussion is that the second option is preferred; it thus becomes a design requirement and is recorded as such:

DR.3   Queries and results will be combined into single structures.

From this point we will also require that the visual modality will be used to present information.

DR.4   Queries and results will be presented via the visual modality.

We have thus ruled out an implementation designed for over-the-phone use. In practice the requirements document and domain model should indicate, at least at a high level, how the system is intended to be used. Irrespective, with these commitments we are in a position to reorganise the evolving specification around two interactors. The first of these describes the structure and behaviour of an individual query - note that this now includes both the search information (template) and the result.

> **interactor** query
>
>   database   - include the database
>
> **attributes**
>
> | vis | template : record   - the query being constructed
>
> | vis | results   : $\mathbb{P}$ record   - current result
>
> **actions**
>
> | any | search   - search the database
>
> | any | update   : attr × value   - update a field on the query

axioms

1   [search] results = {r : records | template matches r}

2   template = T ⇒ [update(a, d)] template = T ⊕ {a ↦ d}

3   boxed(template) in boxed(query)

For the moment we have made no further commitment as to how actions are to be perceived or invoked, so axioms 1 and 2 restate the effect of search and update though now over a simpler model of the state. One requirement that we do impose at this point is that

DR.5   template information should at all times be part of the presentation of a query. Note that the presentation of the query may not itself be perceivable, but when it is, the user must be able to perceive the template.

A model of the overall system is obtained by introducing an indexed collection of queries into a second interactor; note that he collection is given a name (request), and that the query at index 'x' is referred to as 'x.request'. Actions and attributes of specific queries are identified by prefixing their names by some value x in qid; thus x.template refers to the template attribute of the query 'x'. The subset of qid that represent created queries is identified by a state attribute called 'current'. As a result, the effect of the create action is simply to insert a new qid into this set. We have also introduced the idea of an 'active' query. Initially the system creates a query, and once a query has been created it becomes the active one. The user can only invoke actions on the active query, but they can select any of the current queries to become active. Since queries are visual structures we can require that no query should overlap the active one.

interactor system

      request : qid ↪ query   - include a qid-indexed set of queries

attributes

boxed(vis) active : qid   - index of the active query

boxed(any) current : $\mathbb{P}$ qid   - identity of queries in use

actions

boxed(any) create   - create a new query

      select   : qid   - set the active query

      delete   - remove the active query

axioms

1     $\forall$ q, r : qid • q.request.records = r.request.records

2   current = C ⇒ [create] $\left(\begin{array}{l} \text{current} = C \cup \{\text{active}\} \land \text{active} \notin C \\ \text{active.request.template} = \text{null} \end{array} \right)$

3   per(x.update) ⇒ active = x

4   per(x.search) ⇒ active = x

5     $[\text{select}(x)]\ \text{active} = x$

6     $\textbf{per}(\text{select}(x)) \Rightarrow x \in \text{current}$

7     $\square\ \textbf{obl}(\text{system}, \text{create})$

8     $\text{current} = C \Rightarrow [\text{delete}] \left(\begin{array}{l} \text{current} = C - \{\text{active}\} \\ \text{current} \neq \varnothing \Rightarrow \text{active} \in \text{current} \end{array} \right)$

9     $\forall\, q : \text{qid} \bullet \boxed{\text{q.request}} \mathbin{/\!\!/} \boxed{\text{active.request}} \Rightarrow q = \text{active}$

Axioms 3 and 4 place additional constraints on the behaviour of individual queries. In general, the context in which an interactor is embedded can further constrain its behaviour. In the context of requirements engineering, Ryan goes further and defines a theory of default reasoning where axioms expressed in a context such as the system interactor can override those of sub-components such as query [22]. Although not used in this document, ordered defaults appear to be a useful tool for developing structured specifications.

Technical note: Specifications that use axioms similar to 3 and 4 (above) to constrain the behaviour of a 'promoted' structure can be simplified if (1) the same constraint applies to all actions in the promoted components, and (2) if the notation allows reference to the set of actions available within a component. For example, if actions are only allowed on the active window, and 'x_{act}' represents the actions available on component 'x', then the single axiom

$$\forall\, q : \text{qid} \bullet \forall\, a : q.\text{request}_{act} \bullet \textbf{per}(q.a) \Rightarrow \text{active} = q$$

can replace both the original axioms 3 and 4 and any similar axioms that refer to query actions.

4   Interaction Languages and Modalities

Our assumption at this point is that the specification adequately accounts for the users' view of the tasks that the system should support. The next issue we address is *how* those tasks might be performed using specific interaction languages such as direct manipulation or speech. Again, this may be an aspect of the system already prescribed by the requirements documents. For example, the design of the CERD [8], another of the exemplar systems analysed within Amodeus-2, was constrained by highly specific hardware requirements centred on the use of a touch sensitive panel. Similar constraints could apply to our design of MATIS, either in terms of specific hardware or more likely with respect to the software or interface architecture on which the implementation of the system will be based.

Factors that might influence the choice of interaction language include the knowledge and experience of the user community, the work domain, and properties (both qualitative and quantitative) of the information being processed by user and system. For example, direct manipulation may be appropriate for

trained users or a population familiar with similar interfaces, but would probably be unsuitable as a 'walk up and use' system (a touch-panel might be better).
Speech may be useful if the user community is visually impaired, but might be
ruled out if the environment is noisy. Finally, textual rather than symbolic expressions may be necessary for representing values drawn from a large set. In
the context of MATIS it may be feasible to select an airport from a list, but not
a departure or arrival time.

Whatever choices are made, they need to be integrated into the evolving
design, and may in turn require further design decisions. Let us assume that
the system is to support both direct manipulation and natural language. Before
we can represent these decisions in the formal model, we need to have a clear
idea what each entails in terms of attributes and actions. The idea of direct
manipulation is that the user can select representations of values on the (visual)
display. Once selected, the represented value is entered into an appropriate slot
on a query. This raises several design questions, such as:

DQ.2   Which values are represented, and how?

DQ.3   How are values to be associated with slots on a query?

OPT.3.1   There is a notion of current slot on each query, and choosing a value
              updates that slot on the active query.

OPT.3.2   Values are obtained from the slot, e.g. selecting a slot brings up a
              menu of values and once a value is chosen it appears in the slot.

OPT.3.3   Organise values into sets linked to the name of an attribute; se-
              lecting a value from the set associated with name 'a' updates the
              corresponding slot on the active query.

In principle at least a user modelling technique such as Cognitive Task Analysis [1] could be used to assess options from the viewpoint of the user. Intuitively,
option 3.2 has the advantage that the user's focus of attention does not have to
move between the selected slot and the location of the value.

DR.6   For direct manipulation, values are associated directly with each slot
              on a query.

Option 3.3 may have similar properties if the user is simply entering information, but may be more difficult to use if it becomes necessary to look at the
contents of other slots on the active query.

interactor query-dm
    query   - extend the representation of a query

attributes

vis	values	:	$\mathbb{P}$ value	- values that can be used to fill a slot
	slot	:	[attr]	- the slot selected to receive a value

actions

lim	pick-slot	:	attr	- choose a slot
lim	pick-val	:	value	- choose a value for a slot

axioms

1   [pick-slot(a)] $\boxed{\text{values}}$ in $\boxed{\text{query-dm}}$

2   slot $= A \Rightarrow$ [pick-val(v)] **obl**(system, update(A, v))

3   **per**(pick-val(v)) $\Rightarrow$ slot $\neq$ nil $\wedge$ v $\in$ values

Once a slot has been selected, axiom 1 requires that a set of values becomes part of the presentation. At this point we do not say what values are in that set. At this point, all that matters is that the user is allowed to pick a value from the set provided that a slot is selected, and as a result, the system is obliged to update the selected slot on the query with that value. We also need to consider the second interaction language, which is natural language. As with direct manipulation, several questions need to be answered before anything can be represented within the formal model. For example:

DQ.4   Can direct manipulation be used while the user is formulating input in natural language?

DQ.5   Could the user interrupt natural language input to one query to provide natural language input to another? That is, is there one input stream for the system or one for each query?

Our (initial) assumption will be that there is a single natural language stream, but that creation of input on this stream can be interrupted while direct manipulation is used to edit other queries. We are not concerned with the problem of parsing natural language, so the state of the system will represent natural language input as simply a record, that is, the structure that would be obtained after the input was parsed into a set of attribute-value associations. Two actions are introduced; the first adds information to the input stream, and the second takes the input and uses it to update the active query.

interactor system-nl

    system   - include the original system model

    query   : qid $\hookrightarrow$ query-dm   - use the new query defn.

attributes

    parse   : record   - record of parsed values

actions

$\boxed{\text{art}}$ augment : attr $\times$ value   - add natural language input

$\boxed{\text{any}}$ commit   - complete NL query

axioms

1   [] parsed $= \varnothing$

2   parsed $= P \Rightarrow$ [augment] $P \subseteq$ parsed

3   parsed $= P \Rightarrow$ [commit]

$$\forall \, a : \text{dom parsed} \bullet \left(\begin{array}{l} \textbf{obl}(\text{system}, \text{active.query.update}(a, P(a))) \\ \text{parsed} = \varnothing \end{array} \right.$$

One issue highlighted by the specification is the possibility of interference between interaction languages. Suppose that the user begins using natural language input for query A, but then switches to direct manipulation to edit a field on query B. From the earlier specification texts we know that only the active query can be updated, so on resuming natural language input the active query will be B. Now, from axiom 3 above, completed natural language is passed to the active query. Clearly, this design places the onus on the user to reselect the original query when switching modalities. Although we would hope for confirmation from user modellers, our intuition is that this design decision should be examined closely. Options include:

DQ.6   How to mediate between input obtained via direct manipulation (DM) and natural language (NL).

OPT.6.1 Associate NL input with the active query at the start of input, and commit the input to that query regardless of the value of 'active' at the end.

OPT.6.2 Associate a separate NL stream with each query, rather than the system (i.e. reverse the previous design decision).

OPT.6.3 Disallow direct manipulation during NL input.

OPT.6.4 Leave the system as is, i.e. NL input goes to the query that is active on completion.

From the viewpoint of the system model, none of these options is obviously better than the others. Option 6.2 for example may exhibit problems similar to the 'unselected window' phenomenon in direct manipulation, where the user changes the focus of their attention without changing the corresponding focus on the system. Irrespective of outcome, this is a good illustration of how a system model might reveal design options, but the choice between options rests on insight from other disciplines. In the case of DQ.6 a user modeller might suggest that users are unlikely to attend to two tasks (i.e. creating a new query and editing an existing field) in parallel, so OPT.6.3 might well be the preferred.

Interaction between user and system will be enabled through the use of specific devices such as keyboard, mouse, visual display, data glove, speech recogniser etc. Two decisions need to be taken at this point: what devices will the system support, and what will be the relationship between devices and the interaction languages considered above. This discussion is beyond the scope of the present paper, but a similar analysis of the existing MATIS system to the level of interaction devices is to be found in [9].

5   Discussion and Conclusions

In this paper we have shown how the formal representation of an interactive system can be used to document and reason about design trade-offs, in particular those between the goals and tasks that the system will support, and the interaction techniques through which those tasks are achieved. However, we have also indicated points at which formal modelling would need to call on multi-disciplinary insight in order to resolve design issues. In turn, these may need to examine the tasks and work domain in which the system is to be situated. And here is the open issue: in what circumstances would a multi-modal interface be considered appropriate?

In the case of MATIS, one argument that could support use of speech is if the system were to be used by a clerk answering enquiries over the telephone. On being asked for a flight, the clerk could repeat the details back to the customer for confirmation, while at the same time the recogniser uses the spoken response to produce a query. Editing of forms could then be achieved though direct manipulation. More generally, we might expect alternative modalities to be employed in cases where the human expressive systems (primarily speech and gesture) are either incapacitated or required for other tasks. Including a speech recognition facility in parallel with other interaction languages would enable people with motor disabilities to make use of the system. Alternatively, a surgeon or technician interacting with an 'augmented reality' system might employ speech so that their hands are free to manipulate the object (patient/hardware) under investigation. What matters here is that the specific tasks that the user is trying to accomplish may well dictate how design options generated by interaction techniques are reconciled. In this context we mention the work of Paterno' and Leonardi [21] who have described an approach for mapping task descriptions into a collection of interactors.

Although it may seem obvious, formal methods 'work' by making designers think hard about the system they are building, thus prompting questions such as 'when should feedback be available?' or 'what is the effect of this action under these conditions?'. Less obvious, but equally important, it should stressed that we are doing with formal methods in this paper is exactly what scientists or engineers do when confronted with a new problem. They construct a model of the situation in terms of the observable data, where possible using the economy and flexibility of mathematics to express the relationship between the observables. The only differences between the equation

$$\mathbf{F} = \frac{d}{dt} m\mathbf{V}$$

found in a physics textbook, and the axiom

$$8 \qquad \text{current} = C \Rightarrow [\text{delete}] \begin{pmatrix} \text{current} = C - \{\text{active}\} \\ \text{current} \neq \varnothing \Rightarrow \text{active} \in \text{current} \end{pmatrix}$$

taken from the interactor 'system' are (1) that the former uses the language of continuous mathematics to express the relationship while the latter employs discrete mathematics and logic, and (2), that the physical law *describes* observations of an existing system while the axiom *prescribes* legitimate observations of a system to be constructed. In both cases we argue that any understanding of the system rests on the ease and precision with which it can be described. Although there is still a need to assess the utility of formal methods within human-computer interaction, we note that technology such as multi-media presentation and immersive interaction are becoming more commonplace. This technology is likely to enter large scale applications, some safety critical. Safety-critical systems form one design context where the use of formal methods is well known and accepted. The emphasis of rigorous development is on showing that a software component of a complex system satisfies its requirements. The potential for human error (or even difficulty in interaction) to cause serious damage or loss of life means that the design of these systems needs also to be informed by cognitive and domain-oriented perspectives. In this paper we have also shown that use of formalism in the design process can (and should) complement insight from other disciplines.

One problem with the model developed in this paper is that changes or commitments made later in development may necessitate restructuring the specification. Design decisions, for example to employ direct manipulation rather than natural language can cut *across* the interactor structure. That is, the decision involves extending the behaviour of each component and reconstituting the system, rather than simply adding a new interactor or level to the specification. This may well be an unavoidable factor in iterative design, and the cost of modifying a specification is quite small, but it would be convenient to avoid changes that might unnecessarily invalidate any theorems shown to hold on the initial or previous design step. To this end we are examining techniques derived from order-sorted algebraic specifications.

In this particularly case study the starting point was an (assumed) set of domain requirements, and development then proceeded in a top-down manner, with design commitments introducing further structure and constraints on the system. We were effectively at the start of a 'V' model development process [24]. This may not always be feasible in practice. Early commitment or requirements to specific hardware devices may for example severely limit or constrain the options that a designer has for supporting users' tasks. In the worst case, hardware limitations may make it necessary for users to reconsider how certain tasks are performed. We argue that the formal techniques used in this paper can represent such design commitments early in the development process, and by doing so can reduce the costs associated with modifying the design of software later in the development process.

References

1. P.J. Barnard and J. May. Interactions with advanced graphical interfaces and the deployment of latent human knowledge. In *Eurographics Workshop on Design, Specification and Verification of Interactive Systems*. Springer, June 1994. Held in Bocca di Magra, Italy. To appear 1995.

2. J.P. Bowen and M.J. Hinchey. Seven more myths of formal methods. In *FME'94: Industrial Benefit of Formal Methods*, volume 873 of *Lecture Notes in Computer Science*, pages 105–117. Springer-Verlag, 1994.

3. J. Coutaz, L. Nigay, and D. Salber. The MSM framework: A design space for multi-sensory-motor systems. In *Proc. EWHCI'93*, volume 753 of *Lecture Notes in Computer Science*, pages 231–241. Springer-Verlag, 1993.

4. D.J. Duke. Reasoning about gestural interaction. *Computer Graphics Forum*, 14(3), 1995. Conference Issue: Proc. Eurographics'95, Maastricht, The Netherlands.

5. D.J. Duke, G. Faconti, M.D. Harrison, and F. Paterno'. Unifying views of interactors. In *Proc International Workshop on Advanced Visual Interfaces*, pages 143–152. ACM Press, 1994.

6. D.J. Duke and M.D. Harrison. Abstract interaction objects. *Computer Graphics Forum*, 12(3):25–36, 1993. Conference Issue: Proc. Eurographics'93.

7. D.J. Duke and M.D. Harrison. From formal models to formal methods. In *Proc Intl. Workshop on Software Engineering and Human-Computer Interaction*, volume 896 of *Lecture Notes in Computer Science*, pages 159–173. Springer-Verlag, 1994.

8. D.J. Duke and M.D. Harrison. FSM: Overview and worked examples. Technical Report SM/WP44, ESPRIT BRA 7040 Amodeus-2, December 1994. See also the Amodeus-2 Executive Summaries on the World-Wide Web.

9. D.J. Duke and M.D. Harrison. Matis: A case study in formal specification. Technical Report SM/WP17, ESPRIT BRA 7040 Amodeus-2, January 1994. File: sysmod/sm_wp17.ps.

10. D.J. Duke and M.D. Harrison. A theory of presentations. In *FME'94: Industrial Benefit of Formal Methods*, volume 873 of *Lecture Notes in Computer Science*, pages 271–290. Springer-Verlag, 1994.

11. D. Gries. *The Science of Programming*. Texts and Monographs in Computer Science. Springer-Verlag, 1981.

12. A. Hall. Seven myths of formal methods. *Software*, pages 11–19, September 1990.

13. I.J. Hayes. *Specification Case Studies*. Series in Computer Science. Prentice Hall International, second edition, 1992.

14. C.B. Jones. *Systematic Software Development Using VDM*. Prentice Hall International, second edition, 1990.

15. C.B. Jones and R. Shaw, editors. *Case Studies in Systematic Software Development*. Prentice Hall, 1990.

16. S.J. Kent, T.S. Maibaum, and W.J. Quirk. Formally specifying temporal constraints and error recovery. In *Proc. of the IEEE International Workshop on Requirements Engineering*, pages 208–215. IEEE Press, 1993.

17. E.J. Lemmon. *Beginning Logic*. Thomas Nelson and Sons, 1965.

18. A. MacLean, R. Young, V. Bellotti, and T. Moran. Questions, options, and criteria: Elements of design space analysis. *Human-Computer Interaction*, 6(3&4):201–250, 1991.

19. J.-J. Ch. Meyer and R.J. Wieringa, editors. *Deontic Logic in Computer Science: Normative System Specification*. Wiley Professional Computing, 1993.

20. L. Nigay. Conception et modélisation logicielles des systèmes interactifs. Ph.D. Thèse de l'Université Joseph Fourier, Grenoble, 1994.

21. F. Paterno' and A. Leonardi. A semantics based approach for the design and implementation of interaction objects. *Computer Graphics Forum*, 13(3), 1994. Conference Issue: Proc. Eurographics'94, Oslo, Norway.

22. M. Ryan. Defaults in specifications. In *Proc. of the IEEE International Workshop on Requirements Engineering*, pages 142–149. IEEE Press, 1993.

23. M. Ryan, J. Fiadeiro, and T. Maibaum. Sharing actions and attributes in modal action logic. In T. Ito and A.R. Meyer, editors, *Theoretical Aspects of Computer Software*, volume 526 of *Lecture Notes in Computer Science*, pages 569–593. Springer-Verlag, 1991.

70

24. I. Sommerville. *Software Engineering*. Addison-Wesley, fourth edition, 1992.
25. J.M. Spivey. *The Z Notation: A Reference Manual*. Prentice Hall International, second edition, 1992.

Amodeus-2 technical reports are available electronically via
ftp://ftp.mrc-apu.cam.ac.uk/pub/amodeus
or
http://www.mrc-apu.cam.ac.uk/amodeus/amodeus.html

A MATIS: An Informal Description

MATIS (Multi-modal Airline Travel Information System) allows a user to query a database about flight information by specifying search templates using input from modalities such as speech, keyboard, and mouse. Commands can be constructed by combining modalities in a synergistic manner; for example the user may give the spoken command "Show me the flights between London and *this* city" while using the mouse to indicate the city that is intended as the destination [20].

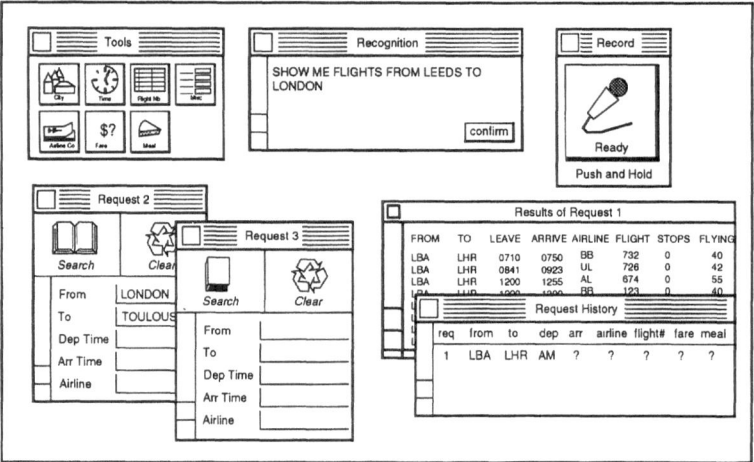

Fig. 2. Screen sketch of the MATIS Implementation.

Figure 2 shows a sketch of the current MATIS interface (after [20]); some of the information in the screen is related to the underlying system and other software components such as the speech recogniser. The features of MATIS that should be noted are:

Requests: MATIS supports multi-threading, that is, there may be more than one request active at one time. Two request windows can be on the left; requests 2 and 3. Each window consists of a set of *slots* and two icons. The slots are used to hold the information against which the database will be searched, for example, request 2 represents a search for lights from London to Toulouse. The 'book' icon is initially closed (and greyed-out). When sufficient information has been entered to make up a possible search the icon becomes the open book and clicking on it sends the template to the database. Selecting the second icon causes the template to be cleared. Not all slots need be completed for a search, and some infrequently used slots are not made available on a blank request. Instead, these are added to a request through the tool palette.

Tools: This is a panel of tools that allows the user to fill slots using the mouse. Clicking on a tool pops up a menu of options from which the user can choose a value to fill in a slot. If the slot is not on the current request then it is added.

Results: Submitting a query to the database results in a new window on the screen showing matching flight information in a tabular format.

Request History: A history of requests is maintained in a window, and can be used to re-issue an old request or, using the cut-and-paste metaphor, to build a new request.

Speech Record: The speech record icon shows the current state of the recogniser: ready (as in the Figure), listening, or searching. To issue a query using speech, the recogniser must first be in the ready state. Clicking on the icon instructs the system to listen for voice input. End of input is signalled by the user clicking on the icon again, and the recogniser then attempts to construct a command.

Recogniser: The recognition component displays the command corresponding to the interpretation of speech input; a natural language query can also be entered directly into the recogniser using the keyboard.

Regarding input, the main feature of MATIS is the (possible) use of multiple modalities to construct requests, and two formalisms for filling search slots with values:

- Natural Language: Input is in the form of a natural language statement that is parsed and used by the system to fill in slots, or
- Graphical: Input is directed to a slot selected by the mouse.

Natural language statements can be provided by speech, using the microphone, or by typing directly into the recognition window. Requests are generated using the graphical formalisms either by using the request tools window to fill in the slots via mouse or by typing directly into a slot. A request can be completed by using a single modality (for example, using the microphone to enter natural language), by using modalities combined sequentially, for example using the mouse and request tools to complete some slots then using the keyboard to enter data into others, or requests can be constructed using deictic expressions where a command is built from multiple modalities, for example, stating "Flights from Boston to this city" while using the mouse to indicate the city intended as the destination.

B Interactors

Formal System Modelling (FSM) at York uses the concept of an interactor to organise the formal description of a system into components. In its most general form, an interactor consists of a state and actions that can be perceived and/or invoked by the environment through a number of well-defined interfaces. In practice it is useful to specialise this view and distinguish one interface, the presentation, as that part of the component (state and actions) that can be perceived by a user of the system. Graphical representations of both of these views of an interactor are shown below.

Fig. 3. Two views of interactors.

Interactors can be used with a range of formalisms, including Z [25], VDM [14], and MAL [23]. A related notion of interactor, developed at CNUCE, uses the process based formalism LOTOS [5]. The Amodeus-2 Executive Summaries [8] summarise the approach and provide other worked examples. We first illustrate the formal description of an interactor through the example of a button on a graphical user interface. The button state is represented by two boolean-valued variables. These indicate whether the button has been selected (e.g. by clicking on it with a mouse) and whether it is enabled. Both variables are annotated with the symbol 'vis'. This indicates that the variable forms part of the presentation, and more specifically, when it can be perceived, it is so through the *visual* modality. Selection might be presented by highlighting or inverting the image; when disabled, the button may appear greyed-out. Two actions are defined, one to change each of the attributes. Actions can be annotated with the modality or channel through which they are performed; the symbol 'any' indicates that no commitment has been made at this point in the design.

interactor button	- comments describe the purpose of structures
attributes	
vis selected : $\mathbb{B}$	- the button can be selected or unselected
vis enabled : $\mathbb{B}$	- and it can be enabled or disabled
actions	
any select	- change whether or not the button is selected
any toggle	- enable or disable the button

axioms

1   enabled $\wedge$ selected = B $\Rightarrow$ [select] selected = $\neg$ B

2   enabled = B $\Rightarrow$ [toggle] enabled = $\neg$ B

3   **per**(select) $\Rightarrow$ enabled

The axioms of the specification are expressed in modal action logic [23, 22]. In each axiom a predicate of the form 'P $\Rightarrow$ [A] Q' should be read as 'provided P is true, performing A results in a state where Q is true'. Thus axiom 1 states that provided the icon is enabled, the effect of 'select' is to negate the value of 'selected'. Here the fact the icon must be enabled defines the precondition within which the effect of the select action is well defined. In general, this is less restrictive than the conditions under which an action is permitted to take place. The latter can be specified using *deontic* predicates like axiom 3 [19]. The axioms states that 'select' is only permitted when the button is enabled. By making this normative condition explicit we can if necessary reason about what happens to a system when permissions are not obeyed, for example if the button is used in a system that tries to select it while disabled. Reasoning about non-normative behaviour is discussed in [16].

For the purposes of practical system development, an important property of interactors is that they can be used to build new interactors. Using two button icons to represent 'up' and 'down' arrows, we can describe a scroll-bar in the following terms:

interactor scrollbar

up, dn	:	button	- we include two copies of button

attributes

vis	min, max	:	$\mathbb{N}$	- range of positions for the 'bar'
vis	posn	:	interval	- the current position of the 'bar'

actions

any	scr-up, scr-dn	- move the bar up or down in its range

axioms

1   posn $\subseteq$ min . . . max

2   posn = P $\Rightarrow$ [scr-up] max(posn) $\geq$ max(P)

3   posn = P $\Rightarrow$ [scr-dn] min(posn) $\leq$ min(P)

4   up.selected $\Rightarrow$ **obl**(scr-up)

5   dn.selected $\Rightarrow$ **obl**(scr-dn)

6   ☐min☐, ☐max☐, ☐posn☐ in ☐scrollbar☐

The data type 'interval' is defined by:

type interval = $\mathbb{N} . . . \mathbb{N}$

An interval is a subsequence of the natural numbers, and in the scrollbar, the position occupied by the bar is expressed as a subinterval within the two endpoints. Following the scroll-up action, the position of the bar is at least its previous position; conversely, scrolling downwards can decrement the position. The reason for not stating that the position must increase (or decrease) is that if a scroll-bar is used to control the position within a (comparatively) larger volume of data, more than one different view onto the data may map onto the same scrollbar position. Thus scrolling upwards may have a perceivable effect on the displayed data, but not on the scrollbar.

Axioms 3 and 4 are further examples of deontic requirements. They state that when the up (or down) button is selected, the scrollbar is obliged to scroll upwards (or downwards). Finally, axiom 5 indicates that the range and position of the bar is always a part of its presentation, i.e. if the scrollbar interactor is perceivable, then these components are also perceivable. If a percept 'p' is available via modality 'm', the expression $\boxed{p}$ refers to the properties of 'p' relevant to the modality. The theory of presentations described in [10] relates visual percepts for example to spatial extents, and we are assuming that the relationship '_ in _' represents spatial containment.

C   Glossary of Notation

The data types and notation used in this paper is based on the mathematical notations of VDM [14] and Z [25] embedded within the structured 'theory' presentation of modal action logic [23, 22]. We assume the existence of the following basic data types:

$\mathbb{N}$	Natural numbers: $\{0, 1, 2, \ldots\}$
$\mathbb{B}$	Boolean values: $\{\text{true}, \text{false}\}$

Logic

Let P and Q be predicates, and x a variable.

$P \wedge Q$	Both P AND Q hold
$P \vee Q$	Either P OR Q (or both) hold
$P \Rightarrow Q$	P IMPLIES Q: If P holds, so must Q
$P \Leftrightarrow Q$	P IF AND ONLY IF Q
$\forall x : S \bullet P$	For all values of x in S, P holds
$\exists x : S \bullet P$	There exists a value of x in S for which P holds

Modal Action Logic

MAL extends classical first order logic with action expressions and a modal operator. Let P be a predicate, and let A an action:

$[A] P$	P must hold after performance of A
per(A)	Permission: the action may occur
obl(A)	Obligation: the action must occur

Sets

Let S and T be sets, P a predicate, E an expression, and t_i terms. Let x_i be variables, and let D be a declaration, e.g. $x_1 : S, x_2 : T$.

∅	Empty set
$\{t_1, \ldots, t_n\}$	Set enumeration: the set of t_1 through to t_n
ℙ S	Power set: the set of all subsets of S
E ∈ S	Membership: the value E is a member of the set S
{D | P • E}	Comprehension: the set of all values of E, such that P holds given D
{D | P}	The set of values for D such that P holds
S ∩ T	Set intersection: the set of values in both S and T
S ∪ T	Set union: the set of values in either S or T
S ⊆ T	Containment: S is a subset of T
S × T	Cartesian product: the set of pairs (x, y) s.t. $x \in S$ and $y \in T$
[S]	Optional type: S ∪ {nil}

Functions

Let S and T be sets, and F and G functions:

{}	Empty function
S → T	The set of functions from S to T
$\{x \mapsto y\}$	The function that maps x to y
dom F	Domain: the set $\{x \mid \exists y • (x, y) \in F\}$
ran F	Range: the set $\{y \mid \exists x • (x, y) \in F\}$
F ⊕ G	Overriding: $(F \oplus G)(x) = G(x)$, if $x \in$ dom G, (x) otherwise

Presentations

Let p and q be percepts, and m a modality:

`any`	Any modality - no commitment to a channel
`vis`	Visual
`art`	Articulatory, e.g. speech
`lim`	Motion or gesture via limbs
`p`	The perceivable component of p
p in q	The spatial extent of p lies within that of q
p ∥ q	The spatial extent of p overlaps that of q
neighbours(p)	The set of spatial extents that surround that of p

This article was processed using the LaTeX macro package with LLNCS style

Revising mental models to accommodate expectation failures in human-computer dialogues

Thomas G. Moher
Victor Dirda

Department of Electrical Engineering and Computer Science
University of Illinois at Chicago, Chicago, IL 60607, U.S.A.

Abstract. Faulty mental models of device operation may lead to expectation failure in human-computer dialogues. This paper presents an integrative modeling formalism for representing users and devices, and employs this formalism to describe a two-phase process of *model strengthening* and *model weakening* in response to expectation failure. During weakening, selected components of the mental model are tagged as "uncertain." The task plan is re-executed on the weakened mental model, and the mental model is strengthened as particular suspicions are eliminated. The revised mental model may then be used as the basis for the development of an alternative task plan.

1 Introduction

More often than not, users have an incomplete or inaccurate understanding, or *mental model*, of the software which they employ [6]. Sometimes this is because the software is entirely novel to them; at other times it is due to the complexity of the software or to the differences among software products which perform similar functions. When the user constructs a plan to use the software using a faulty mental model, execution of the plan may result in failure to satisfy task requirements.

This paper focuses specifically on the issue of mental model repair by considering an example in which a user begins with an imperfect model and proceeds to fail at a specific task. We model the user's response in terms of a two-phase process of *model weakening* and *model strengthening*. In the first phase, the original mental model is weakened relative to the certainty of operations applied to model components identified by the expectation failure. In the second phase, the weakened model is strengthened based on a mental replay (simulation) of the user's immediate past actions. The revised mental model resulting from this process represents the strongest model consistent with actual device behavior, and may (or may not) provide an adequate basis for a revised plan to satisfy task requirements.

The failure of mental models, and their repair, is of interest both in user modeling and in software design. Designers of new software could benefit from an explicit articulation of mental models derived from experience with existing software with which they share functionality; simulation of existing mental models in the context of the actual operation of the new software could provide clues to transfer breakdowns in the performance of common tasks. Prior knowledge of such breakdowns could motivate interface design and documentation and training strategies.

2 Modeling framework

For the purposes of this paper, we adopt a global model (depicted in Figure 1) of an interactive system consisting of two submodels: a device (in this case a text editor) and a user. The user model in turn contains two submodels: a mental model of the device and a plan model for accomplishing a task.

Each submodel includes both event (rectangle) and state (circle) components. In the device model, events correspond to user input affordances, and states may be either observable or hidden. In the plan model, events represent specific physical actions on the part of the user, and states dynamic mental or physical attributes of the user. Mental model components correspond to the user's expectations regarding the behavior of the device.

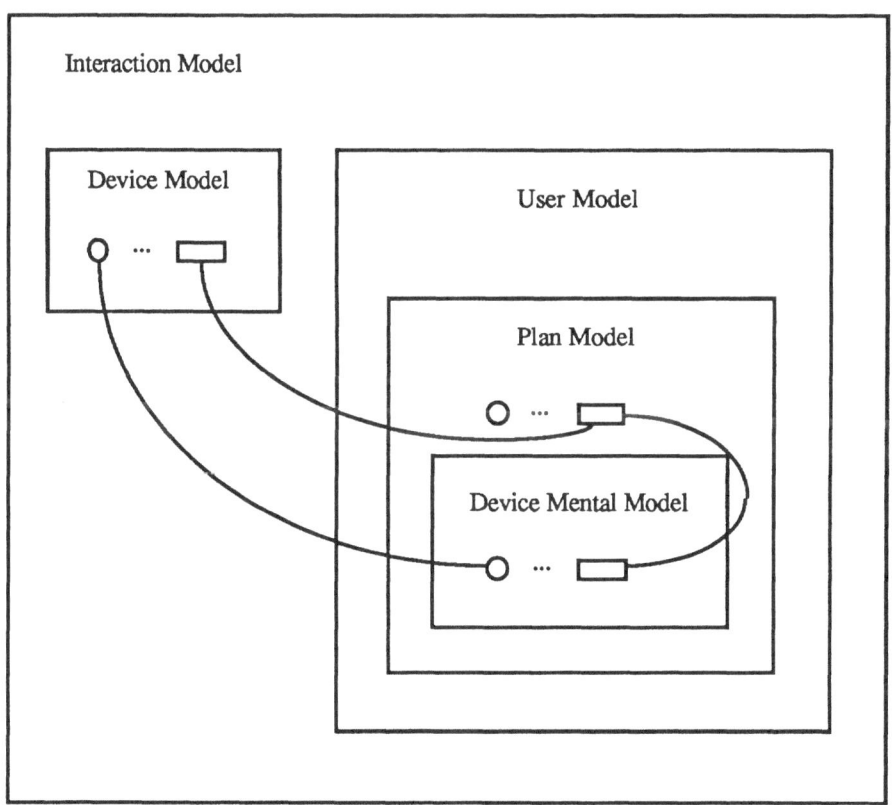

Figure 1. An integrative framework for interaction modeling

The operationality of the global model is established by links. The links between user and device events tie physical actions to input affordances. The links between user and mental model events tie plan model actions to mental model event simulations; the framework assumes that the user predicts editor responses synchronously with the editing actions. Finally, the state-to-state links establish a basis for comparison between actual and expected editor behavior, performed by the user. For the purposes of this paper, we shall leave aside complex issues of perception and assume that comparisons between mental model states and observable device model states are made without error.

The framework we employ is integrative, in the sense of bridging rather than homogenization. Our work is most closely related to Cognitive Complexity Theory (CCT) [16] because of its emphasis on horizontal integration via a bipartite (system and user) model to generate integrated behavior. However, in contrast to CCT, our framework distinguishes distinct device and mental models. In this sense, our framework is similar to the Syndetic Model [11], albeit set at a higher level of detail necessary for the treatment of error detection and remediation.

Interaction Framework [14] adds the notion of normative behavior (our term) by describing the operation of an interactive system without assigning responsibility for the interaction to particular agents of the system; it is not the mission of Interaction Framework itself to describe how the global goals are reflected in the structure of its individual components. In the case of fallible behavior and complex interactions, there may be ambiguity in the idea of global goals. The approach we take is that the expression of intentionality is part of an autonomous agent structure, even though the intentionality may not be achievable by an agent in isolation. That is, the mechanism which the agent uses to achieve a goal in the global context is part of the agent's individual structure.

Our work in effect achieves a horizontal integrative effect by modularizing the integrative approach of CCT, using the partition of a system into interactive agents and the separation of models into composable declarative, procedural and semantic elements. It also works toward vertical integration with high-level goal models by employing explicitly normative models, expressing intent as a predictive mental model. In this manner, the spirit of some high-level integrative approaches such as Design Rationales [2] is suggested. Here the identity of expected effect and intent can be used to give a stronger basis for recommendations.

3 Error detection and correction

Figure 2 presents a simple model of generic task performance with error correction within the integrative framework described above. The gist of the model is that the ubiquitous possibility of error in human tasks invokes a generic and well-practiced error-coping mechanism. According to this model, the user first intends to perform some task and creates or accesses some (possibly oversimplified or defective) plan to accomplish it. The user then matches the plan to the exact situation of the task and creates some structure for keeping track of this particular instance of its performance. In addition, the user generates a predictive mechanism for monitoring the performance and progress of the task. The user proceeds to perform the actions of the plan and to monitor its progress until either successful completion or an unexpected result. The presence of an unexpected result triggers a response which may be directed toward the discrepancy itself (verification and understanding as well as a reorientation to the situation), the causes of the discrepancy (repair of either the plan itself or the mental model upon which the plan was predicated), or the goal or intent of the task (reassessment of its desirability or particular form).

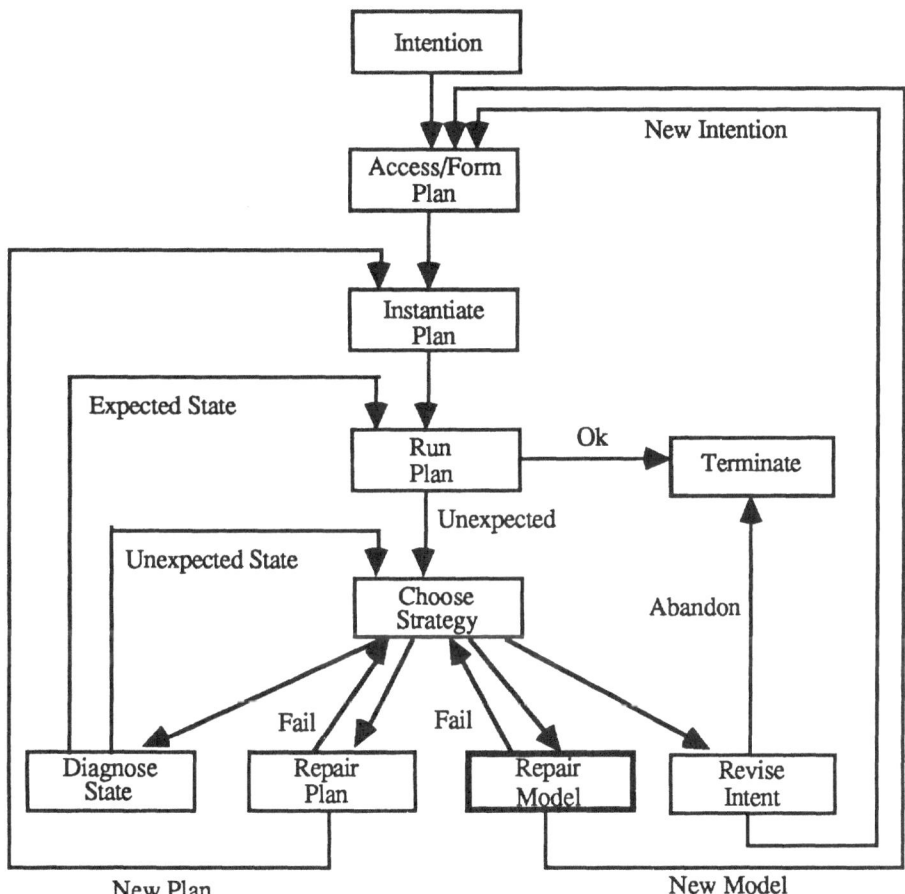

Figure 2. Generic task performance with error correction

Most artificial intelligence approaches to problem solving are based on a foundation of axiomatic knowledge and some deductive engine. In the HCI field, similar approaches include programmable user models [20], the Soar problem solving cognitive architecture [17, 18, 21] and automated systems for creating task plans from tasks and device affordance specifications [3, 5]. Related to these are menu traversal learning models [15] and text editing task planning [4]. These approaches share the assumptions of accurate deductive principles, sufficient facts and operators to achieve a transformation of some initial problem state to a goal achievement, or an exploration-permissive system which allows the success or failure of a solution to drive the learning of particular actions within a static framework of understanding.

An approach based on weaker knowledge (typified by most expert system and empirically-based approaches) depends on what may be called associative knowledge: an association of facts with each other without axiomatic support or principles of generality. The existence of some facts is treated as affecting the probability of the existence of other facts; this approach is also used in truth maintenance systems [9, 10]. The strength of associations may be absolute (in which case the associations have an axiomatic strength) or probabilistic. Such models are used to model troubleshooting behavior in which a spontaneous system change is identified by tracing from manifestations of an abnormal condition to some absent or abnormal state via expected state associations. Here, the underlying framework is assumed to be statically consistent; transient inconsistency is introduced by the spontaneous change of an external system or the application to a new set of observations. The same approach, based on known relations among states related to the task, can be used for diagnosis and learning [12, 13].

In the absence of focal knowledge but the presence of general knowledge of the task domain, a more constructive approach may be used. This is exemplified by the Model Generative Reasoning model [8] for explaining novel phenomena. In this case only a knowledge of models of domain phenomena and their manifestations is used. Models are combined and the net effect of the combination is checked against the observed phenomenon. The approach requires knowledge of "micromodels" of the domain as well as a taxonomy of the domain, which is used to organize the combination to avoid the intractably inefficient strategy of trying all random combinations.

The approach we adopt is based on weak knowledge of the problem domain itself, either statically weak knowledge (the user's "true" state of knowledge is inadequate for strong methods) or functionally weak (the unexpected event has shaken the user's confidence in correct knowledge or the disorientation of the event interferes with recall). In this approach, the original mental model is systematically *weakened* until its predictions include the observed novel behavior, and subsequently *strengthened* for a more precise model. While our goal is to define a plausible (competence) model, this approach may in fact be relatively common, as the complexity of interface functionality often results in lack of specialized feature knowledge (even in the face of general familiarity with the interface), cognitive loading may interfere with the use of stronger methods, and there may be cognitive economy in its simplicity.

A final alternative, not discussed here, is the use of exploratory behavior in which the attempt to model in detail is abandoned and the properties of the interface presentation and responses are used to infer semantics and construct a model from scratch.

4 Task description

The task example is taken from ongoing work described in [4]. The user is presented with the problem of trying to copy some text from one part of a document and to insert it twice later in the same document, replacing text already in place. For this example, we assume that the user does not confuse intended text with actual text by using an overly narrow context of observation, misperception of text, or any other reason. Thus, intended text and insertion point references are treated as parameters of the actual selection editing actions.

We introduce a formal notation to describe the state of the document within the context of the editor. Given a text document of the form $\alpha\beta$ (where α and β are strings of arbitrary length), we denote by $\alpha[]\beta$ the same document with the cursor positioned between text segments α and β. Similarly, for a document of the form $\alpha\beta$ (where X is also an arbitrary string), we denote by $\alpha[X]\beta$ the same document with text X selected (highlighted). Finally, we define $plain(\alpha)$ as the document string α with all brackets removed. The task, then, is to transform document D = $\alpha X\beta Y\gamma Z\delta$ into document D' such that $plain(D') = \alpha X\beta X\gamma X\delta$.

5 Initial mental model

Figure 3 depicts the plausible (but incorrect) mental model of the editor which we ascribe to our user. We use a colored Petri net representation for modeling [1, 19]; this is also the form in which we will later describe the user's plan. *Places* (circles) in the model represent the text document itself and the hidden buffer, and are occupied by *tokens* representing the content value of the place. Potential user actions are represented as *transitions* (rectangles). State changes are effected when transitions fire, at which time tokens are deleted from the transition's input places and generated in its output places. Transitions are *enabled* when their incoming places are occupied with tokens which match the *constraints* represented by annotations on their incoming arcs, at which time the actual value of the token is bound to symbolic variables specified in the constraint. The value of the generated tokens is specified by the annotation on the outgoing arc, employing those bindings.

As an example, consider the Paste operation. Working on the text document $\alpha[]\beta$ and a pre-defined buffer content H, Paste replaces the working text with $\alpha H[]\beta$ and restores the buffer to its prior state. In contrast, the Copy operation, while leaving the document unaffected, destructively replaces the buffer contents(H) with the selected text(X).

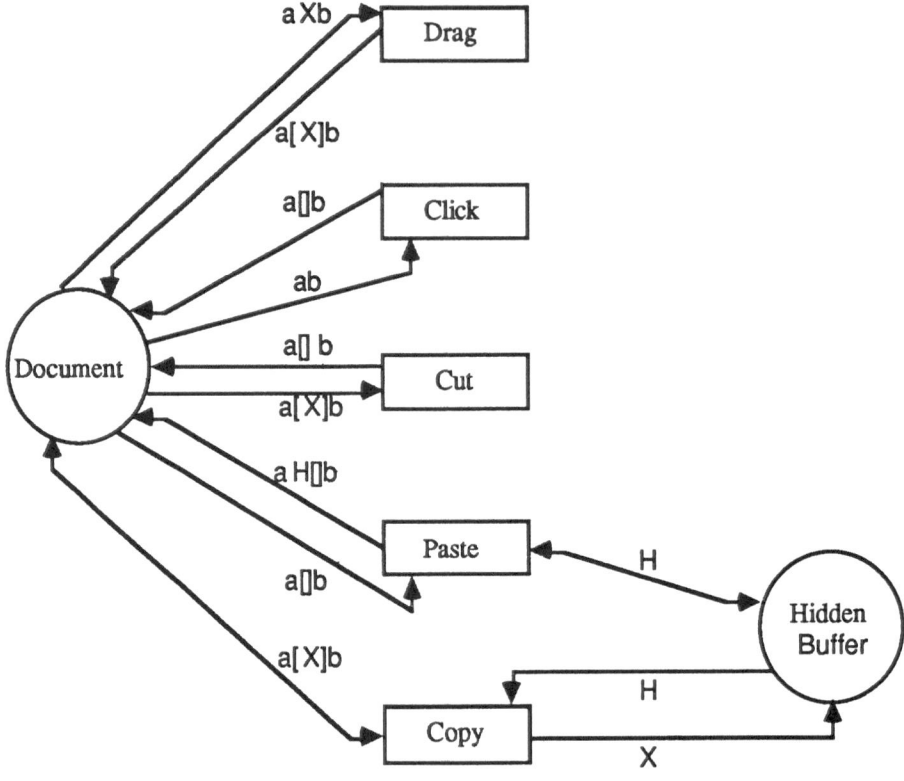

Figure 3. Initial (incorrect) mental model of editor operation

It is important to note that the user's mental model is not necessarily intended to be a description of the user's conscious formulation of how the editor operates or even to reflect how the user might explain the editor to another person. It is intended to indicate the implicit and possibly unarticulated beliefs of the user. There may be an inconsistency of belief, and there may be a difference in the reliability with which the user remembers a given belief. What is of essence, we shall argue, is that a grading of strength might be applied to individual facts comprising the user's understanding, and that these are empirically observable through explicit interrogation, requests for free-form explanation, or decisions where the rationality of choices is dependent upon the underlying belief.

6 Initial plan

The mental model of Figure 3 is sufficient to allow the user to construct a plan for using the editor's operations in such a way as to satisfy the task requirements. Initially, the place labeled Source contains the token X, while the place Targets contains the strings $\beta Y\gamma$ and $\gamma Z\delta$. The *plan model* consists of the following algorithm (shown in Petri net representation in Figure 4).

Select segment X from the source document
Copy X
while Targets is not empty
      Remove string LMN from Targets
      Click to form L[]MN
      Paste to form LX[]MN
      Drag to select LX[M]N
      Cut to form LX[]N
end while

7 Model execution and expectation failure

The plan described above works fine for the first replacement (of Y with X), but produces an unexpected text change when the user attempts to insert X prior to Z. Instead of the expected configuration $\alpha X \beta Y \gamma X Z \delta$, the text produced has the form $\alpha X \beta Y \gamma Y Z \delta$. Expectation failure triggers user error-handling strategies.

Error handling strategies can be divided into three rough categories: performance error handling, knowledge error handling, and reorientation. Performance error handling entails the checking for errors in the execution of the task (or its monitoring) and, if needed, their correction or repair (if possible). Knowledge error handling involves checking for factual or procedural misinformation, generation of appropriate knowledge, and finally its deployment to repair and resume the task and its plan. Reorientation denotes the need to reestablish a new basis for understanding and describing the existing situation when current understanding or description is undermined.

Knowledge error requires less routinized problem solving skills. The factor that makes it particularly hard in general is that the existing state of knowledge may have seemed complete and correct. The process of correcting knowledge errors thus involves putting existing subjective truth into question and resolving which elements of its must be changed. The fundamental challenges of this is that the question may not be resolvable in a unique way. The proposed method is the assignment of strength of belief to a model and adjustment of its weakest elements first possibly adjusting more and more strongly held beliefs until consistency is achieved between the mental model and observations.

In the particular case of this example, the user first considers the possibility of having misread the display. Upon confirming its content, the user then considers the possibility of having failed to perform a paste operation and considers alternative operations. None of the alternative operations would cause text to be added; the user confirms that a paste was indeed performed. Mentally reviewing the task (its performance as well as its monitoring) convinces the user that the task was performed as planned and monitored correctly. Replaying the expectations (from the mental model) convinces the user that the plan, given the underlying assumptions of how the editor works, is sound.

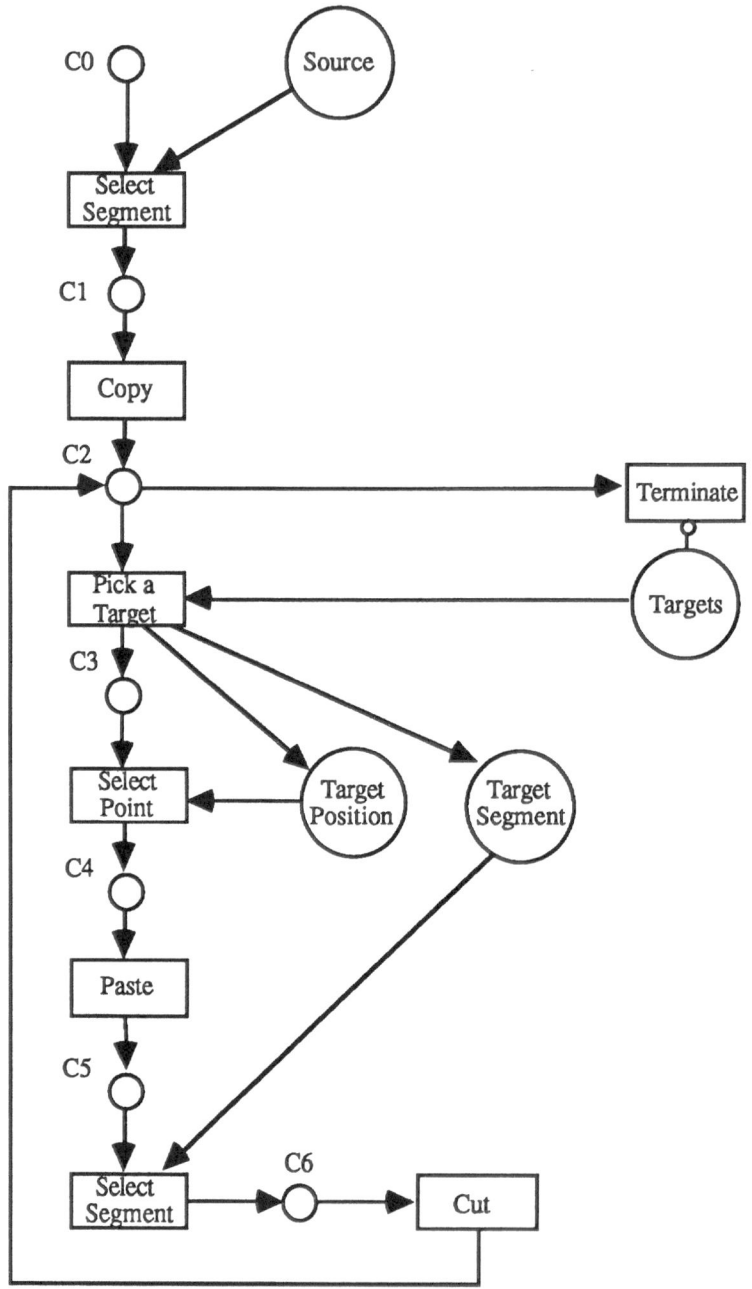

Figure 4. Initial plan model for the substitution task

At this point the user must formulate a new description of what has actually occurred, since his or her original state of knowledge (mental model) is apparently incorrect. The user interprets the content of the display as inserting "garbage" at the insertion point and considers what among his or her current beliefs is weakest. The discrepancy between the content of the hidden buffer as expected and as deduced from the assumption that the last operation was a paste, along with the fact that the paste operates as expected (at least to the extent of inserting the content of the hidden buffer) leads the user to identify the hidden buffer as the *focus* for weakening the model.

8 Weakening the original mental model

The first step in revising the mental model includes an explicit weakening, in this case by placing operations affecting the buffer "under a cloud." In formal terms, this process involves the addition of an "indefinite" attribute to edges in the Petri net representation for operations which already affect the buffer, and the addition of "indefinite" edges between the buffer and operations not affecting the buffer in the original model. Figure 5 depicts the weakened version of the original model relative to buffer operations.

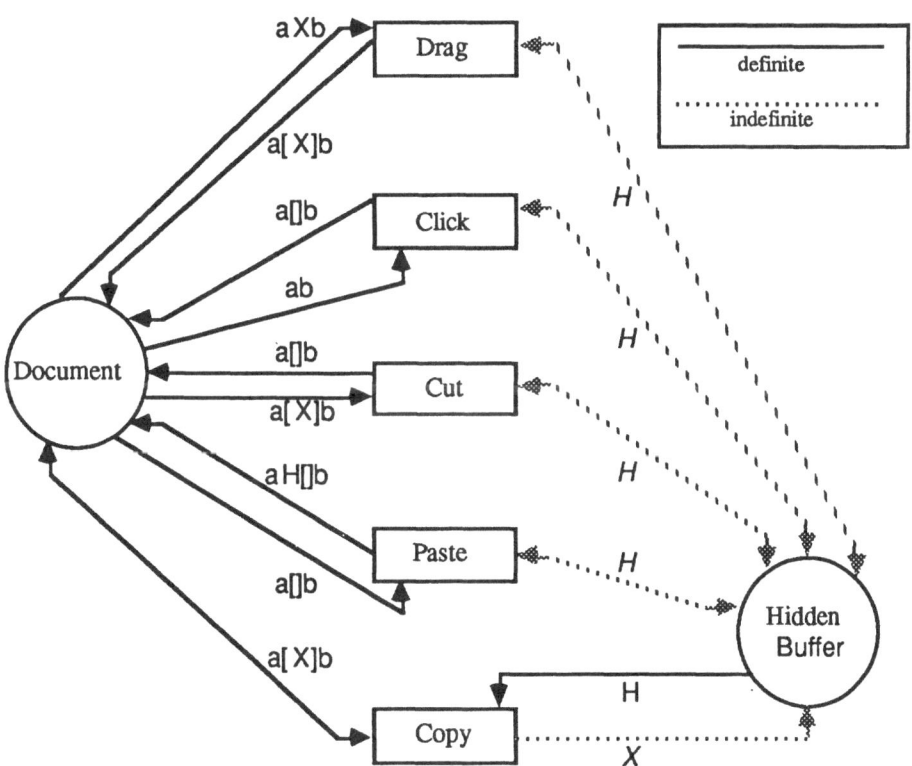

Figure 5. Weakened mental model of editor operation

Consider the Paste operation. In the original model, paste was represented as an operation which performed a non-destructive read of the buffer and copied the buffer contents into the document at the insertion point. There are, however, plausible alternative semantics for the Paste operation, including the possibility that the Paste operation clears the buffer or pastes only a portion of the buffer into the source document. (The latter case might arise, for example, if the buffer were maintained as a stack, with the paste operation performing a pop operation on the buffer and a concomitant insertion into the document.) Since both the content inserted into the document and the resultant content of the buffer are affected, both arcs (input and output) from the Paste transition are marked as "indefinite."

A similar line of reasoning applies to the Copy operation. However, the full uncertainty of effect can be subsumed by uncertainty of what is put into the buffer. There is no need to make the deletion of the current content indefinite since partial deletion can be modeled by complete deletion and reinsertion of part of the original content.

In the case of the last three operations—the Cut, Drag (selection) and Click (set insertion point)—there is no *a priori* belief of relevance, so the weakened model merely includes the possibility that these operations may somehow alter the buffer content.

In some cases, a weakened model might still provide sufficient definite operations upon which to base a revised plan to satisfy the task. In the case of the editor example, however, this is not the case; there is no task plan which could employ the remaining definite operations in the model of Figure 5 to accomplish the objectives.

9 Strengthening the weakened model

The weakened model represents a maximally generalized model template which still includes the original model as an instance. Since the weakened model depends for its construction only on the immediate expectation failure, further retrospective analysis of system performance may provide information which could limit the generality of the weakened model. We call this *model strengthening*.

Strengthening occurs as a byproduct of mental *post hoc* simulation of the weakened model. During this simulation, the ordinary rules of transition firing apply, but uncertain operations use "weak" expectation values. Operations performed in the context of definite expectations are placed on a list of *suspects*. Operations are *exonerated* if observed system performance exactly matches expectations. If performance satisfies the more relaxed requirements of the weakened model, the weakened model is retained, but the list of remaining suspects is used to define a possibly strengthened version of the weakened model.

(The issue is muddied somewhat by the fact that intervening actions may mask initially matching observations. Here we assume that the simplicity of the example permits the hypothetical user to recall observable changes without error.)

The strengthening algorithm—applied to each operation in the task trace—may thus be defined as:

```
if an expectation for the focus exists
        put unverified uses (input) of the focus into the suspect list
perform the operation
if the visible result is unexpected
        abandon the model
if the focus value is observationally verifiable
        if it is verified (matches strict expectations from the initial model)
                mark suspect list members as exonerated
        empty suspect list
if an expectation for the focus exists
        put unverified effects (output) on the focus in suspect list
```

0. At the outset, ignorant of the history of previous operations, there is no expectation regarding the contents of the buffer (focus).

1. The Drag operation initially selecting X has no expected effect on text content and no net effect on an already unspecified buffer content expectation. Performing the operation confirms that the text content is unaffected.

2. The Copy operation on X again has no expected effect upon the text, but does establish an expected value for the buffer, based on the weakened model. The weak expectation of content X is represented by X. The existence of a concrete (but unobservable) expectation causes the effect of the copy operation to be put into the suspect list :

Buffer Contents	Expected Text	Actual Text	Suspect List
X	$\alpha X \beta Y \gamma Z \delta$	$\alpha X \beta Y \gamma Z \delta$	copy.to.buffer: X

3. The Click operation selecting the insertion point just prior to Y has no expected effect on either the text or the buffer, but because there now exists an (unobservable) expectation regarding the buffer contents, it is put in the Suspect List.

Buffer Contents	Expected Text	Actual Text	Suspect List
X	$\alpha X \beta Y \gamma Z \delta$	$\alpha X \beta Y \gamma Z \delta$	copy.to.buffer: X
			click.from.buffer: X
			click.to.buffer: X

4. The Paste operation generates an expectation referring to the content of the buffer which is potentially verifiable: that the text becomes $\alpha X\beta XY\gamma Z\delta$. The expectation is added to the Suspect List *prior* to executing the operation.

Buffer Contents	Expected Text	Actual Text	Suspect List
X	$\alpha X\beta Y\gamma Z\delta$	$\alpha X\beta Y\gamma Z\delta$	copy.to.buffer: X
			click.from.buffer: X
			click.to.buffer: X
			paste.from.buffer: X

The appearance of text segment X after β is sufficient for a match with expectations, allowing the operations on the Suspect List to be cleared of suspicion. The Copy operation is indeed considered to replace the current content with the selected text, the Click operation leaves the buffer unchanged and the Paste uses the full buffer content. (This is unjustified in a strict sense, but the model is being used with a bias towards confirming expectations rather than axiomatic proof.)

The Paste operation, however, does have a suspected effect which is not immediately confirmable and so it is placed on the new Suspect List.

Buffer Contents	Expected Text	Actual Text	Suspect List
X	$\alpha X\beta XY\gamma Z\delta$	$\alpha X\beta XY\gamma Z\delta$	paste.to.buffer: X

5. The Drag operation selecting Y has a potential effect on the buffer content and no expected change on the text; because of the definite expectation it is placed on the Suspect List.

Buffer Contents	Expected Text	Actual Text	Suspect List
X	$\alpha X\beta XY\gamma Z\delta$	$\alpha X\beta XY\gamma Z\delta$	paste.to.buffer: X
			drag.from.buffer: X
			drag.to.buffer: X

6. The Cut operation deleting Y has no net effect on the buffer expectation, but generates an expectation regarding the text, and is placed on the Suspect List. The expected text change matches the actual $\beta X\gamma$ text configuration exactly.

Buffer Contents	Expected Text	Actual Text	Suspect List
X	$\alpha X\beta X\gamma Z\delta$	$\alpha X\beta X\gamma Z\delta$	paste.to.buffer: X
			drag.from.buffer: X
			drag.to.buffer: X
			cut.from.buffer: X
			cut.to.buffer: X

7. The next operation is the Click operation setting the insertion point prior to Z. The Click operation has been deemed verified (see step 4. above) and has no net effect upon either the buffer or text content expectations; since it is already verified, it is not added to the Suspect List.

8. Finally, the last Paste operation is performed. Recall from step 4. that the precondition to the paste (the label on the incoming arc to the transition) has already been verified, and is not added to the Suspect List. It does, however, generate an expectation regarding the text content.

Buffer Contents	Expected Text	Actual Text	Suspect List
X	$\alpha X\beta X\gamma XZ\delta$	$\alpha X\beta X\gamma YZ\delta$	paste.to.buffer: X
			drag.from.buffer: X
			drag.to.buffer: X
			cut.from.buffer: X
			cut.to.buffer: X

Since the expected model text was "weak" (i.e., X instead of X), it is deemed to match the document text (which actually contained a Y where the X was expected). However, since the expectation was not confirmed exactly, the remaining suspects are not exonerated.

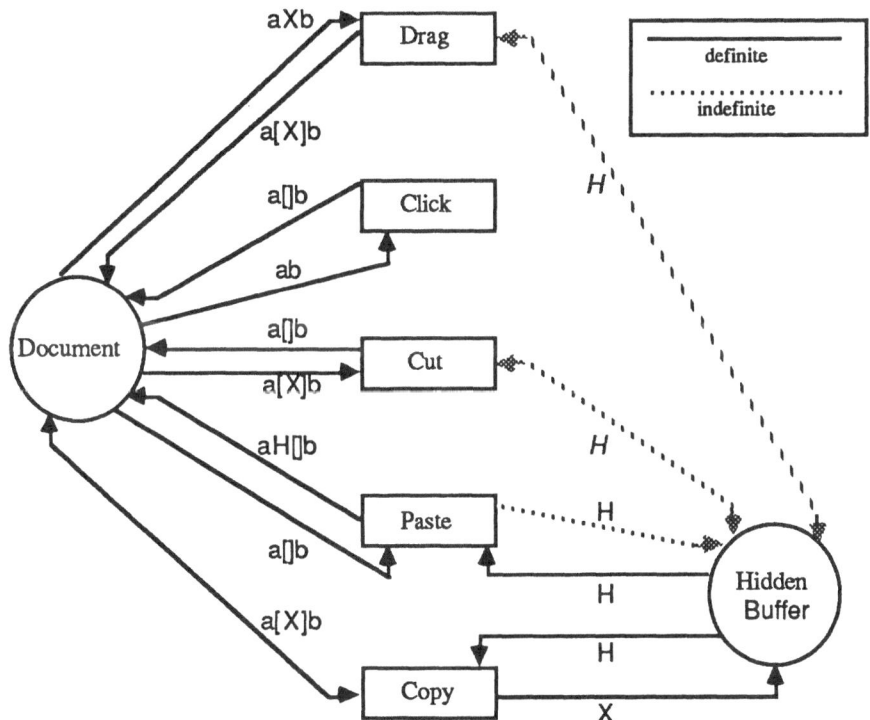

Figure 6. Strengthened mental model of editor operation

Figure 6 depicts the *strengthened model* resulting from the simulation process. A comparison with Figure 5 reveals several significant changes. The indefiniteness of the Paste operation has been refined. It was confirmed that a paste indeed inserts the current buffer contents into the document at the selection point. What is left in question is whether the paste operation leaves the buffer unchanged. Nothing which happened during the simulation could confirm that expectation, and the resulting arc retains its "indefinite" attribute. The semantics of the Copy operation has been resolved; copy indeed replaces the buffer contents with the selection from the text document. The question concerning the Click operation has also been settled; it has no effect on the buffer.

Left completely unresolved are the semantics of the Drag and Cut operations. Nothing which transpired during the simulation would permit us to rule out the possibility that these operations impacted the contents of the buffer.

It is important to note that while the strengthened mental model is significantly more constrained than the weakened mental model, it still serves as a template for a variety of plausible device models, including editors in which (1) the Cut operation loads up the buffer, (2) the Drag operation loads up the buffer, and (3) the Paste operation leaves undefined the contents of the buffer.

Finally, in contrast to the weakened model, the strengthened model is (in this instance) sufficiently definite to allow the development of a plan for satisfying task requirements. By applying additional Drag and Copy operations on either the first or second occurrences of X prior to the final Click operation, the user can be guaranteed that the subsequent Paste will indeed insert X after γ. The plan may be suboptimal with respect to any of the particular editors subsumed under the strengthened model, but it is effective for all such editors. Of course, subsequent experience or explicit experimentation might further refine the mental model and permit the development of an optimal plan.

10 Conclusion

In our view, the value of this work lies not so much in the specifics of the model weakening/strengthening process, but rather in the formulation of a modeling framework in which such an hypothesis may be articulated. We have demonstrated an approach in which discrete models of a device, a user's mental model of that device, and a user's plan for satisfying task requirements may all be expressed within a single representational formalism. Given an actual device and an initial user model, the approach allows for the prediction of the point of expectation failure. In a design context, this might be useful in predicting user errors when transferring between devices of similar (but not identical) functionality.

We view the model weakening/strengthening hypothesis as plausible, and even testable. As computer scientists, our primary goal is not to propose problem-solving strategies, but instead to provide a framework within which cognitive scientists could express such strategies. In the future, we plan to provide software systems to support both the specification and simulation of such processes.

References

1. Bastide, R., Palanque, P.: Petri nets with objects for the design, validation and prototyping of user-driven interfaces, In: Proceedings INTERACT'90, Cambridge: Elsevier, 625-631 (1990).

2. Belotti, V.: Integrating Theoreticians' and Practitioners' Perspectives with Design Rationale, In: Proceedings INTERCHI'93, New York: ACM Press, 101-106 (1993).

3. Blandford, A., Young, R.: Developing Runnable User Models: Separating the Problem Solving Techniques from the Domain Knowledge, Amodeus Document UM/WP6 (1993).

4. Blandford, A., Young, R.: Separating User and Device Descriptions for Modeling Interactive Problem Solving, Amodeus Project Document UM/WP27 (1994).

5. Byrne, M., Wood, S, Sukaviriya, P., Foley, J, Kieras, D.: Automating Interface Evaluation, In: Proceedings CHI'94, New York: ACM Press, 232-237 (1994).

6. Carroll, J., Olson, J.: Mental Models in Human-Computer Interaction, In: Helander M. (Ed.), Handbook of Human-Computer Interaction, North-Holland: Elsevier, 45-65 (1988).

7. Churchill, E., Young, R.: Modeling representations of device knowledge in Soar, In: Steels L., Smith. B. (Eds.), AISB-91: Proceedings of the Eighth Conference on Artificial Intelligence and the Simulation of Behavior, Berlin: Springer, 247-255 (1991).

8. Coombs, M, Hartley, R.: The MGR algorithm and its application to the generation of explanations for novel events, International Journal of Man-Machine Studies, 27, 679-708 (1987).

9. de Kleer, J.: An assumption-based TMS, Artificial Intelligence, 28, 127-162 (1986).

10. Doyle, J.: Truth maintenance systems, Artificial Intelligence, 12, 231-271 (1979).

11. Duke, D., Barnard, P., Duce, D., May, J.: Syndetic Models for Human-Computer Interaction, Amodeus Project Document ID/WP35 (1994).

12. Furuta, K., Kondo, S.: Reasoning on plant process using TMS with temporal constraints, In: Rzevski G. (Ed.), Artificial Intelligence in Manufacturing, Proceedings 4th International Conference on Applications of Artificial Intelligence in Engineering, Berlin: Springer, 313-321 (1989).

13. Furuta, K., Kondo, S.: An approach to assessment of plant man-machine systems by computer simulation of an operator's cognitive behavior, International Journal of Man-Machine Studies, 39, 473-493 (1993).

14. Harrison, M, Barnard, P.: On Defining Requirements for Interaction, In: Finkelstein A. (Ed.), Proceedings IEEE International Workshop on Requirements Engineering, New York: IEEE, 50-54 (1993).

15. Howes, A.: A Model of the Acquisition of Menu Knowledge by Exploration, Proceedings CHI'94, New York: ACM Press, 445-451 (1994).

16. Kieras, D., Polson, P.: An Approach to the Formal Analysis of User Complexity, International Journal of Man-Machine Studies, 22, 365-394 (1985).

17. Newell, A.: Unified Theories of Cognition, Cambridge: Harvard University Press (1990).

18. Polk, T., Newell, A., Lewis, R.: Towards a unified theory of immediate reasoning in Soar, In: Proceedings Eleventh Annual Conference of the Cognitive Science Society (1989).

19. Van Biljon, W.: Extending Petri nets for specifying man-machine dialogues, International Journal of Man-Machine Studies, 34, 437-455 (1988).

20. Young, R., Green, T., Simon, T.: Programmable User Models for Predictive Evaluation of Interface Designs, In: Proceedings CHI'89, New York: ACM Press, 15-19 (1989).

21. Young, R., Whittington, J.: Instruction Language Descriptions and User Models for Aspects of Interactive Systems, Amodeus Project Document D20 (1992).

The Application Of Petri Nets To Represent And Reason About Human Factors Problems During Accident Analyses

Chris Johnson

Department of Computing Science, University of Glasgow,
Glasgow, G12 8QQ.
johnson@dcs.glasgow.ac.uk

Abstract. Accident reports are intended to ensure that failures do not recur. They contain the analysis of many different experts, including human factors and systems engineers. The insights of these investigators are often separated into chapters that reflect the particular concerns and expertise of their authors. Such a separation often makes it difficult for readers to trace the ways in which human and system 'failures' combine to create the necessary conditions for an accident. The following paper argues that mathematically based modelling techniques can be used to overcome this problem. It is hypothesised that the application of formal notations can be extended from the domain of systems engineering in order to represent the findings of human factors analyses. In particular, it is argued that Petri Nets can be used to represent and reason about the concurrent behaviour of multiple operators and their systems. Tool support can be recruited to validate the resulting nets. The sequences of events leading to an accident can be simulated and shown to human factors and systems engineers. This, in turn, may elicit further observations about the causes of an accident. A near collision analysed by the U.K. Department of Transport's Air Accident Investigations Branch (AAIB) is used in order to evaluate this approach.

1 Introduction

We are concerned to identify techniques that support both human factors and systems engineering because the Commission of the European Community [12], the Japanese Fifth Generation Initiative [28] and United States' Presidential Task Forces [25] have all cited operator intervention as a primary factor in the cause and exacerbation of accidents. Unfortunately, many accident reports separate human factors considerations from the findings of systems engineers. They are frequently discussed in different chapters and appendices, for example see Air Accidents Investigations Branch [1, 2] or Worley and Lewis [29]. This paper starts from the premise that such distinctions are artificial. Human 'errors' cannot be fully explained without considering the demands that application functionality places upon its operators. System failures cannot be fully explained without considering the managerial and operational circumstances that affect maintenance and reliability. Some accident reports use tortuous cross-referencing to draw together these strands of analysis. Others leave the reader wondering how the different findings of the experts can form a coherent picture of the events leading to an accident [19]. The following paper intends to show how mathematically-based notations can be used to avoid some of these problems. These notations provide means of capturing the concurrent behaviour of multiple operators and their systems. Analytical techniques can then be applied in order to identify ways in which the interaction between operators and systems jeopardises safety. It is argued that tool support can be recruited to validate the findings embodied in Petri Nets. The sequences of events leading to an accident can be simulated. These animations can be shown to human factors and systems engineers in order to elicit further observations about the causes of an accident.

1.1 Alternative Formalisms

A number of alternative formalisms can be recruited to support human factors and systems engineering. For instance, the tabular form of Failure Mode and Effect Analysis can be used to represent the conditions that lead to an accident [9]. Failure modes, the effects of systems failures and additional observations are enumerated under three columns, this is illustrated in Table 1. These ta-

Component	Failure Mode	Failure Cause	Criticality	Improvement
Pump Blow-back	Blockage	Valve collapse	Medium	Maintenance
Pump Seal	Over-heat	Dried	High	More inspection

Table 1. A Failure Mode, Effects And Criticality Analysis Table.

bles could include both operator and system 'failures'. Unfortunately, they can become large and unwieldy even for accidents with relatively simple causes. Interaction between failures in different parts of the system are not considered. These are significant limitations for analysts seeking to represent interaction between systems and their operators.

Fault-trees can be used to represent the findings of accident investigations. These use 'gates' to represent the logical combinations of events that must occur in order for an accident to take place. The fault-tree notation is analogous to that used to represent electrical circuits. It is in widespread use throughout the process industries. Human factors researchers have used similar notations to support the design of interactive systems [27]. Unfortunately, the European Federation of Chemical Engineering's International Study Group On Risk Analysis concludes:

"Fault-trees have difficulties with event sequences... parts of systems where sequence is important are, therefore, usually modelled using techniques more adept at incorporating such considerations" (Cox, [8]).

This is a significant limitation because event sequences determine the quality of interaction between an operator and their system. The order in which displays are presented and commands issued is an important consideration during the development of human-machine interfaces.

Elsewhere we have argued that traces of interaction can be represented using interval temporal logics [15, 17]. These formalisms extend first order logics to provide operators, such as $\bigcirc$ (read as 'next'), that can be used to represent sequential information. Unfortunately, these notations provide non-formalists with an extremely poor impression of the human-machine interaction leading to an accident. Executable subsets of interval temporal logic can, however, be used to derive prototypes that simulate the behaviour of interactive systems [13]. These simulations can be shown to analysts in order to determine whether the logic accurately models the events that led to an accident. Unfortunately, using temporal logics to construct multi-user, multi-system simulations can be extremely costly in terms of the time and expertise of the analyst.

The following pages intend to demonstrate that Petri Nets can be used to overcome the limitations of formalisms such as fault-trees and executable logics. Some notable attempts have been made to represent human factors requirements using this notation. For instance, Van Biljon [5] exploits Petri Nets to derive formal specifications of interactive systems at a very high level of abstraction. Bastide and Palanque [3] have used this notation to represent the design of an interactive database. Petri Nets have also been used to support the engineering of concurrent systems [20]. Chretienne [7] shows how they can be used to represent and reason about timing properties of system events. Hura and Attwood [11] have used Petri Nets to support accident analysis from the perspective of systems engineering. In contrast, this paper will demonstrate that Petri Nets can be used to analyse the operator-system interaction that can lead to accidents.

1.2 Outline Of The Paper

This section has briefly provided the background to this research and has introduced the main objectives of the paper. Section 2 describes the events that led to a possible collision between two aircraft. The AAIB accident report on this incident is used to illustrate our argument. Section 3 introduces the components of Petri Nets and argues that they can be used to represent the ways in which human and systems 'failures' can contribute towards an accident. Section 4 argues that graphical representations of Petri Nets provide a useful means of describing the event sequences that can lead to loss of life. Section 5 shows how this graphical notation can be used to represent the concurrent behaviour of multiple concurrent systems and their users. It is argued that this provides a means of capturing the many different interactions that frequently lead to accidents. Section 6 argues that Petri Nets can be used to identify potential instances of non-determinism, or conflict, within human-machine systems. The results of this analysis can be used to direct the allocation of design resources in order to avoid the circumstances that lead to accidents. Section 7 shows how hierarchical Petri Nets can be used to capture the more detailed findings of human factors and systems specialists. Sub-networks can represent the fine grained analysis of experts such as cognitive psychologists and avionics designers. It is argued that higher-level Petri Nets provide a cohesive structure, or context, for these more detailed findings. Section 8 briefly introduces Chiola's GreatSPN tool that has been used to produce and validate the networks presented in this paper [6]. Section 9 describes areas for further work and presents the conclusions that may be drawn from this research.

2 The Scenario

We have selected an incident analysed by the AAIB as an example for the remander of this paper [1]. A British Aerospace One-Eleven (BA-1-11) was returning to the United Kingdom from Venice. Its commander sat in the right seat. In the left seat, a first officer was undergoing familiarisation training. As they reached Abbeville, the crew discussed their approach to runway 08L at Gatwick Airport. This was known as the emergency runway. It was held in reserve for situations in which the main runway, 08R, was unavailable. Both pilots were familiar with 08L. Both knew that it would come into operation at 21:00 hrs when the main runway was scheduled to be closed down. At 20:45 hrs they received an Automatic Terminal Information Service radio transmission from their destination. This gave weather details and reported that the current landing runway was 08R. Shortly afterwards, London air traffic control confirmed their clearance for 08L. They also informed the crew that this runway was being opened for them. The crew were cleared by the Tower for a visual landing on "08 LEFT". They replied with "CLEAR TO LAND 08 LEFT". There was then a brief discussion initiated by the co-pilot who was uncertain which runway they were approaching. This caused the commander to change his interpretation of the visual cues on his approach to the airfield. He re-aligned the aircraft with taxiway number 2 instead of the landing runway 08L. The aircraft touched the ground and rolled to a halt on the taxiway after 960 meters.

While the BA-1-11 approached the airfield, the crew of a Boeing 737 (B-737) were preparing to start their engines. They were directed along taxiways 7 and 2. As they turned onto taxiway 2, the crew of the B-737 observed the lights of the BA-1-11 as it came in to land. After a few seconds discussion with his co-pilot, the commander slowed the B-737 and flashed its landing lights. He then made a call to the Control Tower. This call was not acknowledged. The air traffic controller had noticed the BA-1-11's change of course and was busy confirming his observations using the Ground Movement Radar. This system did not extend beyond the airfield's boundary. The controller, therefore, had to wait until the BA-1-11 approached the taxiway before he could gain the necessary confirmation. The crew of the B-737 were told to hold their position as the BA-1-11 approached. Three seconds later the Tower ordered them to move off the taxiway. The fully laden aircraft turned onto the grass verge and its tires became bogged-down in the grass. The tail and left wing of the B-737 were left partially blocking the taxiway. The BA-1-11 stopped one hundred and ninety meters short of the B-737.

3 Petri Nets

Petri Nets can be used to represent the state of a human-machine system in terms of the conditions that are satisfied during intervals of interaction [24]. When particular conditions hold, certain events can occur. If an event takes place then it can alter the state of the human-machine system. Changes in state are represented by the new conditions that hold after an event has occurred. These new conditions enable further events to take place. More formally, Petri Nets are directed graphs; $PN = (P, T, E, M)$. They consist of a set of places, P, transitions, T, edges, E and markings, M.

Places can be used to describe the conditions that hold for operators and their systems during the course of an accident. In particular, they can be used to represent the pre-conditions for disaster. In our scenario, accident analysts might use a place to represent the fact that the BA-1-11 is on taxiway 2. Another place can represent the fact that the B-737 is blocking the path of the BA-1-11. Such places describe the causes of an accident at an extremely high level of abstraction. Places can also be used to represent causes that are specifically related to the human factors or systems engineering of an application. Places can be used to represent human factors observations about the behaviour of individual operators; the air traffic controller is monitoring the Ground Movement Radar. Places might also represent the behaviour of individual systems; the Ground Movement Radar is presenting the new course of the BA-1-11.

Transitions can be used to represent the events that cause accidents. In our scenario, the initiating events leading towards a collision can be identified as the landing of the BA-1-11 and the arrival of the B-737 on taxiway 2. These can be represented as transitions that change the state of the human-machine system into one in which both aircraft are on taxiway 2. Transitions can represent events initiated by both systems and their operators. For instance, human factors observations might indicate that the air traffic controller's decision to move the B-737 was a critical transition in the human-machine system. Similarly, systems engineers might identify the detection of the BA-1-11 by the Ground Movement Radar as an important event in our accident scenario. Isolating these critical transitions provides a focus for subsequent human factors and systems analysis. The air traffic controller might have been trained not to move the B-737 off onto the grass. The Ground Movement Radar might have been re-designed to detect the change in course before the BA-1-11 reached taxiway 2.

Edges connect places to transitions: $E \subseteq \{P \times T\} \cup \{T \times P\}$. They can be used to form the chains of events and conditions that lead to an accident. They can be described in terms of two functions. The function Op maps from each transition to its set of output places. The output places of a transition represent the conditions that hold after an event has occurred. For example, an output place can be used to represent the systems engineering observation that changes in the BA-1-11's approach caused changes to the display of the Ground

Movement Radar. An input place function, *Ip*, maps from each transition to the set of input places for that transition. The input places of a transitions specify the conditions that must hold for an event to occur. The input place of a transition can be used to represent the human factors observation that the Ground Movement Radar's display led the air traffic controller to order the B-737 off taxiway 2.

4 Graphical Notation

Petri Nets can be represented graphically. Events, or transitions, are shown as bars (–). Conditions, or places, are denoted by unfilled circles (○). Edges are shown as arrows linking places and transitions. Figure 1 shows a graphical Petri Net representation for our accident scenario. Rather than show the path of events that actually occurred, this network shows how the incidents reported by the AAIB could have led to a loss of life. Such hypotheses frequently form the focus of accident investigations·in incidents where casualties were 'narrowly' avoided. Figure 1 provides a very high level representation of the events leading to a potential collision. It is intended to show how Petri Nets can provide a framework for subsequent human factors and systems analysis. This high level of abstraction is inappropriate for many of the findings presented in accident reports. Section 7 will show how Petri Nets can be refined to represent a finer level of detail.

In order to model the dynamic behaviour of a human-machine system, tokens are used to mark those places in a Petri Net that are enabled. A place is enabled if its conditions hold. The tokens in a net are said to characterise a marking state and are denoted graphically by filled dots (•). For instance, Figure 2 is marked to show that both the BA-1-11 and the B-737 are on taxiway 2. Analysts can alter the marking of a Petri Net to indicate the different conditions that hold for operators and their systems. These walk-throughs can be used to simulate the sequences of events and states that arise during accident scenarios. A transition can fire if all of its input places contain at least one token. After firing, a token is deposited in each of the output places of a transition. In Figure 2 it is possible for the transition indicating that BA-1-11 establishes a collision course to fire. The transition representing the B-737 turning to block the path of the BA-1-11 can also fire. If these transitions fired then the places indicating that the BA-1-11 is on a collision course and that the B-737 is blocking taxiway 2 would be marked with tokens. The marking of these places would, in turn, enable the collision transition leading to a state in which loss of life occurs.

5 Concurrency

Figure 2 shows how Petri Nets can be used to represent sequential behaviour. The places and transitions that led the B-737 to block taxiway 2 can be traced along a single path of input and output edges. Disasters are, however, often

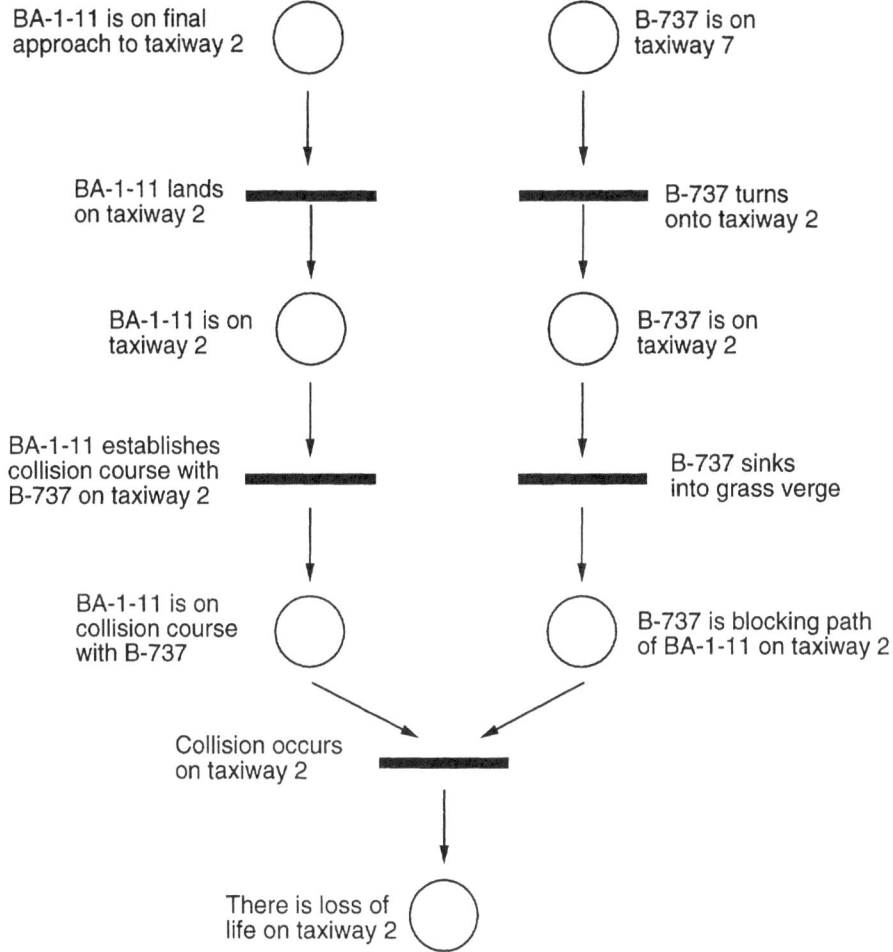

Fig 1. A Simple Petri Net.

caused by the interaction between concurrent users and systems [4]. It is important that Petri Nets can be used to represent the behaviours of these multiple agents. Figure 3 shows the results of a human factors analysis of the communications between the crew of the B-737 and the air traffic controller. The consequences of the controller's intervention are indicated by the input and output edges leading from the place labelled Ground Movement Radar shows BA-1-11's new course for taxiway 2. Figure 3 also shows how Petri Nets can be used to represent the effects of human intervention upon systems engineering. The controller's commands directly led to the B-737 sinking into the grass verge:

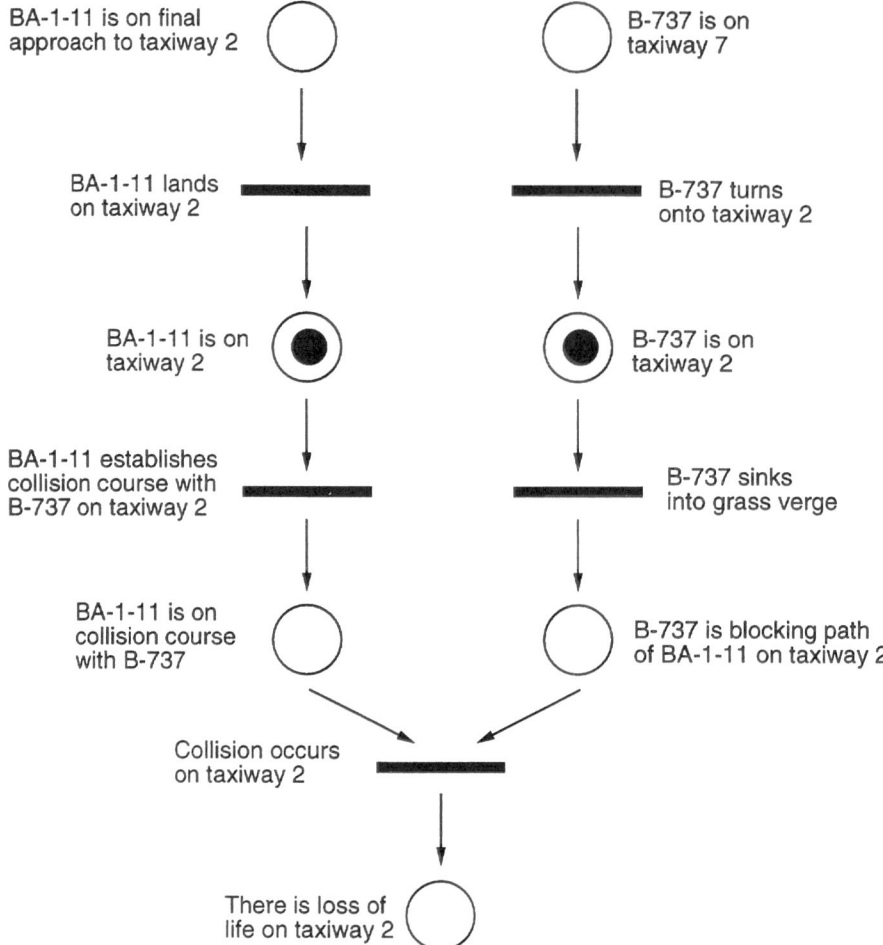

Fig. 2. A Petri Net With Multiple Tokens.

"Because the landing gear (of the B-737) had left the paved taxiing surface, the appropriate inspections were performed. The only damage detected was a fuel leak on the upper surface of the left wing, where sealant within the fuel tank had become loose at a skin joint." (Air Accidents Investigations Branch, [1]).

The damage sustained by the BA-737 is represented by the transition labelled B-737 fuel tank sealant is damaged. In order for this transition to fire both of its input places must be marked. The B-737 must be on taxiway 2 and the air traffic controller must order it off the paved surface. These places, therefore, represent necessary but not sufficient conditions for damage to the B-737. It was the interaction between the concurrent behaviour of the air traffic controller and

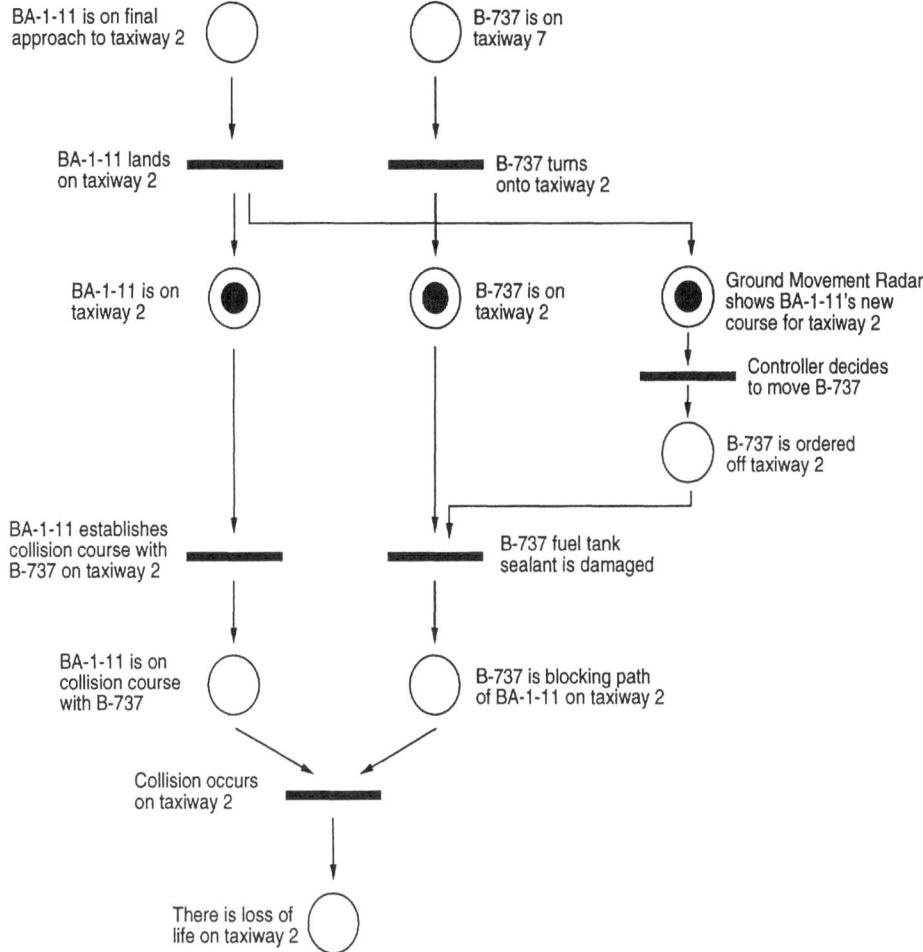

Fig. 3. A Petri Net Showing Concurrent Interaction.

the crew of the B-737 that contributed to the causes of the accident. If the crew had been warned of the BA-1-11 before the turning onto taxiway 2 or if the controller had not ordered the B-737 onto the verge than the B-737 might not have been left blocking the taxiway.

Petri Nets can capture the synchronisation requirements that must be satisfied in order for an accident to occur. For instance, the B-737 must be blocking the taxiway and the BA-1-11 must be on a collision course if loss of life is to occur. This is represented in Figure 3 by the transition that leads to the place labelled `There is loss of life on taxiway 2`. This links the sequences describing the behaviours of the BA-1-11 and the B-737. Such transitions represent interaction between concurrent human-machine systems. They also provide a focus for accident analysis. The ultimate aim of our accident analysis is to ensure that the transition labelled `Collision occurs on taxiway 2` never fires. This can be achieved if its input places are not both marked. In other words, it should never be the case that the B-737 is blocking the path of the BA-1-11 and the BA-1-11 is on a collision course for the B-737. The fact that this is readily apparent from a cursory glance at Figure 3 illustrates an important benefit for Petri Nets as communications tools. It is important to note, however, that Figure 3 simply represents the events that might have led to a possible loss of life. It does not recommend means of avoiding such an incident. This illustrates an important point about the use of formal notations. They provide precise and concise means of capturing the causes of failure in human factors and systems engineering. They provide communications tools and can be shown to the other participants in an enquiry. They do not provide a panacea for the problems of accident analysis. They do not replace the judgemental skills that must be developed by human factors and systems engineers. In our scenario, there is no automatic means of moving between the Petri Net representation and the remedies that can prevent an accident from recurring.

6 Conflict

The previous sections of this paper have shown how Petri Nets can be used to represent the causes of an accident. Human factors and systems engineers can also use Petri Nets to analyse techniques that might prevent a system from failing. For instance, Figure 4 represents two possible outcomes for our scenario. One terminating place shows loss of life. The other shows that the disaster is averted. Analysts can use such networks to focus attention upon techniques that might ensure that loss of life does not occur. Human factors and systems engineering must be exploited so that the transition, labelled `BA-1-11 establishes collision course with B-737 on taxiway 2`, never fires. The reason we are concerned to disable this transition is that it is one possible outcome from what is known as a conflict situation. The place labelled `BA-1-11 is on taxiway 2` is marked and so it is possible to fire either the transition indicating a collision course or the transition representing insufficient velocity. The network does not indicate which of these two possible transitions will fire. Given this marking we can, however, be sure that only one will fire and that they cannot occur simultaneously. Firing the collision course transition would remove a token from the place labelled `BA-1-11 is on taxiway 2`. This would disable the insufficient velocity transition. Petri Nets that include conflict situations are non-deterministic. If many different transitions are enabled then any one of them can be selected for firing. This provides a means of representing the non-determinism that is inherent in many complex multi-user, multi-system applications.

Conflict situations represent critical stages in an accident scenarios. Non-determinism indicates a loss of control over the behaviour of the human-machine system. Human factors and systems engineers can, therefore, seek to improve the design of a system by identifying and removing conflict from Petri Net repre-

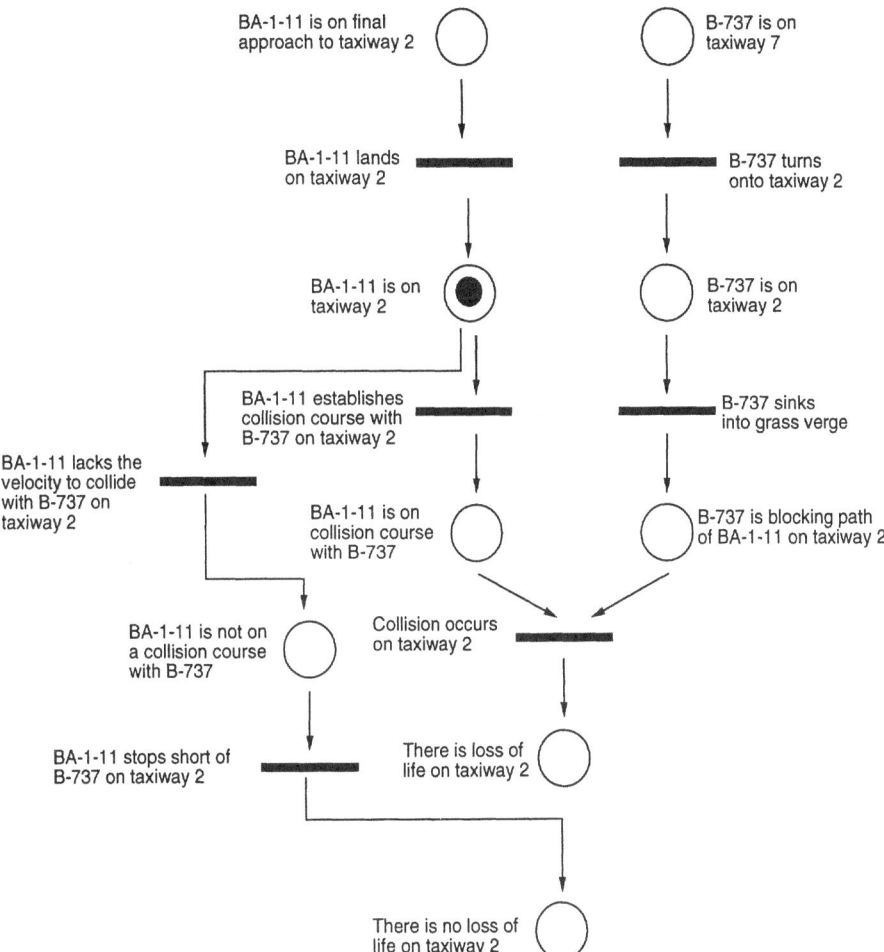

Fig. 4. A Petri Net Showing Conflict.

sentations. In our example, this might be done by ensuring that the air traffic controller issued an earlier warning to the crew of the BA-1-11 as it approached taxiway 2. They, in turn, might have responded by ensuring the prompt and sufficient application of reverse thrust to rapidly reduce their landing speed:

> "Figures calculated by British Aerospace for the ground roll from 121 kt at touchdown to stop, based on a dry runway with full brakes applied for 1.2 seconds after touchdown, did not exceed 490 meters, although the figure achieved depended upon the use of spoilers and the level of thrust applied. The calculated figures were considerably shorter than the 960 meters achieved during the incident by WB (the BA-1-11) and indicate that maximum braking and/or maximum reverse thrust were not used

for the whole of the landing run" (Air Accidents Investigations Branch, [1]).

Human factors and systems engineering must both be recruited in order to achieve the common aim of ensuring that air traffic controllers warn aircraft approaching taxiways. Systems engineering could have extended the range of the Ground Movement Radar. Human factors engineering might have verified that the controller could sample the Ground Movement Radar frequently enough to observe the BA-1-11's change in course. Inhibitor arks provide a means of representing the common aim for both of these disciplines. Transitions that are linked by an inhibitor can only fire if the place from which the inhibitor comes is not marked. Inhibitors are represented graphically as an edge with a small empty circle on one end. In Figure 5 an inhibitor arc is shown running from the place labelled `Air traffic controller is informing BA-1-11 of B-737` to the transition marked `BA-1-11 establishes collision course with B-737 on taxiway 2`. In our example, the place is marked. It has no other output transitions and so the collision course transition cannot be enabled.

7 Hierarchical Petri Nets

The networks in previous sections of this paper represent our scenario at an extremely high level of abstraction. This is inappropriate for many of the findings that emerge from human factors and systems analyses. The exact ways in which systems gather and store data can have a profound impact upon the course of an accident. For example, the Automatic Terminal Information Service at Gatwick did not change the message identifier to indicate that the active runway had changed from 08R to 08L. Detailed cognitive and perceptual factors can influence an operator's response to potential disasters. For instance, the AAIB argued that the interaction between the crew of the BA-1-11 was a prime cause of the near-collision with the B-737. The more dominant and decisive commander was in command. The more contemplative and less assertive individual, who could have questioned the approach to the taxiway, was undergoing training. Petri Nets can also be used to model these details. Places and transitions can be replaced by sub-networks to provide finer grained representations. The place labelled `BA-1-11 is on final approach to taxiway 2` can be refined into the sub-network shown in Figure 6. This captures some of the environmental factors that influenced the actions of the BA-1-11's crew. The fact that the lights on 08L were much brighter than the first officer expected for an emergency runway led him to ask "You are going for the emergency runway, aren't you?". This is represented in the Petri Net by the place, labelled `Lights are much brighter than expected`, followed by the transition labelled with the first officer's utterance. Here the place must be marked in order to enable the transition. In other words, the lights must be brighter than expected for the first officer to make their remark. The Petri Net, therefore, represents the causal link that the AAIB identified between the perceptual cues provided by the taxiway lighting system and the first officer's question:

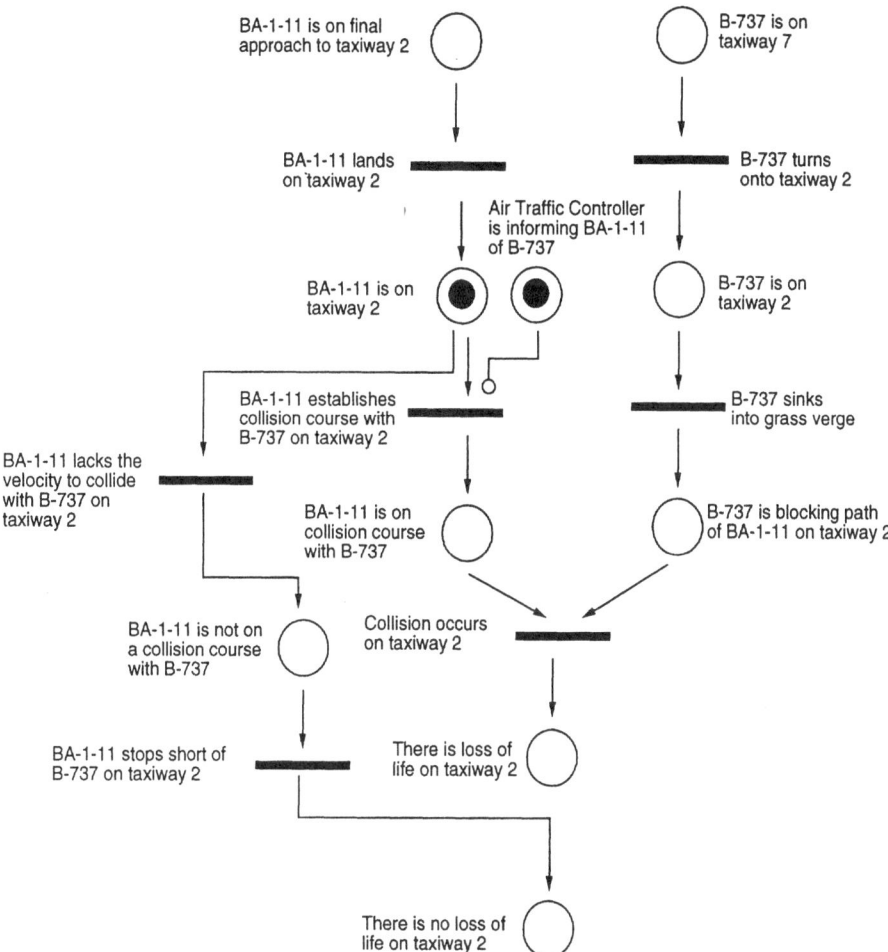

Fig. 5. A Petri Net With An Inhibitor Avoiding Conflict.

"The first officer made this remark because he could see the lights of Gatwick and was a little concerned that the dominant set of lights visible to him (those of 08L) seemed to be of a much higher standard than he was expecting for the 'emergency runway'... These doubts had not crystallised into a clear cut mental model for the first officer and it was certainly in an attempt to provoke some sort of discussion of the situation, and from the discussion to gain a clear model with which he was happy, that he made his remark, 'You are going for the emergency runway, aren't you?'" (Air Accidents Investigations Branch, [1]).

This quotation illustrates the way in which cognitive factors, "mental models", can influence the course of events leading to accidents. Figure 6 also shows how

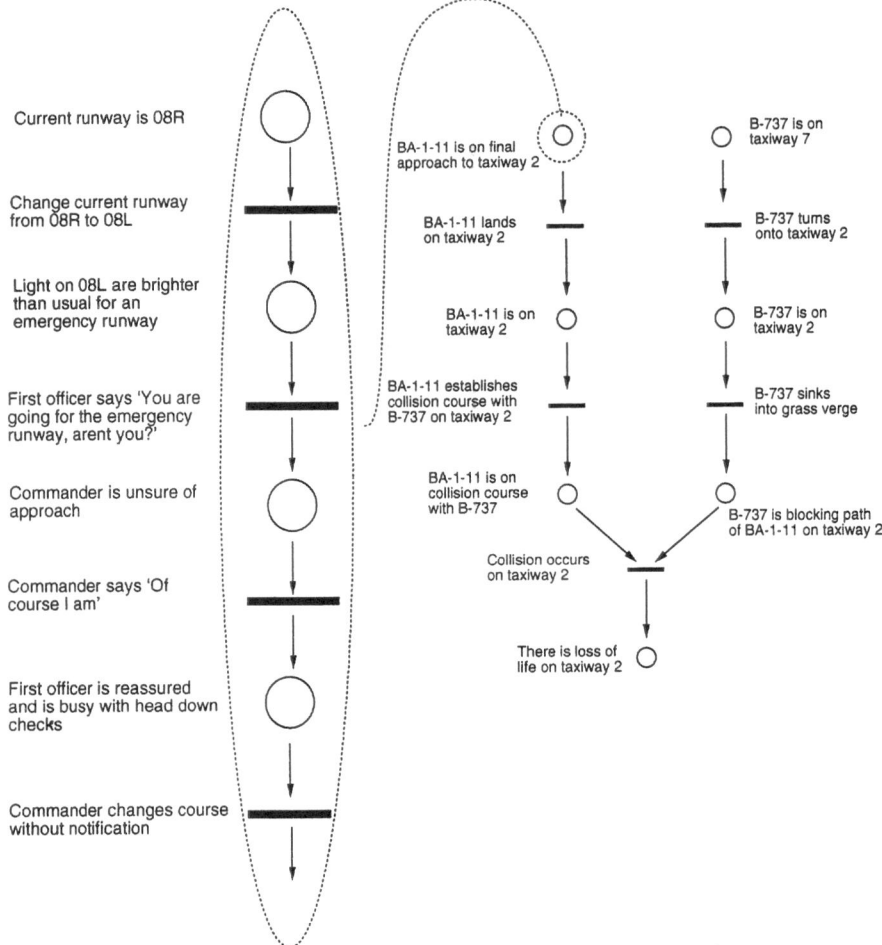

Fig 6. A Sub-Net Showing Crew Interaction.

Petri Nets can represent some of the assumptions that analysts make about the cognitive states of individual participants. In particular, the transition labelled with the first officer's remark enables a place in which the commander is unsure about their approach. Again this illustrates a causal link in the sequence of events investigated by the accident analysts. The commander's change of interpretation was caused by a query from the first officer in an attempt to resolve his uncertainty about which runway was being approached. A similar causal relationship can be seen between the commander's utterance which confirmed that he was sure of his approach and the place which indicates that the first officer is re-assured.

Accident analyses should, ideally, identify techniques that can preserve the safety of human-machine systems. For instance, the first officer might have been made aware of the commander's actions by requiring both crew members to confirm any change of direction during their approach. Operating procedures could stipulate that crew members reach a verbal agreement before issuing certain commands during an approach. The human factors section of the AAIB report stresses the need to improve crew coordination through flight deck management training. Unfortunately, such protocols might not have guaranteed the safety of the aircraft:

> "The nature of the flight deck would have made such an intervention even less likely; an individual being assessed will wish to be very sure of himself before appearing to question the competence of his assessor... The properties of these crew members which made it possible for them to land on taxiway 2 were their ... relative personalities, roles and status: the more dominant and decisive individual was in command and control, with the more contemplative and less assertive individual in a position of both subordination and evaluation." (Air Accidents Investigations Branch, [1]).

The fact that the first officer did not call for an overshoot when he eventually noticed the commander's 'error' confirms the suspicion that that this human factors technique might not have been effective. System support could have avoided such problems. For instance, both the commander and the first officer could have been required to provide input before the approach was changed. Avionics might have required both crew members to 'vote' for certain commands. Figure 7 shows how Petri Nets can be used to represent such systems engineering techniques at finer levels of detail. If the transition representing the first officer's input does not fire then no token will be deposited in the place representing the fact that their command is processed. This, in turn, would prevent the change in direction transition from being fired. Unfortunately, the problems of systems engineering limit the utility of this approach. Not the least of these are the cost and technical complexity of modifying existing avionics systems. There are also human factors limitations. It is inappropriate to enforce voting mechanisms in cockpits where rapid intervention may be required in order to correct the approach of an aircraft, for instance during strong cross-winds. These problems reinforce the point that formal notations need not represent systems that are achievable in the 'real world'. There is no guarantee that they will provide a faithful model of an application domain. This is entirely dependent upon the skill of the analyst and their ability to elicit the salient features of an accident sequence. The power of the Petri Net notation is that it provides a means of explicitly representing these 'salient features'.

8   Simulation

It is important that human factors and systems engineers have a clear understanding of the behaviour of the systems represented by Petri Nets. This task can

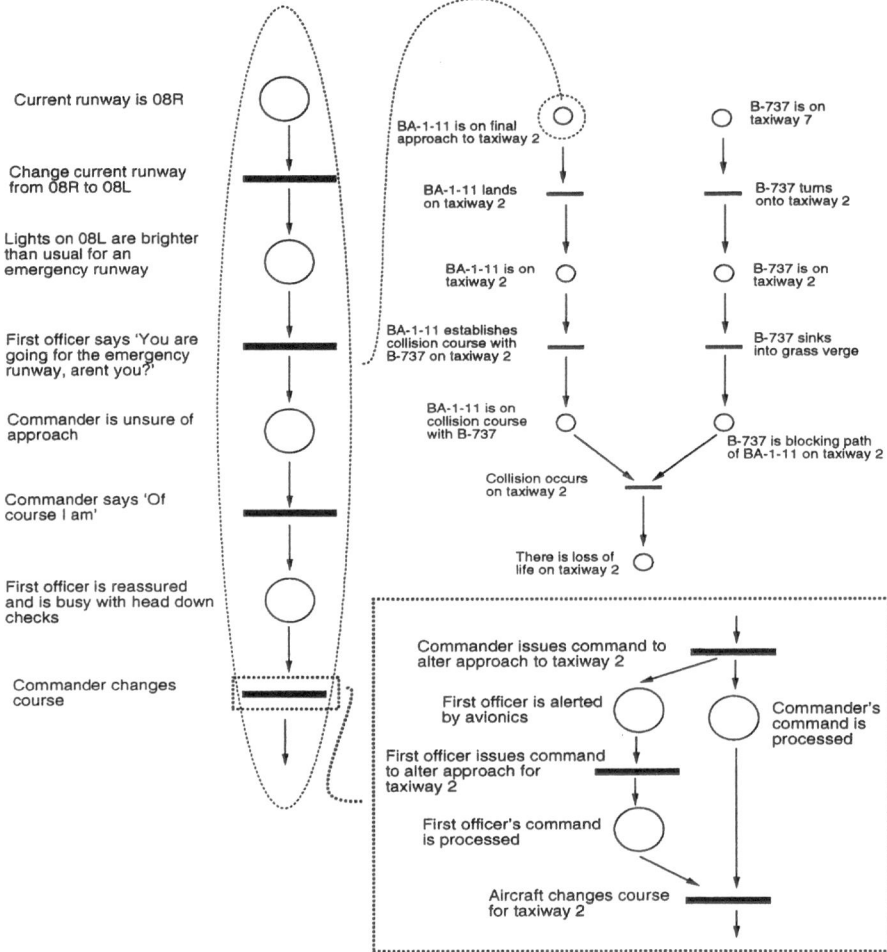

Fig. 7. A Sub-Net Showing A System Command Protocol.

be impaired by the additional complexity that is introduced through the use of sub-networks. It can be difficult to trace the likely passage of tokens through the many places and transitions that might used to represent cognitive, perceptual and environmental details. Fortunately, this task can be eased by tools that animate the enabling and firing of transitions as tokens pass from place to place in a Petri Net. For instance, Chiola's GreatSPN can be used to view tokens as they pass through a network [6]. Human factors and systems engineers can record which places are marked and which transitions are enabled. The "possibility of playing (such) token games highly simplifies the development of correct models, thus eliminating the need for more complex 'net debugging'." A further advantage is that the resulting animations provide powerful communications tools that can be shown to the many different teams that must collaborate during an accident analysis. All of the Petri Nets presented in this paper were generated and checked using the GreatSPN editor. This tool can be used to create arbitrary sub-networks to form hierarchical Petri Nets. Such facilities are vital if complex networks are to be constructed.

9   Conclusions And Further Work

In this paper we have argued that Petri Nets can be used to represent the findings of accident analyses. Petri Nets are well suited to this task because they are capable of representing concurrent interaction between multiple operators and multiple systems. Simple analytical techniques can be applied to these networks in order to identify instances of potential non-determinism. Such situations provide a focus for the allocation of design resources in order to guarantee safety. The use of hierarchical networks provides a means of representing fine grained human and system behaviours. Simulation tools can be used to validate Petri Nets representations of accident scenarios.

This paper is the result of an initial investigation. Much work remains to be done in order to fully explore the potential of Petri Nets as both a design and analysis tool for human-machine systems. In particular, the networks presented in this paper have not described the device or presentation characteristics that can have a profound impact upon the cognitive and perceptual performance of system operators. Previous work, by the author, has shown how these details can gradually be introduced into logic specifications using structured graphics and device abstractions [16]. Future work intends to extend the application of this approach to capture device and presentation information within Petri Nets. It is anticipated that the introduction of these details might provide a means of deriving prototype systems from sub-networks that describe interactive dialogues.

Future work intends to resolve a number of technical problems that limit the utility of our modeling techniques. For instance, we have used transitions to represent the events that contribute towards major accidents. This decision is justified by the observation that both transitions and events affect the state of interaction [18]. Unfortunately, this approach can lead to problems for more complex descriptions. When an event triggers several actions, it must be represented by a number of duplicate transitions. Future research intends to develop an approach suggested by Palanque and Bastide (personal correspondence). They use dedicated places to represent critical events during the course of interaction. This avoids the duplication created by the use of transitions. Similarly, we intend to explore the use of Petri Net composition techniques to separate out both user and system models during accident investigations. This would considerably simplify some of the larger networks shown in this paper.

The networks presented in this paper have not considered the real-time delays that can occur before a transition fires. This is a significant omission because temporal properties frequently have a profound impact upon the safety of human-machine systems. Delays in system responses can lead to frustration and error [21]. It can be difficult for operators to predict the consequences of their interaction if periods of quiescence allow the system to process a backlog of user input [10]. It is, however, possible to explicitly represent temporal properties within a Petri Net. Zuberek [30] associates firing times with transitions in order to model the low-level behaviour of computer hardware. Merlin and Faber [23] have exploited a similar approach by associating minimum and maximum firing times with each transition. Further work intends to show how such techniques might be recruited to enhance the modelling power of Petri Nets for both human factors and systems engineering.

The Petri Nets shown in this paper do not represent probabilistic information. This has not been a severe limitation for our scenario but it might well prove to be significant omission in accidents that are caused by the periodic failure of system components. Researchers have enhanced the Petri Net notation to include probabilistic information. Marsan, Balbo and Conte argue that:

> "With the introduction of Stochastic Petri Nets a link is established between two important classes of computer system models: the above mentioned graph models (e.g., Petri Nets) and the probabilistic models familiar to performance analysts" (Marsan, Balbo and Conte, [22]).

Future work intends to investigate whether a further link might be established between these approaches and human factors techniques. This is important because the probabilistic behaviour of an interactive system can frequently influence the control strategy of its operators [14]. If a component is know to fail frequently then users will, typically, anticipate the failure by devoting greater resources to monitoring its state [26].

10 Acknowledgements

This paper is the result of collaborative research with Dr. Peter Wright of British Aerospace's Dependable Computing Systems Center, University of York and Dr. John McCarthy, Department of Psychology, University of Cork. The members of the Human Computer Interaction Group in the Department of Computer Science, University of York provided valuable advice and encouragement for this research. Thanks are also due to Itana Gimenes who helped to provide access to GreatSPN. This research was supported by a joint British Council/EOLAS grant, number 9284(1992).

11 References

1. Air Accidents Investigations Branch. *Report On The Incident Involving BAC 1-11 G-AYWB and Boeing 737 EI-BTZ On 12 April 1988 At Gatwick Airport*, number 2/89, London, United Kingdom. Her Majesty's Stationery Office, (1989).

2. Air Accidents Investigations Branch. *Report On The Accident To Boeing 737-400 G-OBME Near Kegworth, Leicestershire on 8th January 1989*, number 4/90, London, United Kingdom. Her Majesty's Stationery Office, (1990).

3. Bastide, R. and Palanque, P. Petri net objects for the design, validation and Prototyping of user-driven interfaces. In D. Diaper, D. Gilmore, G. Cockton, and B. Shackel, editors, *Human-Computer Interaction—INTERACT'90*, pages 625–631. Elsevier Science Publications, North Holland, Netherlands, (1990).

4. Bignell, V. and Fortune, J. *Understanding System Failure*. Manchester University Press, Manchester, United Kingdom, (1991).

5. Van Biljon, W.R. Extending Petri nets for specifying man-machine dialogues. *International Journal of Man-Machine Studies*, 28(4):437–455, (1988).

6. Chiola, G. GreatSPN users' manual. Technical report, Departmento di Informatica, Universita' delgi Studi di Turino, Turino, Italy, (1987).

7. Chretienne, P. Timed Petri nets: A solution to the minimum-time-reachability problem between two states of a timed-event graph. *Journal of Systems and Software*, 6(1-2):95–101, (1986).

8. Cox, A.P. editor. *Risk Analysis In The Process Industries: The Report Of The International Study Group On Risk Analysis*. EFCE No. 45. The Institute Of Chemical Engineers, Rugby, United Kingdom, (1985).

9. Davies, K.R. Techniques for the identification and assessment of major accident hazards. In J. Burgoyne, editor, *The Assessment And Control Of Major Hazards*, pages 289–308. Pergamon Press, Oxford, United Kingdom, (1985).

10. Ellis, C.A. and Gibbs, S.J. Concurrency control in groupware systems. *ACM SIGMOD Record*, 18(2):399–407, (1989).

11. Hura, G.S. and Attwood, J.W. The use of Petri nets to analyse coherent fault trees. *IEEE Transactions On Reliability*, 37(5):469–473, (1988).

12. International Atomic Energy Agency and The Commission of the European Community. *Critical Survey of Research On Human Factors And The Man-Machine Interaction*, IAEA-SM-26B/29, Vienna, Austria, (1984).

13. Johnson, C.W. Applying temporal logic to support the specification and prototyping of concurrent multi-user interfaces. In D. Diaper and N. Hammond, editors, *People And Computers VI: Usability Now*, pages 145–156. Cambridge University Press, Cambridge, United Kingdom, (1991).

14. Johnson, C.W. Specifying and prototyping dynamic human-computer interfaces for stochastic applications. To appear in *People And Computers VIII*. Cambridge University Press, Cambridge, United Kingdom, (1993).

15. Johnson, C.W. Using Z To Support The Design Of Interactive, Safety-Critical Systems, BCS/IEE Software Engineering Journal, (10)2:49-60, (1995).

16. Johnson, C.W. and Harrison, M.D. Declarative graphics and dynamic interaction. In F.H. Post and W. Barth, editors, *EUROGRAPHICS '91*, pages 195–207. Elsevier Science Publications, North Holland, Netherlands (1991).

17. Johnson, C.W. and Harrison, M.D. Using temporal logic to support the specification and prototyping of interactive control systems. *International Journal Of Man-Machine Studies*, 36:357–385, (1992).

18. C.W. Johnson, J.C. McCarthy and P.C. Wright, Using A Formal Language To Support Natural Language In Accident Reports. Ergonomics, (38)6:1265-1283, (1995).

19. Kletz, T.A. *What Went Wrong? Case Histories Of Process Plant Disasters.* Gulf, Houston, United States Of America, (1985).

20. Kramer, B. Introducing the GRASPIN specification language SEGRAS. *Journal of Systems and Software*, 15(1):17–31, (1991).

21. Kuhmann, W., Boucsein, W., Schaefer, F. and Alexander, J. Experimental investigation of psychophysiological stress-reactions induced by different system response times in human-computer interactions. *Ergonomics*, 30(6):933 – 943, (1987).

22. Marsan, M.A., Conte, G. and Balbo, G. A class of generalised stochastic Petri nets for the performance evaluation of multiprocessor systems. *ACM Transactions On Computer Systems*, 2(2):93–122, (1984).

23. Merlin, J.A. and Faber, D.J. Recoverability of communications protocols - implications of a theoretical study. *IEEE Transactions On Communications*, COM-24(9), (1976).

24. Peterson, J.L. Petri nets. *Computing Surveys*, 9(3):223 – 252, (1977).

25. President's Task Force On Aircraft Crew Compliment. *United States' Government Report On Aircraft Crew Compliment*, Washington DC, United States of America (1981).

26. Reason, J. *Human Error.* Cambridge University Press, Cambridge, United Kingdom, (1990).

27. Wagenaar, W.A. and Groeneweg, J. Accidents at sea : Multiple causes and impossible consequences. In E. Hollnagel, G. Mancini, and D.D. Woods, editors, *Cognitive Engineering In Complex Dynamic Worlds*, pages 133 – 144. Academic Press, London, United Kingdom (1988).

28. Watson, I.A. Review of human factors in reliability and risk assessment. In J. Burgoyne, editor, *The Assessment And Control Of Major Hazards*, pages 323–337. Pergamon Press, Oxford, United Kingdom (1985).

29. Worley, N. and Lewins, J., editors. *The Chernobyl Accident And Its Implications For The United Kingdom - Report Number 19 Of The Watt Committee on Energy.* Elsevier Applied Science, London, United Kingdom (1988).

30. Zuberek, W.M. Timed Petri nets and preliminary performance evaluation. In *Proceedings Of The 7th Annual Symposium On Computer Architecture*, pages 88–96. ACM and IEEE, New York, United States of America (1980).

This article was processed using the LaTeX macro package with LLNCS style

Requirements For The Next Generation Of User Interface Specification Languages

Phil Gray and Chris Johnson

Department of Computing Science,
University of Glasgow,
Glasgow, G12 8QQ.
{pdg,johnson}@dcs.glasgow.ac.uk

Abstract. Many existing interface specification notations cannot capture the temporal properties that characterise interaction with distributed systems, such as the Internet browsers Mosaic and Netscape. This paper presents a range of formalisms that avoid this limitation. We present a spectrum of approaches that range from the purely textual constructs of branching time logics, through the mixed graphical and textual notation of Extended User Action Notation (XUAN) to the fully graphical representations of Petri Nets. It is concluded that each notation highlights different aspects of the interaction problems that arise when using distributed systems. It is also argued that these notations all suffer from significant usability problems. The paper ends by presenting an agenda for future research into the development of temporal notations for the design of human computer interfaces.

1 Introduction

The increasing popularity of Internet browsers, such as Mosaic and Netscape, has created a new user population who have little knowledge of the communications mechanisms that support distributed information retrieval [2, 17]. Issues of propagation delay, network bottlenecks and data fusion have little relevance to their tasks. The physical and engineering constraints of international communications networks prevent designers from eliminating these problems [4]. This has created a range of usability problems that, in many instances, frustrate attempts to exploit the Internet to its greatest potential. Unfortunately, many existing notations that might be used to represent and reason about these usability problems cannot easily be applied to analyse temporal properties of interaction.

1.1 The Limitations Of Existing Notations

Many notations that support the specification of user interfaces are poorly equipped to represent and reason about temporal properties of interaction. For example, a number of authors have been forced to develop complex extensions to the Z schema calculus in order to represent the flow of interaction over time [23]. Such enhancements create hybrid notations that require considerable skill and expertise. Designers must learn about temporal logics or Hoare's CSP in addition to the Z formalism [14]. There are further problems. Most existing notations provide non- formalists with little impression of what it would be like to interact with complex distributed systems [6, 10, 11]. This paper explores these limitations in more detail. A series of case studies is presented. Existing interface specification notations are applied to represent and reason about interaction with dynamic, distributed systems. Our experience with these case studies is then used to identify requirements for future interface specification notations.

1.2   Outline Of The Paper

This section has argued that the recent growth of dynamic, distributed systems poses considerable challenges for existing interface specification languages. Section 2 builds upon this argument by describing the temporal properties that frustrate the use of Internet browsers, such as Mosaic and Netscape. Section 3 argues that first order logic must be extended with some notion of time in order to represent and reason about such problems. Unfortunately, it can be extremely difficult to trace the properties described by clauses of textual notations, such as branching time temporal logics. Section 4 introduces a formalism that avoids this limitation. User Action Notation provides tabular structuring mechanisms that focus upon system and operator requirements during complex tasks. This formalism is extended to represent complex temporal properties of interaction. The resulting XUAN notation still relies heavily upon the use of textual annotations as a means of representing temporal properties of interaction. Section 5 argues that these annotations can be reduced to a minimum by exploiting Petri Nets. The spatial cues provided by this notation can help non-formalists to interpret the requirements that are embodied within formal specifications. Section 6 performs a brief comparative analysis of the three notations: branching time temporal logics; XUAN and Petri Nets. A set of requirements are developed for future generations of interface design notations. Section 7 presents the conclusions that can be drawn from this work.

2   The World Wide Web

Figure 1 characterises the interaction architecture with distributed information retrieval systems over the Internet. Users exploit browser programs to request and retrieve information from remote sites. We are interested in these applications because they typify a growing range of systems that are introducing users to usability problems that rarely occur on stand-alone machines. For example, Internet browsers hide the details of the underlying networks from the user. This leads to unpredictability because without this information it is difficult to determine whether retrieval commands will be successful. Remote site failure prevents information from being returned to the browser. Communications bottlenecks can delay the transmission of data between the browser and the remote servers.

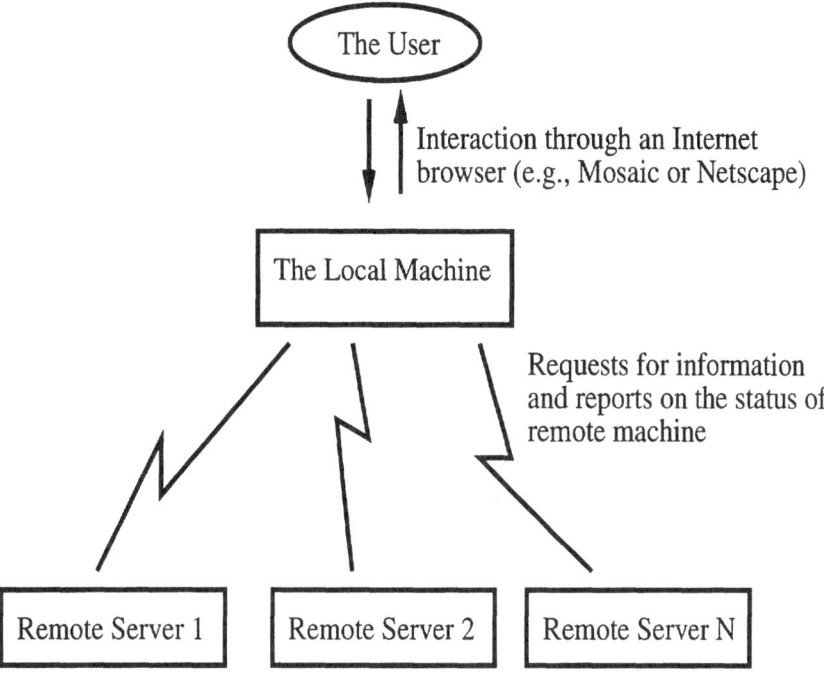

Fig. 1. Information Retrieval Over A Distributed Network

Figure 2 shows the user interface to the National Centre for Super-Computer Applications' Mosaic browser. This system and its commercial successor, Netscape, are used to illustrate this paper. Users typically request information by selecting labelled buttons, such as `Playing Backgammon On The Internet`. The browser then assembles the requested information by sending messages to local or remote servers. Graphical images, sounds, video clips and pages of text are referenced by what are known as Uniform Resource Locators (URLs). The URL of the page in Figure 2 is:

`http://www.statslab.cam.ac.uk/~sret1/backgammon/main.html`

The http refers to the transfer protocol that is used to convey the information from remote sites. The machine that the information is retrieved from is specified after the protocol. In our example, it is the Internet site at `statslab.cam.ac.uk`. The location of the information on that machine is given after the address of the site; `~sret1/backgammon/`. The important point here is that users can access vast resources of information by the selection of labelled buttons. Users are not required to understand the underlying architecture that supports the various protocols and URL retrieval mechanisms.

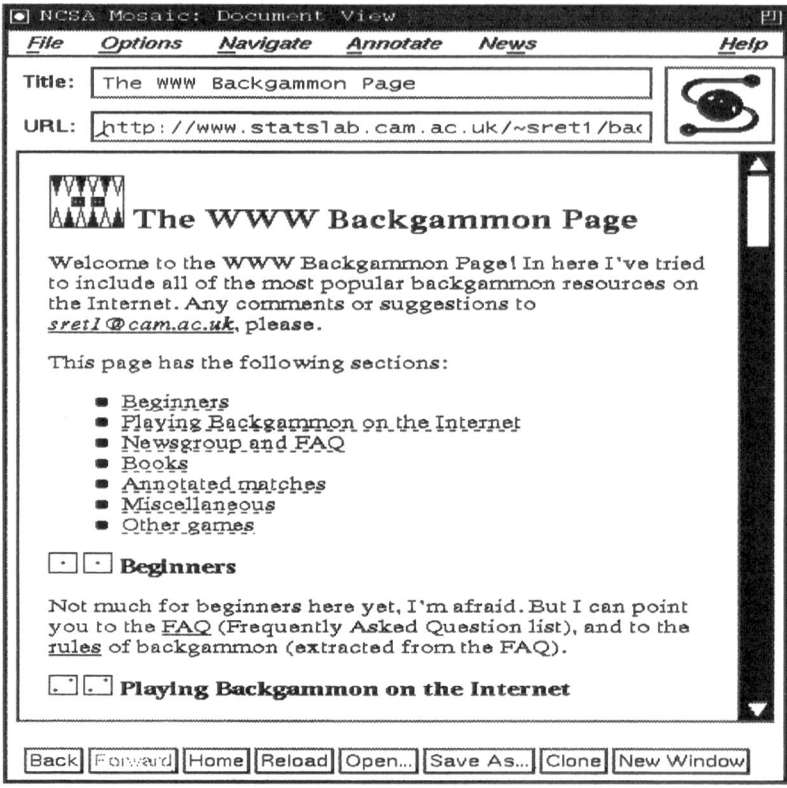

Fig. 2 The User Interface To The Mosaic Browser

3 A Textual Notation: Branching Time Temporal Logic

Unpredictable delays can occur when users attempt to access information over distributed networks. Bottlenecks can form in the passage of information back to the browser. These problems can increase or can be resolved as the loading on the network changes over time. A number of studies have shown that users find it difficult to complete retrieval tasks under such circumstances, especially if they only have a fixed amount of time at their disposal [20]. Other studies have shown that variable delays in system responses lead to frustration and error [16]. It is important, therefore, that designers can represent and reason about the impact of these problems. For instance, logic can be used to specify that a page will be displayed if the user selects an area of text that is linked to that page. The following clause helps to clarify the point that delays can occur during the retrieval process, *fetch*(*Http_address*, *Page*), or during presentation, *present(Page)*, if the resource requires considerable processing:

$$display\_page(Page) \Leftarrow$$
$$user\_selects(Text) \wedge linked(Text, Http\_address) \wedge$$
$$fetch(Http\_address, Page) \wedge present(Page) \qquad (1)$$

There are a number of limitations with such requirements. For example, there is no notion of sequence in classical logic; formula (1) would be true if the user requested the page after it had already been presented. This is clearly not what the designer intended. A further limitation for our purposes is that it does not capture the potential delay between the user selecting the text and the page being returned from a remote machine. Such problems can be avoided by introducing models of time into the notation. Clarke and Emerson's [3] Computation Tree Logic is an example of this approach. CTL is based upon a branching model of time; it can be used to describe alternative future traces of interaction. Johnson [13] discusses the formal underpinnings of the notation. Intuitive readings for CTL clauses will be given throughout the paper. The intention is to focus upon the application of the formalism to support interface development. Figure 3 provides an illustration of the way in which designers might view CTL's model of time. In this diagram two possible futures lead from the user selecting the text.

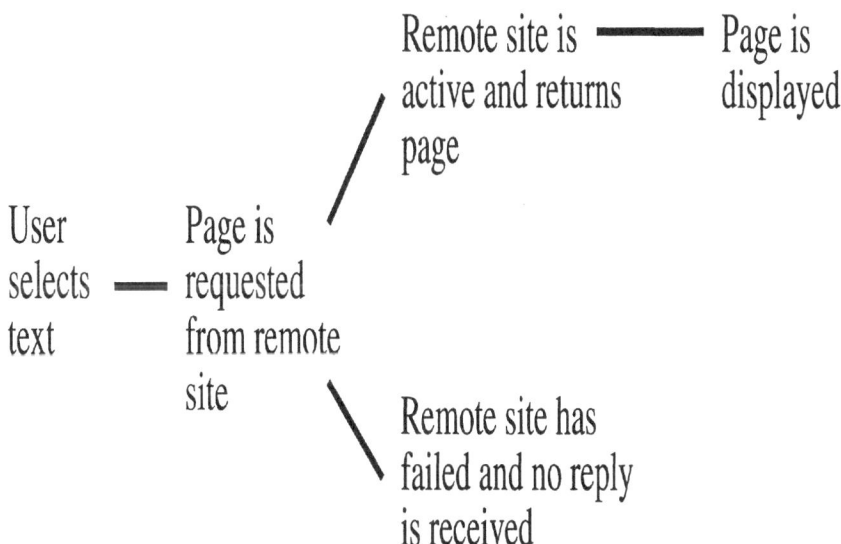

Fig. 3. A Branching View Of Possible Futures

In one path, the page is successfully retrieved from a remote site. In another path it cannot be retrieved because the remote site is unavailable. The following clause illustratés the way in which designers can exploit CTL's textual notation to introduce the sequential information that was missing from clause (1). The AX operator specifies that the page is retrieved in all possible paths after the user selects the text. If this clause could be satisfied then the user would be able to predict that all requests would be immediately successful. This describes the situation on stand-alone machines:

$$display\_page(Page) \Leftarrow$$
$$user\_selects(Text) \wedge linked(Text, Http\_address) \wedge$$
$$AX(fetch(Http\_address, Page) \wedge present(Page)) \qquad (2)$$

This formula does not, however, represent the potential delay that can lead to unpredictability in Web browsers. Given existing communications technology it is not possible to guarantee that all pages will be retrieved immediately after they have been requested. Site failure and heavy network loading can delay the transmission of information. It is only possible to specify that there are some traces in which the page is immediately presented after it has been requested. This requirement can be represented using the EX operator (read as 'there exists some next state'):

$$display\_page(Page) \Leftarrow$$
$$user\_selects(Text) \wedge linked(Text, Http\_address) \wedge$$
$$EX(fetch(Http\_address, Page) \wedge AXpresent(Page)) \qquad (3)$$

Such clauses provide a framework for subsequent development. They can be used to identify critical phases during interaction with a complex system. In this case, designers must develop techniques that provide users with sufficient context to enable them to predict the behaviour of their application. For instance, it might be specified that a warning should be displayed as soon as the failure of a request is detected:

$$failure\_warning(Page) \Leftarrow$$
$$user\_selects(Text) \wedge linked(Text, Http\_address) \wedge$$
$$EX(notfetch(Http\_address, Page) \wedge AXpresent(request\_failure)) \qquad (4)$$

The way in which warnings, such as *request_failure*, are presented can have a profound impact upon the usability of an interface. For instance, Mosaic displays 'Unable to connect to remote host' when a request has not been acknowledged by the server. The warning is presented in a small bar approximately two thirds of the way up the window. This is easily over-looked. Designers might, therefore, seek alternative solutions. For instance, logic abstractions can be used to specify that the user must provide input to confirm that they have read about the failure of their request. This approach is exploited by Netscape. In the following clause, the CTL $\mathcal{U}$ operator (read as 'until') is used to describe the duration of the warning:

$$acknowledge\_failure\_warning(Page) \Leftarrow$$
$$user\_selects(Text) \wedge linked(Text, Http\_address) \wedge$$
$$EX(notfetch(Http\_address, Page) \wedge$$
$$AX[present(request\_failure)\mathcal{U}user\_selects(request\_failure)]) \tag{5}$$

Unfortunately, a number of usability problems restrict the utility of branching time temporal logics. It can be difficult for designers to exploit such notations; a training in discrete mathematics is required in order to understand the formal underpinnings of the language. It can also can be extremely difficult to construct the complex chains of interaction that arise between a system and its user. Individual clauses, such as $present(request\_failure)$, may themselves contain further temporal operators. Each trace must, therefore, be painstakingly built from many individual clauses. The following section introduces a formalism that avoids these limitations.

4 A Semi-Textual Notation: XUAN

The Extended User Action Notation, XUAN [7] is a semi-formal notation for describing the actions of human and computer participants in interactive tasks. It is based on the User Action Notation [8].

4.1 The Tabular Layout of Task Descriptions in XUAN

Both UAN and XUAN organise the actions comprising a task into categories based on the agent which executes them and their function in the task. These categories define the columns of a tabular layout of the actions making up the task. For example, Figure 4 presents the UAN specification of clicking a typical screen button widget. A XUAN task is, like a UAN task, a set of the actions comprising the task, separated out into columns (or types) for some communicative purpose. However, the categories have been systematised in order to make clearer their roles and their relationship to one another[1]. The left/right-top/down ordering of the table elements may be viewed as a partial representation of temporal ordering on actions and the columnar organisation as modelling the task agents.

One consequence of treating user and system function similarly in the task description is that the somewhat ad hoc nature of system annotations of user actions is replaced by a symmetrical treatment of each task agent. Both perform visible actions and (hypothesised) invisible internal actions. These internal actions for the system have already been considered (dialogue state, application action); those for the user are similar (changes to short term memory, long term

---

[1] The UAN tabular layout is used as one way of writing a XUAN description. The description can also be expressed entirely textually; with only a 1D rather than a 2D ordering of the actions [7].

User actions	Interface Feedback	Interface State	Connection to Computation
Move to screen button	Cursor tracks		
Mouse button down	Screen button hilited	Button selected	
Mouse button up	Screen button unhilited		Execute button action

Fig. 4. UAN Task Description

memory, planning and other cognitive actions). From this standpoint XUAN resembles Memory-Cognition-Action tables [22].

Within a column, the temporal ordering among elements in the action set is specified using the *UAN action language*. For example, if task T contains the user action set a1,a2, the relationship of strict sequence would be expressed by:

    a1, a2 (usually separated by a newline in UAN)

Order independent execution of the set (i.e., all must be executed, but in any order) is shown with the operator '&' :

    a1 & a2

A full description of the action language can be found in Hix and Hartson [8] but briefly the main temporal relations are:

```
,           strict sequence
&           Order independence
||          Concurrent with
->          Interruptible by (as indicated by direction of arrow)
<->         Mutually interruptible
<|>         Interleavable
```

User actions are either primitive actions, typically manipulations of physical input devices (pressing a key, moving a mouse), or tasks. Additionally, and optionally, a UAN action specification may be annotated with information about system feedback (viz., perceivable changes in system state), non-perceivable changes to user interface state and application-significant operations. This approach, although possessing the virtues of simplicity and readability, is overly

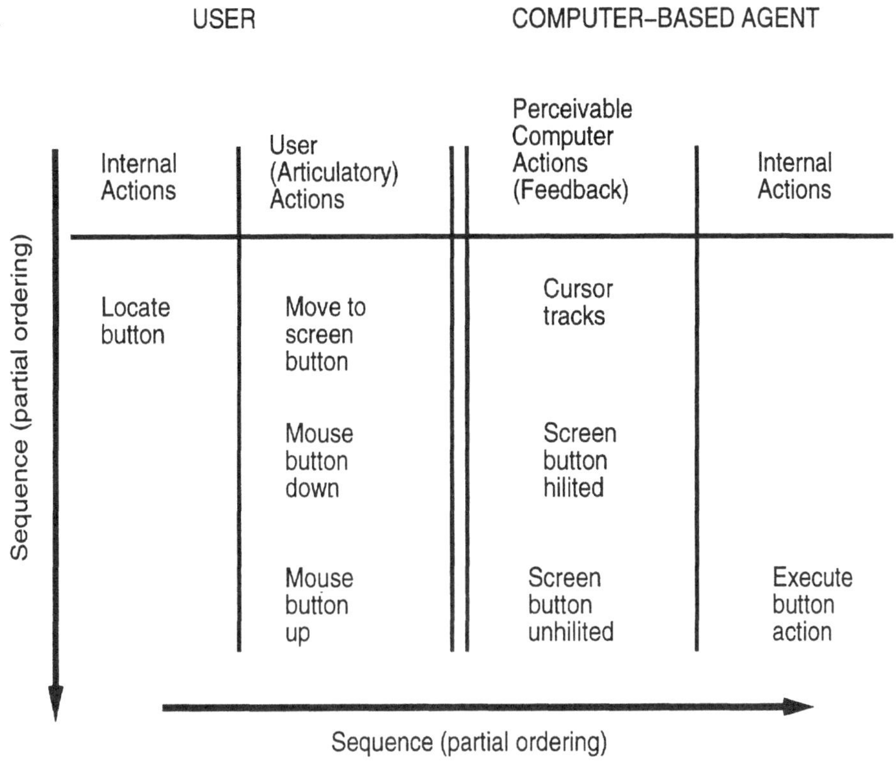

Fig. 5. XUAN Task Description

restrictive when attempting to deal with complex temporal relationships between actions in different categories. In particular, the tabular layout assumes that each feedback element (immediately) follows the action to which it is attached. Consider specifying type-ahead or mouse-ahead using this UAN table:

```
k1                echo k1
k2                echo k2
```

If we follow strict left-right/top-bottom sequencing, then type ahead would not be possible, since k2 must occur after echo k1. Instead, we require partial orderings of the actions:

```
k2 follows k1
echo k1 follows k1
echo k2 follows k2
```

This set of temporal constraints can be satisfied by an interaction in which type-ahead may occur; that is; the constraints may be true even though

```
k2 follows echo k1
```

is false. In order to accommodate these features systematically in XUAN, we treat each assertion about the temporal relationships among actions as a temporal constraint partially definitive of the task. That is, a task may be defined as a tuple of (1) a set of agent actions and (2) a set of temporal constraints on that action set:

```
task = (agent actions, temporal constraints)
```

Some of the temporal constraints may be shown in the conventional UAN tabular format, using UAN operators and syntax. However, the set of constraints may also be represented as a list, each constraint self-contained. We can express the type- ahead example more succinctly with the following textual format:

```
TASK: keypress
actions = press key : USER, echo key: SYSTEM FEEDBACK
constraints = press key , (echo key || keypress)
```

Notice that in this specification it is only guaranteed that the echo for a particular key will follow that key pressing action. The temporal ordering of the press-echo pairs is left undetermined, thus allowing for any degree of type-ahead.

4.2 Dealing With System Delays in the World Wide Web

Type-ahead is a desirable feature in cases of unpredictable feedback delays when the user knows what is wanted and the system can accommodate the input regardless of the state of the interaction. However, when the system interpretation of the user action depends on the information feedback or on the result of previous user actions, problems can arise if the user is allowed to generate input too soon. This is especially a problem in distributed systems, like the World Wide Web.

Mosaic for the Macintosh, for example, allows a user to select embedded buttons while the system is still engaged in fetching the page in which the buttons are located. A user may see part of the new page, locate a button and attempt to select it before the entire page has been downloaded. Such premature user input is ignored, often resulting in disorientation. A XUAN description can help to elucidate the source of the problem. The actual sequence from the user's point of view (i.e., what the user thinks is happening) can be described as shown in Figure 6. However, a more accurate description of the interaction (i.e., what should happen) is shown in Figure 7. We can see that the problem has arisen because the user's second select button action has taken place too early. Typically, this is because the display of the new page begins, and hence button are visible, before the download is complete. The message which indicates that the download has been completed is quite small and may be overlooked by the user. Two solutions to this problem are immediately apparent from the task description, as illustrated in Figure 8. First, one could lock out user input until the download is complete, viz., disallow a select button action before the download complete occurs. The X version of Mosaic enforces this option. This does

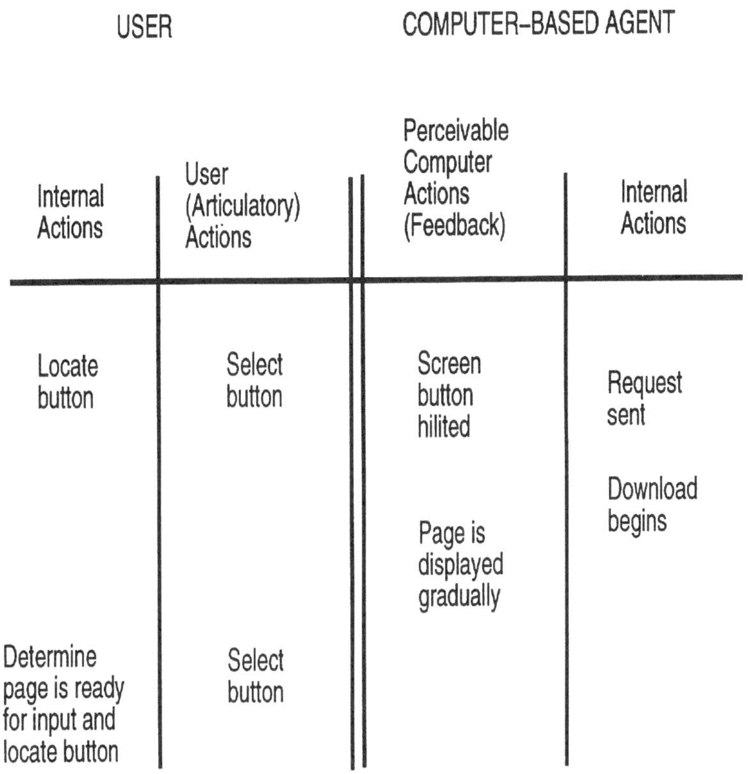

USER   COMPUTER–BASED AGENT

Internal Actions	User (Articulatory) Actions		Perceivable Computer Actions (Feedback)	Internal Actions
Locate button	Select button		Screen button hilited	Request sent
				Download begins
			Page is displayed gradually	
Determine page is ready for input and locate button	Select button			

Fig. 6 Selecting an Embedded Button: The User's Mistaken View

not provide any information from which the user may determine that the page has been completely downloaded. However, Mosaic also uses the cursor shape to provide feedback; during downloading the cursor has a watch shape and when the download is complete, it returns to an arrow. Since the cursor is usually in the focus of the user's attention during this task, it serves as a more effective indication of system state than the textual 'Download complete' message. This example demonstrates the way XUAN can be used to identify and reason about interaction problems arising from delays introduced by distributed systems like the World Wide Web. We have used task descriptions to specify what the user thinks is happening (a hypothetical but false description) and to compare that with what should happen, shown as alternative descriptions. An important element of the use of XUAN for such analyses is the ability to annotate actions and their relationship with design-significant assertions.

The tabular layout of UAN and XUAN is more accessible to a non-formalist than the textual clauses of branching time temporal logic. It is important to emphasise, however, that a number of usability problems still restrict the application of the XUAN notation. In particular, it can be difficult to trace prolonged

	USER		COMPUTER–BASED AGENT	
Internal Actions	User (Articulatory) Actions		Perceivable Computer Actions (Feedback)	Internal Actions
Locate button	Select button		Screen button hilited	Request sent
			Page is displayed gradually	Download begins
				Download complete
			"Download Complete" message	
Determine page is ready for input and locate button	Select button			

Fig. 7 Selecting an Embedded Button: What Should Happen

periods of interaction through the columns of many different tables. Graphical notations, such as Petri Nets, provide means of reducing such problems [1].

5 A Graphical Notation: Petri Nets

Petri Nets have been used to support the engineering of concurrent systems [15, 5]. They have also been used to represent human factors requirements. Bastide and Palanque [1] exploit Petri Nets to derive formal specifications of interactive systems at a very high level of abstraction. Johnson, McCarthy and Wright [9] have shown that Petri Nets can be used to represent the operator-system interaction which can lead to accidents. This section builds upon this work and shows how Petri Nets might be used to represent and reason about interaction with distributed systems.

Petri Nets represent the conditions that are satisfied during intervals of interaction [21]. When particular conditions hold, certain events can occur. If an event takes place then it can alter the state of the human-machine system. Changes in state are represented by the new conditions that hold after an event has oc-

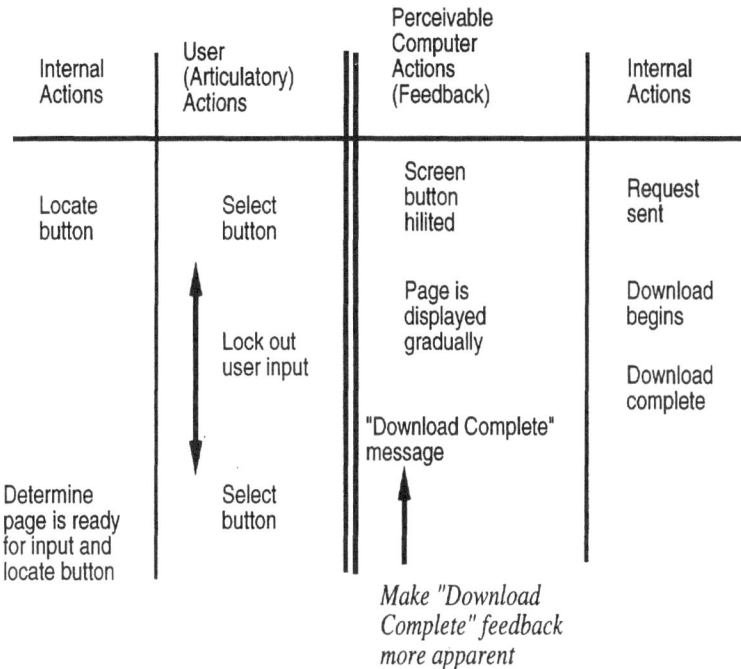

Fig. 8. Selecting an Embedded Button: Design Annotations

curred. These new conditions enable further events to take place. More formally, Petri Nets are directed graphs; $PN = (P, T, E, M)$. They consist of a set of places, P, transitions, T, edges, E and markings, M.

Places can be used to describe the properties that hold during particular intervals of interaction. For instance, a place might represent the fact that the system is presenting the "download complete" message. Alternatively, places can also be used to represent facts about the system operator. For instance, a place might be used to represent the fact that a user is reading the information displayed by the system.

Transitions can be used to represent the events that alter the state of interaction. They can represent events initiated by both systems and their operators. For instance, a transition might be used to represent input events; such as the user selecting a button. They can also be used to indicate the events that occur when the system receives information from remote sites. Isolating these critical transitions provides a focus for subsequent human factors and systems analysis. Previous sections have argued that delays between a request and the presentation of information can have a profound impact upon usability.

Edges connect places to transitions: $E \subseteq \{P \times T\} \cup \{T \times P\}$. They can be used to form the chains of events and conditions that characterise the course of interaction with a distributed system. They can be described in terms of two functions. The function Op maps from each transition to its set of output places. The output places of a transition represent the conditions that hold after an event has occurred. For example, an output place might be used to represent the observation that the "download complete" message is displayed after information has been retrieved. An input place function, Ip, maps from each transition to the set of input places for that transition. The input places of a transitions specify the conditions which must hold for an event to occur. The input place of a transition might be used to represent the human factors observation that the presentation of the message led to the user requesting another page of information .

Petri Nets can be represented graphically. Events, or transitions, are shown as bars. Conditions, or places, are denoted by unfilled circles. Edges are shown as arrows linking places and transitions. Figure 9 shows a simplified graphical Petri Net representation for interaction with a web browser. It is derived from the XUAN description in Figure 8. It illustrates the way that the spatial layout of Petri Nets can be used to represent temporal properties of interactive systems. In order to model the dynamic behaviour of a human-machine system, tokens are used to mark those places in a Petri Net that are enabled. A place is enabled if its conditions hold. The tokens in a net are said to characterise a marking state and are denoted graphically by filled dots. For instance, Figure 10 is marked to show that the system is retrieving URLs and that the watch icon is being presented instead of the arrow for the cursor. Designers might alter the marking of a Petri Net to indicate the different conditions that hold for users and their systems. These walk-throughs can be used to simulate the sequences of events and states that are identified during critical traces of interaction. A transition can fire if all of its input places contain at least one token. After firing, a token is deposited in each of the output places of a transition. In Figure 10 it is possible for the transition indicating that the first resource is retrieved to fire. If this transition fired then the place indicating that the system is incrementally updating its display would be marked with a token. This, in turn, would enable the transition labelled 'System presents "download complete" message' to fire as both of its input places would now be marked.

The markings in a network can also be used to represent concurrent properties. For instance, users might make another selection in the interval between an initial request and the retrieval of the resources associated with that request. In the XUAN of Figure 8 this was not possible because the user was locked out of the system. Figure 11 annotates the Petri Net to show an alternative approach. Here, the user has selected a second button before the tokens produced by the first selection have "cleared" the network. In other words, the user has ignored the watch icon and has typed ahead to make further retrieval requests. Experience with Computer Supported Co-operative Work systems suggests that arbitrary locking mechanisms can lead to frustration and error [18]. Expert users benefit from the potential offered by type ahead mechanisms. Our point here is

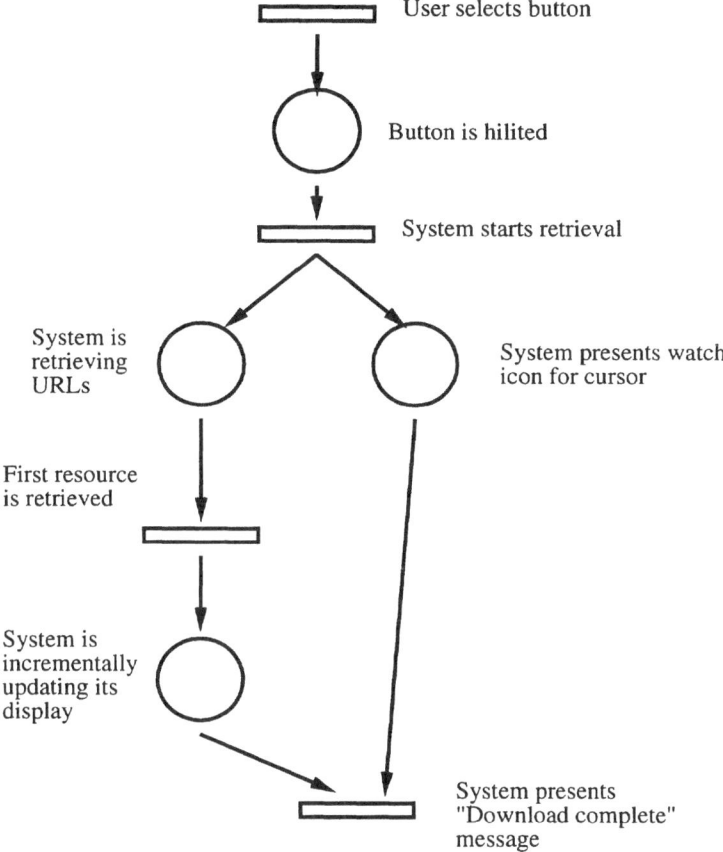

Fig. 9 A High Level Petri Net

not that one solution or another provides a panacea for usability problems in distributed systems. Rather it is that new generations of design notations must be used to represent and reason about such applications. Petri Nets address some of the problems that arise when tracing temporal properties in XUAN tables and temporal logic clauses. There are, however, limitations with this graphical formalism. Extensive tool support is required in order to construct and maintain complex networks. A further limitation is that it is almost impossible to represent and reason about undo facilities using Petri Nets. Designers must provide highly elaborate networks that reconstruct previous markings after the undo has been selected. This is a significant limitation if the graphical formalism is to represent and reason about changes to distributed data rather than simple browsing mechanisms.

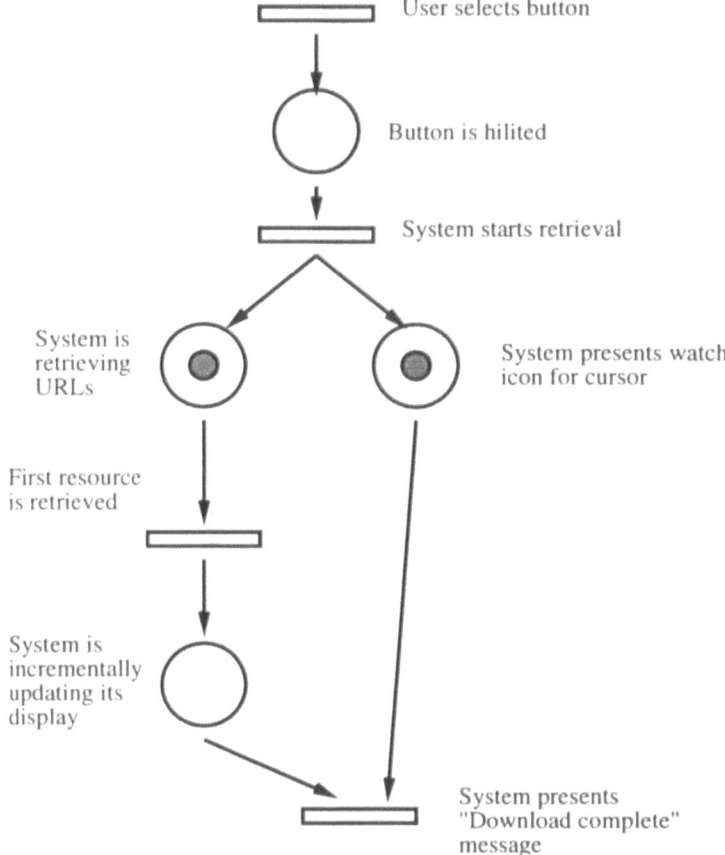

Fig. 10. A Marked Petri Net

6   An Agenda For Future Research

Previous sections have used a number of formalisms to represent temporal properties of interaction with distributed systems. These notations form a continuum from purely textual specification languages, through table based approaches to graphical formalisms. This section builds upon our analysis and identifies requirements for future generations of interface specification languages.

6.1   Requirements for Temporal Notations To Support Interface Design

An adequate notation must capture a variety of types of information about interaction:

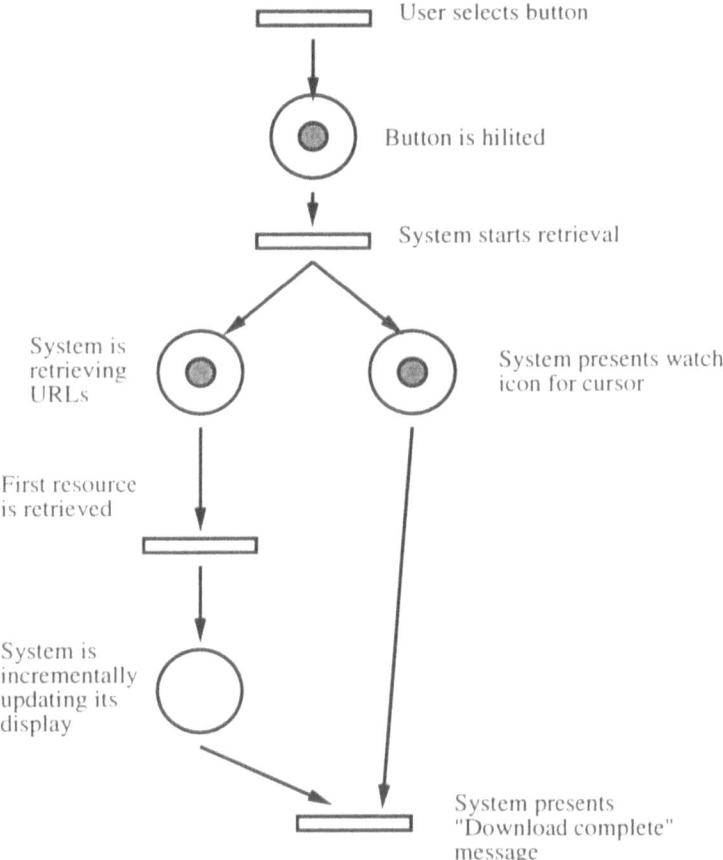

Fig. 11. A Marked Petri Net Showing Type ahead

- it must offer sufficient expressiveness so that any temporal property of the interaction that is relevant to designers may be described. Problems in representing and reasoning about undo clearly limit the application of Petri Nets;

- it must capture the salience of temporal properties during interaction; it must be relatively easy to identify usability problems from their temporal representation. This can be difficult in purely textual notations such as temporal logic;

- it must have, at least for the temporal aspects of the description, a well-found semantics. Designers must be able to determine that particular sequences of interaction are or are not logically possible. The lack of any complete, formal under-pinning for XUAN created significant problems in constructing the analysis presented in this paper;

- it must support the integration of temporal representations with other relevant properties of interaction, such as the state of the display and the physical properties of input/output media.

Figure 12 summarises the properties of the three notations examined in this paper against the requirements listed above: It should be stressed that the eval-

	Expressiveness	Salience	Semantics	Integration
Temporal Logic	High	Low	High	Medium
XUAN	High	Medium	Low	High
Petri Nets	High	Medium	High	Low

Fig. 12 Subjective Comparisons Between Notations

uations in this table are subjective estimates based upon our experience in applying the notations. Some of the findings may have been biased by the particular applications under investigation. Of course, the list of desirable properties is incomplete as well.

6.2   Potential Solutions

From Figure 12, it can be seen that none of these notations satisfies all of our requirements. There are at least two potential means of addressing this problem:

- create an entirely notation avoiding the weaknesses of existing formalisms;
- develop a hybrid notation from the best features of several existing formalisms.

The first approach seems to be fraught with difficulty. Many years of research are required in order to identify and develop appropriate language constructs. Once this has been done, it remains a non-trivial task to built a consistent and complete semantics for those constructs.

   In anticipation of this work, the second alternative would seem to offer a more cost- effective solution. For instance, the task allocations in XUAN tables might be used to identify critical incidents during interaction between a system and its user. The graphical structures of the Petri Net notation might then be used to analyse concurrency and synchronisation requirements. The additional semantic support of textual formalisms, such as temporal logics, might then be recruited if formal reasoning were required in order to establish safety properties. This integration might be achieved in a number of ways. One might annotate XUAN descriptions using Petri Nets. Places and transitions might be annotated with logic clauses. In fact, several of these approaches may turn out to be appropriate in different design contexts. Some work towards these hybrid approaches is currently underway at Glasgow and in Toulouse [19]. Many questions remain to be addressed by this research. In particular, tools and techniques must be developed so that designers can establish the consistency of multiple design notations for complex and dynamic user interfaces.

7 Conclusion

This paper argues that many existing approaches to interface design cannot easily be used to capture the temporal properties that characterise interaction with distributed systems. This paper introduces a range of specification notations that avoid this limitation. We present a spectrum of approaches that range from the purely textual constructs of branching time logics, through the mixed graphical and textual notation of Extended User Action Notation (XUAN) to the graphical representations of Petri Nets. It is concluded that each notation highlights different aspects of the interaction problems that can arise when using distributed, dynamic systems. It is also argued that these notations suffer from significant usability problems. The paper ends by presenting an agenda for future research into the development of temporal notations for human computer interface design.

Acknowledgements

NCSA Mosaic is a trademark of the National Centre for Computer Applications. Netscape is a trademark of the Netscape Communications Corporation. This work was conducted as part of the Temporal Aspects of Usability project SPG9201233, funded by the Joint Council Initiative in Cognitive Science and Human Computer Interaction.

References

1. Bastide, R. and Palanque, P. (1990) Petri Net Objects For The Design, Validation And Prototyping Of User-Driven Interfaces. In D. Diaper, D. Gilmore, G. Cockton and B. Shackel, editors, *Interact'90*, pages 625-631, Elsevier Science Publishers, North Holland.

2. Berners-Lee, T.J., Cailliau, R. and Groff, J.-F. (1992) *The World Wide Web*, Computer Networks And ISDN Systems, (25):454-459.

3. Clarke, E.M. and Emerson, E.A. (1982) The Design And Synthesis Of Synchronisation Skeletons Using Branching Time Temporal Logic. In D. Kozen (ed.) *Logic Of Programs 1981*, 52-71, LNCS 131, Springer Verlag, Berlin, Germany.

4. Coulouris, G., Dollimore, J. and Kindberg, T. (1994) *Distributed Systems: Concepts And Design*, Addison Wesley, Wokingham, United Kingdom.

5. Deng, Y., Perkusich, A., Figueired, J. and Chang, S.K. (1993) Integrating Software Engineering Methods And Petri Nets For The Specification And Prototyping Of Complex Information Systems. In *Proceedings of the 14th International Conference On The Application And Theory Of Petri Nets*, Chicago, USA, June 1993, pp. 206-223.

6. Dix, A. (1991) *Formal Methods For Interactive Systems*, Academic Press, London, United Kingdom.

7. Gray, P.D., England, D. and McGowan, S. (1994) XUAN: Enhancing UAN To Capture Temporal Relations Among Actions. In G. Cockton, S.W. Draper and G.R.S. Weir, editors, *People And Computers IX*, pages 301-312, Cambridge University Press, Cambridge, United Kingdom.

8. Hix, D. and Hartson, H.R. (1993), *Developing User Interfaces*, John Wiley and Sons, London, 1993.

9. Johnson, C.W., McCarthy, J. and Wright, P.C. (1995) *Using Petri Nets To Support Natural Language In Accident Reports*. To appear in Ergonomics.

10. Johnson, C.W. (1991) Declarative Graphics And Dynamic Interaction. In F.H. Post and W. Barth, editors, *Eurographics '91*, 195-207. Elsevier, North Holland.

11. Johnson, C.W. (1992) A Formal Approach To The Integration Of Human Factors And Systems Engineering, DPhil thesis, University Of York, York, United Kingdom. Available as technical report YCST 95/05.

12. Johnson, C.W. (1993) A Formal Approach To The Presentation of CSCW Systems. In J.L. Alty, D. Diaper and S. Guest, editors, *People And Computers VIII*, 335-352, Cambridge University Press, Cambridge, United Kingdom.

13. Johnson, C.W. (1993a) *A Probabilistic Logic For The Development Of Safety-Critical Interactive Systems*, International Journal of Man-Machine Studies, (38)2:333-351.

14. Johnson, C.W. (1995) *Using Z To Support The Design Of Interactive, Safety-Critical Systems*. The Software Engineering Journal, (10)2:49-60.

15. Kramer, B. (1991) *Introducing The GRASPIN Specification Language SEG-RAS*, Journal Of Systems And Software, 15(1):17-31.

16. Kuhmann, W. (1989) *The Stress Inducing Properties Of System Response Times*, Ergonomics, (32)3:271-280.

17. Martin, J.L. (1993) *Travels With Gopher*, IEEE Computer, (26)5:84-7.

18. Miles, V., Johnson, C.W., McCarthy, J. and Harrison, M. (1991) Supporting Prediction In Complex Dynamic Systems. In D. Diaper and N. Hammond (editors), *People And Computers VI*, 133-144, Cambridge University Press,

Cambridge, United Kingdom.

19. Palanque, P. (1995), Integrating UAN and Object Petri Nets, Personal Correspondence.
20. Pejtersen, A.M., (1989) *A Library System For Information Retrieval Based On A Cognitive Task Analysis And Supported By An Icon Based Interface.* In ACM SIGIR Proceedings, Boston. ACM Press, New York, United States of America.
21. Peterson, J.L. (1977), *Petri Nets*, Computing Surveys, 9(3):223-252.
22. Sharratt, B. (1990), Memory-Cognition-Action Tables: A Pragmatic Approach To Analytical Modelling. In D. Diaper, D. Gilmore, G. Cockton and B. Shackel, editors, *Interact'90*, pages 271-275, Elsevier Science Publishers, North Holland.
23. Sufrin, B. and He, J. (1990), Specification, Refinement And Analysis Of Interactive Processes. In M. D. Harrison and H. W. Thimbleby, editors, *Formal Methods in Human Computer Interaction*, pages 153-200, Cambridge University Press, Cambridge, United Kingdom, 1990.

This article was processed using the LaTeX macro package with LLNCS style

Exploring Design Options Rationally

Chris Bramwell, Bob Fields and Michael Harrison

Human-Computer Interaction Group,
Department of Computer Science,
University of York, York, YO1 5DD, U.K.
Email: {cjb bob mdh}@minster.york.ac.uk.

Abstract. This paper describes a design technique for interactive systems that allows designs to be specified and refined formally, using a notation based on Action Systems. The rationale underlying the choices made by designers is recorded in a style based on the "Questions, Options, Criteria" notation. The means of capturing formal specifications and the reasoning behind design decisions are presented as parts of a uniform framework; a formal account is given of how design options satisfy criteria and how design options can be combined to answer larger design questions.

1 Introduction

The use of formal specification techniques and development methods has been widely advocated as a means of meeting the levels of integrity demanded of computer-based systems. For many interactive systems, the satisfaction of overall objectives and requirements of functionality and dependability depends crucially on the system's usability. For this reason, formal specification and development techniques are making inroads into the area of interactive systems design (see, for instance, [6]).

The work described in this paper addresses two main questions. Firstly, how can specifications and designs of interactive systems be recorded in a way that aids communication between designers and which capitalises on work in the software engineering community on formal development and refinement? Secondly, how can the rationale behind a particular design be recorded to aid maintenance and inform future development efforts?

A formal notation based on *Action Systems* [2, 9] and *Interactors* [4, 5] is used to specify both a system and several ways of designing an extension to it. The account of how designs are discovered, what design issues are being addressed by each option and the means by which a designer picks one option over another, is in accord with the Design Space Analysis framework and the QOC (Questions, Options, Criteria) notation [8]. Using QOC, design proceeds by posing *design questions* (problems for which some solution is required). In response to a question, a number of *design options* are devised. In order to select among these different options, a set of *criteria* are formulated which test the acceptability of the various options. In principle, design questions may be decomposed into a number of smaller questions; the options for the sub-questions may be composed into options for the larger question. As Section 4 demonstrates, this composition is itself formally straightforward, but the way in which criteria at the sub-question level can be "lifted" to apply at the question level is far from simple. A contribution of the current paper is to investigate issues surrounding the formal semantics of this lifting of criteria. QOC is an informal development process, imposing few constraints on the formulation and consistency of its design questions, options and criteria. This process is sometimes seen as being contrary to the philosophy of formal development methods; a further contribution of this paper is to show how QOC development techniques can be integrated coherently with formal methods.

A common problem in *real* systems development, frequently ignored in the literature on formal development methods, is that a system is rarely designed from scratch, rather additional (or different) requirements are expressed on an existing system. The example in this paper involves extending an existing specification by the addition of a new feature. The existing system is a simple text editing application and the new requirement is for an "undo" facility whereby the effect of editing actions may be reversed and earlier states retrieved. Although such functionality has been discussed at length elsewhere, both from the point of view of design (for example in [3] or [12]) and in empirical terms, it is still a rich enough domain to illustrate the current work. A similar problem area is tackled in [15], where the requirements for a multi-user undo facility are examined using a number of techniques including QOC and formal specifications (though no integration of techniques is proposed).

The paper is structured as follows. Section 2 introduces an example Interactor specification and discusses the notation and its semantics. In Section 3 the issue of extending this specification with additional features is explored. Design questions are posed and alternative options to satisfy the questions are proposed. In Section 4, criteria that allow the different options to be evaluated are described and in Section 5 it is shown how preferences that are placed over particular criteria can lead to design decisions between options. Finally, Section 6 draws some conclusions about the work presented here. The reader is referred to the Appendix for a glossary of the specification notation used in the body of the paper.

2 Initial Specification of a Text Editor

The basic functionality of the text editor is to manipulate text objects represented by the *TEXT* datatype as a sequence of characters.

$[CHAR]$
$TEXT == seq\ CHAR$

The text editor is described by an Interactor *TextEd* which maintains two state variables *text* and *cursor* and two externally presented variables *left* and *right*. The variable *text* is the content of the document currently being edited and *cursor* is the current location of the cursor in the document. The variables *left* and *right* contain the text presented via some output medium to the user at the left and the right of the cursor, respectively; together they allow at most N characters to be presented. Initially, the state of the system is such that the text is an empty sequence of characters, the cursor is at the zero position and no text is presented to the user. Actions are provided to insert and delete characters and to reposition the cursor.

interactor *TextEd*

alphabet *insert?c* : *CHAR*, *delete*, *cursor?x* : N, *present*

var *text* : *TEXT*
  cursor : N

pres *left*, *right* : *TEXT*

initially
$$text, cursor, left, right: \begin{bmatrix} text = \langle \rangle \wedge cursor = 0 \\ left = \langle \rangle \wedge right = \langle \rangle \end{bmatrix}$$

action *insert?c* $\widehat{=}$
$$text, cursor: \begin{bmatrix} text = text_0[0..cursor_0] \frown \langle c \rangle \frown text_0[cursor..\#text_0] \\ cursor = cursor_0 + 1 \end{bmatrix}$$

action *delete* $\widehat{=}$
$$text, cursor: \begin{bmatrix} text = text_0[0..cursor] \frown text_0[cursor_0 + 1..\#text_0] \\ cursor = cursor_0 \ominus 1 \end{bmatrix}$$

action *cursor?x* $\widehat{=}$ $(x \in 0..\#text) \rightarrow cursor: [cursor = x]$

$$action\ present\ \widehat{=}\ left, right: \begin{bmatrix} \#left + \#right = min(N, \#text) \\ left = text[cursor \ominus \#left..cursor] \\ right = text[cursor + 1..cursor + \#right] \end{bmatrix}$$

The alphabet clause of an interactor identifies the set of all actions in which it may engage. The var and pres clauses introduce the internal variables and the presentation variables of the Interactor, respectively. The initially clause specifies a program to initialise the interactor and each action clause specifies the behaviour of an action; the actions of the *TextEd* interactor have the following meaning. The *insert?c* action places a new character c at the current cursor position, shifting the remainder of the document and incrementing the cursor position. The action *delete* removes the current character and decrements the cursor. The action *cursor?x* sets the current cursor position to be x, leaving the text unchanged. This action is "guarded" by a predicate (to the left of the arrow "$\rightarrow$"), indicating that the new cursor position must refer to a valid location in the document. The *present* action defines how the presentation variables are updated; refinements of this interactor could specify particular strategies for invoking this action (such as causing it to be executed periodically or after every user action). It is assumed that the system is responsible for the presentation strategy, so the *present* action is not in the user's alphabet.

In general, actions consist of a *name* followed by a number of *arguments*. An optional *guard* and an action *body*. If a guard is not present, it is assumed to be *true*.

$$\text{action } ActionName?(Args) \mathrel{\hat{=}} Guard \to Body$$

An action's body is defined using a version of Morgan's *specification statement* [10] of the form $w : [post]$ where w is a list of variables that the body may change and *post*, the post-condition, is a predicate specifying the values of the state variables after execution. Following Morgan, any predicates that are *stacked* are assumed to be conjoined and 0-subscripted variables refer to their *initial* values before execution of the body. The behaviour of an Action System Interactor proceeds according to three rules:

- First, the initialisation clause is executed.

- Then any action whose guard evaluates to *true* in the current state may be executed, causing a state change. This rule is re-applied repeatedly if possible, otherwise,

- if a state is reached where no actions' guards are enabled, the interactor is said to have *deadlocked* and the system can execute no further.

These rules give an intuition about the semantics of Action Systems in terms of the sequences of actions they may perform. The second rule provides an *external* choice between system actions that can be executed in a current state. That is, any choice made between actions in the set $\{insert?c, delete, cursor?x\}$ in the second rule is made by the applier of the rules who is, in this case, the user of the system.

The rules of execution described above allow some sequences of actions to execute, and cause others to deadlock because execution leads to a state where the guard of the next action is *false*, and the execution sequence cannot proceed. For example, the action sequence $\langle init, insert?\underline{a}, delete\rangle$ is permitted whereas $\langle init, insert?\underline{a}, cursor?3\rangle$ is disallowed by the *TextEd* specification because the guard of *cursor?3* is not satisfied. The *traces* of an Action System Interactor are defined to be the set of all permitted sequences of actions for that Interactor. A trace *tr* is executed on the internal and presented variables of an Action System Interactor by applying the execution operator $\widehat{tr}$ as defined by Morgan [9].

Definition: The execution of a sequence of actions. For any two non-empty sequences s and t and an action a, sequence execution is defined by

$$\widehat{\langle\rangle} \mathrel{\hat{=}} \textbf{skip}$$

$$\widehat{\langle a\rangle} \mathrel{\hat{=}} a$$

$$\overline{tr_1 \mathbin{^\frown} tr_2} \mathrel{\hat{=}} \widehat{tr_1};\ \widehat{tr_2}$$

$\square$

For example, the effect of inserting a character $\underline{a}$ then deleting it is the same as just executing the **skip** command (which has no effect). More formally, this is represented by the following equivalence:

$$\overline{(insert?\underline{a}, delete)} \equiv \textbf{skip}$$

3 Questions and Options: Extending the Specification

With the specification of the text editor above, it is now possible to begin to discuss how the extension to add an *undo* operation might be defined. Informally, an undo facility must allow the effects of actions to be reversed, so that the user may revert to earlier states of the system. In order to specify such an operation, a record of past system states must be maintained. This is achieved by defining the type *HISTORY* to be a sequence of *text* and *cursor* values.

$$HISTORY == seq(TEXT \times \mathbb{N})$$

The system must retain a record of past states; this is done by adding the internal variable *history* to the state of the *TextEd* interactor:

$$history : HISTORY$$

and adding the condition that the history is empty to the initialisation clause of the *TextEd* interactor, making it:

$$\text{initially } text, cursor, left, right, history: \begin{bmatrix} text = \langle \rangle \wedge cursor = 0 \\ left = \langle \rangle \wedge right = \langle \rangle \\ history = \langle \rangle \end{bmatrix}$$

The interactor is forced to record historical information by sequentially prepending the *STORE* program onto the bodies of the *insert* and *delete* actions, causing the text and cursor position immediately prior to the execution of these actions to be added to the history.

$$STORE \mathrel{\widehat{=}} history: \left[history = (text, cursor) \mathbin{\frown} history_0 \right]$$

It is interesting to note that a lower level of granularity for *undo* is achieved by also prepending the *STORE* program onto the body of *cursor?x*. This design issue is not discussed further here.

The undo functionality will be achieved by the addition of an extra *undo* action to the *TextEd* interactor. The new action has the form:

$$\text{action } undo?n : \mathbb{N}_1 \mathrel{\widehat{=}} \cdots$$

The parameter *n* indicates how many steps back in the history to go. The details of the "$\cdots$" is a design question that can be decomposed into two simpler questions, each of which may be analysed in isolation, and the results combined to provide a more complete *undo* solution. The general design question:

Q: What does the *undo* action do?

can be decomposed into two seemingly orthogonal questions, Q1 and Q2, which will, at least initially, be examined separately.

Q1: How many steps may be undone at once?

Q2: Following an *undo*, what is the result of the next *undo*? In other words, what effect does *undo* have on the history?

Question Q1: How many steps may be undone at once? In order to answer this question, two design options are suggested.

O1.1: A single step undo (so the parameter n to the *undo* action is constrained to be 1).

O1.2: A user specified number of steps.

Option O1.1: A single step undo. The first option is a very restrictive solution, allowing only a single step to be undone at once. For this reason, the undo action has a guard allowing it to be performed only when the parameter $n = 1$ and the history is non-empty.

$$\begin{pmatrix} n = 1 \\ history \neq \langle \rangle \end{pmatrix} \rightarrow text, cursor, history: \left[(text, cursor) = head(history_0) \right]$$

Option O1.2: A user specified number of steps. The second option is more general than the first, allowing arbitrary numbers of steps to be undone. The only condition imposed by the guard is that the history contains at least enough items for the requested number of undo steps.

$$(\#history \geqslant n) \rightarrow text, cursor, history: \left[(text, cursor) = history_0[n] \right]$$

Question Q2: What is the result of the next undo? Again, many possible options exist for this question, and just two are considered here.

O2.1: The current state.

O2.2: The previous state in the undo history.

Option O2.1: The current state. With this option, the effect of the *undo* action is to add the current text and cursor values to the history, making undo manipulate the history in the same way as any other command does.

$$text, cursor, history: \left[history = (text_0, cursor_0) \frown history_0 \right]$$

Option O2.2: The previous state in the undo history. The second option ensures that the history is shortened so that the next "undone" state is the previous state in the undo history. The guard ensures that there are enough history elements to do this.

$$(\#history \geqslant n) \rightarrow text, cursor, history: \left[history = history_0 \text{ after } n \right]$$

3.1 Combining Options

A complete solution to the general design question Q : "What does the *undo* action do?" consists of a selection of the above options; one of O1.1 and O1.2 and one of O2.1 and O2.2. How are the meanings of the four possible combinations defined? As an example, the combination of options O1.1 and O2.2 is specified as follows:

$$\begin{pmatrix} n = 1 \\ history \neq \langle\rangle \end{pmatrix} \rightarrow text, cursor, history\mathbf{:} \begin{bmatrix} (text, cursor) = head(history_0) \\ history = history_0 \ after \ n \end{bmatrix}$$

The above program allows only single steps to be undone at once (by having $n = 1$ in the guard) and ensures that after an undo is executed in some state, a further undo invocation will cause the next state in the undo history to be established.

More generally, an operator $(\_ \sqcup \_)$ for combining options can be defined. The combination of two actions yields a third, which achieves both post-conditions (if possible) and can be executed whenever both guards are satisfied.

Definition: Combining actions. For two actions of the form $G_1 \rightarrow w : [post_1]$ and $G_2 \rightarrow w : [post_2]$, their combination is defined by

$$(G_1 \rightarrow w : [post_1]) \sqcup (G_2 \rightarrow w : [post_2]) \mathrel{\widehat{=}} (G_1 \wedge G_2) \rightarrow w : [post_1 \wedge post_2]$$

$\square$

The action combinator defined above always produces a more refined action [13] and is sufficient to guarantee trace refinement of Action Systems as defined by Woodcock and Morgan [14] where one process P is refined by another Q if both processes have similar alphabets and P is capable of executing all the traces that Q is capable of executing.

4 Evaluating the Options

The previous section identified a number of design options as candidate solutions to the design questions raised. In this section, some criteria are presented that allow a designer to compare and differentiate between the options, providing a justification for selecting one option above the others. In general, the criteria originate in two ways. Either they are mechanisms used by the designer to select and document courses of action; they are therefore internal to the design process and reflect the designers' priorities and knowledge of the application area. Alternatively, the criteria may represent requirements, and therefore arise as a result of the iterative requirements capture and negotiation process between customer and designer. Informally, the four criteria investigated are:

C1: The user can always *undo* knowing the earlier state.

C2: Work can be restored if the user knows the number of steps to be undone.

C3: No work done by the user is ever lost.

C4: Short interaction paths when performing undos.

The interpretation of the informal criteria and their relationship to individual and combined options isn't immediately obvious from their informal descriptions. However, by formalising the criteria as logical properties, it is possible to determine whether a particular criterion supports or falsifies an option. The relationship between options and criteria is then logical.

The definitions of criteria C1, C2 and C3 are based on the variables depicted in Figure 1 below. Typically, the user has executed a sequence of actions tr_1, for which there is a current value of *text* (t) and *cursor* (c). Then, another valid sequence of actions tr_2 is executed, so that the values of *text* and *cursor* then become t' and c'. The undo task consists of the user formulating and executing an "undo program" whose effect is to restore the values of *text* and *cursor* to be t and c. Criteria C1, C2 and C3 are conditions on how the user does this and what information they require in order to do so. Satisfaction of criterion C2 means an undo sequence can be constructed from a knowledge of the length of the action sequence tr_2. Similarly C1 means that the undo program depends on knowledge of t and c. C3 allows arbitrary information about the history of commands and states to be used in the undo construction.

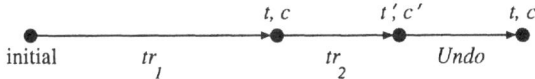

$$t, c \qquad t', c' \qquad t, c$$

initial $\qquad tr_1 \qquad\qquad tr_2 \qquad$ Undo

Fig. 1. Undoing previous work

All the criteria defined below rely on an equivalence relation on the execution of traces, based only on the values assigned to *text* and *cursor*, defined as follows.

Definition: Weaker equivalence of programs based on text and cursor values. For any two programs P and Q,

$$P \approx Q \;\hat{=}\; \|\; \mathbf{var}\; \mathit{left, right, history} \bullet P \;\| \;\equiv\; \|\; \mathbf{var}\; \mathit{left, right, history} \bullet Q \;\|$$

The variables *left*, *right* and *history* are all "hidden" by declaring them to be local to a program block delimited by the $\|\; \ldots \;\|$ brackets. $\qquad\qquad\square$

The criteria C1, C2 and C3 are formalised as follows.

Criterion C1: The user can always undo knowing the earlier state. Given that the user has a desired earlier state, it should be possible them to infer an interaction sequence to perform the undo. Here, the sequence of actions tr_2 represents a piece of work done by the user (not containing *undo* actions). After executing tr_2, is the user able to construct an undo sequence to return to the previous state, given that they can only remember what the contents of that state? Criterion C1 is formalised as follows.

$$\forall tr_1 : Traces, tr_2 : NoUndos \mid tr_1 \frown tr_2 \in Traces \bullet$$
$$init; \widehat{tr_1}; \;\|\; \mathbf{con}\; t, c \mid \begin{pmatrix} t = text \\ c = cursor \end{pmatrix} \bullet \widehat{tr_2};$$
$$\mathbf{while}\; \neg \begin{pmatrix} text = t \\ cursor = c \end{pmatrix} \rightarrow undo!1\; \mathbf{end}\; \|$$
$$\approx init; \widehat{tr_1}$$

Options	Description
O1.1, O2.1	Only a single step can be undone at once and a subsequent undo command will restore the current state.
O1.1, O2.2	Only a single step can be undone at once and a subsequent undo command will restore the previous state in the undo history.
O1.2, O2.1	Multiple steps may be undone with a single command and a subsequent undo command will restore the current state.
O1.2, O2.2	Multiple steps may be undone with a single command and a subsequent undo command will restore the previous state in the undo history.

Table 1. Combined design options

The definition of this criterion makes explicit use of the values of t and c so they are defined as logical constants in a block of the form $\|[\ \mathbf{con}\ t, c\ |\ \cdots\ ]\|$. The user's strategy here is to repeatedly execute single step undos $undo!1$ until the required state is retrieved.

This criterion does not distinguish any single options but both combinations (O1.1, O2.2) and (O1.2, O2.2) satisfy it. The meanings of the combined design options are summarised in Table 1.

To illustrate how one might prove that a design option satisfies a particular criterion a sketch of the proof that the option combination (O1.1, O2.2), defined in Section 3.1, satisfies criterion C1 is given as follows.

Proof: Option combination (O1.1, O2.2) satisfies criterion C1. In this proof, it is sufficient to show that the program:

$$\widetilde{tr_2};\ \mathbf{while}\ \neg \begin{pmatrix} text = t \\ cursor = c \end{pmatrix} \rightarrow undo!1\ \mathbf{end}$$

terminates with t, c as the current values of *text* and *cursor*, respectively. To do this, it is established that the weakest pre-condition of the above program achieving the predicate $t = text \wedge c = cursor$ evaluates to *true*.

Typically, weakest pre-condition proofs step backwards through the execution of a program, as follows.

Considering the weakest pre-condition of the while loop: the weakest pre-condition for which the **while** loop achieves the predicate $t = text \wedge c = cursor$ is that $t = text \wedge c = cursor$ on initial execution of the loop or there exists a (t, c) element in the undo history.

Considering the weakest pre-condition of the execution of tr_2:

Case I. If the trace tr_2 is empty then the body of the while loop cannot execute (as its guard is not satisfied) and equivalence (with respect to $\approxeq$) between the two programs on either side of the equation above is guaranteed.

Case II. If the trace tr_2 is non-empty then the execution of the first *undo* action of tr_2 ensures that (t, c) is an element of the history at that point. The trace tr_2 does not contain any actions of the form $undo!n$. By examination of the specifications of *insert?c*, *delete*, *cursor?x* and *present* it is clear that they all preserve the history (that is, leave it unchanged or prepend another item.) Therefore, the weakest pre-condition that $\widehat{tr_2}$ achieves the predicate (t, c) *in history* is *true*, observing the weakest pre-condition of the while loop given above. This mean that the while loop is guaranteed to find and set *text*, *cursor* to t, c respectively. Hence, equivalence (with respect to $\approxeq$) between the two programs on either side of the equation above is guaranteed.

□

Criterion C2: Work can be restored if the user knows the number of steps to be undone. Here, the sequence of actions tr_2 represents a piece of work done by the user (not containing *undo* actions). Is it possible for the user, after executing tr_2, to revert to the previous state, given that the length of tr_2 is known? Criterion C2 is defined more formally as follows.

$$\forall tr_1 : Traces, tr_2 : NoUndos \mid (tr_1 \frown tr_2 \in Traces) \bullet$$
$$init;\ \widehat{tr_1};\ \widehat{tr_2};\ undo(\#tr_2) \approxeq init;\ \widehat{tr_1}$$

where *Traces* is the set of execution traces *TextEd* (augmented with the design option or options under consideration) is capable of performing; *NoUndos* is the set of all sequences of actions not containing actions of the form *undo!n*; *init* is the initialisation program of *TextEd*; and *undo(n)* defines an "undo strategy" for *TextEd* so that $(tr_1 \frown tr_2 \frown undo(n)) \in Traces$. For instance, with the option combination (O1.1, O2.2) from the previous section *undo(n)* yields traces containing n instances of *undo!1*.

Criterion C2 can be used to distinguish O1.1, which fails to satisfy the criterion, and O1.2, which satisfies the criterion. When applied to the combined options, the combinations (O1.1, O2.2), (O1.2, O2.1) and (O1.2, O2.2) satisfy the criterion whereas the combination (O1.1, O2.1) does not.

Criterion C3: No work done by the user is ever lost. Satisfaction of this property requires that the user can always construct a sequence of *undo* actions to retrieve any previous *text* and *cursor* state of the system. As before, the sequence of actions tr_2 represents any intermediate work done by the user.

$$\forall tr_1 : Traces, tr_2 \mid tr_1 \frown tr_2 \in Traces \bullet$$
$$\exists tr_3 : Undos \mid tr_1 \frown tr_2 \frown tr_3 \in Traces \bullet$$
$$init;\ \widehat{tr_1};\ \widehat{tr_2};\ \widehat{tr_3} \approxeq init;\ \widehat{tr_1}$$

where *Undos* is a set of action sequences just containing actions of the form *undo!n*. Criterion C3 does not distinguish between any of the initial four options; when applied to the combined options, however, only the combination (O1.2,O2.1) is satisfied.

Criterion C4: Short interaction paths when performing undos. This property is simple to formalise, given a representation for the length of interaction sequences (for example, a size function operating on sequences of actions). The property distinguishes between options O1.1 (where the *undo!1* operation is performed n times) and O1.2 (where a single *undo!n* is possible). The distinction is carried through to the combined options, where (O1.1, O2.1) and (O1.2, O2.2) are distinguished from (O1.2, O2.1) and (O1.2, O2.2) as one would expect. The distinction is, however, not particularly illuminating, and the criterion is not formalised.

4.1 Observations

Figure 2 summarises which criteria support or deny which design options. A line joining an option and a criterion indicates that the option satisfies the criterion, and no line implies the converse. No lines at all between a criterion and options of a particular question means that the criterion is unsatisfied by all options of that question. The same information is also presented in Table 2.

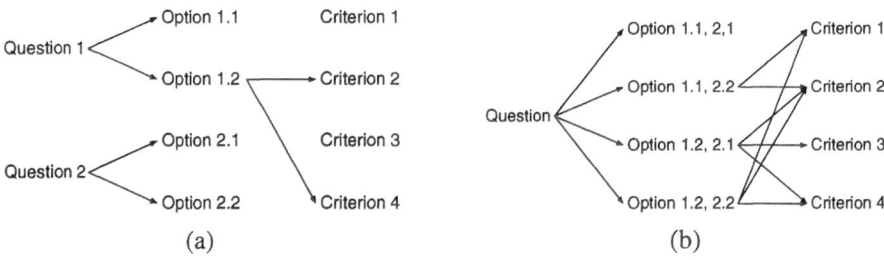

Fig. 2. Questions, Options and Criteria

Criterion	O1.1	O1.2	O2.1	O2.2	O1.1,O2.1	O1.1,O2.2	O1.2,O2.1	O1.2,O2.2
C1					✓			✓
C2		✓			✓	✓	✓	
C3							✓	
C4		✓					✓	✓

Table 2. Criteria and design options

It is interesting to note that the formulae above represent user-significant features of the system in their structure. Each of the formulae has the form

$$\forall tr_1, tr_2 \mid tr_1 \frown tr_2 \in \textit{Traces} \bullet \textit{init}; \widetilde{tr_1}; \widetilde{tr_2}; \textit{PROG}(f(tr_1, tr_2)) \approx \textit{init}; \widetilde{tr_1}$$

The user's behaviour is described by a program *PROG*, which is dependent on some function f of the bound variables tr_1 and tr_2. For example, in criterion C2, the user program depends only on the length of tr_2 and in C1 it depends on the text and cursor values immediately prior to the execution of tr_2. The function f can be thought of as characterising what the user needs to know (or remember) about the history of interactions or system states in order to behave as described by *PROG* and achieve the undo goal. The fs used in the different criteria, therefore capture factors that are related to the usability of the various designs.

5 Making a Decision

In the previous section, a number of criteria for selecting design options were identified and formalised. These criteria do not, however, allow an unambiguous selection of a design to be made, because there is no single option satisfying all criteria. The situation is typical of real-world developments where decisions are guided as much by the need to make engineering judgements and compromises between conflicting objectives as by the formal refinement of requirements into systems. The final step in the method allows the "tradeoff" between different criteria to be captured.

In order to make a selection from the proposed options, the criteria may be ranked in order of desirability or importance and used to reject options until the space of available options has been reduced in size, preferably to leave exactly one option.

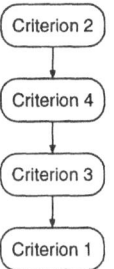

Fig. 3. Total ordering of criteria

The total ordering depicted in Figure 3 means that satisfying Criterion C2 is more important or desirable that satisfying C4, which is in turn more important than C3, and so on.

Informally, the overriding preference for C2 rules out the combination (O1.1, O2.1). The next preference for C4 rules out the combination (O1.1, O2.2). Finally, the Criterion C3 rules out the combination (O1.2, O2.2) leaving only the combination (O1.2, O2.1), which will be used in the design. Not only has a design decision finally been made, but the *rationale* for having made this particular decision has been documented by recording the criteria and preference ordering.

If, on the other hand, neither C1 nor C3 is preferred over the other, then the preference is described by the partial ordering in Figure 4. The mechanism for selecting options does not uniquely determine a result, preferring the combinations (O1.2, O2.1) and

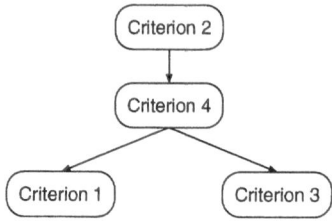

Fig. 4. Partial ordering of criteria

(O1.2, O2.2) equally. In a case such as this, either the preference ordering must be adjusted, new and better options devised, additional criteria defined or the choice may be left to the implementer. Either way, a facility is provided for expressing preferences and recording the reasoning that went into the designer's decision-making process.

6 Conclusions

In conclusion, this paper has made two main contributions. The first is a demonstration of how a standard specification notation from the formal methods domain can be used to specify the behaviour of interactive systems. This is in contrast to other approaches (such as those described in [1] or [5]) where hybrid notations are defined for this purpose. The Action System notation comes complete with a proof theory and a formalised theory of refinements which can be adopted, with only minor alterations, for Action System Interactors.

The second contribution is an integration between formal specification, development methods and a *design rationale* technique (based on the first author's current research). The decision points made during a development are recorded and the reasons for selecting one design option over another. Formality is therefore introduced into the process of constructing specifications, as well as refining one specification into another.

In terms of the development process, the kind of design rationale used here has several rôles. High level questions capture the customer's requirements; decompositions into sub-questions correspond either to the customer providing more detail in the requirements statement or to the developer deciding to split the problem up in a particular way. Options correspond to the designer's proposals for solving the problem, and are of no particular direct interest to the customers. Criteria form the basis for discussion or negotiation between the customer with a view to clarifying the meaning of questions or identifying and filling gaps in requirements. It is in this way that the customer is involved as the development proceeds.

On the face of it, the technique described in this paper would seem to demand a large amount of effort for it to be applied in a real development. However, two factors would tend to mitigate against the high cost. Firstly, there will be situations where the space of design options is large and confusing and the necessity to record rationale behind decisions for the benefit of future developers is paramount. Secondly, in application areas with a significant safety critical or business critical dimension, formally-based techniques are already being used, irrespective of whether rationale underlying design decisions is captured.

Finally, the approach to design space exploration and the recording of the rationale behind design decisions could have been presented using similar formal specification techniques to Morgan's refinement calculus or Action Systems, for example variations on Z [11] and VDM [7]. The decision to use the particular particular notation presented here was made for purely pragmatic reasons.

Acknowledgements

The first author has received funding from an EPSRC Case Studentship Award from Rank Xerox (92566197) and the second is funded as part of the British Aerospace Dependable Computing Systems Centre. The authors would like to thank Roger Took and the anonymous referees for their comments on an earlier version of this paper.

References

1. G. D. Abowd. *Formal Aspects of Human-Computer Interaction*. PhD thesis, University of Oxford Computing Laboratory: Programming Research Group, 1991. Available as Technical Monograph PRG-97.

2. R.J.R. Back and K. Sere. From action systems to modular systems. In M. Naftalin, T. Denvir, and M. Bertran, editors, *Proceedings of FME'94: Industrial Benefit of Formal Methods*, number 873 in Lecture Notes in Computer Science, pages 1–25. Formal Methods Europe, Springer-Verlag, October 1994.

3. A.J. Dix. *Formal Methods for Interactive Systems*. Computers and People. Academic Press, 1991.

4. D. Duke and M. Harrison. Abstract interaction objects. *Computer Graphics Forum*, 12(3):25–36, 1993.

5. B. Fields, M. Harrison, and P. Wright. Modelling interactive systems and providing task relevant information. In F. Paternò, editor, *Proceedings, EUROGRAPHICS Workshop on the Design, Specification, Verification of Interactive Systems, Bocca di Magra, Italy*, Eurographics Seminar Series. Springer-Verlag, 1995.

6. M. Harrison and H. Thimbleby, editors. *Formal Methods in Human-Computer Interaction*. Cambridge, 1990.

7. C.B. Jones. *Systematic Software Development Using VDM*. International Series in Computer Science. Prentice-Hall International, 2nd edition, 1990.

8. A. MacLean, R. Young, V.M.E. Bellotti, and T. Moran. Questions, options, and criteria: Elements of design space analysis. *Human-Computer Interaction*, 6:201–250, 1991.

9. C. Morgan. Of wp and CSP. In A.J.M. Feijen, D. van Gasteren, D. Gries, and J.Misra, editors, *Beauty is our business*, chapter 36, pages 319–326. Springer-Verlag, 1990.

10. C. Morgan. *Programming from specifications*. International Series in Computer Science. Prentice-Hall International, 1990.

11. J.M. Spivey. *The Z notation : A reference manual*. Prentice-Hall International, second edition, 1992.

12. H. Thimbleby. *User Interface Design*. Frontier Series. ACM Press, 1990.

13. M. Utting and K. Robinson. Towards an object-oriented refinement calculus. *Australian Computer Science Communications*, 13(1), February 1991.

14. J.C.P. Woodcock and C. Morgan. Refinement of state-based concurrent systems. *Lecture Notes in Computer Science 428, Springer-Verlag*, pages 340–351, 1990.

15. R.M. Young and G.D. Abowd. Multi-perspective modelling of interface design issues: Undo in a collaborative editor. In G. Cockton, S.W. Draper, and G.R.S Weir, editors, *HCI'94 Conference*, People and Computers IX. BCS HCI Specialist Group, Cambridge University Press, 1994.

Appendix

The tables below describe some of the formal notation used in the paper for defining predicates on numbers and sequences and constructing action systems.

Numbers	
$\mathbb{N}$	The set of natural numbers.
$\mathbb{N}_1$	The set of natural numbers greater than zero.
$n \ominus m$	Non-negative subtraction. Zero if $m \geq n$, or $n - m$ otherwise.
$m..n$	The set of integers from m to n .
$min(m,n)$	The least number of m and n.
$max(m,n)$	The greatest number of m and n.

Sequences	
$seq\ X$	The type of sequences of elements of type X (including the empty sequence).
$\langle\rangle$	The empty sequence.
$\langle e \rangle$	The sequence with a single element e.
$s \frown t$	The concatenation of two sequences.
$\#s$	The number of elements in sequence s.
$s\ after\ n$	A sequence after n elements. The empty sequence if n is too large.
$s[n]$	The nth element of a sequence s.
$s[m..n]$	The sub-sequence of s between m and n (or vice versa if $n < m$): $[s[min(m,n)], ..., s[max(m,n)]]$.

Action Systems and Refinement Calculus	
$name?(args) \widehat{=} guard \rightarrow body$	Action definition.
while $guard \rightarrow body$ **end**	Whole loop.
$\lVert$ **var** $v \bullet ... \rVert$	Program block with local variables, v.
$\lVert$ **con** $v \bullet ... \rVert$	Program block with local constants, v.
$w\text{:}\ [post]$	Specification statement, with write frame w and a post-condition *post*.
$var := exp$	Variable assignment.

Moving Between Contexts

Alan Dix

School of Computing and Mathematics
University of Huddersfield
Queensgate
Huddersfield, UK, HD1 3DH
email: alan@zeus.hud.ac.uk

Abstract. Any action is performed in a particular context. So what does it mean to do the 'same' thing in a different context? There is no simple answer to this question , it depends on the interpretation of the operation and even then may be ambiguous. This is not a purely theoretical problem, but occurs in practical computational problems. This paper examines this issue looking at three different problems: multi-user undo, distributed update and the simultaneous development of a document in multiple formats. In each case, we find formal rules which any sensible translation must obey. We also see that dynamic pointers, a generic specification and implementation concept defined in previous work, can be used to generate default translation rules which suffice in many circumstances. This is because dynamic pointers can themselves be seen as a translation of location information between different contexts.

1 Introduction

In this paper we are going to look at three different situations where operations which have been formulated in one context have to be reinterpreted in another. If you stand up in the morning, it is pretty clear what it means to do the same thing in the evening. But, if you face the east in the morning, what is the equivalent action in the evening? Do you still face east, or do you face west towards the setting sun? As is evident, a general answer to the question involves the meaning and purpose of an operation. However, we will see that there are many situations where there is an obvious and computable meaning to this concept.

The first situation we will consider is the issue of undo in a multi-user interactive system. One of the solutions to this involves switching the order of commands. So, the first command has to be understood in the context before the second and vice versa.

In the second example, we will consider the simultaneous update of the same object in a distributed environment. In order to merge these updates it is necessary to reinterpret updates as if they had been performed one after another, rather than simultaneously.

Finally, and perhaps most exciting, we will look at the parallel development of related documents in different formats. One of the most difficult things about cooperative writing is finding a single word-processor or text proocessing package to use. Often one resorts to using plain ASCII files! However, we will see that it is possible to work on different formats translating updates formulated in one format into equivalent ones on the other.

Throughout the paper, we will consider the general properties required of different forms of translation between contexts. In addition, we will see how dynamic pointers, which encapsulate the translation of location information between contexts, can be used as a generic mechanism to aid in the production of appropriate translation rules. The properties of dynamic pointers are dealt with in detail elsewhere [3] and their application to multi-user interface issues has also been developed [2]. In this paper we will summarise sufficient of this background to make the paper self-contained.

2 Group and long-term undo

2.1 The problem

Providing undo support has been a challenge for several synchronous multi-user editors [8]. The principal problem is as follows:

Two users, Alison and Brian, are editing a document. First Alison performs action a, then Brian performs action b, finally Alison presses the undo button – what happens? There are two options.

global undo – the very last action b is undone
local undo – Alison's last action a is undone

The meaning of global undo is clear and, although it is often expensive to implement, at least you know what to do. Unfortunately, in all but the most tightly coordinated editors this is not the behaviour a user would expect. Local undo is what they want.

Although the description of this problem is in terms of group undo, it is important to note that the same problem arises in single user systems. If you had done both actions yourself and then realised that the first was wrong you would be in exactly the same situation.

2.2 Commutativity

Gregory Abowd and I examined the general issues using a formal model of group undo [1]. The formal model allowed us to clarify when local undo could be given a sensible meaning. This was when the users' commands commute. If the result of ab is the same as ba, then one can simply pretend the commands happened the other way round and effectively use global undo.

Figure 1 shows this process. You can think of this as rewriting history! It is rather similar to the serialisation conditions familiar in database theory.

In fact, it is not necessary that the operations commute in all contexts, but merely that when applied to the particular state s_0 where we started. That is, if $doit$ is the state update function, we require that:

$$doit(a, doit(b, s_0)) = doit(b, doit(a, s_0))$$

It is certainly safe, if we can sow that commands commute in all circumstances, but this is conservative. We might find that some pairs of commands commute only sometimes and if we can detect these we can undo them in the circumstances where they do commute.

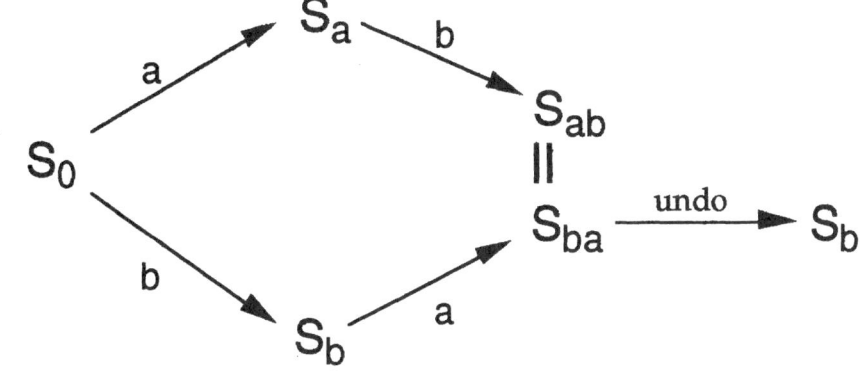

Fig. 1. Local undo = rewrite history + global undo

Unfortunately, not all comands commute, so we also considered various ways of making commands more likely to commute. These include locking (which prevents people performing non-commuting actions), and structuring the document into sub-objects so that updates to different objects can commute. The hardest case is free text. This is because an update in the text affects the offsets of characters in the whole of the rest of the document. No implemented group undo system of which I am aware caters for multiple actions to the same text object.

Happily, there are ways of representing operations on text so that they are more likely to commute. This was explored in [1] when we suggested the use of a variant of Ellis and Gibbs distributed update algorithms and also in [2] where the dynamic pointer solutions were explored in detail. In both methods the operations are translated when they are reversed. For example, imagine the operations were as follows (a sort of mutual admiration society):

s_0 = "Alison⎵is⎵⎵and⎵Brian⎵is⎵."
a = insert(24,"beautiful")
b = insert(10,"adorable")
s_{ab} = "Alison⎵is⎵adorable⎵and⎵Brian⎵is⎵beautiful."

If we reverse these operations the effect is disasterous.

s_{ba} = "Alison⎵is⎵adorable⎵and⎵Bbeautifulrian⎵is⎵."

Both the use of Ellis and Gibbs algorithm and dynamic pointers effectively modify the first operation slightly to give:

b = insert(10,"adorable")
a' = insert(32,"beautiful")
$s_{ba'}$ = "Alison⎵is⎵adorable⎵and⎵Brian⎵is⎵beautiful."

Just what we wanted!

2.3 Levels of interpretation

There is something very strange happening here. Surely operations either commute or they don't? How can you change the representation of something and make it commute when it didn't before? Let's go back. We said that undo is possible if two operations a and b commute, that is if:

$$doit(a, doit(b, s_0)) = doit(b, doit(a, s_0))$$

However, in the example we gave, the operations on either side were not the same – we rewrote one of them to give a'. We cheated! The original operations didn't commute, we just invented some different operations which had the same effect. This sounds like very shaky ground on which to stand.

In fact, the problem is more fundamental. It is not clear that the original concept of commuting updates is well formulated. If you asked anyone what it would mean to do the two insertions a and b in the opposite order they would give the dynamic pointers answer, not the one based on the literal operation. Of course, if we had instead described the operations as:

a = insert(at Alison's cursor, "beautiful")

b = insert(at Brian's cursor, "adorable")

Then we would have expected that Alison's cursor would be in a different position before and after Brian's operation. (In fact, this is effectively how dynamic pointers work.) In any system there will be multiple interpretations of the same user action at different levels in the system. At the physical level we will have interpretations like 'click mouse at 117, 523', a little deeper, this would be interpreted as 'click the "delete" button', this would then translate to the internal operation 'delete the text at the selection', which finally might become 'remove characters 573 to 597 from the text'. Of course, in the user's head this might just be 'oops, didn't mean to hit the paste key'. So, the same operation may be described in different ways and, depending on which we choose, the 'same' operations may or may not commute.

Arguably the best interpretation will be the one the user means. However, there is evidence that the user's idea of what is being undone differs from that of the system designer, certainly at the level of the grouping of actions for undo [10]. Also, not all users have the same interpretation and so there is no gold standard.

2.4 Changing contexts

How come these different levels of interpretation differ so much in their meaning when we consider undo? Are systems poorly managing the translation between user's intentions and the realisation within the machine? While this may be the case, it is not the fundamental problem here. In the above description of different levels, each interpretation meant the same thing – in the context in which they acted. But, if we want the 'same' operation in a different context, the problems start. At each level of interpretation, we can see changes in context which invalidate the description.

(i)   click mouse at 117, 523   —   the window has been moved
(ii) click the "delete" button   —   the button has changed its function
(iii) delete the text at the selection —   the user has selected a different piece of text
(iv) remove characters 573 to 597   —   text has been inserted or deleted before position
                                            573

So, whatever level of interpretation we pick we need to translate the operation as we move it beween contexts. So, our original formulation of commutativity was flawed, it is normally meaningless to talk of:

$$a\,b = b\,a$$

The second operation b was formulated in the context *after* a was performed (s_a) and so cannot simply be performed in the context before. Similarly, a was formulated in the original context s_0 and so also needs transformation. The result is more like:

$$a\,b = b'\,a'$$

However, the translation that changes a to a' is different from that which changes b to b', so we introduce specific notation for the two translations:

$\overset{\leftarrow a}{b}$ — b moved back to execute before a

$\overset{\rightarrow b}{a}$ — a moved forward to execute after the translated b

These translations must obey the commutativity law making the diagram in figure 2 commute. These translations may also depend on the original context, but in all the examples we will deal with they turn out to be independent of it. Note also that translations will in general be partial – there will be some pairs of operations for which there is no sensible reversal. This happens when commands interfere with one another and we will see an example of this below.

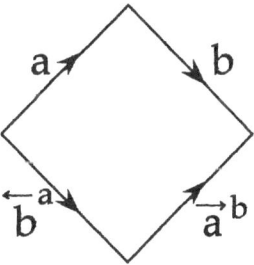

Fig. 2. Undo translations commute

Given this complexity, surely one should design systems so that commands do not depend on context? The design of relational databases means that updates are usually expressed in an apparently context independent fashion. Rather than say 'update that record', you say 'change the salary of employee no. 573 to £17,000'. First, this sort of descriptive formulation is hardly what one would expect of a modern interactive system!

Also the context independence is partly illusory. If a previous update had been 'change the employee no. of 235 to 573', then we would have had similar problems to positional commands.

2.5 Example translations

Independent objects. The very simplest translation scheme is not to allow any reordering, that is, the translation is not just partial, it is empty! One step better are translation schemes which divide the document[1] into separate objects. Updates to each object commute with those for other objects and no translation is necessary. If two updates refer to the same object then they are deemed incompatible and no translation is given. Of course, the objects may themselves be split into independent sub-objects or attributes and then updates to different attributes of the same object would be allowed.

For example, in a drawing package each shape on the screen is a different object. Each shape has various attributes: colour, position, width, height. These attributes are changed by direct manipulation and turned into internal operations:

   (i) select blue in colour menu — `set_attr(#179,colour,blue)`
  (ii) drag circle across screen — `set_attr(#63,position,(356,813))`
 (iii) press delete key — `delete(#432)`
 (iv) select box in new menu — `create(#112,box)`

The numbers in each operation refer to the internal reference for the relevant objects. In the cases of (i) and (iii), these would be of the currently selected object and in the case of (ii) it would be whatever object was dragged. The final example (iv) is different in that the reference would not be part of the original command, but would be generated when the object was created. However, it would need to be remembered in any history which is used for undo purposes. The translation alters no operations, but some translations are not allowed (the translation is the identity over a restricted domain). The forbidden combinations are:

$$\text{create}(n, shape) \ \& \ \text{set\_attr}(n', attr, val) \quad - \quad \text{if } n = n'$$
$$\text{create}(n, shape) \ \& \ \text{delete}(n') \quad - \quad \text{if } n = n'$$
$$\text{set\_attr}(n, a, v) \ \& \ \text{set\_attr}(n', a', v') \quad - \quad \text{if } n = n' \text{ and } a = a' \text{ and } v \neq v'$$
$$\text{set\_attr}(n, a, v) \ \& \ \text{delete}(n') \quad - \quad \text{if } n = n'$$

If we assume that the program never reuses reference numbers, then combinations such as `delete(n)` followed by `create(n, shape)`, could never occur and so all `delete`–`create` and `delete`–`set_attr` are compatible.

Text editing. As we noted earlier, independent objects are easy. It is text which causes problems. We'll consider only single character insertions and deletions. The two operations are:

    `insert(n, c)` — insert the character c just after the nth character.
    `delete(m)` — delete the mth character.

First some of the simple rules:

---

[1] The word document here refers to the whole thing being updated, whether it is a database, spreadsheet or text

(i) $a \quad = \texttt{insert}(n, c) \qquad b \quad = \texttt{insert}(m, c') \qquad - n < m$

$\quad \overleftarrow{b}^{a} = \texttt{insert}(m+1, c') \quad \overrightarrow{a}^{b} = \texttt{insert}(n, c)$

(ii) $a \quad = \texttt{insert}(n, c) \qquad b \quad = \texttt{insert}(m, c') \qquad - n > m$

$\quad \overleftarrow{b}^{a} = \texttt{insert}(m, c') \quad\;\; \overrightarrow{a}^{b} = \texttt{insert}(n+1, c)$

(iii) $a \quad = \texttt{insert}(n, c) \qquad b \quad = \texttt{delete}(m) \qquad\;\; - n > m$

$\quad \overleftarrow{b}^{a} = \texttt{delete}(m) \qquad\;\; \overrightarrow{a}^{b} = \texttt{insert}(n-1, c)$

The nasty examples are where insertions and deletions happen at exactly the same place. Some of these obviously do not admit a sensible reversal, for example, an insert followed immediately by a deletion at the same location. The only reasonable translation is for both to become no-ops.

(iv) $a \quad = \texttt{insert}(n, c) \; b \quad = \texttt{delete}(n+1)$

$\quad \overleftarrow{b}^{a} = \epsilon \qquad\qquad\qquad \overrightarrow{a}^{b} = \epsilon$

However, it would seem better to simply regard these as undefined.

The other combinations have sensible translations, for example:

(v) $a \quad = \texttt{insert}(n, c) \quad b \quad = \texttt{insert}(n, c')$

$\quad \overleftarrow{b}^{a} = \texttt{insert}(n, c') \quad \overrightarrow{a}^{b} = \texttt{insert}(n, c)$

(vi) $a \quad = \texttt{insert}(n, c) \quad b \quad = \texttt{insert}(n+1, c')$

$\quad \overleftarrow{b}^{a} = \texttt{insert}(n, c') \quad \overrightarrow{a}^{b} = \texttt{insert}(n, c)$

(vii) $a \quad = \texttt{delete}(n) \qquad b \quad = \texttt{delete}(n-1)$

$\quad \overleftarrow{b}^{a} = \texttt{delete}(n-1) \; \overrightarrow{a}^{b} = \texttt{delete}(n-1)$

It is easy to verify that all these rules obey the commutativity property.

3   Merging updates

A similar problem arises when several users are editing an object on a distributed platform. If network speeds allow, the updates can be routed through a central server. In this case there is one document and the only problems which arise are the inevitable race conditions (e.g., two people attempt to type at the same position and get their typing mixed up). However, often the loss of interactive performance for a centralised architecture makes it impractical. Instead, each user's copy of the application will hold a local copy of the shared document. In these cases, one must either lock the objects so that only one person can edit at once, or else accept the risk that two people will edit the same object. If this happens, then the local copies of the documents on the two user's machines will be in conflict, neither will be the 'most up to date' and if one is taken rather than the other, one user's updates will be lost. The problem is how to perform updates on each copy in order to resynchronise the two copies, but in such a way that the two updates are merged, rather than one lost.

In the Grove editor, Ellis and Gibbs designed an algorithm to recover from this situation [5]. Imagine that one user has performed an operation a and the other has perfomed b. Their algorithm finds operations a' and b' such that the diagram in figure 3 commutes. They define translation rules similar to those we have seen for undo. This depends on the order in which the operations 'should' have happened. We will assume that a is the first. For example, the rule for insert–insert is:

156

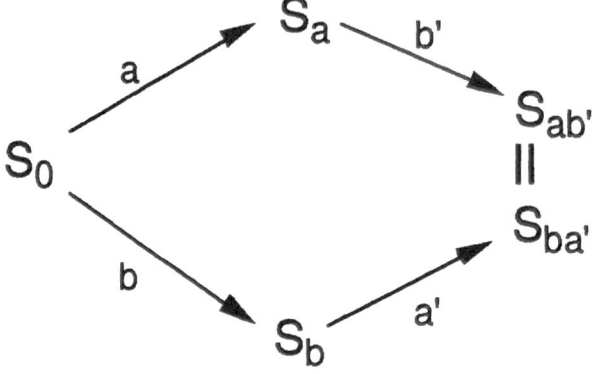

Fig. 3. Ellis and Gibbs' translations

$$a = \text{insert}\,(n, c) \qquad\qquad b = \text{insert}\,(m, c')$$

$$b' = \begin{cases} \text{insert}(m, c') & \text{if } n > m \\ \text{insert}(m, c') & \text{if } n = m \\ \text{insert}(m + 1, c') & \text{if } n < m \end{cases} \qquad a' = \begin{cases} \text{insert}(n, c) & \text{if } n > m \\ \text{insert}(n + 1, c) & \text{if } n = m \\ \text{insert}(n + 1, c) & \text{if } n < m \end{cases}$$

Notice that the rules for a' and b' differ. This is because if the two users insert at the same location the result depends on which we regard as happening first. Basically, we have to decide whether the final text has cc' or $c'c$. The rules above produce the latter result. Rules for the former would be the other way round, but still a' and b' would differ.

3.1 Moving between contexts

Again we have the problem of translating operations formulated in one context into a different one. This time the commands a and b are formulated in the context of the original state, s_0. We wish to translate a into the context of s_b and b into that of s_a, remembering that a should happen 'first'. As these translations are similar to those for the undo case, we will introduce similar notation.

$\underset{\leftarrow a}{b}$ — b, which should have happened after a, moved forward to execute after a

$\underset{\rightarrow b}{a}$ — a, which should have happened before b, moved forward to execute after b

Any translation for this sort of context change should obey the following law, and hence make the diagram in figure 4 commute.

$$a\,\underset{\leftarrow a}{b} = b\,\underset{\rightarrow b}{a}$$

As with the translations for undo, it is not clear that these translations can be total. In general we would expect to find some conflict. Ellis and Gibbs managed to develop a complete set for single character operations, but more complex block oriented operations are bound to lead to incompatible updates. For example, suppose Alison performed a global substitution of 'transformation' to 'change' and Brian simultaneously substituted

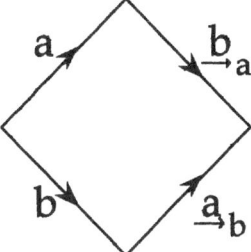

Fig. 4. Moving between contexts for simultaneous actions

'translation' to 'transformation'. In this case, one can think of translations which obey the relevant properties, but it is not at all clear that they are sensible.

In a synchronous editor, it would be very disconcerting to have some of your updates suddenly disregarded, but very intrusive for the system to request clarification on problematic merges. In such systems it is probably best to employ locking for potentially conflicting updates, but only where translations cannot be found. Note that this means analysing in advance those circumstances under which conflicts can arise – it's no good asking for the lock *after* the user has done the operation!

3.2 Long term interaction

A similar problem arises in more long term interactions. For example, two users have portable machines which are not connected to a network. When they meet and connect their machines any inconsistencies between their data must be resolved. Systems which support this sort of activity, for example Lotus Notes, Laplink or the CODA distributed filesystem [7], work by keeping one copy or other of the data. At best, they detect that an inconsistency has occurred and either warn the user or, in the case of Lotus Notes, keep both copies. One way to tackle the problem is to use translation techniques similar to those above. However, in the case of long term interactions, it is likely that there will be many incompatible updates. This is acceptable as the process of merging can afford to be more heavy weight than in the synchronous case. It is important here that the merging process is made as easy for the user as possible using translation to suggest the most likely form of the merged version. One possibility is to use version managment techniques to allow the users to maintain the different versions of the document [4]. This enables the users to see the history of changes and also gives the system suitable information to present merging in a helpful manner.

3.3 They are all different

The similarity between the different translations suggests that it might be possible to get away with less than four different translations. That is having constructed, say, the two undo translations, one might be able to generate one or other of the merge translations.

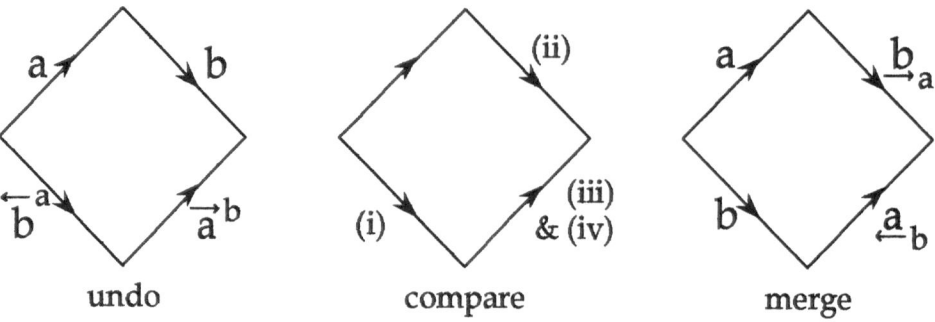

Fig. 5. Comparing translations

If we examine the two commuting diagrams (figure 5), we can focus on different arcs and obtain the following putative identities.

(i) $\overset{\longleftarrow a}{(\underset{\longrightarrow a}{b})} = b$

(ii) $\overset{\longleftarrow a}{(b} \underset{\longrightarrow a}{)} = b$

(iii) $\overrightarrow{a}^{(\underset{\rightarrow a}{b})} = \underset{\leftarrow b}{a}$

(iv) $a \underset{\leftarrow(\underset{b}{})}{\leftarrow a} = \overrightarrow{a}^{\rightarrow b}$

These all sound reasonable, but unfortunately *none of them* hold. The problem is that the translations lose information:

- The undo translations lose information when a is an insert, because in the context before a, the difference between the locations either side of the inserted text is lost.
- The merge translations lose information when a is a delete, because in the context after a the difference between locations either side of the deleted text is lost.

The problem cases are shown in figures 6 and 7. Each figure shows two commuting diagrams. In figure 6, we see that in an insert–insert scenario you cannot predict the right hand side of the diagram from the left, whilst figure 7 shows that in a delete–insert scenario you cannot predict the bottom from the top.

In the insert-insert secenario, identities (i) and (iii) hold. This is because they depend on *first* translating b forward. This does not lose information. However, in (ii) and (iv), b is first translated backwards, which loses information, and hence both fail. In the delete-delete scenario the opposite is true and it is (i) and (iii) which fail. The full counter-examples are given in appendix 1.

4 Composing translations

So far, we have only seen examples of translations applied to single operations. In fact, for both undo and merge this is sufficient. If you have produced *atomic* translations for each

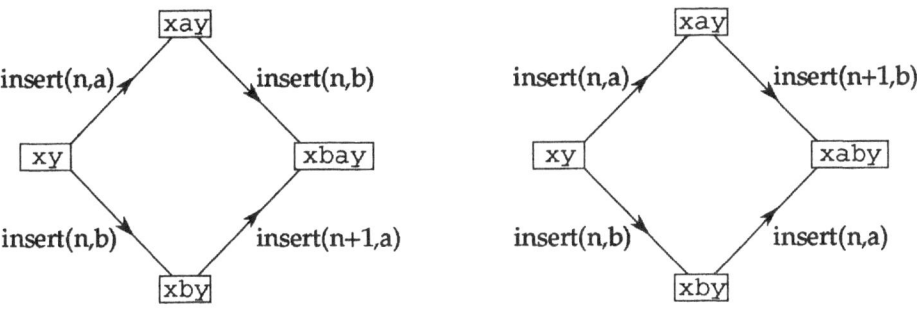

Fig. 6. Problem: the insert–insert scenario

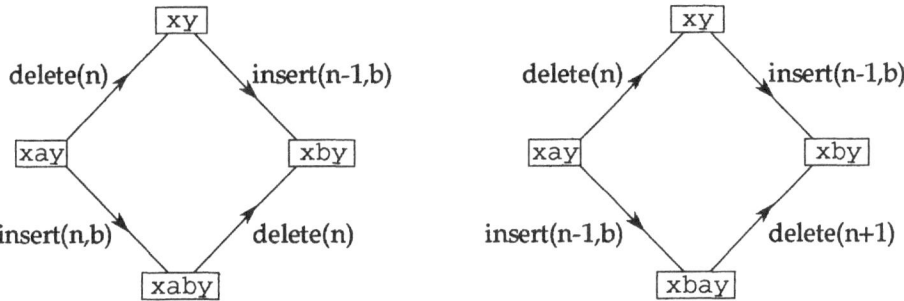

Fig. 7. Problem: the delete–insert scenario

pair of individual commands, then it is possible to construct the composite translations for sequences of commands. These composite translations can easily be built by diagram chasing.

4.1 Undo composition

Consider figure 8. We are trying to find the operations a', b', c' such that:

$$a b c = b' c' a'$$

By simply chasing the atomic translations through the commuting diagram we obtain:

(i) $\overrightarrow{a}^{(bc)} = (\overrightarrow{a}^{b})^{\overrightarrow{}c}$

(ii) $\overleftarrow{bc}^{a} = \overleftarrow{b}^{a} \overleftarrow{c}^{a} (\overrightarrow{a}^{b})$

Similarly, by chasing the commuting diagram in figure 9 we get:

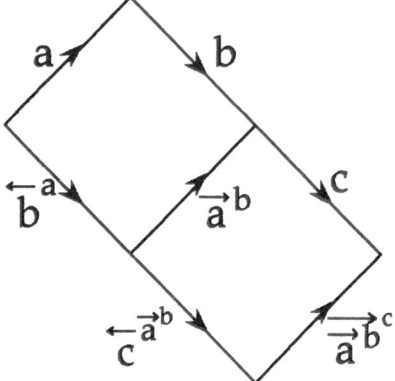

Fig. 8. Composing undo translations – a(bc)

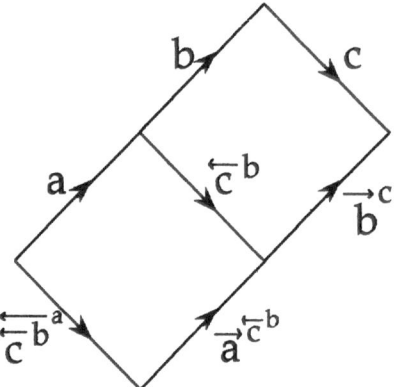

Fig. 9. Composing undo translations – (ab)c

(iii) $\overrightarrow{ab}^{c} = \overrightarrow{a}^{(\overleftarrow{c}^{b})}\overrightarrow{b}^{c}$

(iv) $\overleftarrow{c}^{(ab)} = (\overleftarrow{c}^{b})^{\overleftarrow{}a}$

Repeated application of these formulae allow us to calculate the appropriate translation for arbitrary large sequences of commands. Furthermore, they are not just a formal tool, but can be evaluated at run time – an algorithm as well as a definition. Regard each formulae as a rewrite rule left to right and take any expression involving translations and sequences. If we apply the rewrite rules, then we will eventually move the sequence terms to the outermost level and end up with an expression which is a sequence of atomic translations. Each atomic translation can be performed using the given rules and then the elements of the sequence perfomed in turn.

It is important that these formulae are sound. For example, take an expression like:

$$\underset{ab}{\overset{\longrightarrow cd}{}}$$

We expect to get the same answer no matter what order we reduce expression it. This is pretty clear from the mode in which they were obtained, but a proof that these rules are indeed confluent is found in appendix 2.

4.2 Merge composition

Composition of merge translations follows in a similar manner. The relevant formulae are:

(i) $\quad \underset{\leftarrow (bc)}{a} = \underset{\longleftarrow c}{(\underset{\leftarrow b}{a})}$

(ii) $\quad \underset{\longrightarrow a}{bc} = \underset{\longrightarrow a}{b}\ \underset{\longrightarrow a}{c}(\underset{\leftarrow b}{a})$

(iii) $\quad \underset{\leftarrow c}{ab} = \underset{\leftarrow c}{a}\ \underset{\leftarrow c}{b}(\underset{\longrightarrow b}{c})$

(iv) $\quad \underset{\longrightarrow (ab)}{c} = \underset{\longrightarrow b}{(\underset{\longrightarrow a}{c})}$

Notice that the composition formulae for backwards and forwards translation are duals of one another. This reflects the symmetry of the commuting diagram (figure 4). This means that proofs need tackle only one case, instead of the two needed for undo. Furthermore, (i) and (ii) are identical (swopping appropriate translations) with the cases (i) and (ii) for undo, but I can see no immediate use of this fact.

5 Dynamic pointers

Developing translations for every new operation is obviously a pain. Most of the translations follow a simple pattern. The translated operation is the same as the original, but with the location information modified slightly.

Dynamic pointers are a technique originally developed for coping with single-user interface design [3] and have recently been applied to some of the multi-user problems dealt with in this paper [1, 2]. They encapsulate the way locational information is modified after operations. That is, they capture the translation of pointers between contexts. With any object there is an associated set of pointers wich refer to locations within that object. For example, in the case of text these might be the positions of the gaps between the characters: pointer n refers to the gap between the nth and $n + 1$th characters and pointer 0 is before the first character in the text. As well as pointers to individual locations within the object, there may be more complex pointers, for example, in pointers to blocks of text or pointers to sets of records in a database.

5.1 Updates – the pull function

For every operation a corresponding 'pull' function is defined. This says how the pointers should be updated. For any operation op we will write $pull_{op}$ or simply $pull$ if the operation is obvious. Similarly for any set of objects Obj we write Pt_{Obj} for the set of pointers for those objects or Pt for short. The signatures of the corresponding functions are then:

$op : Params \times Obj \rightarrow Obj$

$pull_{op} : Params \times Obj \rightarrow (Pt \rightarrow Pt)$

The operation will involve some extra parameters (e.g., the text to be inserted) and these have been written generically as $Params$. Note that these parameters will often themselves involve positional information, that is, pointers. This is important later. The pull function needs the same parameters as the operations itself as the partciular form of the update depends on both the parameters (e.g., where the update happens) and the state of the object (e.g., for a delete word operation how big the word is). However, the operation and its parameters will often be obvious from context and so we will usually treat the pull function as a mapping from pointers to pointers.

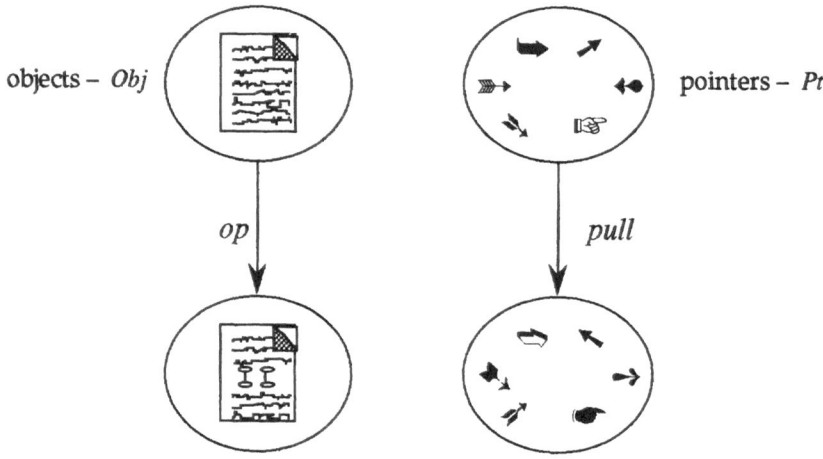

objects – Obj pointers – Pt

op $pull$

Fig. 10. Dynamic pointers – the pull function

Pull functions for the two character operations are as follows.

$$insert(n, c) \quad - \quad pull_{insert}(p) = \begin{cases} p & \text{if } p \le n \\ p+1 & \text{if } p > n \end{cases}$$

$$delete(n, c) \quad - \quad pull_{delete}(p) = \begin{cases} p & \text{if } p < n \\ p-1 & \text{if } p \ge n \end{cases}$$

Note that it is not clear what the insertion's pull function should do at the point of the insertion. The choice here (the 'leave 'em behind' strategy) is one option, the other being to increment the pointer. In [2] these are called $pull_-$ and $pull_+$ respectively. In older work, the latter choice was taken as the default, but it became apparent from the multi-user situations that this was not the best behaviour and hence more recent work has used $pull_-$ as the primary pull function. A similar problem arises with $pull_{delete}^{-1}$ and this comes in '$-$' and '$+$' versions. This ambiguity is directly related to the failure of the putative identities in section 3.3.

5.2 Using dynamic pointers for translations

It is evident that the rules for dynamic pointer update closely resemble those required for operation translation. This is reasonable, dynamic pointers transform locations between contexts and the operations are defined in terms of locations. Given an operation op defined in terms of pointers from Pt and a pull function $pull$, we can translate the operation to $pull(op)$ by transforming each pointer in the description of op. We can use this to generate default rules for the various translation operations:

$$\overset{\leftarrow a}{b} = pull_a^{-1}(b)$$
$$\overset{\rightarrow b}{a} = pull_{\leftarrow a}(a)$$
$$\underset{\rightarrow a}{b} = pull_a(b)$$
$$\underset{\leftarrow b}{a} = pull_b(a)$$

These default rules work everywhere except the immediate area of the change. For the special cases you either have to disallow translations or work out the precise rules by hand. Some of these can be filled in by simply choosing whether you want the $-$ or $+$ versions of the pull functions, but each case has to be checked as this behaviour may not be exactly as required. For undo, it is probably best to signal the conflict rather than guessing, especially if the system also offers more extensive support for the user's own undoing of actions [1]. The synchronous distributed editing situation does demand that all updates are performed silently – the aim is to make the users feel as if they are interacting with a single document. As Ellis and Gibbs show, the rules can be filled in completely for single character edits [5], but for more complex operations this can not be guaranteed. In the case of more long term distributed work, the effort of re-merging can be made explicit and so partial translations are more acceptable.

5.3 More properties of dynamic pointers

Projections. Updates take one object to another of the same type. In addition, we often need to deal with two different kinds of objects with a relationship between them. For example, in an interactive system, we may want to deal with the relationship between a document and its image on the screen. In fact, this is very similar to the update operations. We'll call the two object types Obj and Obj' and the relationship $proj$. There will be corresponding functions relating the two sets of pointers Pt and Pt'.

$proj: Params \rightarrow (Obj \leftrightarrow Obj')$
$fwd: Params \times Obj \times Obj' \rightarrow (Pt \rightarrow Pt')$
$back: Params \times Obj \times Obj' \rightarrow (Pt' \rightarrow Pt)$

As with the pull function, we will normally drop the initial parameters to the fwd and $back$ functions as these will be obvious from context. The two functions fwd and $back$ translate the pointers in each direction (like $pull$ and $pull^{-1}$) and are weak inverses of one another (i.e., they are inverses on their respective ranges). The two notions could be unified completely, but for compatibility with older work the separate notation is retained here.

Locality of change and sub-object projections. As well as a pull function, each operation can have an associated block pointer representing the extent of the changes in the operation.

If this locality of change is supplied for each operation, then it can be used to detect possible incompatibilities. If the locality of change of two operations do not intersect then they can be safely transformed using the default pull translations. The locality of change information can be used statically to determine which combinations require special treatment, or at run time, actually returned as part of the operation allowing detection of incompatibility.

Another extension primarily used during analysis are sub-object projections. These are special projections where one object is apart of another. Sub-object projections can be used to determine the 'normal' behaviour of translations. The definitions we gave allow the possibility of silly translations. For example, for any pair of operations a and b, we can define the translations:

$$\overleftarrow{b}^{a} = a\,b$$
$$\overrightarrow{a}^{b} = \epsilon$$

These obey the commutativity law and are otherwise acceptable, except they are clearly not sensible.

Let L_a and L_b be the locality of change for a and b. Let s_a be any sub-object block pointer which does not intersect L_a and s_b be any which does not intersect $pull_a^{-1}(L_b)$. We write $proj_s$ for the projection which extracts the sub-object at the block s. Then, we expect that:

$$proj_{s_a} \circ \overleftarrow{b}^{a} = proj_{pull_a(s_a)} \circ b$$
$$proj_{pull_{\overleftarrow{b}^{a}}(s_b)} \circ \overrightarrow{a}^{b} = proj_{s_b} \circ a$$

This basically says that $\overleftarrow{b}^{a}$ behaves 'the same' as b except within the locality of change of a and vice versa.

The full details of the locality of change and sub-object projections are found in [3].

6 Parallel development

6.1 Working together

One of the most difficult decisions in collaborative writing is choosing a common electronic format. Everyone has a favourite wordprocessor or text-processing program, and each package has its own advantages. Not only do these differ in the way they store information, but more important, they differ in the sort of information they store.

For example, let's consider RTF, SGML and LaTeX. An RTF document (as produced by Microsoft Word) is largely a definition of how a document *looks* – although styles are given names, these are largely an encapsulation of appearance. In contrast, an SGML or HTML document records the structure only, presentation is left to the browser or editor. Somewhere between is LaTeX, popular among computing academics, which has some structure and some layout, although it is certainly not a superset of the other two.

People who are cooperating will want to use their own system when working on the text, but will need to transfer drafts to and from each other. Often this happens at the level of ASCII text (often sent by email). This is a least common denominator representation, throwing away all the advantages of each package. Even with ASCII text there are numerous character set problems due to the different platforms used. Note that we can see this as another form of moving between contexts, this time the contexts are particular software 'worlds': the RTF world, LaTeX world etc.

6.2 Translators

A more sophisticated alternative is to use translators between formats. For example, there are converters for RTF to LaTeX, RTF to HTML and LaTeX to SGML. Within a particular platform (PC or Mac) individual wordprocessors will read in many different file formats and there are usually a host of tools to do other translations. If one has a complete set of converters (figure 11) then anyone can work in their preferred format in the knowledge that, if they want to pass it on to another member of the team, they can simply put it through the relevant converter. Unfortunately, as each representation has its own model of text, information is lost during the translation process. Depending on the scenario of use this can be mildly annoying or disastrous.

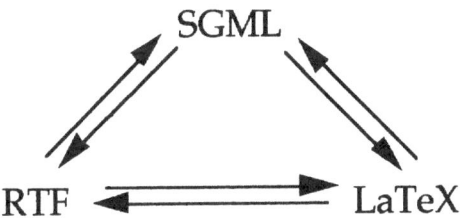

Fig. 11. Individual translators

Imagine first that Alison, Brian and Clarise are working on a book together. Alison works in formal methods and is using LaTeX, Brian is in a psychology department and is using MS Word (RTF), and Clarise is working on an Esprit project which is committed to using international standard products and so is using SGML.

In the first scenario each is responsible for particular chapters. When they want comments on a chapter they put it through the relevant converters and send copies to each of their colleagues. As information is lost their colleagues see a slightly different version than the chapter's author. For example, when Brian sends Alison a copy of his chapter, the voice annotations are lost from the Word document, and when Alison sends Brian a copy of hers some of the cross referencing and optional page breaks disappear. The lack of a common appearance and loss of certain features is annoying, but is better than exchanging ASCII.

In our second scenario, the authorship of chapters is shared. One chapter is being worked on by Brian and Clarise. After Brian has worked on a chapter for a while he passes it on to Clarise. Later Clarise will pass the amended version back to Alison. To avoid dealing with merging issues we assume that they make sure that only one person is working on a chapter at a time! When the RTF document is converted to SGML, much of the presentation formatting information is lost. If the translator is quite clever it will parse the style names intelligently in order to produce good markup, but much is bound to be lost. When the reverse translation is done, more will be lost, any mark-up that Clarise added will be lost. Even if Clarise does no changes and one simply performs a translation forward and back, the resulting document will have lost a lot of information. With translations back and forth to LaTeX as well, the situation gets worse. One is effectively reduced to the intersection of the features in all the supported formats. Not much better than ASCII.

Another problem with this approach is that one needs translators for each pair of formats. For n formats we need $n(n - 1)$ translators! If these are produced by different vendors, using different translation conventions, then it is even more likely that information will be lost when several are used one after another

6.3   A common format

One alternative is to look for some common format that can be used for interchange. Indeed that is one of the purposes of SGML DTDs and other standards such as ODA [9]. We then need only translators to and from each format to the common format. This format can either be a minimal format (like ASCII again!) which only supports common features, or a super, all-embracing format that has every feature that is in any of the others.

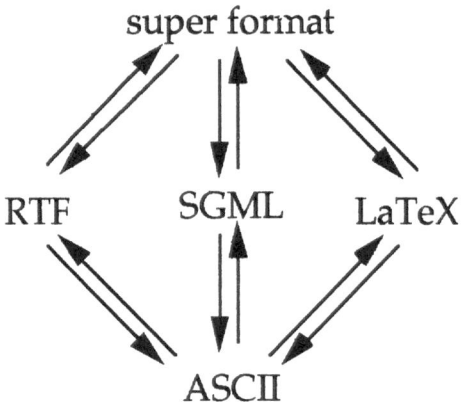

Fig. 12. A common format

Using a super format means that only $2n$ translators are needed, and, so long as the two translators to and from each format are written properly (i.e., inverses), they are more likely to be more consistent. Also, when you translate to the super-format you no longer lose any information – great. Unfortunately, when you take documents back into a representation that can be used, oops, it's all lost again. Imagine you perform the translation:

$$\text{RTF} \rightarrow \text{super format} \rightarrow \text{LaTeX}$$

There is no reason to expect the result to be better than a direct RTF to LaTeX conversion. By the time you translate back and forth a few times you are back to the minimal information again.

6.4 Maintaining an invariant

What is required is a way of working such that information which has been added in one format, but which cannot be translated is recovered when the reverse translation is performed. That is, one effectively keeps a model of the document in each of the formats. When a document is changed in one format, then only the part that changes is updated in the other formats. Similar issues have been heavily studied in the context of continuously maintained mappings between the internal state of an interactive system and its display [6]. That is a functional relationship, but the principal is similar. At any time we expect that all the copies of the document in the different formats satisfy an invariant. This can most easily be expressed in terms of a common format, for example, that the ASCII version of all of them is the same. Then, when one is updated, one looks for an equivalent update to each of the others which maintains the invariant (see figure 13).

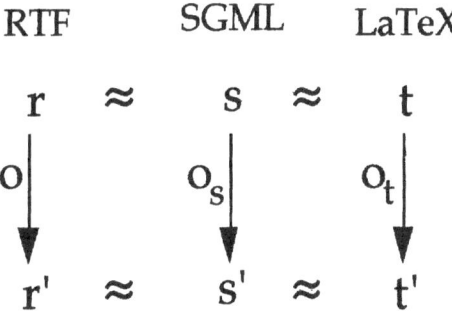

Fig. 13. Parallel translations

Formally we can phrase this as follows. Given documents r, s and t such that $inv(r, s, t)$ and an operation o on r find operations o_s and o_t, such that $inv(o(r), o_s(s), o_t(t))$. The generation of the equivalent updates o_s and o_t will in general not be a simple function of o, but also include information stored about the documents and their relationship.

6.5 Using dynamic pointers

This is just the sort of thing dynamic pointer projections were designed for! We'll concentrate on just two of the documents r and s. We'll assume we have a translator between the document formats, which can work on fragments (with known context) – that is an incremental translator. This translator can be developed in an ad hoc fashion or be based on translation to and from a common format. In addition, we demand that these translators are projections, they supply us with a mapping between the pointers in each document format. For example, the RTF to SGML converter would have signature:

$$trans \quad : Params \rightarrow (RTF \rightarrow SGML)$$
$$fwd_{trans}: Pt_{RTF} \rightarrow Pt_{SGML}$$
$$back_{trans}: Pt_{SGML} \rightarrow Pt_{RTF}$$

We will use these (in a manner described below) to maintain continuously a projection between r and s. This projection is essentially the invariant (saying they have the same content) together with a pointer mapping saying which parts of the documents are equivalent.

$$inv \quad : Params \rightarrow (RTF \leftrightarrow SGML)$$
$$fwd_{inv}: Pt_{RTF} \rightarrow Pt_{SGML}$$
$$back_{inv}: Pt_{SGML} \rightarrow Pt_{RTF}$$

Now, given any operation o on r we can obtain its locality information loc_o. First of all, we know that any part of s which does not intersect $fwd_{inv}(loc_o)$ is unchanged by the operation. To build the rest of s', we simply use the translator on the portion of r within loc_o. The translated bit is 'glued' into place and the new SGML document is complete. Any mark-up on the unaltered bits is preserved. The changed bits may need some additional repair by the user as they will simply have the default mark-up generated by the translator, but the effort is minimal compared to the other alternatives.

One final thread to tie up is the pointer part of the new invariant, fwd'_{inv} and $back'_{inv}$. This is repaired as follows. It is easy to build a pull function for o_s (outside of $fwd_{inv}(loc_o)$) based on the difference in and location of the updated part. The pointers outside loc_o are then related by:

$$fwd'_{inv} = pull_{o_s} \circ fwd_{inv} \circ pull_o^{-1}$$
$$back'_{inv} = pull_o \circ back_{inv} \circ pull_{o_s}^{-1}$$

This is basically shifting around the existing pointer mapping. Finally, the fwd and $back$ maps for loc_o itself are repaired by 'gluing' in the pointer map generated by fwd_{trans} and $back_{trans}$ restricted to loc_o.

6.6 Generating pull functions

The above method relies on having a pull function for update operations and 'fwd' and 'back' mappings for translations. The latter requires some rewriting of the translators, but is not too difficult. The former is more of a problem as this information would ideally be maintained by the relevant editors. However, even if Microsoft do not bring out a dynamic pointer compatible version of Word in the near future, all is not lost! The pull function can be generated by a modified file difference utility. Obviously this would need to be tuned for any particular file format, but would be useful for other purposes (such as version control) anyway.

7 Conclusions

We have seen that three different problems can all be seen as manifestations of a single phenomenon, translating operations between contexts. In each case we have needed operations which were originally formulated in one context to be used in another. The first two situations, undo and merge, were particularly similar. However, we found that there were subtle but important differences between all the translation operations. We also found that it is only necessary to define atomic translations, that is translations of single operations. Translations for sequences of operations can be generated from these atomic translations by chasing commuting diagrams.

Dynamic pointers can also be regarded as a form of translation between contexts, in this case translating locations rather than operations. However, the part of an operation which requires changing between contexts is often locational and hence dynamic pointers can be used to describe or even implement translation policies. This further eases the problem of defining suitable translations.

An important new application of dynamic pointer techniques has been described, where different representations of a document can be maintained in parallel. This offers a better hope for inter-application compatibility than the definition of common formats as it allows each to develop their own strengths, rather than being ossified in a fixed standard.

References

1. Gregory D. Abowd and Alan J. Dix. Giving undo attention. *Interacting with Computers*, 4(3):317–342, 1992.
2. A. J. Dix. Dynamic pointers and threads. *Collaborative Computing (accepted for publication)*, 1994.
3. A.J. Dix. *Formal Methods for Interactive Systems*. Academic Press, 1991.
4. Alan J. Dix and Victoria C. Miles. Version control for asynchronous group work. Technical Report YCS 181, Computer Science Dept., University of York, U.K., 1992. (Poster presentation HCI'92: People and Computers VII).
5. C.A. Ellis and S.J. Gibbs. Concurrency control in groupware systems. *SIGMOD Record*, 18(2):399–407, June 1989. 1989 ACM SIGMOD International Conference on Management of Data.
6. M. D. Harrison and A. J. Dix. Modelling the relationship between state and display in interactive systems. In P.Gornay and M.J.Tauber, editors, *Visualisation in Human–Computer Interaction*, volume LNCS 439, pages 241–249. Springer-Verlag, 1990.
7. J. J. Kistler and M. Satyanarayanan. Disconnected operation in the coda file system. *ACM Transactions on Computer Systems*, 10(1):3–25, February 1992.
8. Atul Prakash and Michael J. Knister. Undoing actions in collaborative work. In *CSCWU92 – Proceedings of the Conference on Computer-Supported Cooperative Work*, pages 273–280. ACM Press, 1992.
9. A. Schill. *Cooperative Office Systems*. Prentice Hall, 1995.
10. P. Wright, A. Monk, and M. Harrison. State, display an undo: a study of consistency in display base interaction. Technical report, University of York, 1992.

Appendix 1 – Differences between transations

In section 3.3, we discussed several putative identites which look as though they might hold between undo and merge translations. We now give the counter examples showing that the translations cannot easily be obtained from one another by use of simple identities. The identities we proposed based on comparing the two commuting diagrams were were:

(i) $\overset{\longleftarrow a}{\underset{\longrightarrow a}{(\,b\,)}}{}^{a} = b$

(ii) $\overset{\longleftarrow a}{\underset{\longrightarrow a}{(\,b\,)}} = b$

(iii) $\overset{\longrightarrow}{a}{}^{(\underset{\rightarrow a}{b})} = a_{\overset{}{\leftarrow b}}$

(iv) $a_{\overset{\leftarrow a}{\leftarrow(\,b\,)}} = \overset{\rightarrow b}{a}$

Figures 6 and 7, showed the problematic insert–insert and delete–insert diagrams. We use these to build the counter-examples. As sort hand, we will write 'dn' for $delete(n)$ and 'dn+1' for $delete(n + 1)$. Similarly, we will use 'in', 'in-1' an 'in+1' for insertions. The character to insert is obvious from context and is irrelevant in the examples.

Insert–insert cases

We need to look at two instances of undo translations (note that these are laid out to resemble the diagram order):

(u1) $a = in$ $b = in$

      $\overset{\leftarrow a}{b} = in$ $\overset{\rightarrow b}{a} = in+1$

(u2) $a = in+1$ $b = in$

      $\overset{\leftarrow a}{b} = in$ $\overset{\rightarrow b}{a} = in$

There is only one merge rule (which is precisely the problem!). Recall that there were two possible rules for merging two inserts at the same location. The alternative rule is shown in brackets. We will track it also as we follow through the examples, an we will see that whichever merge rule is adopted counter-examples can be found.

(m1) $a = in$ $\underset{\rightarrow a}{b} = in$ [in+1]

      $b = in$ $\underset{\leftarrow b}{a} = in+1$ [in]

In section 3.3, we said that (i) and (iii) are true for the insert–insert scenario. This can easily be verified. So, we will look at (ii) and (iv). First for the case with $a = $ 'in' and $b = $ 'in+1':

(ii) $\overset{\longleftarrow in}{\underset{\longrightarrow in}{(in+1\,)}} = \underset{\rightarrow in}{in}$

                $= in - NO$ [in+1 – OK]

(iv) RHS: $\overset{\rightarrow in+1}{in} = in$

     LHS: $in_{\overset{\leftarrow in}{\leftarrow(in+1\,)}} = \underset{\leftarrow in}{in}$

                $= in+1 - NO\ [in - OK]$

These counter-examples seem to favour the alternative merge rules, but if we look at the case with both a and b equal to 'in' we see that this rule doesn't work either.

(ii) $\overset{\longleftarrow in}{\underset{\longrightarrow in}{(in\,)}} = \underset{\rightarrow in}{in}$

                $= in - OK$ [in+1 – NO]

(iv) RHS: $\overset{\rightarrow in}{in} = in+1$

     LHS: $in_{\overset{\leftarrow in}{\leftarrow(in\,)}} = \underset{\leftarrow in}{in}$

                $= in+1 - OK\ [in - NO]$

So, whichever merge rule is chosen, neither identity holds in general.

Delete–insert cases

This time we need consider only one instance of the undo rule. However, like the case of the merge rule above, it is not clear which of two options should be chosen. This is because it is unclear whether an insertion following a delete belongs just before or after the deleted characters. We will again trace through both alternatives.

(u3) a = dn $\qquad\qquad\qquad b$ = in-1

$\overset{\leftarrow a}{b}$ = in [in+1] $\qquad\qquad \overset{\rightarrow b}{a}$ = dn [dn+1]

In counter-symmetry to the insert–insert scenario, we now hae two merge cases. Happily, there are no different alternatives for these!

(m2) a = dn $\qquad\qquad \underset{\rightarrow a}{b}$ = in-1

$\quad b$ = in $\qquad\qquad \underset{\leftarrow b}{a}$ = dn

(m3) a = dn $\qquad\qquad \underset{\rightarrow a}{b}$ = in-1

$\quad b$ = in-1 $\qquad\qquad \underset{\leftarrow b}{a}$ = dn+1

This time identities (ii) and (iv) are OK, but (i) and (iii) will fail. Again, we will consider two cases, first a = 'dn' and b = 'in-1':

(i) $\qquad \overset{\leftarrow dn}{(\underset{\rightarrow dn}{\text{in-1}})} = \overset{\leftarrow dn}{\text{in-1}}$

$\qquad\qquad\qquad$ = in – NO [in-1 – OK]

(iii) RHS $\underset{\leftarrow \text{in-1}}{\text{dn}}$ = dn+1

$\qquad$ LHS $\overset{\rightarrow\text{(in-1}}{\text{dn}}\,\,\overset{}{\rightarrow\text{dn)}}$ = $\overset{\rightarrow\text{in-1}}{\text{dn}}$

$\qquad\qquad\qquad$ = dn – NO [dn+1 – OK]

Again, this case seems to favour the alternative for undo. But, now consider the case where a = 'dn' and b = 'in':

(i) $\qquad \overset{\leftarrow dn}{(\underset{\rightarrow dn}{\text{in}})} = \overset{\leftarrow dn}{\text{in-1}}$

$\qquad\qquad\qquad$ = in – OK [in-1 – NO]

(iii) RHS $\underset{\leftarrow \text{in}}{\text{dn}}$ = dn

$\qquad$ LHS $\overset{\rightarrow\text{(in}}{\text{dn}}\,\,\overset{}{\rightarrow\text{dn)}}$ = $\overset{\rightarrow\text{in-1}}{\text{dn}}$

$\qquad\qquad\qquad$ = dn OK [dn+1 – NO]

So, whichever alternative we choose for the undo rule, both (i) an (iii) are invalid.

Appendix 2 – Soundness of compositon laws

In section 4, we looked at sequence definitions of the various forward and backward translation operators. These allowed us to extend the atomic translation definitions to work on sequences of operations. These definitions are intended to work for any atomic translations satisfying the basic translation laws:

$ab = \overset{\leftarrow a}{b}\,\overset{\rightarrow b}{a} \qquad\qquad a\underset{\rightarrow a}{b} = b\underset{\leftarrow b}{a}$

We noted that it is important that the composition rules are sound, in the sense that all rewrites of an expression using the rules get to the same result, a confluence property. This will ensure that the sequence rules are conservative, that is they do not give rise to additional equations for the atomic translations. We will show that this is true for the undo laws. The proof for merge is similar.

Recall that the laws for undo are:

(i) $\overrightarrow{a}^{(bc)} = (\overrightarrow{a}^{b})^{\overrightarrow{}c}$ (iii) $\overrightarrow{ab}^{\rightarrow c} = \overrightarrow{a}^{(\overleftarrow{c}^{b})}\overrightarrow{b}^{\rightarrow c}$

(ii) $\overleftarrow{bc}^{\leftarrow a} = \overleftarrow{b}^{\leftarrow a}\overleftarrow{c}^{(\overrightarrow{a}^{b})}$ (iv) $\overleftarrow{c}^{(ab)} = (\overleftarrow{c}^{\overleftarrow{}a}^{b})$

The only way rewrites can fail to be confluent is when there are two ways of reducing the outermost operator. In the case of the above laws, this can only happen in the cases: $\overrightarrow{ab}^{(cd)}$ and $\overleftarrow{cd}^{\leftarrow ab}$

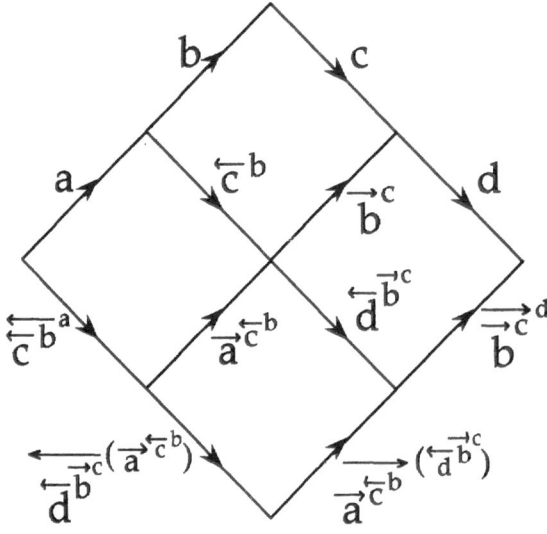

Fig. 14. Checking correctness of compositional definitions

Concentrating on the first, this can be reduced in two ways. Either by (i) or by (iii). We show that both lead to the same cannonical form.

$\overrightarrow{ab}^{(cd)} = (i)\ \overrightarrow{ab}^{\overrightarrow{}c}{}^{\overrightarrow{}d} = (iii)\ \left(\overrightarrow{a}^{(\overleftarrow{c}^{b})}\overrightarrow{b}^{\rightarrow c}\right)^{\overrightarrow{}d}$

$= (iii)\ \overrightarrow{a}^{(\overleftarrow{c}^{b})}\overrightarrow{d}^{\overleftarrow{}(\overrightarrow{b}^{c})}\overrightarrow{b}^{\overrightarrow{}d}{}^{\overrightarrow{}c}$

$= (iii)\ \overrightarrow{a}^{(\overleftarrow{cd}^{b})}\overrightarrow{b}^{\rightarrow cd} = (ii)\ \overrightarrow{a}^{(\overleftarrow{c}^{b}\overleftarrow{d}^{(\overrightarrow{b}^{c})})}\overrightarrow{b}^{\rightarrow cd}$

$= (iii)\ \overrightarrow{a}^{(\overleftarrow{c}^{b})}\overrightarrow{d}^{\overleftarrow{}b}{}^{\overrightarrow{}c}\overrightarrow{b}^{\overrightarrow{}d}{}^{\overrightarrow{}c}$

The second case is similar. It can be reduced by (ii) or (iv), but again both reduce to the same cannonical form.

$$\overleftarrow{cd}^{(ab)} = (ii)\ \overleftarrow{c}^{ab}\ \overleftarrow{d}^{(\overrightarrow{ab}\,)^{\overrightarrow{c}}} = (iii)\ \overleftarrow{c}^{ab}\ \overleftarrow{d}^{(\overrightarrow{a}^{(\overleftarrow{c}^{\overleftarrow{b}}\,)}\,\overrightarrow{b}^{\overrightarrow{c}}\,)}$$

$$= (iv)\ \overleftarrow{c}^{\overleftarrow{b}^{\overleftarrow{a}}}\ \overleftarrow{d}^{(\overrightarrow{b}^{\overrightarrow{c}}\,)^{\overleftarrow{a}^{(\overrightarrow{c}^{\overleftarrow{b}}\,)}}}$$

$$= (iv)\ \overleftarrow{cd}^{\overleftarrow{b}^{\overleftarrow{a}}} \qquad = (ii)\ \left(\overleftarrow{c}^{\overleftarrow{b}}\ \overleftarrow{d}^{(\overrightarrow{b}^{\overrightarrow{c}}\,)}\right)^{\overleftarrow{a}}$$

$$= (ii)\ \overleftarrow{c}^{\overleftarrow{b}^{\overleftarrow{a}}}\ \overleftarrow{d}^{(\overrightarrow{b}^{\overrightarrow{c}}\,)^{\overrightarrow{a}^{(\overleftarrow{c}^{\overleftarrow{b}}\,)}}}$$

The intermediate results of these two proofs are shown on the commuting diagram in figure 14. The proof for the merge case is similar, but slightly simpler as the two merge translations are duals of one another and hence only one case need be considered.

This article was processed using the LaTeX macro package with LLNCS style

Combining Formal Techniques and Prototyping in User Interface Construction and Verification

Peter Bumbulis[1], P.S.C. Alencar[2], D.D. Cowan[1], C.J.P. Lucena[3]

[1] Computer Science Department, University of Waterloo, Waterloo, Ontario, Canada
[2] Departamento de Ciência da Computação, Universidade de Brasília, Brasília, Brazil
[3] Departamento de Informática, Pontifícia Universidade Católica do Rio de Janeiro, Rio de Janeiro, Brazil

Abstract. In this paper we investigate a component-based approach to combining formal techniques and prototyping for user interface construction in which a single specification is used for constructing both implementations (prototypes) for experimentation and models for formal reasoning. Using a component-based approach not only allows us to construct realistic prototypes, but also allows us to generate a variety of formal models. Rapid prototyping allows the designs to be tested with end users and modified based on their comments and performance, while formal modeling permits the designer to verify mechanically specific requirements imposed on the user interface such as those found in safety- or security-critical applications.

1 Introduction

A wide variety of toolkits[4] have been developed to allow user interface designers to prototype graphical user interfaces (GUIs) rapidly. Unfortunately it is difficult to verify that GUIs built with such toolkits behave as intended (in the sense that they possess certain formally expressed properties); this is a serious concern for safety- and security-critical applications. In this paper we propose a new approach to addressing this concern.

One technique often used for gaining confidence in GUI implementations is testing [14, 46]. However testing on its own is usually not adequate for safety- and security-critical applications. There is always the possibility that an untested case will produce an error. In this paper we present a complementary approach to detecting faults[5] in GUIs. Essentially our idea is to derive formal models from GUI implementations automatically and then verify mechanically that these models possesses the required properties. Mechanization is important for two reasons: not only does it increase confidence in the verifications (and their significance) [9, 16], but it also has the potential for reducing the amortized cost

---

[4] We use the term toolkit to refer not only to interface libraries such as Motif [39] but to tools such as Visual Basic [34] and Tk/Tcl [41] as well.

[5] Our terminology follows that of Young and Taylor: "Software may contain *faults*, which may cause *errors* in executions of that software, possibly manifested in *failures* in the system of which the software is part." [55].

of the verification effort. GUIs are not static, they evolve over time. Indeed, it is likely that a significant fraction of the total GUI development effort will be expended after the initial implementation. If models are automatically generated from implementations then producing new models for implementations as they evolve will require little effort. If reasoning is also mechanized, then there is a chance that subsequent verifications will be able to reuse significant portions of previous ones.

Unfortunately the structure of most GUI implementations makes it difficult to derive models suitable for mechanical verification automatically. Our approach to this problem is to introduce the necessary structure into GUI implementations as follows:

1. Fashion a component-oriented [37, 47] toolkit based on the GUI toolkit(s) that we are interested in using.[6] This consists of building a set of primitives and devising an interconnection language, IL. We also construct formal model(s) for each of the primitives providing more abstract descriptions of their behavior.
2. Describe user interfaces using IL and from these descriptions derive both implementations and corresponding formal models, as illustrated in Fig. 1.

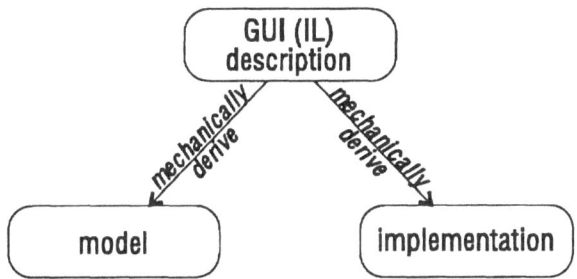

Fig. 1. IL-based user interface development.

We restrict our attention to callback-based toolkits as most commercially available toolkits (including the Windows SDK [31], the Macintosh Toolbox [48] and the Motif [39] UI toolkit) are callback-based. Implementing component-oriented presentation primitives given a callback-based toolkit requires little or no work; the existing toolkit primitives can be used essentially unchanged.[7] Using these primitives in a component-oriented fashion simply involves following the convention that callbacks are restricted to the methods (operations) supplied by components. Rather than being coded in callbacks, application functionality is now encapsulated in *application interface* components. The process of generating

---

[6] For economic reasons, most GUIs are constructed using some toolkit [35].

[7] A wrapper that provides a new interface to the existing functionality likely will be required.

implementations from IL descriptions simply consists of calling routines to build components and add callbacks.

Note that we will need models for the application interface primitives as well. It is generally accepted that user interfaces are best described as *reactive systems* [20]; what is of interest is how they interact with their environment. Many notations have been devised for modeling reactive systems; a number have been based on Dijkstra's guarded command language [12]. Examples of such notations include Chandy and Misra's Unity [7], Manna and Pnueli's diagram language [28] and Holzmann's PROMELA [22]. We introduce a similar notation for modeling user interfaces. Unlike the previously mentioned notations, ours does not provide any means for expressing concurrency (although it could easily be extended for this purpose); the user interfaces that we are concerned with have strictly sequential descriptions. The problem is not in describing concurrency but reasoning about it: omitting this feature simplifies verification.

If we are to have confidence in our reasoning about such models we will need tool support. One possibility would be to use a model checker such as SMV [30] or a reachability analysis tool such as SPIN [22]. Indeed, our modeling formalism is similar to the sequential subset of the SPIN modeling language PROMELA. Unfortunately, a drawback of these tools is that, because of the possibility of state explosion, constructing useful models is a challenging task (cf. [54].) As a result, we investigate the possibility of using mechanical theorem proving for this purpose. We model implementations and express properties as terms and formulas in *higher-order logic* [17] as mechanized by the HOL system [18]. Higher-order logic is essentially predicate calculus enriched with the typed λ-calculus: variables can range over functions and the arguments and results of functions can themselves be functions.[8] One advantage of using higher-order logic is that callbacks can easily be modeled using higher-order functions. As well, the expressiveness of higher-order logic allows us to embed logics to simplify reasoning about specific types of properties, thus avoiding the need to develop specialized verification tools. This expressiveness does not come without a price: reasoning can never be fully automated. Fortunately, many proof assistants (including HOL) provide powerful meta-languages that allow the mechanization of significant portions of proofs. Further, there still is the possibility of reusing existing proofs as implementations evolve.

2 IL

In the remainder of this paper we will use the name IL to denote one specific formalism that we have devised for describing GUIs. IL is a component-oriented formalism: GUIs are described as a hierarchy of interconnected component instances. IL components are either *composite* or *primitive*. Composite components consist of an interconnected collection of simpler components. Primitive components come in three flavors: presentation (menus, buttons, sliders, and the like),

---

[8] Appendix B contains a brief introduction to the HOL logic.

application interface (file and database accessors, for example), and connectors. While component-oriented formalisms have long been popular for addressing reusability and ease of use concerns, their attraction for us is the prospect of being able to construct models easily for corresponding implementations. If we can model interconnection then we can construct models for composite components given models for each of their constituent components and a description of their interconnection. If we have models for each of the primitive components, then we can automatically generate a model for any implementation.

We give a taste of IL by example. Figure 2 is a screen snapshot of a simple

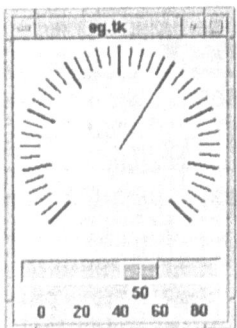

Fig. 2. A simple user interface.

user interface that has been automatically generated from an IL description.[9] The user interface consists of a dial and a slider that have been connected so that they track each other; whenever one moves so does the other.

The IL description of this user interface is shown in Figure 3. An IL de-

```
Frame primitive
Dial changed> set< primitive
Slider changed> set< primitive

Main {
    f:Frame f.d:Dial f.s:Slider

    f.d.changed --> f.s.set
    f.s.changed --> f.d.set
}
```

Fig. 3. An IL description of the user interface in Fig. 2.

scription consists of the definition of a number of components. By convention,

---

[9] (Most of) the code implementing Figure 2 can be found in Appendix A.

the user interface described consists of a single instance of a component named Main. The first three lines of Fig. 3 describe the interfaces of components defined elsewhere:[10] Dials and Sliders have changed and set ports that provide (>) and require (<) values, respectively. The remaining lines define a (composite) component named Main. Main consists of a Dial, a Slider and a Frame. The changed port of the dial is connected to the set port of the slider, and vice versa. Structured names are used to indicate visual containment: the dial (f.d) and the slider (f.s) are visually contained in the frame (f). Frames are used to group presentation components visually. To understand the behavior of the user interface described in Fig. 3 we need to understand the behavior of Dials and Sliders (and Frames.) The value of a Dial or Slider instance is set (at runtime) either by direct manipulation (by the user) or as the result of a value appearing at the set port. If this changes its value, the new value is sent out the changed port. Frame instances do not have any associated behavior. This example makes use of only some of IL's features; however, the features presented will be sufficient to illustrate our approach to modeling GUI implementations.

IL is a very restrictive formalism; a legitimate concern is whether such a formalism can be used to describe GUIs in practice. To address this concern we have patterned IL on similar formalisms implicitly provided by a growing number of commercially available GUI construction tools such as PARTS Workbench [11], Visual Age [23] and Visual AppBuilder [45]. For example, Fig. 4 shows

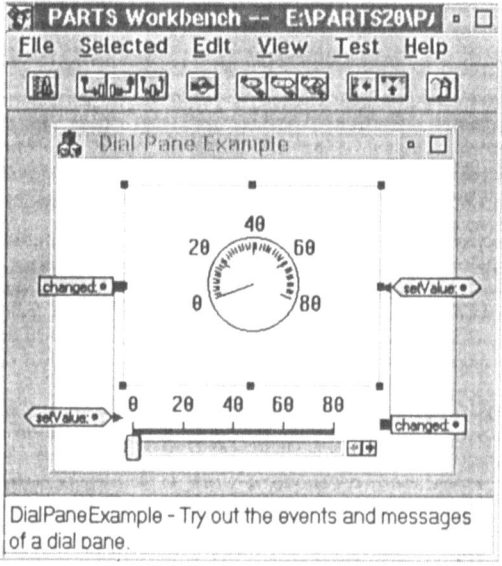

Fig. 4. PARTS Workbench implementation.

---

[10] These declarations are analogous to **extern** declarations in C [24].

one step in the construction of a user interface similar to that presented in Fig. 2 using PARTS Workbench. This user interface was constructed by simply dragging and dropping a window, slider and dial from a palette of components and then making the necessary connections via direct manipulation.

The formalism that we use, while similar, is not identical to any of the existing formalisms. IL differs from the existing formalisms primarily in the choice of relationships explicitly represented with connections and containment; these differences primarily were motivated by the desire to simplify modeling and reasoning. Patterning IL on these commercially available formalisms has a number of advantages including: 1) there is empirical evidence that GUI designers find such formalisms easy to understand and use, and 2) manuals for (tools that use) these formalisms provide a wealth of documentation on how to construct practical GUIs using them.

What makes such component-oriented approaches possible is the increasing standardization of WIMP[11]-based GUIs. On most platforms, the need to adhere to look and feel guidelines[12] not only greatly constrains the appearance and behavior of presentation components but also encourages limiting the choice of presentation primitives to a small (pre-defined) set. As a result, it is not too surprising that the previously mentioned tools not only provide similar sets of presentation primitives but also provide similar options for their customization and interconnection. While IL differs from the formalisms used by the previously mentioned tools, it is similar enough so that we can (in theory) provide similar primitives. It should be noted that these GUI construction tools (and IL) can be used for applications with more specialized presentation requirements as well: all provide mechanisms for the introduction of new primitives.

Note that the user interface shown in Fig. 2 is not very useful; it consists of only presentation components. To be of some use a GUI must contain application interface components as well. However, as the introduction of such components does not affect our approach to modeling behavior nor our techniques for reasoning about it, we will continue to use such simple examples. The focus of our research is on developing one possible technique for formally modeling and reasoning about user interfaces, not on detailing how to construct useful implementations using formalisms such as IL. This topic already has been addressed in detail in manuals such as [11], [38], and [23].

3   IL-Based Development

Figure 5 illustrates one possible IL-based development process. As indicated by the diagram, the approach presented here has more to offer than just the possibility of user interface verification. For example, the models generated from

---

[11] Window, icon, menu, and pointer.

[12] For example, comprehensive guidelines exist for Windows- [32, 33], Macintosh- [2, 3], and Motif-based [40] user interfaces. A more extensive list of user interface guidelines can be found in Vanderdonckt's "Tools for Working with Guidelines" bibliography [53].

180

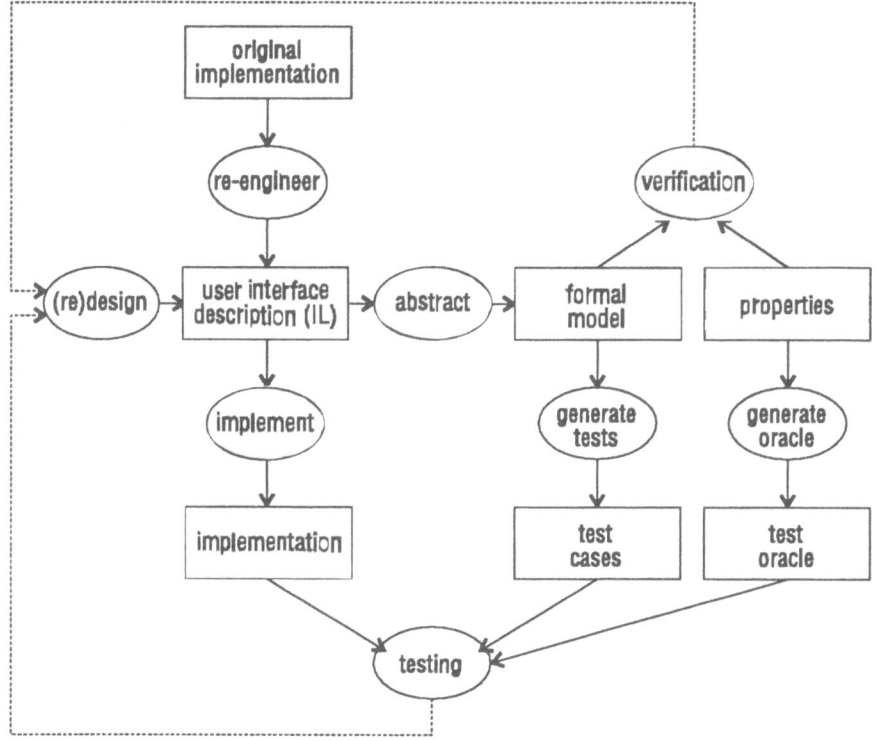

Fig. 5. An IL-based development process.

IL descriptions could be used to aid in the testing process either by serving as a basis for test case generation (say by using ideas of Korel [26]) or by providing a means for measuring test coverage. However, in this paper we restrict our attention as indicated by the shading, with the more heavily shaded areas receiving greater emphasis.

3.1 Roles in IL-Based Development

There are three different roles associated with the development of IL-based user interfaces: the *user interface designer*, or just *designer*, the *developer*, and the *verifier*[13]. The tasks of the designer and developer can be characterized as using and constructing primitive components, respectively. The designer typically requires greater problem domain understanding but less programming skill than the developer. The designer constructs IL descriptions of user interfaces using primitive components supplied by the developer. User interface construction simply consists of selecting and connecting components.[14] If a required component

---

[13] There may be many people in each role or one person may perform several roles.

[14] Construction of an interface builder for IL descriptions (such as provided by PARTS Workbench) should be straightforward.

is not available the designer provides the developer with its specification; the developer then uses traditional software development techniques to construct the actual implementation. Designing the primitive components with reuse in mind reduces the amortized cost of development.

The verifier works in concert with the designer and the developer and is responsible for ensuring that prototypes meet formally expressed requirements. The verifier generates formal models from the IL descriptions and uses these as the basis for verification. To have confidence in the results obtained, the verifier must ensure that models are accurate, and that reasoning is sound. The task of ensuring that models accurately reflect implementations can be reduced to ensuring that the primitive components are accurately modeled. If the software development technique used to construct the primitives does not provide the necessary assurance, testing can be used [50, 27]. To ensure that reasoning is sound, mechanical verification is used.

4 Constructing Models

We tackle the problem of modeling GUIs in HOL in two parts: we first mechanize (the semantics of) a guarded command language in HOL and then use this mechanization in expressing the semantics of components. We discuss both in turn.

4.1 Guarded Command Language

We model behavior using a notation based on Nelson's extension [36][15] of Dijkstra's guarded command language [12]. Our notation is best viewed as a simple, non-deterministic, programming language; statements in the language are also referred to as commands. Each statement in the language has an associated state predicate called a *guard*; a statement can only be activated in a state if its guard is true in that state. If its guard is false then activation fails without changing the state of the computation. We denote the guard of a statement c as grd c. Only two primitive statements are provided:

> skip   no-op
> assign E when activated in state s, results
>   in a state $E\,s$

These primitives never fail, i.e., their guards are defined to be true in all states. The assign statement simultaneously updates all state variables; single variable updates are implemented by having E fix all variables but the one of interest. More complex statements can be built using a number of operators. Operational definitions of the fundamental operators are as follows:

---

[15] Nelson's extension allows for partial commands and drops the law of excluded miracle.

$$c_1 \,[\!]\, c_2 \quad \text{activate either } c_1 \text{ or } c_2$$
$$c_1 \,\mathring{,}\, c_2 \quad \text{activate } c_1, \text{ then activate } c_2$$
$$P \longrightarrow c \quad \text{activate } c \text{ if in a state where } P \text{ is}$$
$$\text{true (fail otherwise)}$$
$$\text{do\_od } c \quad \text{activate } c \text{ until it fails}$$

More conventional programming language constructs can be built from these. For example, "if P then c_1 else c_2" can be implemented as

$$(P \longrightarrow c_1) \,[\!]\, (\neg P \longrightarrow c_2) \ .$$

We model commands as predicates on behaviors and model *behaviors* as state sequences.[16] Behaviors can be finite or infinite; finite behaviors must have at least one element. We denote finite behaviors as $\langle s_1, \ldots, s_n \rangle$ and infinite behaviors as $\langle s_1, \ldots \rangle$. If b is a behavior, then $\text{length}\, b \in \mathbb{N} \cup \{\omega\}$ denotes the number of states in the behavior, with $\text{st}\, b\, i$ denoting the ith state. We also use $\text{first}\, b$ to denote the first state of the behavior and, if b is finite, $\text{last}\, b$ to denote the last state. We define the composition of two behaviors $b_1 \bullet b_2$ to be b_1 if b_1 is infinite, and the sequence obtained by appending all but the first element of b_2 to b_1 if b_1 is finite and $\text{first}\, b_2 = \text{last}\, b_1$. If b_1 is finite and $\text{first}\, b_2 \neq \text{last}\, b_1$ then $b_1 \bullet b_2$ is undefined. At times it will be convenient to ignore the intermediate states of a behavior; we introduce the notation $\text{atom}\, b$ for this purpose. We define $\text{atom}\, b$ to be $\langle \text{first}\, b, \text{last}\, b \rangle$ if b is finite and $\langle \{\text{first}\, b, \}^\omega \rangle$ if b is infinite.

We define the semantics of the primitives and fundamental operators in terms of state sequences using an approach inspired by that of Tredoux [52]:[17]

$$\text{skip}\, b \stackrel{\text{def}}{=} \exists s.\, b = \langle s \rangle$$

$$(\text{assign}\, E)\, b \stackrel{\text{def}}{=} \exists s\, b.\, b = \langle s, E\, s \rangle$$

$$(c_1 \,[\!]\, c_2)\, b \stackrel{\text{def}}{=} c_1\, b \vee c_2\, b$$

$$(c_1 \,\mathring{,}\, c_2)\, b \stackrel{\text{def}}{=} \quad c_1\, b \wedge (\text{length}\, b = \omega)$$
$$\vee\ \exists b_1\, b_2.\, c_1\, b_1 \wedge c_2\, b_2 \wedge (b = b_1 \bullet b_2)$$

$$(P \longrightarrow c)\, b \stackrel{\text{def}}{=} P\, (\text{first}\, b) \wedge c\, b$$

$$\text{do\_od}\, c \stackrel{\text{def}}{=} \quad (\exists n.\, \text{iter}\, c\, n \,\mathring{,}\, (\neg\, (\text{grd}\, c) \longrightarrow \text{skip}))$$
$$[\!]\ (\text{infrep}\, c)$$

For example, for any behavior b, $\text{skip}\, b$ holds iff b is of the form $\langle s \rangle$, for some state s. The definition of do_od is considerably more involved than the rest and makes use of a number of constants not yet defined: $\text{iter}\, c\, n$ represents c composed with itself n times, $c \,\mathring{,}\, \ldots \,\mathring{,}\, c$, and $\text{infrep}\, c$ represents an infinite composition of cs, $c \,\mathring{,}\, c \,\mathring{,}\, \ldots$. Also, '$\exists$' and '$\neg$' are just the logical operators '$\exists$' and '$\neg$' "lifted"

---

[16] This is a simplification; we actually model behavior as an alternating sequence of states and actions.

[17] Infix notation is used for binary predicates such as '$[\!]$' to improve readability.

to work on predicates: for all b, $(\exists i.\, R\, i)\, b = (\exists i.\, R\, i\, b)$ and $(\neg P)\, b = \neg(P\, b)$. It can be verified that our sequence-based semantics agrees with the usual semantics for guarded command languages (by deriving Dijkstra's calculus of predicate transformers, for example.)

4.2   Modeling GUIs

Our idea is to model the behavior of a GUI with a statement essentially of the form $\mathsf{do\_od}(c_1 \,[]\, \ldots \,[]\, c_n)$ where each c_i characterizes the possible behavior resulting from the use of a particular component. For example, we model the behavior of the user interface of Fig. 2 with a statement of the form $\mathsf{do\_od}(c_{\mathrm{dial}} \,[]\, c_{\mathrm{slider}})$, where c_{dial} and c_{slider} are statements characterizing the possible behavior resulting from a single action by the user involving the dial and slider, respectively. A possible expression for c_{slider} might be $\exists v.\, set\, v$, where $set\, v$ describes the results of setting the slider to the value v. This expression can be viewed as shorthand for $(set\, v_1) \,[]\, (set\, v_2) \,[]\, \ldots$ where the v_i enumerate the possible values to which user can set the slider.[18] In turn, we can model set with a function like

$$\lambda v.\, ((\lambda(s,d).\, s = v) \longrightarrow \mathsf{skip})$$
$$[]((\lambda(s,d).\, s \neq v) \longrightarrow (\mathsf{assign}\, (\lambda(s,d).\, (v,d))\, ;\, changed\, v))\ .$$

The semantics of commands generated by this function can be stated informally as *"if the value of the slider is equal to v then do nothing; else set its value to v and then execute 'changed v'."* Note that we model state with tuples: the first component gives the value of the slider, and the second the dial. Also note that in HOL predicates are boolean-valued functions. For example, $\lambda(s,d).\, s = v$ is true in a state iff the first component of the state (i.e. the value of the slider) is v.

Modeling components. The challenge is to devise a way of expressing components such that we can automatically construct (equivalents of) such expressions. Our solution is to express components as a set of code fragments: a fragment for each port requiring values (in the case of Sliders, just set) and one fragment for expressing component behavior. For example, (ignoring initial conditions) the definition of a slider[19] might be given as follows:

$$
\begin{aligned}
&\mathsf{slider}\, cmd\, s\, q\, set\, changed = \\
&\qquad (set = (\lambda v. \\
&\qquad\qquad\qquad (q\, (\lambda n.\quad (n = v)) \longrightarrow \\
&\qquad\qquad\qquad\qquad \mathsf{skip}) \\
&\qquad\qquad\qquad [](q\, (\lambda n.\, \neg(n = v)) \longrightarrow \\
&\qquad\qquad\qquad\qquad\qquad (\mathsf{assign}\, (s\, (\lambda n.\, v))\, ;\, changed\, v)))) \\
&\qquad \wedge (cmd = (\exists v.\, set\, v))
\end{aligned}
$$

---

[18] Recall that '$\exists$' is just '$\exists$' "lifted" to work on predicates: for all b, $(\exists i.\, R\, i)\, b = (\exists i.\, R\, i\, b)$.

[19] Dials are modeled similarly.

A complication that arises is the need to provide component instances with local state. We deal with this by parameterizing component models with functions that convert operations on local state to corresponding operations on global state. In the above example, the parameters s and q serve this purpose: they convert local assignments and queries to global ones, respectively. Examples of functions instantiating such parameters can be found in the definition of gui below.

Connecting components. When generating models for composite components, existentially quantified variables are used to effect connections. For example, a simplified version of the model generated for the user interface of Fig. 4 is:

$$\text{gui } cmd = (\exists cmd_s\ cmd_d\ set_s\ set_d.$$
$$\text{slider } cmd_s\ (\lambda f\ (s, d).\ (f\ s, d))\ (\lambda P\ (s, d).\ P\ s)\ set_s\ set_d$$
$$\wedge\ \text{dial } cmd_d\ (\lambda f\ (s, d).\ (s, f\ d))\ (\lambda P\ (s, d).\ P\ d)\ set_d\ set_s$$
$$\wedge\ (cmd = cmd_s\ []\ cmd_d))$$

Note the use of the choice operator '[]' to express the behavior of gui in terms of the behaviors of its constituent components. While this model might look unwieldy, is easy to automatically generate from an IL description and mechanically manipulate using HOL.

While models and implementations are automatically generated for composite components they must be supplied (by the developer) for primitive components. To make this a more reasonable proposition, a more accessible notation for expressing models could be defined; HOL terms would then be generated from models expressed in this notation. The notation could be executable; for example, note the similarity between the model for the slider described above and the Tcl code used to implement the slider in Appendix A.

5   Properties

Not only do we have to construct models but we have to formalize properties as well. While formalizing safety and security properties (as well as some generic properties[20]) is relatively straight-forward, formalizing exactly what constitutes a good user interface is an open problem. Many different formalisms and methodologies have been proposed to address this issue; indeed many of the references cited in the section on related work can be viewed as approaches to addressing this problem. To take advantage of this body of work one of our goals is to be able to verify that our models possess properties expressed in such formalisms. To this end, we are currently investigating the verification of properties directly expressed as finite state machines [43].

---

[20] For example, most of the presentation components that we are working with can be explicitly enabled or disabled. A simple generic property that can be checked is that at all times some component is enabled.

6 Verification

We are interested in reasoning about how GUI-based applications interact with their environment; for example, we would like to prove that certain state invariants are maintained when reacting to a user's (the environment's) actions. For example, one such invariant is that the dial and slider in Fig. 2 track each other. Due to the nature of the Tk toolkit implementation it is reasonable to model the values visibly displayed by the slider and dial with the values of the corresponding state variables at certain points in the execution of the model; namely after completely handling a user (environment) action. If gui is as defined in Sect. 4.2, then gui c will be true iff do_od (atomic c) models the behavior of Fig. 2 [21]. Assuming that P is a predicate on state sequences (behaviors) that expresses the required property [22] then to verify that the GUI in Fig. 2 possesses this property we have to prove a theorem of the form

$$\vdash \forall c.\, \text{gui}\, c \supset (\forall b.\, (\text{do\_od}\, (\text{atomic}\, c))\, b \supset P\, b) \ .$$

We have constructed a logic for verifying such properties based on Francez's forward predicate transformers [15]; constructing proofs using this logic is akin to symbolic execution [25].

7 Related Work

Specification-based approaches to constructing reliable user interfaces have received much attention; these approaches typically come under the heading of dialogue specification in the literature. In these approaches to GUI development, specifications that meet formally expressed requirements (properties) are first constructed; these are then used as blueprints for implementations. Almost all of the formalisms that have been proposed for dialogue specification are based on some notation originally developed for concurrency analysis including Statecharts [29], CSP [1], Esterel [8], Petri nets [4], LOTOS [44] and DisCo [51]. Carneiro-Coffin's thesis [6] contains a good survey of such formalisms. While progress has been made with regard to the specification of user interfaces using these formalisms, the issue of constructing implementations from such specifications has yet to be satisfactorily addressed. Dialogue implementation with most GUI toolkits consists of coding callback routines. Manually coding a collection of callback routines to produce behavior as described by a specification given in one of the above mentioned formalisms is often difficult and in practice usually not attempted. The possibility of automatically generating the appropriate

---

[21] If we are not interested in the intermediate states occurring during the course of handling individual user (environment) actions, we can model the GUI behavior as do_od atomic(c_1 [] ... [] c_n). The atomic operator elides intermediate states: for any statement c, (atomic c)b holds iff there is some behavior b' such that $c\, b'$ and $b = \text{atom}\, b'$.

[22] i.e. in all states in the sequence the value of the dial and the slider are the same.

callback routines directly from dialogue specifications[23] is being investigated: an early report of such work by Palanque *et al.* can be found in [42]. Work in this area is still preliminary; some fundamental issues have yet to be addressed. For example, it is not yet clear how to reuse (parts of) user interfaces constructed in such a fashion; the difficulty being that two very different formalisms are used in their construction.

One perceived drawback of many dialog specification formalisms is that they are difficult to use by non-specialists. This is of some concern as GUI designers typically are not well versed in formal methods. Recently d'Ausbourg and Roche [10] in a position paper have proposed to address this issue using an approach very similar to our own: they propose to have GUI designers specify user interfaces using some familiar formalism; models of behavior are then derived and analyzed. This work is still preliminary: while the formalism to be used for modeling behavior has been decided upon (the synchronous dataflow language Lustre [19]), the specification language has yet to be selected. They propose to use an existing prototyping language such as UIL [21] for this purpose. Using such a language would have a number of advantages: not only are designers already familiar with the notation, but it also allows proposed designs to be more fully evaluated with respect to human factors concerns. In outline, our work and the work proposed here differs for the most part only in the choice of implementation language and modeling formalism; each could possibly be used to address the others goals. It will be interesting to see what the actual differences are when their approach is more fully developed.

8 Summary and future work

In this paper we have presented the basis for an alternative approach to constructing reliable user interfaces. We have constructed a prototype of the system described in this paper: currently this consists of IL to Tk/Tcl [41] and IL to HOL translators, and a number of HOL theories and tactics. All of the basic features of the proposed framework have been implemented. Concurrently, we are investigating how to mechanize the various proofs that arise.

A   Appendix: An Implementation

We have implemented the examples presented in this paper using Tk/Tcl. Tcl (tool command language) is a simple scripting language for controlling and extending applications: the Tcl interpreter is designed to be easily extended with

---

[23] It should be noted that dialogue specifications are useful for purposes other than serving as blueprints for implementations; good examples can be found in [13] and [5]. In addition, there are other approaches to generating implementations (prototypes) from dialogue specifications. For example, an interpreter can be constructed for the particular formalism, as described in [1]. However, due to (human) resource constraints, implementations produced using this approach are often rudimentary and usually only suitable as prototypes.

```
# Slider'build name:  Create a slider named "name".

proc Slider'build {name} {

    # These should be attributes.

    set V0              0          ;# Minimum value for slider.
    set V1              80         ;# Maximum value for slider.
    set tickInterval    20         ;# Spacing between tick marks.
    set Length          160        ;# Length (in screen units) of slider.

  # Construct the physical representation.

    scale $name -orient horizontal -from $V0 -to $V1 \
        -tickinterval $tickInterval -length $Length -command $name'set
    pack $name

  # Construct the model.

    # Create variable that will hold value of the slider.

    global $name'value
    set $name'value ""

    # If the value of the slider changes $name'set will update the
    # position of the pointer and then invoke $name'changed.

    proc $name'set {value} "
        global $name'value
        if \"!\[cequal \$\{$name'value\} \$value\]\"  \{
            set $name'value \$value
            $name set \$value
            $name'changed \$value
        \}
    "
}
```

Fig. 6. Slider in Tk/Tcl.

application specific commands. Tk extends Tcl with commands for building
Motif-like user interfaces. It is probably best to think of Tcl as a very simple programming language and Tk as a Motif-like toolkit for it. We use Tk/Tcl
for primarily two reasons: 1) the high-level nature of Tk/Tcl makes it easy to
generate implementations, and 2) the free availability of the Tk/Tcl source allows implementation details to be readily ascertained. The approach presented
in this paper does not depend on any particular properties of Tk/Tcl; adapting
it for use with more conventional languages and toolkits is trivial.

Figure 6 contains the code for building Sliders. The code for building Dials

is essentially the same except that, as Tk/Tcl does not provide a suitable dial
widget, we build one using other widgets. Figure 7 contains the code generated

```
#!/xhbin/wishx -f
source external.tk

proc Main'build {root} {
    Frame'build $root.f
    Dial'build $root.f.d
    Slider'build $root.f.s
    proc $root.f.d'changed {value} "$root.f.s'set \$value"
    proc $root.f.s'changed {value} "$root.f.d'set \$value"
}
Main'build ""
```

Fig. 7. Generated Tk/Tcl code for the example.

for the IL description in Fig. 3. (`external.tk` contains the code for the primitives.) Note that as Tcl provides no mechanism for encapsulating data, we do
so by giving each component instance a unique name and using this as a prefix
for the names of all variables and procedures associated with that instance.

B   Appendix: The HOL logic

The following is a brief introduction to the HOL logic; a complete formal definition can be found in the reference manual [49].

Terms in the HOL logic are expressions that denote values and have syntax

$$t ::= c \mid v \mid (t\,t') \mid \lambda v.\, t$$

where c ranges over constants, v over variables, and t and t' over terms. $t\,t'$
denotes the value obtained by evaluating the function denoted by t at t'; $\lambda v.\, t$
denotes the function whose value at x is obtained by substituting x for v in t.

To prevent inconsistencies such as Russell's paradox syntactically well-formed
terms must be well-typed, i.e. have types consistent with the types of their
subterms. Types in the HOL logic are expressions that denote sets[24]: a term of
type σ denotes an element of σ. If t is a term we write t: σ to denote that t has
type σ. Such explicit type information will usually be omitted, however, when it
is clear from form or context what the type must be. Types have syntax

$$\sigma ::= c \mid v \mid (\sigma_1, \dots, \sigma_n)op$$

where c ranges over atomic types, v ranges over type variables, op ranges over
type operators and σ, along with its subscripted variants, range over types. Type

---

[24] Strictly speaking this is not true; the presence of type variables complicates matters.
Full details can be found in [49].

constants and type variables can be distinguished syntactically: the names of type variables must begin with the symbol '*'. To improve readability, a number of commonly used binary type operators have infix forms. For example, '$\rightarrow$' is a distinguished (infix) type operator that constructs function spaces between types. The HOL logic contains only two primitive types: :bool (just the truth values T and F) and :ind (an infinite collection of distinct elements). All other types must be constructed from these using '$\rightarrow$'. For convenience, the HOL system comes with a variety of derived types and type operators.

Features to note about the HOL logic include:

- Formulas are represented with terms of type :bool; predicates are represented with functions with range :bool. For example, if P is defined to be $\lambda n. \exists m. n = 2 \times m$ then $P x$ is true if and only if x is an even natural number.
- A Milner-style polymorphic typing discipline is used. Type variables may be free in a term of the logic, but quantification over type variables is not allowed.

Binding conventions are used to reduce the number of parenthesis needed in terms and types. Function applications associate to the *left*: the term $f_1 f_2 \ldots f_n x$ is parenthesized as $(\ldots((f_1 f_2)f_3) \ldots f_n)x$. In types, '$\rightarrow$' associates to the *right*: $\sigma_1 \rightarrow \sigma_2 \rightarrow \ldots \rightarrow \sigma_n \rightarrow \sigma$ is parenthesized as $\sigma_1 \rightarrow (\sigma_2 \rightarrow (\ldots \rightarrow (\sigma_n \rightarrow \sigma)\ldots))$. In terms with variables bound by '$\forall$', '$\exists$', 'ε', or 'λ', the scope of the binder extends as far to the right of the '.' as possible. For example, the term $(\forall x. x = \lambda y. xy)$ is parenthesized as $(\forall x. (x = \lambda y. xy))$ not $((\forall x. x) = (\lambda y. xy))$.

References

1. Heather Alexander. Formally-based techniques for dialogue design. In *Proceedings of the HCI'87 Conference on People and Computers III*, Systems and Interfaces, pages 201–213, 1987.
2. Apple Computer, Inc. *Apple Macintosh Human Interface Guidelines*, 1992.
3. Apple Computer, Inc. *Human Interface Guidelines: The Apple Desktop Interface*, 1992.
4. Remi Bastide and Philippe Palanque. Petri net objects for the design, validation and prototyping of user-driven interfaces. In *Proceedings of IFIP INTERACT'90: Human-Computer Interaction*, Detailed Design: Construction Tools, pages 625–631, 1990.
5. L.M.F. Carneiro-Coffin, D.D. Cowan, C.J.P. Lucena, and D. Smith. An experience using JASMINIUM – formalization assisting with the design of user interfaces. In Richard N. Taylor and Joëlle Coutaz, editors, *Software Engineering and Human-Computer Interaction; ICSE'94 Workshop on SE-HCI: Joint Research Issues*, volume 896 of *Lecture Notes in Computer Science*, pages 141–158, Sorrento, Italy, 16–17 May 1994. Springer-Verlag.
6. Luiza Maria Fonseca Carneiro-Coffin. *Jasminum: Joining ADVs and State Machines in a Notation for User-Interface Modeling*. PhD thesis, University of Waterloo, 1994.
7. K. Mani Chandy and Jayadev Misra. *Parallel programming*. Addison-Wesley Pub. Co., 1988.

8. Dominique Clément and Janet Incerpi. Specifying the behavior of graphical objects using esterel. In *TAPSOFT '89*, volume 2, pages 111–125, Barcelona, Spain, March 1989.

9. Avra Cohn. The notion of proof in hardware verification. *Journal of Automated Reasoning*, 5(2):127–140, June 1989.

10. Bruno D'Ausbourg and Pierre Roche. Specifying formally or deriving a formal model from an informal description of user interfaces? In Christopher Rouff, editor, *CHI 95 Workshop Formal Specification of User Interfaces Position Papers*, Denver, Colorado, May 7–8 1995.

11. Digitalk. *PARTS Workbench User's Guide*, 1992.

12. Edsger W. Dijkstra. *A Discipline of Programming*. Prentice-Hall, Englewood Cliffs, New Jersey, 1976.

13. D.J. Duke and M.D. Harrison. From formal models to formal methods. In Richard N. Taylor and Joëlle Coutaz, editors, *Software Engineering and Human-Computer Interaction; ICSE'94 Workshop on SE-HCI: Joint Research Issues*, volume 896 of *Lecture Notes in Computer Science*, pages 159–173, Sorrento, Italy, 16–17 May 1994. Springer-Verlag.

14. Kevin J. Farley. Software testing for windows developers. *Data Based Advisor*, 11(11), November 1993.

15. N. Frances. A case for a forward predicate transformer. *Inf. Proc. Lett.*, 6(6):196–198, December 1977.

16. Stephen J. Garland, John V. Guttag, and James J. Horning. Debugging larch shared language specifications. *IEEE Transactions on Software Engineering*, 16(9):1044–1057, September 1990.

17. M. Gordon. Why higher-order logic is a good formalism for specifying and verifying hardware. In *Formal Aspects of VLSI Design: Proceedings of the 1985 Edinburgh Workshop on VLSI*, pages 409–417. North-Holland, 1986.

18. M. J. C. Gordon and Tom F. Melham. *Introduction to HOL: a theorem proving environment for higher order logic*. Cambridge University Press, New York, 1993.

19. Nicholas Halbwachs, Paul Caspi, Pascal Raymond, and Daniel Pilaud. The synchronous data flow programming language LUSTRE. *Proceedings of the IEEE*, 79(9):1305–1320, September 1991.

20. D. Harel and A. Pnueli. On the development of reactive systems. In Krzysztof R. Apt, editor, *Logics and Models of Concurrent Systems*, volume 13 of *Series F: Computer and System Sciences*, pages 477–498. Springer-Verlag, 1985.

21. Dan Heller, Paula Ferguson, and David Brennan. *Motif Programming Manual*, 2nd edition, February 1994.

22. Gerard J. Holzmann. *Design and Validation of Computer Protocols*. Prentice Hall, Englewood Cliffs, N.J., 1991.

23. IBM. *VisualAge: Concepts & Features*, 1994.

24. Brian W. Kernighan and Dennis M. Ritchie. *The C Programming Language, 2nd Ed.* Prentice Hall, 1988.

25. Ralf Kneuper. Symbolic execution: a semantic approach. *Science of Computer Programming*, 16:207–249, October 1991.

26. Bogdan Korel. Automated software test data generation. *IEEE Transactions on Software Engineering*, 16(8):870–879, August 1990.

27. D. C. Luckham, D. P. Helmbold, S. Meldal, D. L. Bryan, and M. A. Haberler. Task sequencing language for specifying distributed ada systems. In *CRAI Workshop on Software Factories and Ada*, Capri, Italy, May 26–30 1986.

28. Zohar Manna and Amir Pnueli. *The temporal logic of reactive systems: Specification*. Springer-Verlag, 1992.

29. Lynn S. Marshall. *A formal description method for user interfaces*. PhD thesis, University of Manchester, 1986.

30. K. L. McMillan. *The SMV system*, February 1992.

31. Microsoft Corp. *Windows 3.1 Programmer's Reference, Volume 1: Overview*, 1992.

32. Microsoft Corp. *Windows Interface: An Application Design Guide*, 1992.

33. Microsoft Corp. *The GUI Guide: International Terminology for the Windows Interface*, 1993.

34. Microsoft Corporation. *Microsoft Visual Basic Programmer's Guide*, 1993.

35. Brad A. Myers. User interface software tools. Technical Report CMU-CS-94-182, School of Computer Science, Carnegie Mellon University, August 1994.

36. Greg Nelson. A generalization of Dijkstra's calculus. *ACM Transactions on Programming Languages and Systems*, 11(4):517–561, October 1989.

37. Oscar Nierstrass, Simon Gibbs, and Dennis Tsichritzis. Component-oriented software development. *Communications of the ACM*, 35(9):160–165, September 1992.

38. Novell, Inc. *Visual AppBuilder: User's Guide*, 1994.

39. Open Software Foundation. *OSF/Motif Programmer's Reference, Revision 1.1*, 1991.

40. Open Software Foundation. *OSF/Motif Style Guide, Revision 1.2*, 1992.

41. John K. Ousterhout. *Tcl and the Tk Toolkit*. Addison-Wesley, 1994.

42. Philippe A. Palanque, Rémi Bastide, and Valérie Sengès. Automatic code generation from a high-level petri net based specification of dialogue. In *EWHCI94: The Fourth East-West International Conference on Human-Computer Interaction*, St. Petersburg, Russia, 2–6 August 1994.

43. David L. Parnas. On the use of transition diagrams in the design of a user interface for an interactive computer system. In *Proceedings of the 1969 National ACM Conference*, pages 379–385, 1969.

44. F. Paternó and G. Faconti. On the use of LOTOS to describe graphical interaction. In A. Monk, D. Diaper, and M. D. Harrison, editors, *Proceedings of the HCI'92 Conference on People and Computers VII*, pages 155–173. Cambridge University Press, September 1992.

45. Stephen W. Plain. Novell's visual appbuilder (sidebar to: "radical development"). *PC Magazine*, 13(19), November 1994.

46. Stephen R. Quinn, John C. Ware, and John Spragens. Tireless testers: automated tools can help iron out the kinks in your custom gui applications. *InfoWorld*, 15(36), September 1993.

47. M. D. Rice and S. B. Seidman. A formal model for module interconnection languages. *IEEE Transactions on Software Engineering*, 20(1):88–101, January 1994.

48. Caroline Rose and Bradley Hacker et al. *Inside Macintosh*. Addison-Wesley, 1985.

49. SRI International under contract to DSTO Australia, Cambridge, England. *The HOL System: Reference*, 1989.

50. Howard Sturgis. An effective test strategy. Technical Report CSL-85-8, Xerox Palo Alto Research Center, November 1985.

51. Kari Systä. Specifying user interfaces in DisCo. *SIGCHI Bulletin*, 26(2):53–58, 1994. Presented at a Workshop on Formal Methods for the Design of Interactive Systems, York, UK, 23rd July 1993.

52. G. Tredoux. Mechanizing execution sequence semantics in HOL. *South African Computer Journal*, 7:81–86, July 1992. Proceedings of the 7th Southern African

Computer Research Symposium, Johannesburg, South Africa. Also available as part of the HOL distribution: ftp://lal.cs.byu.edu/pub/hol/holsys.tar.gz.

53. Jean Vanderdonckt. The "tools for working with guidelines" bibliography. ftp://arzach.fundp.ac.be/pub/papers/jvdd/Tools_fww_guidelines.txt, March 1994.

54. P. Wolper. Expressing interesting properties of programs in propositional temporal logic (extended abstract). In *Proceedings, Thirteenth Annual ACM Symposium on Principles of Programming Languages*, pages 184–193, St. Petersburg Beach, Fla., January 1986.

55. Michal Young and Richard N. Taylor. Rethinking the taxonomy of fault detection techniques. Technical Report TR62P, Software Engineering Research Center, Department of Computer Sciences, Purdue University, September 1991. An earlier version of this paper appeared in *Proceedings of the 11th International Conference on Software Engineering*, Pittsburgh, May 1989.

This article was processed using the LaTeX macro package with LLNCS style

Modelling and Generation of Graphical User Interfaces in the TADEUS Approach

Thomas Elwert, Egbert Schlungbaum

University of Rostock, Department of Computer Science, D-18051 Rostock, Germany
{Thomas.Elwert,Egbert.Schlungbaum}@informatik.uni-rostock.de

Abstract. The goal of the TADEUS-approach (*TA*sk-based *DE*velopment of *US*er interface software) is the task-oriented and user-centred development of graphical user interfaces (GUI). For this reason TADEUS is a methodology as well as a supporting environment for GUI development. An overview about the TADEUS approach is given in this paper. The TADEUS Dialogue graph, a new specification technique for GUI, and the generation of GUI based on Dialogue graphs are described.

1 Introduction

1.1 Motivation

Better interactive software systems (ISS) are one of the research goals in the human-computer interaction area. Hartson [10] shows three ways to achieve this goal, firstly to produce systems with better interfaces, secondly to develop new systems in order to support particular types of work (e.g., group work), thirdly to develop better tools for the support of the development process of ISS. The third way is based on the premise that better software systems are influenced by their development process which is supported by tools. This article is related to the third way.

During the last few years, significant advances have been made in the field of tools for user interface development. The fourth generation of user interface management systems (UIMS) has been developed [11]. Compared to programming with user interface toolkits, the user interface designer is better supported by these systems in the design and implementation of GUI [15].

The development of a GUI is still a time-consuming activity. With the tools commercially available today, each user interface object has to be created and laid out explicitly. Dialogue control specifications have to be added by using a programming language or by using a specialised language, which can require a large effort and needs specific knowledge.

Furthermore it is difficult to follow existing user interface guidelines and style guides like [5], [25], [17] and to maintain the internal consistency across the user interface as well as the external consistency with other applications if the dialogue designer uses currently available user interface tools. In addition, most available tools do not give support for selecting appropriate interaction objects for a specific task.

Independent and unharmonised specification methods for the data and function models on one hand and the specification methods for the dialogue model on the other have been used in the past of software engineering for the development of ISS. The dialogue designer has to solve this difficult and extensive task to achieve consistency and completeness within an ISS description if he uses different methods during the development process from the requirements analysis to the user interface design. In addition, this task has many sources of errors for the dialogue designer [9]. Therefore, it is important to use analysis results like the task model or the data model as inputs for user interface development tools.

The UIMS technology offers the advantage of separation between the application core and the user interface for the implementation of ISS. The task-oriented and user-centred development of dialogue systems requires a homogeneous and continuous development process, for example [4], [6], [26].

The work described in this paper is related to the fields of research mentioned above. A methodology and a supporting environment - the TADEUS system (*TA*sk-based *DE*velopment of *US*er interface software) - have been developed for the specification of user interfaces with direct exploitation of the results from the requirements analysis and for the automatic generation of GUI from the model specifying the ISS. After a discussion of related work, we will give an overview of the TADEUS approach and furthermore we will describe the new dialogue specification technique - the TADEUS Dialogue graph - and the generation of GUI from it.

1.2   Related work

Model-based user interface design with automatic generation. A number of research systems, which automatically generate the user interface from higher level specifications, are documented in the literature. Two directions may be observed, first the systems which use their own notation of higher level specification, and second the systems which use notations of specifications that are well known from software engineering. The importance of the second direction consists of the requirements description of an interactive application from an earlier phase of the software development which can be used for the development of the GUI.

In UIDE [27] the designer has to specify an application model and a dialogue model on the basis of application actions, interface actions and interaction techniques. The user interface is generated during the runtime from these models by means of the UIDE-runtime system. In MIKE [16] and in the UofA*UIMS [24] the initial design specification and implementation of the user interface are generated from a description of the application commands. The interface designer is enabled to improve its appearance and effectiveness by an interactive refinement process. In JADE [28] a look-and-feel database is used to generate the presentational design from frame-like, look-and-feel independent dialogue descriptions. If necessary, the dialogue designer can edit the resulting dialogue description using a graphical editor. These changes will be considered by JADE just like the changes of the original text specification.

In JANUS [1] a GUI is generated from the application requirements which are specified by an OOA model. The resulting user interface can be displayed and animated by means of a UIMS. In GENIUS [14] a user interface for a database-oriented application is generated from a data model, which is specified by extended entity relationship diagrams and dialogue nets, a Petri net based technique for dialogue specification. In both systems the output is generated for an existing UIMS.

All these systems except JADE use an application model or a data model to describe the interactive application. Only the UIDE and the GENIUS systems use in addition a dialogue model which is used by dialogue designers to specify more details of the dialogue. This approach allows a flexible mapping of application task to different interaction styles and different interaction objects.

A motivation for the TADEUS approach is the task-oriented model-based approach of Stary [26]. He claims that the software development for interactive applications needs the elaboration and integration of the task, user, problem domain and interaction models.

Techniques for dialogue specification. There are many approaches to dialogue specification, such as transition networks, grammars or events [8]. The possibility of a visualization of a notation or ideally the interactive, graphical processing of the notation is an important feature of a dialogue specification [3].

The transition networks and their extensions are well known, frequently used graphical dialogue specifications. They tend to emphasise the states of the user interface and the sequence of transitions from one state to another. Certainly transition networks are unsuited to the description of GUI. They are useful and powerful for the specification of non-graphical user interface, but they have to modified in order to handle direct manipulation within a user interface. Jacob [12] extends state transition diagrams by multiple parallel diagrams. However, the global relations of concurrent dialogues cannot be visualised by this approach.

A further approach to graphical specification of user interfaces is the use of Petri nets or Petri net based techniques, like the event graphs from Roudaud et.al. [19], the Petri net objects from Bastide et.al. [2] or the dialogue nets from Janssen [13]. Compared to the user interface specification with transition networks, the advantage of Petri nets is that they already have in the basic form a concept for the specification of concurrence that is needed for the description of window-oriented GUI. Event graphs can be used to describe the dynamic visibility of objects within a graphical interaction application. Petri net objects are more powerful for the description of the general object flow and the object manipulation. But they are more complex than event graphs and less suited for the earlier design phases. Dialogue nets are similar to event graphs. Compared with event graphs, they offer some extensions like hierarchical dialogue structuring and the declaration of modal dialogue windows.

The dialogue nets are based on the condition/event nets, which are working with a single unnamed token. This is the disadvantage in the use of dialogue nets. They do not allow the modelling of multiple instances of a window. The technique used in our approach, the TADEUS Dialogue graph is an extension of the dialogue net. The Dialogue graph is based on the individual-token net [18], a most general form of the Petri net.

2 An Overview of the TADEUS Approach

A main goal of the TADEUS approach is the task-oriented and user-centred development of interactive applications. Several purposes are observed:

- The software for an interactive application is developed in continuous steps from the requirements analysis to the generation of a user interface proto-type, where any step is based on the results of the previous one.
- The development of the interactive application requires the elaboration of four domain models, the task, the user, the problem domain, and the dialogue models.
- The task, the user, and the problem domain models are used to document the results of the requirements analysis. Software engineering methods should be used for these models as soon as possible.
- The dialogue model, whose initial state is generated from the task and problem domain models, is used to specify detailed requirements for the user interface.
- The dialogue model should allow the specification of window-oriented GUI. The Dialogue graph, a new graphical specification technique, has been developed for it.
- A prototype of the user interface is automatically generated from the elaborated models by using software-ergonomic knowledge. This generation should be for an existing UIMS.

The TADEUS approach offers a methodology and a supporting environment for the development of GUI. The methodology includes the *processes* that define a complete and continuous approach for developing such interactive applications, the *action model* that describes the steps done by the dialogue designer based on the processes, the *related meta-models* on which the processes are based, the *models* that are created as a result of the related processes (they are instances of the meta-models) and the *interactive tools* that support the processes and help the dialogue designer to build the GUI in an automated and computer-aided way. The dialogue designer does not need specific programming skills. The GUI produced with the TADEUS environment is used by an end user.

The action model and the domain models. The TADEUS approach contains a well defined action model which subdivides the user interface development process into three phases, the requirements analysis, the dialogue design, and the realization (see figure 1). During the user interface development process the dialogue designer has to elaborate the four domain models — the task, the problem

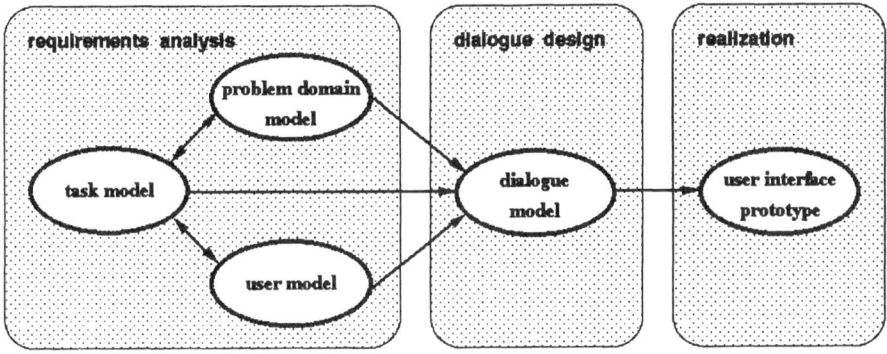

Fig. 1. Relationship between domain models

domain, the user, and the dialogue models. The domain models are defined by meta-models [23].

The *requirements analysis* builds the foundation of our methodology. The task model is represented as a hierarchical goal structure. In this case the concept goal is defined in the following way. A goal is reached if the corresponding task is carried out. A goal consists of three parts: task (one), roles (one or more) and optional secondary objects. The problem domain model is represented as a class hierarchy and/or a class library like the object model from the OOA by Rumbaugh [20]. It consists of the description of the primary and secondary objects. The user model is used to characterise the potential or the existing end users by roles. Each end user is assigned to a role. The tasks, the roles, and the role-task relations are described by attributes and their values. The attribute values will be used for the generation of the dialogue model.

During the *dialogue design phase* the dialogue designer develops the dialogue model whose initial state is generated from the task, user, and problem domain models. Therefore he identifies views in the task and/or in the problem domain models. A view represents the possibilities for task processing which are related and which should be presented at the user interface simultaneously. In general, a view is presented by a single window in a UIMS. We distinguish two dialogue types within the dialogue model: the *navigation dialogue* and the *processing dialogue*. The navigation dialogue defines the sequencing between views. The processing dialogue describes the interaction within a view and the call of application functions [29].

During the *realization phase* a prototype of the user interface description is generated from the dialogue model and the other domain models by using a knowledge base. The prototype is generated for an existing UIMS, for example, the ISA Dialog Manager.

A comprehensive description of the TADEUS approach is given in [23].

Illustration with a small example. Our example explains a part of the user interface of the TADEUS environment, the user modelling component. The necessary parts of the task model and the problem domain model for the user modelling component are shown in figure 2.

This example includes one elementary dialogue structure of a GUI of an information system (e.g., database application) which represents the following task of the end user: he wants to process a set of objects of the same type. Therefore the problem domain model contains a class description (object type) which is transformed into two views in the dialogue model. This means that the dialogue designer as the end user of the TADEUS system, needs for the task processing *user modelling*, two windows, firstly, a so-called "class-window" for the manipulation about the instances of the class and secondly, a so-called "instance-window" for the manipulation of each instance. This is one case to generate parts of the dialogue model from the problem domain model.

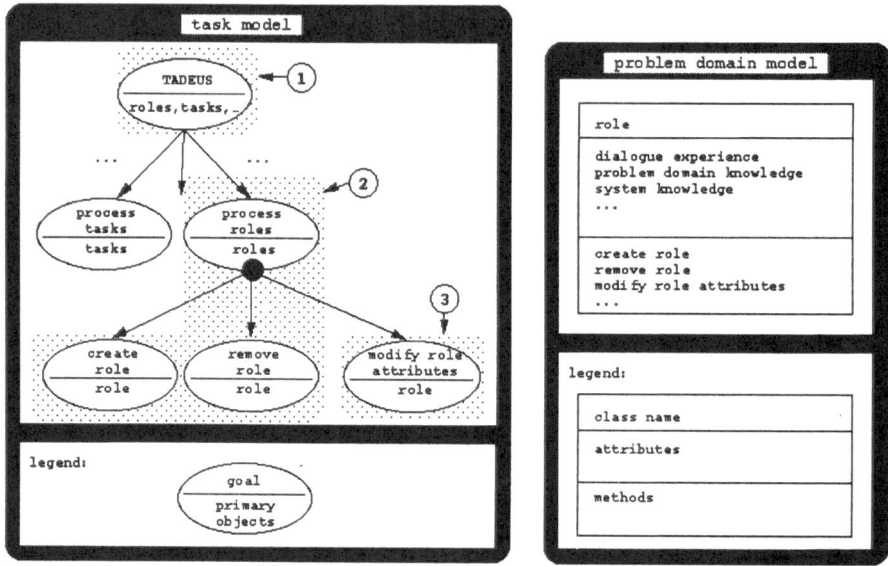

Fig. 2. TADEUS - user modelling component: Task and problem domain models

The dialogue designer has to identify views within the task model in order to generate the dialogue model from the task model. In our example they are grey shadowed (figure 2): the view (1) *TADEUS* for the main window, the view (2) *User Model* for the class-window, and the view (3) *Role* for the instance-window (for the dialogue model see figure 4).

In general, only one instance exists for a class-window and one or more instances exist for an instance-window.

3 Specification of Graphical User Interfaces

3.1 Description of the main components of a Dialogue graph

Nodes and transitions. A Dialogue graph consists of nodes, which represent dialogue views or dialogue objects, and transitions, which represent the possible interactions between these nodes.

The *nodes* are drawn as circles or ellipses labelled with a name. There are non-modal, modal and complex nodes. In analogy to the Janssen's dialogue net [13] a non-modal node is drawn with a normal circle, a modal node with a big circle and a complex node with a double circle. The non-modal node describes a dialogue view. This node type contains neither refinement nor interaction limitations unlike the modal node. The modal node is a starting point for a modal dialogue. If the end user achieves this node by an interaction he must first complete this modal dialogue in order to continue the other dialogue. A complex node allows the dialogue designer to refine a dialogue view.

The end user navigates from the starting view S_1 to the destination view S_2 by interactions represented by *transitions*. The direction of a transition is additionally explained with the black point drawn near by the destination view. Between two nodes there can exist a concurrent transition, a sequential transition, an object-related concurrent transition, a modal transition or a closing transition. The behaviour of transition is described by control rules in a paragraph below. The representations of the transitions are shown in figure 3.

Tokens. In order to specify the state of a user interface the Dialogue graph nodes are marked. The marking of a node describes the state of the related dialogue view (in detail: the state of the user interface window associated with a concrete dialogue view). The Dialogue graph with all it's nodes and their markings describes the total state of the modelled user interface. The tokens represent the properties of a dialogue view. The following properties are distinguished and should be represented with tokens on a node:

- **a** active — The corresponding dialogue view is visible and was activated. This means that this view has the input focus.
- **v** visible — The corresponding dialogue view is visible.
- **m** manipulable — The corresponding dialogue view is visible and can be activated.

Furthermore there exist *variable tokens* which are set during the runtime of the ISS in order to handle multiple window instances. The value of these tokens depends on the result of the related end user interaction.

There are some rules about the existence of the described tokens, which will be used for dialogue modelling:

1. Only one dialogue view can have the input focus in a GUI at the same time. That means only one a-token can exist within the Dialogue graph.
2. If a dialogue view is active then it is also visible and manipulable.

transition type	graphic symbol	behaviour
concurrent transition		t_1: S_1: (a,v,m) S_2: - t_2: S_1: (v,m) S_2: (a,v,m)
sequential transition		t_1: S_1: (a,v,m) S_2: - t_2: S_1: - S_2: (a,v,m)
object-related concurrent transition		t_1: S_1: (a,v,m) S_2: - t_2: S_1: (v,m) S_2: (a,v,m,X)
modal transition	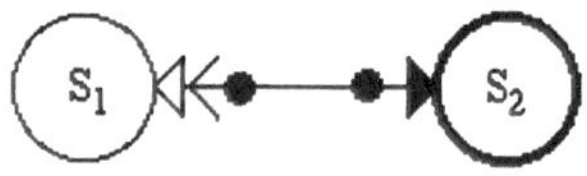	t_1: S_1: (a,v,m) S_2: - t_2: S_1: (v) S_2: (a,v,m) t_3: S_1: (a,v,m) S_2: -
closing transition	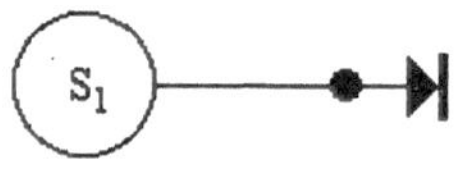	t_1: S_1: (a,v,m) t_2: S_1: -

Fig. 3. Dialogue graph: graphical representation and behaviour of the transitions

3. If a dialogue view is visible and manipulable then this view can get the input focus through a user interaction (These interactions are not shown in the Dialogue graph).
4. If a dialogue view is visible but not manipulable then it cannot be activated. That means a modal dialogue view is active.
5. A non-marked dialogue view means that the corresponding view is invisible.

Control rules - semantics of transitions. As shown in figure 3, each transition has its own behaviour. The existence rules are used to define the control rules, which are explained in a verbal form.

Concurrent transition. The view S_1 is active. After the execution of a related end user interaction, the concurrent transition is carried out and the view S_1 will become visible and manipulable and the view S_2 will become active.

Sequential transition. The view S_1 is active. After the execution of a related end user interaction, the transition is carried out and the view S_1 will become invisible. The view S_2 will become active.

Object-related concurrent transition. The behaviour of this transition is similar to the concurrent transition. After the related end user interaction, the views S_1 and S_2 are visible. An important property of this transition is the possibility to create one or more instances of the view S_2. Each instance of view S_2 is an instance-window and represents one object of the related class. The related end user interaction is connected with the selection of an object represented by the variable token X because the concrete object name is only available during runtime.

Modal transition. The view S_1 is active. It is possible to change to the view S_2 by a related end user interaction. Then the modal view S_2 is active. At the same time, all the other visible views have to lose the property manipulable (**m**-token) in order to enable the modal behaviour of S_2 (see rules 3 and 4). If the modal dialogue is finished, all visible views except view S_2 get the **m**-token back.

Closing transition. The view S_1 is active. If the transition fires, the current dialogue is finished.

3.2 Continuation of the small example

The Dialogue graph is used for the description of navigation dialogue. On the basis of the views identified within the task model (see figure 2) the initial state of the Dialogue graph is created automatically. As shown in figure 4, there exists a concurrent transition between the views *TADEUS* and *User model* and an object-related concurrent transition between the views *User Model* and *Role*.

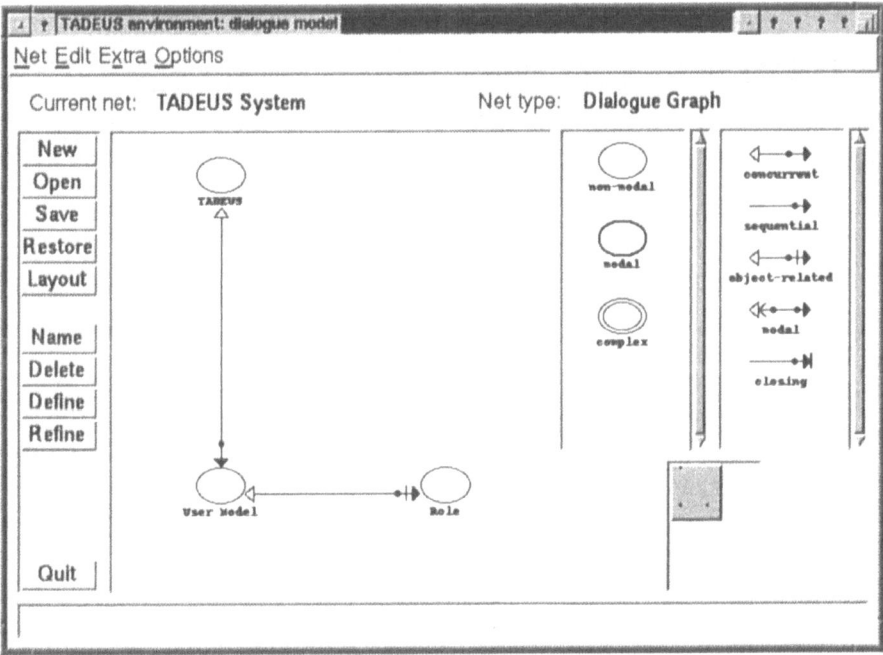

Fig. 4. Dialogue model of the user modelling component

The dialogue designer has to extend the Dialogue graph in order to create the necessary requirements for the automatic generation of the GUI. A possible scenario with the use of the GUI generated from this Dialogue graph is described later.

3.3 Further details of Dialogue graphs

Description of processing dialogues. It is also possible to describe the processing dialogue by the Dialogue graph notation. But the resulting dialogue graph is very complex and is difficult to handle. In order to find a better solution we favour the interaction table to describe the processing dialogue at the current time. In extention of our example the interaction table of the view *User Model* is represented in table 1. Each starting point of a processing dialogue is related to one row in the interaction table. The transitions within the interaction table are generated from two sources the task model and the styleguide information. Now the dialogue designer specifies the related dialogue form for each transition. Furthermore he has the possibility to enter additional information in order to improve the GUI generation (e.g., grouping).

Table 1. Interaction table for the view *User Model*

transition	dialogue form	type	group	group position
create role	data input	free	1	1
remove role	function call		2	2
modify role	function call		2	1
help	function call		3	1
quit	function call		3	2

Complex dialogue — refinement. In order to create and develop complex and detailed dialogue description, it is necessary to refine a given Dialogue graph. This task is performed by a special node — the complex node. This node allows the dialogue designer to make a token-preserving refinement of a node which is based on the work of Reisig [18].

Modal dialogue. A modal node describes a starting point for a modal dialogue in the navigation dialogue. The description of a modal dialogue is necessary if the end user has to carry out a special task or to confirm a message. In this case it must be impossible to change to another dialogue view.

The end user must finish all interaction in the modal dialogue and only then can he work in other dialogue views.

For the Dialogue graph we can write down rules about the behaviour of the tokens if the end user reaches a starting point of a modal dialogue:

1. If a modal node becomes active, all visible nodes of the entire Dialogue graph lose the property manipulable. (If an a-token reaches a modal node, all nodes with a m-token lose this token.)
2. After the modal dialogue all visible nodes get the property manipulable back. (All nodes which lost the m-token get the m-token back.)
3. There is no way to change the activity to a node which is not in the modal dialogue.

Furthermore with the help of refinement a modal node can be refined to a sub-net describing a modal dialogue.

3.4 Mapping to a Petri net

As mentioned above our Dialogue graph is based on a special type of Petri net, the individual-token net [18]. If we can map the Dialogue graph to an individual-token net, there is a possibility to use an existing simulation and analysis tool which allows us to check the correctness, the existence of deadlocks and the liveliness of the Dialogue graph. Furthermore we can reduce the time for the development of a tool handling our Dialogue graph specification. For each Dialogue graph transition there exists an equivalent individual-token net [22].

Composition of language primitives. Currently we investigate the composition of different individual-token net parts into an entire net which is an equivalent representation of the Dialogue graph. The first step is the transformation of each transition of the Dialogue graph. The second step is the composition of these parts. There exist well defined rules in order to combine such individual-token net parts. For example, if there are concurrent transitions with the same starting point (primary view) and some target views (secondary views), then additional transitions are necessary in order to model the change of the activity between the secondary views.

3.5 Tool for Dialogue graphs

A tool supporting the manipulation of Dialogue graphs is under construction. The implementation of the Dialogue graph editor is finished. Figure 4 gives an expression of this editor. The snapshot shows the Dialogue graph of our example.

4 Generation of the GUI

The development of the dialogue model and the generation of the user interface prototype are closely related. The exactness of the dialogue model influences the effort for the generation of the user interface. If there is missed information in the dialogue model, the dialogue designer has to answer some questions during the generation process. The generation process contains seven steps (in extention to [21]):

1. Defining the default layout description.
2. Evaluating the default layout description concerning the fulfilment of software ergonomic criteria.
3. Selection of abstract interaction objects and the bindings to the dialogue forms.
4. Mapping from abstract interaction objects to concrete interaction objects.
5. Defining the layout of concrete interaction objects by using the default layouts.
6. Placing the concrete interaction objects inside the views automatically. (Thus, the additional information of the interaction table is used.)
7. Creation of the dynamics (dialogue structure) from the Dialogue graph.
8. Generation of the user interface description file for an existing UIMS.

In general, the dialogue designer performs the first two steps for each project only once. The possible repeated generation process begins at step 3.

The information about the dialogue forms is used to choose abstract interaction objects (AIO) by rules which are derived from table 2. In the following step the abstract interaction objects are mapped to concrete interaction objects (CIO) by rules which are derived from table 3.

Table 2. From the dialogue form to the AIO (some examples)

dialogue form	type	AIO
function call		action trigger
data input	free	input field; input group
	1:n	single selector
	m:n	multiple selector
data output		output field; output group

In the next step each concrete interaction object is extended by layout parameters. This task can be solved by the usage of a default layout description. This description contains knowledge about layout parameters of each concrete interaction object type (e.g.: foreground colour, background colour).

The default layout description is defined by the dialogue designer at the starting point of the user interface development. When he has changed the default layout description he can use a knowledge-based support to evaluate them (step 1 and 2). The knowledge base about the colour usage is based on the German standard DIN 66234 [7].

The dynamics of the user interface are generated from the final dialogue graph. The transitions are used to generate rules for an existing UIMS, in our case the ISA Dialog Manager. An example for the sequential transition and the concurrent transition is shown in figure 5.

Table 3. From the AIO to the CIO (some examples)

AIO	type	CIO
input field		edit text
single selector	1:n (n = const., $n \leq 7$)	group box + radio button
	1:n (n = const., $n > 7$)	list box
	1:n (n = variable)	list box
multiple selector	m:n (n = const., $n \leq 7$)	group box + check boxes
	m:n (n = const., $n > 7$)	list box
	m:n (n = variable)	list box

Table 4. Default layout description

AIO	background	foreground	font	cursor type
mask	white	black	mask font	arrow cursor
object group	grey	black	mask font	arrow cursor
input field	white	blue	text font	text cursor
action trigger	dark grey	black	button font	action cursor

Finally the internal data structure is transformed into a dialogue description file for the UIMS which is used to animate the resulting user interface and to demonstrate the prototype of the interactive software system. Figure 6 shows the GUI for the views *User Model* and *Role*.

Scenario of the use of the generated GUI. The end user dialogue starts with the TADEUS-window generated from the view *TADEUS* (here without representation). By an interaction in the TADEUS-window he starts to carry out the task *user modelling*. The User Model-window is opened. The snapshot of this window in figure 6 shows the state after the creation of the roles *clark* and *secretary*. Now the end user is creating the role *manager*. Furthermore he opened the Role-window for the role secretary in order to modify values of role attributes. He could open the Role-window for another role, e.g. the role *clerk*.

Finally we give the marking of the Dialogue graph for the described state of the GUI:

1. The view *TADEUS* is marked with (**v,m**).
2. The view *User Model* is marked with (**a,v,m**).
3. The view *Role* is marked with (**v,m**, secretary) and (**v,m**, clerk).

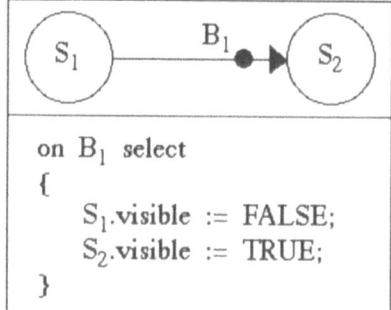 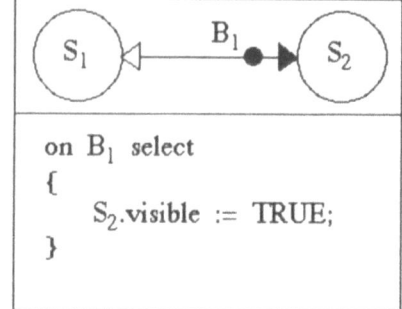

Fig. 5. Generation pattern

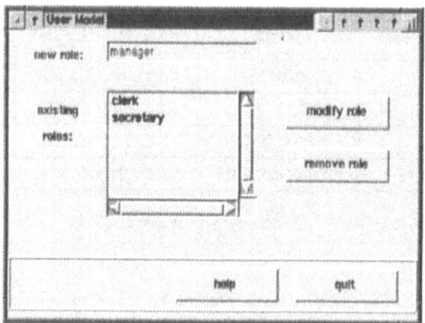 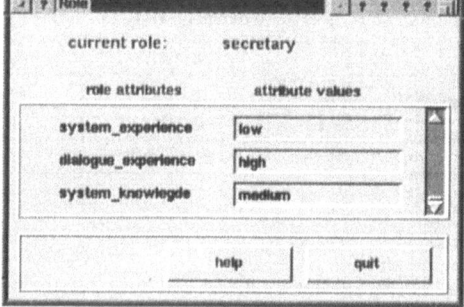

Fig. 6. GUI generated from the dialogue model

5   Conclusions

The TADEUS approach, a model-based approach for the development of GUI has been introduced briefly. It supports a homogeneous and continuous development process from the requirements analysis for an interactive software system to the generated user interface prototype. An explicit dialogue model is used. This approach allows the dialogue designer firstly, to use the results of the requirements analysis for the GUI-design directly, and secondly, to specify the dialogue structure in detail by using the TADEUS Dialogue graph. It is a high level and adequate graphical specification technique for window-oriented GUI. The specification can handle multiple window instances. Thirdly, a participatory design approach is only allowed by the automatic user interface generation, because the elaborated models are insufficient for direct end user involvement.

Another important aspect is the usage of existing software tools to implement the TADEUS environment. A Petri net tool will be used for the implementation of the Dialogue graph simulation. This is possible because the Dialogue graph can be mapped to an individual token net. With it the dialogue designer can check the quality of the specified Dialogue graph (e.g., correctness, deadlocks, liveliness). The mapping allows the dialogue designer to simulate the modelled user interface in an early state by an existing tool. Model errors can be found earlier, software production cost will become smaller. The GUI is generated for an existing UIMS (ISA Dialog Manager).

To sum up it can be said that the TADEUS approach offers a step to the direction of integration of user interface development in the field of software engineering.

Acknowledgements. This work is partially influenced by the EXPOSE research project. The project EXPOSE was supported by a grant from the Federal Ministry of Research and Development in Bonn under the Research Program "Arbeit und Technik" (01 HK 291). The work ideas are based on discussions with Peter Forbrig. The authors would like to thank Almut Brauer for the figures and Torsten Gebert, Olaf Gschweng and Marko Klein for the implementation of the graphical net editor.

Furthermore the authors would like to thank the anonymous reviewers for their helpful comments which contribute to the quality of this paper.

References

1. Balzert, H.: Das JANUS-System - Automatische, wissensbasierte Generierung von Mensch-Computer-Schnittstellen. Informatik Forsch. Entw. 9, 22–35 (1994).
2. Bastide, R., Palanque, P.: Petri Net Objects for the Design, Validation and Prototyping of User-Driven Interfaces. INTERACT'90 Conference Proceedings. Amsterdam: North-Holland 1990 (pp. 625–631).
3. Bay, C.: Analyse von Spezifikationsmitteln für graphische Dialoge zur Weiterentwicklung des THESEUS-Dialogmodells. Studienarbeit. TH Darmstadt, FB Informatik 1988.
4. Bodart, F., Hennebert, A.-M., Leheureux, J.-M., Vanderdonckt, J.: A Model-based Approach to Presentation: A Continuum from Task Analysis to Prototype. Proceedings 1. EG-Workshop on Design, Specification and Verification of Interactive Systems, Pisa 1994 (pp. 25–39).
5. CUA: Systems Application Architecture: Common User Access - Guide to User Interface Design, Advanced Interface Design Reference. IBM 1991.
6. deBaar, D.J.M.J., Foley, J.D., Mullet, K.E.: Coupling Application Design and User Interface Design. CHI '92 Conference Proceedings. New York: ACM 1992 (pp. 259–266).
7. DIN 66234 Bildschirmarbeitsplätze. Deutsches Institut für Normung. 1988.
8. Green, M.: A Survey of Three Dialogue Models. ACM Transactions on Graphics 5, 245–275 (1986).
9. Greutmann, T.: Datenmodellierung und aufgabengerechte Dialoge: ein Synchronisationsproblem. Proc. Software-Ergonomie '93. Stuttgart: Teubner 1993 (pp. 99–109).
10. Hartson, H.R., Boehm-Davis, D.: User interface development processes and methodologies. Behaviour & Information Technology 12, 98–114 (1993).

11. Hix, D.: Generations of User Interface Management Systems.
    IEEE Software 9, 77–87 (1990).
12. Jacob, R.J.K.: A Specification Language for Direct Manipulation User Interfaces.
    ACM Transaction on Graphics 5, 283-317 (1986).
13. Janssen, C.: Dialognetze zur Beschreibung von Dialogabläufen in graphisch-inter-
    aktiven Systemen. Proc. Software-Ergonomie '93. Stuttgart: Teubner 1993 (pp.
    67–76).
14. Janssen, C., Weisbecker, A., Ziegler, J.: Generating User Interfaces from Data
    Models and Dialogue Net Specifications. CHI '93 Conference Proceedings. New
    York: ACM 1993 (pp. 418–423).
15. Myers, B.A., Rosson, M.B.: Survey on User Interface Programming. CHI'92 Con-
    ference Proceedings. New York: ACM 1992 (pp. 195-202).
16. Olsen, D.R.: MIKE: The Menu Interaction Kontrol Environment. ACM Transac-
    tion on Graphics 5, 318–344 (1986).
17. OSF: OSF/Motif Style Guide Release 1.1. Open Software Foundation, 1991.
18. Reisig, W.: A Primer in Petri Net Design. Berlin: Springer 1992.
19. Roudaud, B., et.al.: A New Generation UIMS. INTERACT'90 Conference Pro-
    ceedings. Amsterdam: North-Holland 1990 (pp. 607–612).
20. Rumbaugh, J., et.al.: Objectoriented Modelling and Design. Englewood Cliffs:
    Prentice Hall 1991.
21. Schlungbaum, E., Schmidt, M.: Automatische Erzeugung von Beschreibungen für
    Benutzungsoberflächen. Rostocker Informatik Berichte 15, 97–106 (1994).
22. Schlungbaum, E., Elwert, T.: Modellierung von Graphischen Benutzungsober-
    flächen im Rahmen des TADEUS-Ansatzes. Proc. Software-Ergonomie '95.
    Stuttgart: Teubner 1995 (pp. 331–348).
23. Schlungbaum, E., Elwert, T.: TADEUS - a model-based Approach to the Devel-
    opment of Interactive Software Systems.
    Rostocker Informatik Berichte 17, 93–104 (1995).
24. Singh, G., Green, M.: Automating the Lexical and Syntactic Design of Graphical
    User Interfaces: The UofA* UIMS.
    ACM Transaction on Graphics 10 213–254 (1991).
25. Smith, S., Mosier, J.: Guidelines for Designing User Interface Software. Mitre Cor-
    poration 1986.
26. Stary, C.: Interaktive Systeme: Software-Entwicklung und Software-Ergonomie.
    Braunschweig, Wiesbaden: Vieweg 1994.
27. Sukaviriya, P., Foley, J.D., Griffith, T.: A Second Generation User Interface De-
    sign Environment: The Model and The Runtime Architecture. CHI '93 Conference
    Proceedings. New York: ACM 1993 (pp. 375–382).
28. van der Zanden, B., Myers, B.A.: Automatic, Look-and-Feel Independent Dialog
    Creation for Graphical User Interfaces. CHI '90 Conference Proceedings. New York:
    ACM 1990 (pp. 27–34).
29. Ziegler, J.: Entwurf graphischer Benutzungsschnittstellen. Ziegler, J., Ilg, R. (eds.)
    Benutzergerechte Software-Gestaltung: Standards, Methoden und Werkzeuge.
    München: Oldenbourg 1993 (pp. 145–169).

This article was processed using the LaTeX macro package with LLNCS style

Four different measures to quantify three usability attributes: 'feedback', 'interactive directness' and 'flexibility'

Matthias Rauterberg

Work and Organisational Psychology Unit (IfAP)
Swiss Federal Institute of Technology (ETH)
Nelkenstrasse 11, CH–8092 Zuerich, Switzerland
Tel: +41-1-63-27082, Email: rauterberg@ifap.bepr.ethz.ch

Abstract. One of the main problems of standards (e.g., DIN 66234, ISO 9241) in the context of usability of software quality is, that they can not be measured in product features. We present a new approach to measure user-interface quality in a quantitative way. First, we developed a concept to describe user-interfaces on a granularity level, that is detailed enough to preserve important interface characteristics, and is general enough to cover most of known interface types. We distinguish between different types of 'interaction-points'. With these kinds of interaction-points we can describe several types of interfaces (CUI: command, menu, form-fill-in; GUI: desktop, direct manipulation, multimedia, etc.). We carried out two different comparative usability studies to validate our quantitative measures. The results of one other published comparative usability study can be predicted. Results of six different interfaces are presented and discussed.

Keywords: user-interfaces, utility functions, testability, quantification

1 Introduction

One of the main problems of standards (e.g., DIN 66234, ISO 9241 Part 10) to quantify software quality of usability is, that they can not be measured in product features [11]. Four different views on human computer interaction to measure interactive qualities currently exists (cf. [1], [17]).

(1) The *interaction-oriented view:* usability quality is measured in terms of how the user interacts with the product ("usability testing"). This view is the most common one. All kinds of usability testing with "real" users are subsumed in this category [8].

(2) The *user-oriented view:* usability quality is measured in terms of the mental effort and attitude of the user ("questionnaires" and "interviews").

(3) The *product-oriented view:* usability quality is measured in terms of the ergonomic attributes of the product itself (quantitative measures).

(4) The *formal view:* usability is formalised and simulated in terms of mental models (formal concepts). Karat [10] describes formal methods in the context of "theory-based" evaluation.

The interactive qualities of user-interfaces currently are quantified in the context of *interaction-oriented view* and *user-oriented view*, but these both approaches are time consuming and more or less expensive [9].

It would be helpful if usability attributes could be quantified in such a way that the extent of each attribute could be measured in product features. Levels of measurement

210

are classified in different scales as follows (cf. Tab. 1): (1) *nominal scale* (to classify or grouping interfaces), (2) *ordinal scale* (to compare different types of interfaces and to put categories in order), (3) *interval scale* (meaningful measure of the distance between categories), and (4) *rational scale* (interval scale with an absolute null) (cf. [12]).

Tab. 1. Levels of measurement of usability attributes

level	examples in the context of Human-Computer Interaction	reference
nominal	Type of interface (e.g., command, menu, desktop, etc.)	[18]
ordinal	Experimental comparison study (e.g., summative evaluation)	[3] [7] [15]
interval	Checklist (e.g., expert evaluation)	[11] [18]
rational	Quantitative measure	[16]

2   A descriptive concept of interaction-points

We present a new approach to measure user-interface quality in a quantitative way. First, we developed a concept to describe user-interfaces on a granularity level, that is detailed enough to preserve important interface characteristics, and is general enough to cover most of known interface types (command language, CUI, GUI, multimedia, etc.). Different types of user-interfaces can be quantified and distinguished by the general concept of "interaction-points". Regarding to the interactive semantic of "interaction-points" (IPs), different types of IPs must be discriminated (cf. [4]).

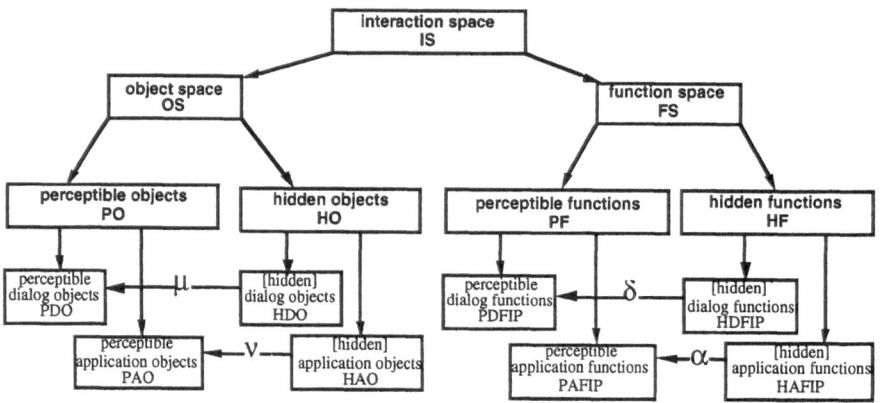

Fig. 1. The interaction space (IS) consists of the object space (OS) and the function space (FS); both spaces can be distinguished in perceptible and hidden interactive elements.

An interactive system can be distinguished in a dialog and an application manager. So, we distinguish between dialog objects (DO, e.g. "window") and application objects (AO, e.g. "text document"), and dialog functions (DF, e.g. "open window") and application functions (AFIP, e.g. "insert section mark"). Each function f∈ FS, that changes the state of the content of an application object, is an *application function*. All other functions are *dialog functions* (e.g., window operations like move, resize, close). The complete set of all description terms is shown in Fig. 1 and defined in Tab. 2.

Tab. 2. The interaction space (IS) consists of the object (OS) and the function (FS) space

IS := OS x FS	[interaction space]
DC ∈ IS	[dialog context]
OS := PO ∪ HO	[object space]
FS := PF ∪ HF	[function space]
PO := PDO ∪ PAO	[(perceptible) representations of objects]
HO := HDO ∪ HAO	[hidden objects]
PF := PDFIP ∪ PAFIP	[(perceptible) representations of functions]
HF := HDFIP ∪ HAFIP	[hidden functions]
PDFIP := {(df, pf) ∈ HDFIP x PF: pf = δ(df)}	[(perceptible) represented DFIP]
PAFIP := {(af, pf) ∈ HAFIP x PF: pf = α(af)}	[(perceptible) represented AFIP]
IP := DFIP ∪ AFIP	[interaction-points]
DFIP := PDFIP ∪ HDFIP	[IPs of dialog functions]
AFIP := PAFIP ∪ HAFIP	[IPs of application functions]

δ := mapping function of a df ∈ HDFIP to an appropriate pf ∈ PF.
α := mapping function of an af ∈ HAFIP to an appropriate pf ∈ PF.

PDO := {(do, po) ∈ HDO x PO: po = μ(do)}	[(perceptible) represented DO]
PAO := {(ao, po) ∈ HAO x PO: po = ν(ao)}	[(perceptible) represented AO]

μ := mapping function of a dialog object do ∈ DO to an appropriate po ∈ PO.
ν := mapping function of an application object ao ∈ AO to an appropriate po ∈ PO.

A dialog context (DC) is defined by all available objects and functions in the actual system state. If the set of available functions changes in the actual DC, then the system changes from one DC to another. In the actual DC all dialog objects (functions, resp.) are *perceptible* (PO, PF) or *hidden* (HO, HF). Four different mapping functions relate perceptible structures to hidden objects or functions (see Fig. 1).

Each interaction-point (IP) is related to at least one interactive function. If both mapping function's δ and α are of the type 1:m(any), then the user-interface is a command interface (see Fig. 2). If both mapping function's δ and α are of the type 1:1, then the user-interface is a menu or direct manipulative interface where each f∈FS is related to a perceptible structure PF (see Fig. 3). The perceptual structure (visible, audible, or tactile) of a function (PF) can be, e.g., an icon, earcon, menu option, command prompt, or other mouse sensitive areas.

The intersection of PF and PO is sometimes not empty: PF ∩ PO ≠ ∅. Icons of graphical interfaces are elements of this intersection, e.g., PDFIP "copy" ≡ PDO "clipboard", PAFIP "delete" ≡ PAO "trash" (see Fig. 3). Each interaction-point (IP) is related to at least one interactive function (see Fig. 4).

3 Four quantitative measures of interface attributes

One important difference between user-interfaces can be the "interactive directness". A user-interface is 100% *interactively direct*, if the user has fully access in the actual dialog context to all f∈FS (see [13], e.g. [20]). This is the case for all command language interfaces (cf. Fig. 2). Another important interface attribute is the amount of "feedback". Good interface design is characterised by optimising the multitude of

DFIPs (e.g. "flatten" the menu tree; see [14]) and by allocating an appropriate PDFIP to the remaining HDFIPs (cf. [2]).

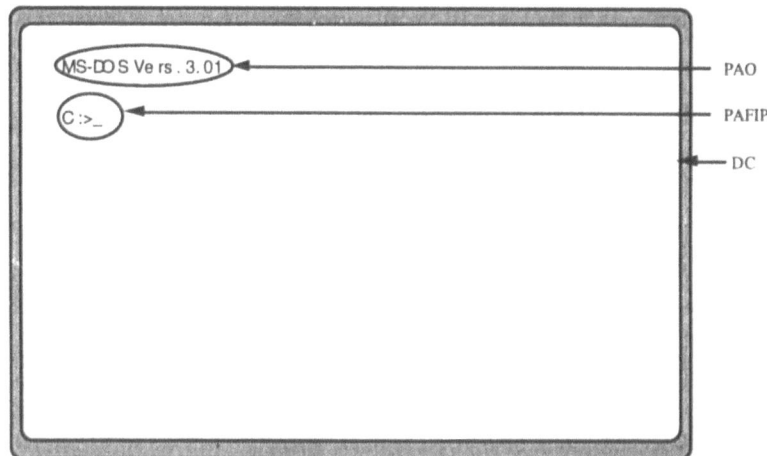

Fig. 2. An actual dialog context (DC) of the operating system MsDOS with a command language interface (PAFIP: command entry point).

One disadvantage of snapshots (cf. Fig. 2 and Fig. 3) is that all hidden structures could not be referenced. To describe the hidden functionality a schematic view is needed (cf. Fig. 4).

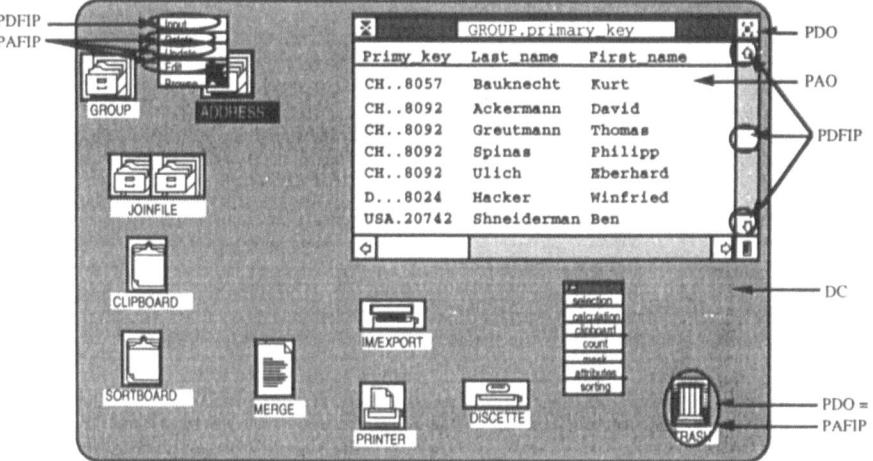

Fig. 3. An actual dialog context (DC) of a direct manipulative interface with the representation space of the interactive object (PAO: e.g., data window; PDO: e.g., trash), and the representation space (PF: marked by circles) of the interactive functions (PAFIP: e.g., pop-up menu, trash; PDFIP: e.g., window scrolling).

To estimate the amount of "feedback" of an interface a ratio is calculated: "number of PFs" (#PF = #PDFIP + #PAFIP) divided by the "number of HFs" (#HF = #HDFIP +

#HAFIP) per dialog context. This ratio quantifies the average "amount of functional feedback" of the function space (FB; see Formula 1). We abbreviate the number of all different dialog contexts with D. A GUI has often a very large number of DCs. To handle this problem we take only all task related DCs into account. Doing this, our measures will give us only a lower estimation for GUIs.

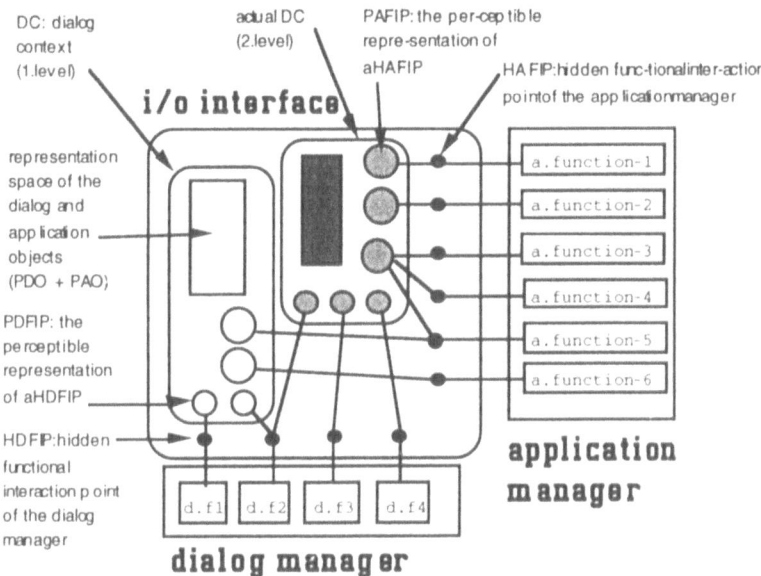

Fig. 4. A schematic presentation of the I/O interface, the dialog and the application manager of an interactive system with a menu tree of two levels.

The average length of all possible sequences of interactive operations (PATH) from the top level dialog context (DC, e.g., 'start context') down to DCs with the desired HAFIP or HDFIP can be used as a possible quantitative measure of "interactive directness" (ID, see Formula 2). The measure ID delivers two indices: one for HAFIPs and one for HDFIPs. A PATH has no cycles and has not more than two additional dialog operations compared with the shortest sequence. An interface with the maximum ID of 100% has only one DC with path lengths of one dialog step. We abbreviate the number of all different dialog paths with P.

Functional feedback:
$$FB = \frac{1}{D} \sum_{d=1}^{D} (\#PF_d/\#HF_d) * 100\%$$
(1)

Interactive directness:
$$ID = \left\{ \frac{1}{P} \sum_{p=1}^{P} \ln(PATH_p) \right\}^{-1} * 100\%$$
(2)

To quantify the flexibility of the application manager we calculate the average number of HAFIPs per dialog context (DFA; see Formula 3). To quantify the flexibility of the dialog manager we calculate the average number of HDFIPs per dialog context

(DFD; see Formula 4). A modeless dialog state has maximal flexibility (e.g., "command" interfaces, or Oberon; [20]).

Application flexibility: $$DFA = \frac{1}{D} \sum_{d=1}^{D} (\# HAFIP_d) \qquad (3)$$

Dialog flexibility: $$DFD = \frac{1}{D} \sum_{d=1}^{D} (\# HDFIP_d) \qquad (4)$$

Let us apply the five measures to our example in Fig. 4. The average amount of functional feedback is:
FB = (4/4 + 6/9) / 2 * 100% = 83.3 %.

The average amount of interactive directness is:
$ID_{HAFIP} = ((2*1 + 5*2) / 7)^{-1} * 100\% = 58.3 \%$;
$ID_{HDFIP} = ((2*1 + 3*2) / 5)^{-1} * 100\% = 62.5 \%$.

The average amount of flexibility is:
DFA = (2 + 5) / 2 = 3.5 and
DFD = (2 + 3) / 2 = 2.5.

To interpret the results of our measure's appropriately empirical studies are necessary.

4 Results and discussions of three empirical studies

We carried out two different comparative usability studies to validate our measures ([3] [15]). A third external comparative study [7] was used for a cross-validation. All three investigated software products have the same application manager, but two different dialog managers each.

4.1 Experiment-I

Method. Rauterberg [15] compared a traditional menu-driven interface (character-oriented user-interface: CUI; cf. Fig. 5) of a relational database management system with a modern desktop interface (graphic-oriented user-interface: GUI; cf. Fig. 6) of the same application manager. We chose this program, because there are two different types of interfaces for the same database machine running on the same hardware (DOS PCs). Both types of interfaces are distributed as standard software on the European market.

Subjects. Twelve paid beginners (novice and naive, see [5]) took part in this study. The twelve experts (experienced and expert) had been working with the respective user-interface for several years in their daily work; they were chosen from the address list of the software company. The experts did not receive any payment; the beginners were paid. The previous experience was carefully measured with a questionnaire during a semi structured interview (average duration for the interviews with the experts: 40-50 min).

CUI-beginners: average age of 27 years; 4 women, 2 men; 31 hrs. of general previous experience with EDP; 1.5 hrs. of instruction.

CUI-experts: average age of 38 years; 6 men; 7.500 hrs. of general previous experience with EDP; 1.736 hrs. of experience with specific user-interface (menu-selection).

GUI-beginners: average age of 21years; 2 women, 4 men; 68 hrs. of general previous experience with EDP; 1.5 hrs. of instruction.

GUI-experts: average age of 38 years; 6 men; 3.700 hrs. of general previous experience with EDP; 1.496 hrs. of experience with specific user-interface (desktop).

Independent Factors. The test design is characterised by three independent factors: (1) two diffent interfaces (Factor-A: CUI vs. GUI), (2) ten different tasks (Factor-B: task-1, task-2, ..., task-10), and (3) the different experience of the test subjects (Factor-C: beginners vs. experts).

The CUI interface consists of a strict hierarchical menu tree with exact three levels (like MsWord, cf. Fig. 3). Starting with the main menu (level 1) the user can make active each module (level 2) by pressing the corresponding letter key. In the dialogue context of a module the different routines (level 3) can be activated by pressing another letter key. On main menu or module level only, help, global switches, the active data base file, and redirection input or output could be activated or changed using the function keys. In an activated routine context the dialogue control could be achieved alone by pressing function keys.

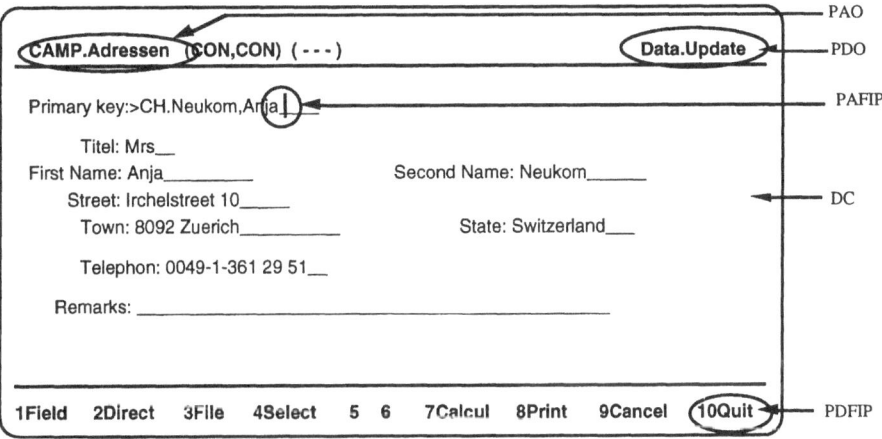

Fig. 5. The CUI interface of the data base management system with the representation space of the interactive objects (PAO: e.g., data file name; PDO: e.g., module name.routine name), and the representation space of the interactive functions (PAFIP: e.g., text entry point; PDFIP: e.g., function key F10).

The GUI interface is implemented under GEM on DOS PCs (cf. Fig. 6). The screen of the desktop interface is divided into four different areas. The row at the top of the screen contains the semantic labels of all pull-down menus (first area). The second row just below is an output or 'info area' (second area). The biggest part is the desktop area with all icons, windows, and dialogboxes (third area). The bottom row is a string of all semantic labels for all function keys. Each label field (F1 to F10) is a mouse sensitive area, too (fourth area). The dialogue of this typical type of desktop interface can be controlled by pull-down menus and partly by function keys, as well.

Dependent measures. The dependent variable was the pure 'task solving time' of each user according to logfile record excluding system response time; the control variables were: the number of hours of general previous experience with EDP (included specific experience with the two different systems).

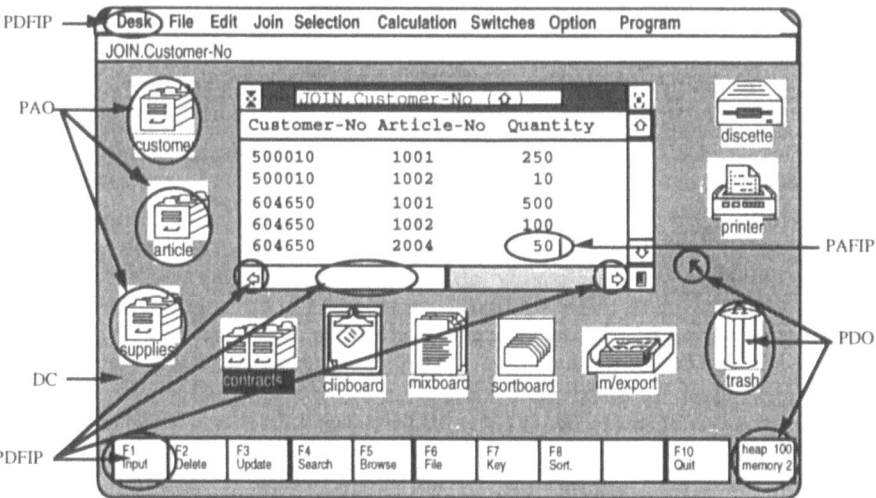

Fig. 6. The GUI interface of the data base management system with the representation space of the interactive objects (PAO: e.g., data files; PDO: e.g., mouse pointer, trash), and the representation space of the interactive functions (PAFIP: e.g., data entry point; PDFIP: e.g., pull down menu, function key F1, scroll bar areas).

Tasks. Ten tasks were selected according to whether they allowed the subjects to use exactly the same functionality of the application manager with both types of interfaces and to use those operations which are most common in daily data base work. The test data base consisted of three files, which contained all necessary attributes to manage a camping place. Tasks 9 and 10 were selected to test whether the design of the user-interface was appropriate for these types of tasks, too.

Task 1: "Please find out how many data records are in the file ADDRESS, in the file PLACE, and in the file GROUP." The user has to activate a specific menu option ("File info...") of the desktop interface; resp. "Datafile" in module "Info" of the menu interface) and to read the file size (file: ADDRESS - 280 data records, PLACE - 17 data records, GROUP - 27 data records).

Task 2: "Delete only the last data record of the file ADDRESS, the file PLACE, and the file GROUP (sorted by the attribute 'namekey')." The user has to open (sorted according to the given attribute), select and delete the last data record (file: PLACE, ADDRESS, GROUP).

Task 3: "Search and select the data record with the namekey 'D..8000C O M' in the file ADDRESS, and show the content of all attributes of this data record on the screen. Correct this data record for the following attributes: State: D, Place offer: 07, Remarks: The system dealer can give a demonstration." The user must select a certain data record (file: ADDRESS), correcting the data record with regard to three attributes.

The seven remaining tasks are completely described in [15].

Results. At the start the results were analysed from the point of view of a three-factorial design across only the first six tasks (Factor-A "interface", Factor-B "task (1-6)", and Factor-C "expertness"). In the 90 minutes most of the beginners were not able to finish more than the first six (or eight at most) of the tasks given, so that the tasks 8 to 10 were excluded from this analysis. Almost all experts were able to finish all the ten tasks given.

Tab. 3. Results of the dependent variable 'task solving time' of the comparison study CUI vs. GUI; the alpha-error is abbreviated with p

Dependent variable: 'Task solving time'	Mean ± Standard Deviation		Effect
	CUI (N=6)	GUI (N=6)	p
beginners	1073 s ± 590 s	670 s ± 490 s	< .002
experts	414 s ± 245 s	201 s ± 137 s	< .001
total	683 s ± 556 s	418 s ± 437 s	< .001

The main result of this empirical investigation was, that the mean task solving time with the GUI (experts: 201 s, beginners: 670 s) is significantly shorter than with the CUI (experts: 414 s, beginners: 1073 s) interface for beginners and experts, too (see Tab. 3). For all the first six tasks the users of the GUI interface needed less time to solve the tasks than the users with the CUI interface.

Discussion. Contrary to the often voiced opinion that a desktop interface with direct manipulation is good for beginners only, it is the expert group with the desktop interface who has profit of GUI's, too. Compared to them the beginners with menu selection had particularly bad results.

No specific dependency between the previous experience with EDP and the different types of tasks can be assumed. Generally it was not clear in which way the restriction on database handling applied in this investigation was responsible for the results found in this study.

On the whole it is to be emphasised that a desktop interface with direct manipulation by means of the "mouse" as a general element of interaction was superior to the conventional user-interface with menu selection by means of the "function keys". This is true particularly for users with long previous database experience (experts).

How can we explain the observed advantage of the GUI? Our first interpretation of this outcome was the supposed different amount of 'transparency' [19]. One aspect of 'transparency' is 'feedback' (see [6] pp. 318-321). But, if we take the results of our quantification into account, then we can assume that the different amount of flexibility is the critical quality.

4.2 Experiment-II

Method. The second experiment was run on a PC with colour screen. The standard Windows 3.0 environment with a multimedia information system of a German bank association with a hierarchical dialog structure was used. The original version was developed by the German multimedia software house ADI Inc. in Karlsruhe (D). The second version of this multimedia system was redesigned and programmed at our usability laboratory to get a system with a net-shaped dialog structure.

Subjects. A total of 12 beginners participated. Group-A consists of one woman and five men with the average age 24.2 ± 0.4 years. Group-B consists of two women and four men with the average age 22.5 ± 0.8 years. Group-A tested first the original version and in a second trial the redesigned version. Group-B tested both systems in reverse order.

Independent Factors. The test design is characterised by three independent factors: (1) two different interfaces (Factor-A: graphical interface with a hierarchical dialog structure GUI_{hier} vs. graphical interface with a net-shaped dialog structure GUI_{net}), (2) nine different tasks (Factor-B: task-1, task-2, ..., task-9), and (3) the different sequence of testing both systems (Factor-C: GUI_{hier} ->GUI_{net} vs. GUI_{net} ->GUI_{hier}).

The original version consists of 62 different screens (masks) with on average 11.6 ± 5.1 objects per screen (number of all objects is 721; cf. Fig. 7). The second version consists of 51 different screens (masks) with on average 13.2 ± 4.9 objects per screen (number of all objects is 672).

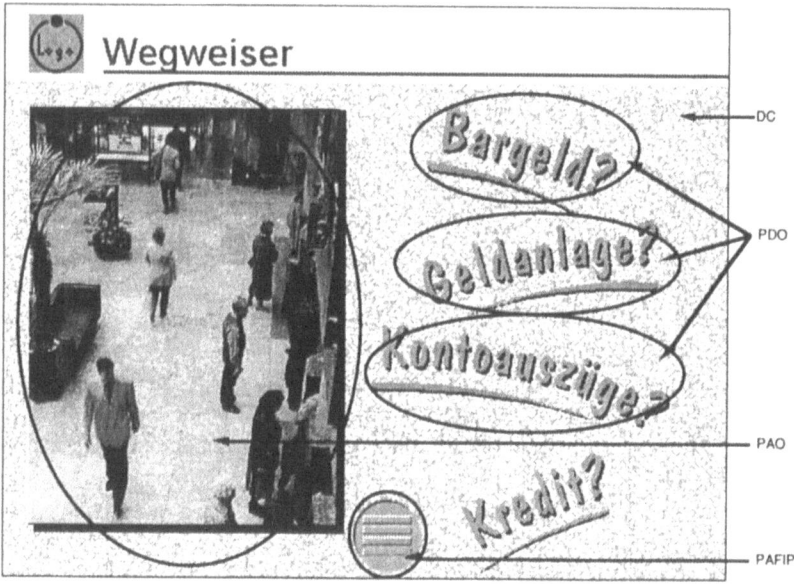

Fig. 7. The graphical interface of the multimedia information system with the representation space of the interactive objects (PAO: e.g., picture of entrance hall; PDO: e.g., several topics), and the representation space of the interactive functions (PAFIP: e.g., button to next screen).

Dependent measures. The two dependent variables were 'task solving time' per task and 'number of masks successions' over all nine tasks.

Tasks. Subjects were instructed to solve nine tasks: «(1) Search a house for a price of 450,000.– DM. (2) Who is responsibly for the sales talk about an estate? (3) Where is the office of this person located in the building? (4) To buy the house you need a mortgage. Where can you get this? (5) Where can you get information about buying and selling of securities? (6) The bank offers different events of entertainment. You have a free day (April, 7th, 1993). Which events are offered? (7) You have not enough cash and you are nearby the main station. Where is the next cash service? (8) Where is the cash counter located in the building? (9) Which spectrum of services are available at the cash service desk?»

Results. The multimedia information system with the net-shaped dialog structure (GUI$_{net}$) is not superior to the system with the hierarchical dialog structure (GUI$_{hier}$). It seems to be that the users of the 'more flexible' system need more time to solve the tasks (cf. Tab. 4).

To make sure that this result is not biased by an unknown aspect the experiment was carried out a second time. The results are exactly the same as in the first investigation.

Tab. 4. Results of the two dependent variables of the comparison study GUI$_{hier}$ vs. GUI$_{net}$; the alpha-error is abbreviated with p

Dependent variable:	Mean ± Standard Deviation		Effect
	GUI$_{hier}$ (N=6)	GUI$_{net}$ (N=6)	p
'Task solving time'	9.7 min ± 3.8 min	10.8 min ± 4.3 min	< .085
'#masks successions'	54 ± 15 masks	56 ± 19 masks	< .625

Discussion. The comparison of both multimedia interfaces could not show an empirical provable difference between the hierarchical and the net-shaped dialog structure. The amount of feedback is for both interfaces identically: each HF has at least one PF. If we could show a performance difference then this difference must be caused by the type of dialog structure. But, we can not find a difference between both versions in task solving time or in number of masks successions (cf. Tab. 4).

4.3 Experiment-III

Method. The study of Grützmacher [7] was carried out to investigate research questions in the context of how to control a complex domain ('development aid for a fictive society in Africa') with the simulation tool "Moro". Two different dialog structures (hierarchical vs. net-shaped) with the same CUI interface were compared (cf. Fig. 8). The program was implemented on a host computer and could be used during six months. This host computer was installed for public access at the University of Zurich. Each session was automatically recorded. Only the first simulation session is included in the further analysis. All second or more sessions are excluded.

Subjects. The sample consists of 20 unknown users with the hierarchical dialog structure (average age 25 ± 3 years) and 15 unknown users with the net-shaped structure (average age 28 ± 6 years).

Independent Factors. One independent factor was varied: the dialog structure (Factor A: hierarchical CUI$_{hier}$ versus net-shaped CUI$_{net}$ dialog structure). This simulation tool was implemented on a mainframe computer system with character oriented terminals (IBM 3270). The simulation tool was controlled by several parameters (e.g., 'number of inhabitants', 'number of cows', 'capital stock', etc.).

Dependent measures. At the end of each simulation run the absolute difference between the actual value and the targeted value of all eight parameters was calculated and divided by the targeted value ('percental difference'). The dependent variable 'target discrepancy' was the average of all eight percental differences.

Tasks. The user was instructed to meet several targets, one for each of eight different parameters (e.g., 'number of inhabitants' = 800, 'number of cows' = 4000, etc.). To control the simulation the user could change 49 different parameters. In CUI$_{net}$ each of all 49 parameters was presented in exactly one mask per parameter. In CUI$_{hier}$ several parameters could be changed in more than one mask.

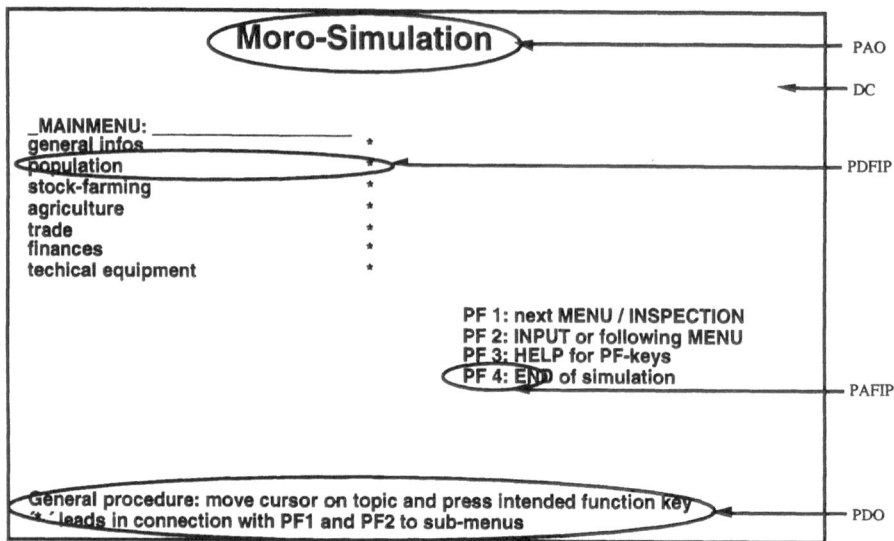

Fig. 8. The CUI-interface of the simulation tool with the representation space of the interactive objects (PAO: e.g., name of the tool; PDO: e.g., context sensitive help text), and the representation space of the interactive functions (PAFIP: e.g., function key END; PDFIP: e.g., menu option).

Results. The net-shaped dialog structure was not superior to the hierarchical dialog structure (cf. Tab. 5). This study showed similar results as in the second experiment.

Tab. 5. Results of the dependent variable 'target discrepancy' of the comparison study CUI_{hier} vs. CUI_{net}; the alpha-error is abbreviated with p

	Mean ± Standard Deviation		Effect
Dependent variable:	CUI_{hier} *(N=20)*	CUI_{net} *(N=15)*	*p*
'Target discrepancy'	49% ± 15%	48% ± 18%	< .825

The average number of 'simulation years' was for CUI_{hier} = 19 ± 7 and for CUI_{net} = 27 ± 10 'years' (T-test, p < .043). The users played significantly 'longer' with CUI_{net} than with CUI_{hier}.

Discussion. The hypothesis of Grützmacher [5] was that the net-shaped dialog structure is superior to the hierarchical structure. The study showed no differences between both dialog structures measured with "target discrepancy" as a performance measure. Grützmacher presented no explanation for this negative result.

5 Results of applying the measures

Interesting is the fact, that the GUI of experiment-I supports the user with less "visual feedback" (FB = 66%, see Tab. 6) on average than the CUI (FB = 73%). This amount of FB of the CUI is caused by 22 small DCs with FB = 100%; the GUI has only 14 DCs with FB = 100%. The amount of functional feedback seems not to be related to the advantage of GUIs. There must be another reason.

The "interactive directness" is not quite different between both interfaces:
CUI: ID = 24.7% for AFIPs and 23.2% for DFIPs versus
GUI: ID = 22.5% for AFIPs and 25.5% for DFIPs (see Tab. 6).

Only the two measures of "flexibility" show an important difference:
CUI: DFA = 12.1 and DFD = 10.1 versus
GUI: DFA = 19.5 and DFD = 20.4 (see Tab. 6).

In the hierarchical dialog structure of the multimedia information system (experiment-II) only one way is given to reach an AFIP. In the net-shaped version several ways are possible to navigate through the dialog structure. But, what is an AFIP in the context of a multimedia system? What is the application kernel?

We define the *application kernel* of a multimedia information system as the set of all masks with a relevant information in the sense of the main purpose of the information system (e.g., concrete information's about bank services in the context of a bank information system); all other masks are part of the dialog manager. A PAFIP is therefore each mouse sensitive area that changes the system to a mask of the application kernel; all other buttons or mouse sensitive areas are DFIP's.

Tab. 6. Comparison our three empirical validation studies relating to the quantitative measures ID, FB, DFA, and DFD. P is the number of all different dialog PATHs for an AFIP or a DFIP; D is the number of all different DCs

Expe-riment	Interface type and dialog structure	$P_{(AFIP)}$	$ID_{(AFIP)}$ %	$P_{(DFIP)}$	$ID_{(DFIP)}$ %	D	FB %	DFA	DFD
I	CUI-hierarchical	434	24.7	362	23.2	36	73	12.1	10.1
I	GUI-hierarchical	547	22.5	570	25.5	28	66	19.5	20.4
II	Multimedia-hierarchical	241	25.1	34	28.1	68	100	3.6	0.5
II	Multimedia-net shaped	276	40.7	87	46.3	65	100	4.2	1.3
III	CUI-hierarchical	720	20.9	693	23.9	363	86	2.0	1.9
III	CUI-net shaped	490	15.8	1053	21.9	389	90	1.3	2.7

With the generous support of Grützmacher we were able to analyse all 752 dialog contexts for both interfaces of the simulation tool 'Moro' (cf. experiment-III). For the hierarchical CUI we get the following results: DFA = 2.0 and DFD = 1.9; for the net-shaped CUI: DFA = 1.3 and DFD = 2.7 (see last two rows in Tab. 6). These results for DFA and DFD of both CUI interfaces give us a strong empirical evidence that the following assumptions are correct:

(1) The dialog flexibility can be quantitatively measured in a task independent way, and
(2) the values of DFA and DFD must exceed the threshold of 15.

6 Discussion

If our interpretation of the outcome of experiment-I is correct then we can not find a significant performance difference for dialog structures that remain under the assumed threshold of 15. To control the factor of feedback we carried out the second experiment with a multimedia information system that has 100% functional feedback for both interfaces [3].

We picked out a multimedia information system with a hierarchical dialog structure where DFA and DFD are clearly under 15. We implemented a comparable system with a net-shaped dialog structure where DFA and DFD have nearly the same ratio of flexibility as in experiment-I:

$DFA_{GUI} / DFA_{CUI} = 1.6$ and $DFA_{MMnet} / DFA_{MMhier} = 1.2$;

$DFD_{GUI} / DFD_{CUI} = 2.0$ and $DFD_{MMnet} / DFD_{MMhier} = 2.6$.

As we predicted, we can not find a significant performance difference between both types of dialog structures (see Tab. 4). To make sure that our results are not biased by our own expectations, we carried out a cross validation study. To do this, (1) we need the outcomes of an external independent comparison study between two different interfaces and (2) the possibility to apply our quantitative measures to all DCs of both interfaces. The empirical investigation of Grützmacher [7] fulfils both conditions.

Given our interpretation of the last two experiments we expected and found a value for DFA and DFD under 15. We interpret the negative result of experiment-III to the effect that flexibility must exceed a threshold to be effective (DFD, DFA > 15).

7   Conclusion

Using the quantitative measures for "feedback", "interactive directness" and "flexibility" to measure the interactive quality of user-interfaces, we are able to classify the most common types: command, menu, desktop. The command interface is characterised by high interactive directness, but this interface type has a very low amount of visual feedback. Especially graphical interfaces (e.g., multimedia) can support users with sufficient interactive directness. GUIs are characterised by high dialog flexibility.

The presented approach to quantify usability attributes and the interactive quality of user-interfaces is a first step in the right direction. The next step is a more detailed analysis of the relevant characteristics and validation of these characteristics in further empirical investigations. In the context of standardisation we can use our criteria to test user-interfaces for conformity with standards.

Acknowledgements: We have to thank the following persons for their generous support: Dr. Karl Schlagenhauf and Raimund Mollenhauer at ADI Software Inc., Karlsruhe (D), Prof. Kurt Bauknecht at the University of Zürich, Andreas Grützmacher and Prof. Eberhard Ulich at the ETH, Zürich (CH).

8   References

1. Bevan, N., J. Kirakowski and J. Maissel: What is Usability? In: H-J. Bullinger (ed.): Human Aspects in Computing: Design and Use of Interactive Systems with Terminals. Amsterdam: Elsevier 1991, pp. 651-655.
2. Bodart, F. and Vanderdonckt, J. M.: On the problems of selecting interaction objects. In: G. Cockton, S. Draper & G. Weir (eds.): People and Computers IX. Cambridge: Cambridge University Press 1994, pp. 163-178.
3. Brunner, M. and M. Rauterberg: Hierarchische oder netzartige Dialogstruktur bei multimedialen Informationsystemen: eine experimentelle Vergleichsstudie. Technical Report MM-2-93. Institut für Arbeitspsychologie, Zürich: Eidgenössische Technische Hochschule (1993).

4. Denert, E.: Specification and design of dialogue systems with state diagrams. In: E. Morlet and D. Ribbens (eds.): International Computing Symposium '77. Amsterdam: North-Holland 1977, pp. 417-424.

5. Fisher, J.: Defining the novice user. Behaviour and Information Technology 10(5), 437-441 (1991).

6. Dix, A., J. Finlay, G.: Abowd and R. Beale: Human-Computer Interaction. New York: Prentice Hall (1993).

7. Grützmacher, B.: Datenpräsentation und Lösungsverhalten in einer komplexen, simulierten Problemsituation. Unpublished Master Thesis. (Philosophische Fakultät I, Psychologisches Institut, Abteilung Angewandte Psychologie). Zürich: Universität Zürich (1988).

8. IFIP: Report of the 1st Meeting of the European User Environment Subgroup of IFIP WF 6.5. German National Center for Computer Science (GMD), P.O. 1316, D-5202 Sankt Augustin (Germany) (1981).

9. Jeffries, R. and H. Desurvire: Usability testing vs. heuristic evaluation: was there a contest? SIGCHI Bulletin 24(4), 39-41 (1992).

10. Karat, J.: Software Evaluation Methodologies. In: M. Helander (ed.): Handbook of Human-Computer Interaction. Amsterdam: Elsevier 1988, pp. 891-903.

11. Kirakowski, J. and M. Corbett: Effective Methodology for the Study of HCI. In: H. Bullinger and P. Polson (eds.): Human Factors in Information Technology vol. 5. Amsterdam: North-Holland (1990).

12. Kleinbaum, D. and Kupper, L.: Applied Regression Analysis and other Multivariate Methods. Belmont: Wadsworth (1978).

13. Laverson, A., K. Norman and B. Shneiderman: An evaluation of jump-ahead technique in menu selection. Behaviour and Information Technology 6(2), 97-108, (1987).

14. Paap, K. and R. Roske-Hofstrand: Design of menus. In: M. Helander (ed.): Handbook of Human-Computer Interaction. Amsterdam: Elsevier 1988, pp. 205-235.

15. Rauterberg, M.: An empirical comparison of menu-selection (CUI) and desktop (GUI) computer programs carried out by beginners and experts. Behaviour and Information Technology 11(4), 227-236 (1992).

16. Rauterberg, M.: Quantitative Measures to Evaluate Human-Computer Interfaces. In: M. Smith and G. Salvendy (eds.): Human-Computer Interaction: Applications and Case Studies. Amsterdam: Elsevier 1993 (Advances in Human Factors/ Ergonomics vol. 19A, pp. 612-617).

17. Rengger, R.: Indicators of usability based on performance. In: H-J. Bullinger (ed.): Human Aspects in Computing: Design and Use of Interactive Systems with Terminals. Amsterdam: Elsevier 1991, pp. 656-660.

18. Shneiderman, B.: Designing the user-interface. Amsterdam: Addison-Wesley (1987).

19. Ulich, E., M. Rauterberg, T. Moll, T. Greutmann and O. Strohm: Task orientation and user-oriented dialog design. International Journal of Human-Computer Interaction 3(2), 117-144 (1991).

20. Wirth, N. and J. Gutknecht: Project Oberon - The design of an operating system and compiler. Reading (MA): Addison-Wesley (1992).

Proving the Correctness of
Formal User Interface Specifications

Bernhard Bauer

Institut für Informatik, Technische Universität München,
Arcisstr. 21, D-80290 München, Germany

Abstract. Formal grammars, task action grammars and attribute grammars are widely accepted approaches for the specification of dialogues of interactive systems. In this paper we present a formal specification technique - based on attribute grammars - coupling dialogue specifications with application and layout specifications. For this specification formalism a proof principle and an analyzing technique is provided and applied to a user interface specification of an ISDN telephone. Properties can be shown between the interaction of a user and the behaviour of the system. The used specification technique allows e.g. to show that there are dialogues such that a special action can be performed, e.g. a menu-item can be selected and e.g. that the application has a special state after a distinguished action.

1 Introduction

Nowadays nearly every software project has to deal with the implementation of user interfaces, since the end-users of such systems are often computer novices using only the program with little or less knowledge about the computer technology. But the development of a graphical user interface is a very critical point in the software engineering process, since the complete interaction between the user and the application is via the user interface. Having a correct proven application and an incorrect user interface the result would be damnable. Therefore formal methods must be designed in the framework of user interface development to consider correctness aspects. These methods must be supported by tools to be usable in real projects. Using formal methods allows further the generation of user interfaces out of a declarative description (model) of the properties of an interactive application. Those generation aspects can be found in the model based user interface tools (e.g. [4, 5, 6, 14, 15, 20, 27, 28]). The specification formalism applied in this paper can be used (under some restrictions) as an input for the system presented in [27, 28] for the generation of a presentation and dialogue control component of an interactive system.

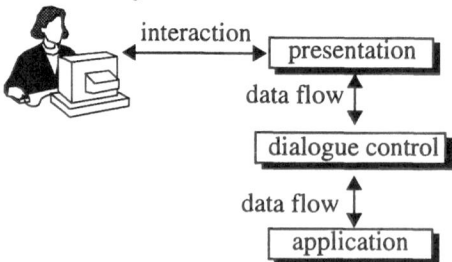

fig. 1 visualization of the three layers of a program with a user interface

Considering a whole application with a user interface three layers have to be distinguished (see fig. 1):

- The specification of the *presentation* (layout) the user is interacting with.
- The specification of the *dialogues* or *tasks* (dynamics) describing all possible dialogues, independent of the layout as in [13].
- The specification of the *application* offering an appointed functionality which must be supported by the user interface.

This paper focuses on the formal specification of dialogues and its effects on the application. Therefore it is possible to prove properties not only about the dialogues but also about its effects on the application. The new specification formalism is a mixture of attribute grammars and algebraic specifications. Formal grammars were already used in [26] for the description of dialogues. [19, 25, 29] developed (extended) task action grammars, being special cases of attribute grammars, encoding more semantical informations in grammars. Specifying the semantic functions of an attribute grammar algebraically, i.e. by axioms, theorem proving techniques can be applied. Having on the one side the mechanizable theorem proving techniques of algebraic specifications and on the other side the analyzing techniques for grammars allows the development of powerful tools for the consideration of correctness aspects of user interfaces.

The new aspects presented in this paper are: Using attributed algebraic specifications for the linking of dialogue descriptions to applications, a mechanizable proof principle for the specification formalism which is more powerful than the other approaches for attribute grammars and algebraic specifications. Standard techniques for grammars are adapted to user interface verification.

Interesting correctness aspects for user interface specifications are:

- does the dialogue description offer all (exported) application functions,
- is it possible to perform an action at all,
- is an action reachable from another action,
- does the application have a given state before/after a special action is performed,
- does a special property hold before an action is performed,
- does the dialogue description ensure the applicability of an application function,
- does the validity of local context conditions result in the validity of global context conditions.

The first three items can be shown by the analyzing technique outlined in section 3.1 (signature flow analysis) and the other items by the proof principle of section 3.2 (attributed term induction).

The rest of the paper is organized as follows: In section 2 we describe how user interfaces can be specified by attributed algebraic specifications. Starting with an intuitive example in section 2.1. Section 2.2 deals with the theoretical background of the specification technique. Section 2.3 shows an example specification. Correctness aspects of user interface specifications are considered in section 3. Starting with the analyzing technique and its application to correctness aspects of user interfaces (section 3.1) and in section 3.2 a new proof principle for attributed algebraic specifications is defined. Some concluding remarks are given in section 4.

2 Specifying User Interfaces with Attributed Algebraic Specifications

In this chapter the specification of user interfaces with attributed algebraic specifications is provided, starting with an intuitive example. After the theoretical background is given the specification of a user interface for an ISDN telephone is explained.

2.1 An Intuitive Example

Performing a call with a user interface for an ISDN telephone is shown in fig. 2. The session starts with the initial telephone (2.1). Clicking on the receiver starts a telephone call. Now a telephone number, e.g. 2021, can be entered (2.2, 2.3). Afterwards with the called person can be talked (2.4). To end the call on the receiver place must be clicked (2.5).

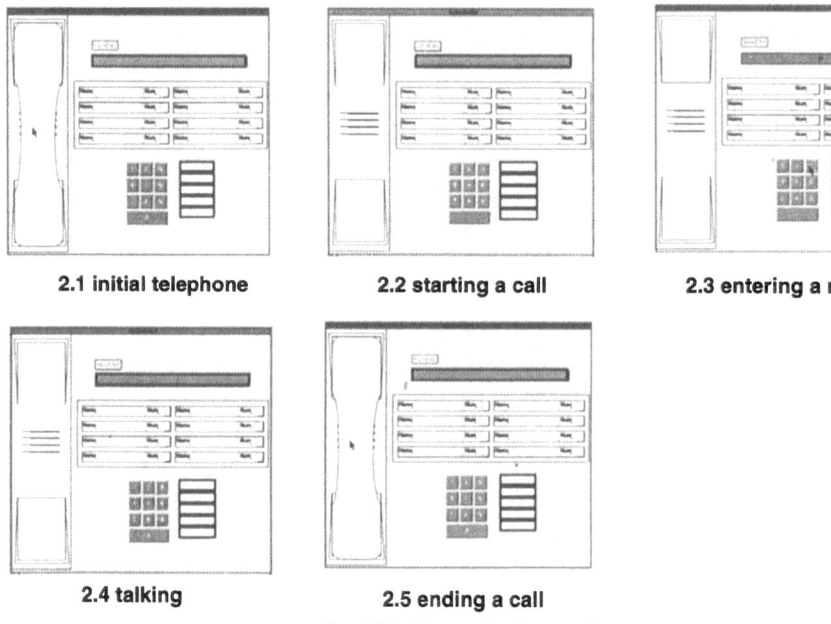

2.1 initial telephone   2.2 starting a call   2.3 entering a number

2.4 talking   2.5 ending a call

fig. 2 Making a telephone call

Viewing the telephone call in an abstract way the sentence

    CALL 2021 END

was built such that *CALL* is the token delivered from the presentation by clicking on the receiver, *2021* is the token delivered by entering the phone number and *END* by clicking on the receiver place. Therefore we have an abstract description of our telephone call independent of the actual presentation. The distinction between the abstract specification of the dialogue and the concrete presentation (layout) allows to have one dialogue specification and several concrete user interfaces, e.g.:

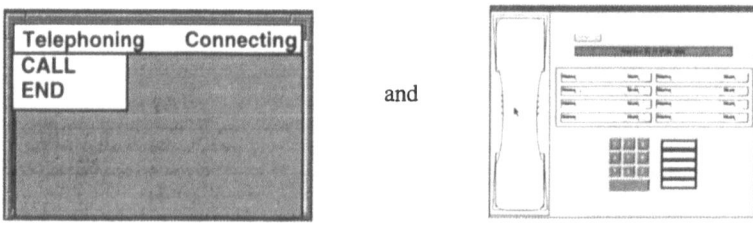

and

fig. 3 two alternative concrete presentations

such that *CALL* is delivered when the menu-item *CALL* is selected and so on.

Now we can define an abstract grammar or signature for the specification of the above dialogue. The abstract syntax tree for the above sentence is shown in fig. 4 corresponding to the term *mkCallTask(mkCall(CALL, mkEnterTNumber(2021)), END)*:

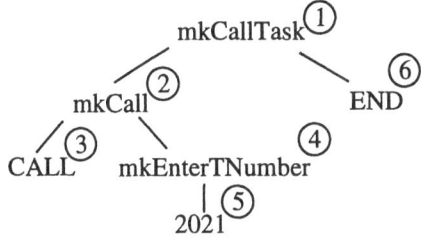

fig. 4 dialogue

As a next step we associate with each node of the syntax tree, i.e. ①, ②,..., ⑥, special informations (attributes). In the example we associate to each node the attributes *statebefore* and *stateafter* describing the state of the application before and after performing a subdialogue. To calculate attribute values rules have to be defined how the information, i.e. the attribute values, of a node can be computed using application functions and attribute values of other nodes. For the specification of the application functions algebraic specifications are used leading to a unifying approach for the application and user interface development. The dialogue state of a user interface is the tree and the state of the application is stored in the attribution. Proving properties of a user interface is therefore a proof over all attributed trees. With the proof principle presented in section 3.2 it can be shown that the application has a special state at distinguished nodes. E.g. the attribute *stateafter* at node ② is a realized telephone call.

Thus an attributed algebraic specification for describing a user interface consists of: the algebraic specification of the application (*semantics* part), the dialogue description (*syntax* part) and its effects on the application (*attribution* part). In the attribution part the calculation of the actual *layout* can be specified, too.

2.2 Attributed Algebraic Specifications

We assume the reader to be familiar with the basic notions of algebraic specifications such as *signature* $\Sigma = (S, F)$, Σ-*terms* $T_\Sigma(X)_{s \in S}$, *ground terms* T_Σ, *(ground) substitutions* σ (for more details see [12, 32]).

The new specification technique of attributed algebraic specifications is an extension of algebraic specifications allowing informations to be assigned to nodes of a term. Consequently to a given (syntax) term a set of *occurrence terms* is associated denoting the occurrences in a term. Given the syntax term of fig. 4

    mkCallTask(mkCall(CALL, mkEnterTNumber(2021)), END)

the associated occurrence terms are

occ(mkCallTask(mkCall(CALL, mkEnterTNumber(2021)), END)), denoting the root ① of fig. 4, mkCallTask(*occ*(mkCall(CALL, mkEnterTNumber(2021))), END), denoting the node ②, mkCallTask(mkCall(*occ*(CALL), mkEnterTNumber(2021)), END), denoting the node ③, mkCallTask(mkCall(CALL, *occ*(mkEnterTNumber(2021)), END)), denoting the node ④ and so on.

The notion of occurrence terms is used to express occurrences in a term where attributes are associated with. An attribute is a function taking an occurrence term as an argument and the value of the attribute as result.

E.g. statebefore(occ(mkCallTask(mkCall(CALL, mkEnterTNumber(2021)), END))) denotes the attribute *statebefore* at the root of the tree in fig. 4.

To define occurrence terms in a formal way we need the notion of a context:

A Σ-*context* is any term $c[z_s] \in T_\Sigma(\{z_s\} \cup X)$ over the signature Σ containing a distinguished variable z_s of some sort $s \in S$ such that z_s occurs exactly once in $c[z_s]$. The application of a context $c[z_s]$ to a term $t \in (T_\Sigma(X))_s$ is defined by substituting the context variable z_s by t. To shorten notation $c[t / z_s]$ is abbreviated by $c[t]$.

With the notion of a context the occurrence term

mkCallTask(*occ*(mkCall(CALL, mkEnterTNumber(2021))), END)

can be written as $c[occ(r) / z_{Call}]$ or for short $c[occ(r)]$ with the context $c[z_{Call}] = mkCallTask(z_{Call}, END)$ and a term $r = mkCall(CALL, mkEnterTNumber(2021))$.

A *scheme identifier* $sv\,[z]$ of sort s with identifier $z \in \{z_s \mid s \in S \}$ is a place holder for any term $t \in (T_\Sigma(\{z\} \cup X))_s$, such that z occurs exactly once in t.

By $T_\Sigma(X, SV)_s$ we denote terms of sort s allowing scheme identifier $sv[z] \in SV$.

A Σ-*occurrence term* (for short: *occurrence term*) is any term $c[occ_s(t)]$ with some context $c[z_s] \in T_\Sigma(\{z_s\} \cup X, SV)$ and some term $t \in (T_\Sigma(X))_s$ of sort s. By $T_\Sigma^{occ_s}$ the set of all occurrence terms with occ_s is denoted. If the sort of occ_s is uniquely determined the abbreviation occ is used.

An example for an *occurrence term* with scheme identifier $sv[z_{Call}]$ would be:

sv[occ(mkCall(CALL, mkEnterTNumber(n)))]

matching *mkCallTask(occ(mkCall(CALL, mkEnterTNumber(2021))), END)* with

sv[z_{Call}] = mkCallTask(z_{Call}, END) and n = 2021.

Let $\Sigma_{syn} = (S_{syn}, F_{syn})$ and $\Sigma_{sem} = (S_{sem}, F_{sem})$ be signatures and F_{Attr} a set of attribute functions, with F_{Attr} a function *nodesorts* : $F_{Attr} \rightarrow \mathcal{P}(S)$ is defined representing the sorts of the occurrences the attributes are associated with, *rootsort* $\in S$ a distinguished sort, $SV = (SV(Z)_s)_{s \in S}$ a family of sets of schema identifier with identifiers in $Z = \{z_s \mid s \in S\}$, $X = (X_s)_{s \in S}$ a family of sets of identifiers. The set of *attributed terms* over Σ of sort s with identifiers in X and SV is denoted by $AT_\Sigma(X, SV)_s$ and is inductively defined by:

(1) each term $t \in \left(T_{\Sigma_{syn} \cup \Sigma_{sem}}(X) \right)_s$ is an attributed term of sort s.

(2) if $t \in T_{(S, F_{syn})}^{occ_{s'}}(X, SV)$, $(f_{Attr}\colon rootsort \rightarrow s) \in F_{Attr}$ and

   $s' \in nodesorts\,(f_{Attr})$ then $f_{Attr}(t)$ is an attributed term of sort s.

(3) if $t_1, t_2, ..., t_n$ are attributed terms of sort $s_1, s_2, ..., s_n$ ($n \geq 0$) and $f \in F_{syn} \cup F_{sem}$

with $f: s_1, s_2, ..., s_n \rightarrow s$, then $f(t_1, t_2, ..., t_n)$ is an attributed term of sort s.

The set of attributed terms is denoted by $AT_\Sigma(X, SV)_{s \in S}$ and abbreviated by $AT_\Sigma(X, SV)$.

With the notion of an attributed term attribute equations, i.e. equations defining the calculation of attribute values using application functions and attribute values of other nodes, can be defined.

E.g. the attribute equation

stateafter(sv[occ(mkCall(CALL, mkEnterTNumber(n)))]) =
call(n, statebefore(sv[occ(mkCall(CALL, mkEnterTNumber(n)))])),

(the left-hand side and right-hand side of the equation are attributed terms) describes the attribute value of the attribute *stateafter* at an arbitrary node marked with *mkCall* and children *CALL* and *mkEnterTNumber(n)* as the result of the application function *call* with the telephone number (here: the entered telephone number n) and a state, being the attribute value of the attribute *statebefore* at the same node, as arguments. Having the attribute equation and the term of fig. 4 the instantiated attribute equation is

stateafter(mkCallTask(occ(mkCall(CALL, mkEnterTNumber(2021))), END)) =
call(n, statebefore(mkCallTask(occ(mkCall(CALL, mkEnterTNumber(2021))), END)))

The formal definition of an attributed algebraic specification is:

Attributed Algebraic Specifications

An *attributed algebraic specification* is a tuple $ASpec = (\Sigma_{syn}, Attr, Spec_{sem})$ whereby

(1) $\Sigma_{syn} = (S_{syn}, F_{syn})$ is the syntax-signature consisting of a set S_{syn} of syntax-sort symbols and F_{syn} is a set of syntax-function symbols (see also see [7, 8]);

(2) $Attr = \left(\left(F_{Attr_s} \right)_{s \in S_{syn}}, Ax_{Attr} \right)$ defines the attribution. $\left(F_{Attr_s} \right)_{s \in S_{syn}}$ is a family of sets F_{Attr_s} of attribute-function symbols. Ax_{Attr} is a set of axioms describing the attribute equations of the form $t = r$ with $t, r \in AT_\Sigma(X, SV)$.

(3) $Spec_{sem} = <\Sigma_{sem}, Ax_{sem}>$ is the algebraic specification of the semantic functions whereby $\Sigma_{sem} = (S_{sem}, F_{sem})$ ($\Sigma_{syn} \subseteq \Sigma_{sem}$ is allowed) consists of a set of semantic-sort symbols S_{sem} and a set of semantic-function symbols F_{sem} used in the attribute equations. The properties of the semantic functions are specified by the equations Ax_{sem}.

The *root sort* of an attributed algebraic specification $ASpec$ (denoted by *rootsort(ASpec)*) is a distinguished sort of the syntax-signature comparable with a distinguished start symbol of a grammar.

The semantics of an attributed algebraic specification is the model class, i.e. the set of all algebras over the used signature satisfying the axioms. For more details on the theory of attributed algebraic specifications see [2].

Using attributed algebraic specifications of interactive systems the algebraic specification of the application is the semantics part $Spec_{sem}$ of $ASpec = (\Sigma_{syn}, Attr, Spec_{sem})$. By Σ_{syn} all performable dialogues are specified. The attribution $Attr$ specifies how the application is effected by the performed dialogue and how the dialogue is effected by the application. In the following all performable dialogues are called *dialogue state*. An element of the dialogue state is described by an attributed tree storing information about the already performed dialogue (in the *syntax tree*) and the semantics of it (in the *attribution* of the syntax tree), i.e. the changes of the application state. The actual state is the actual attributed tree. We take the following view (for more details see the example below):

- The end-user's interactions, e.g. the selection of a menu-item, produce a stream of tokens changed into a tree by a parser.
- The actual state of the application is handled as an attribute describing how the user interactions change the application.[1]

2.3 User Interface Specification of an ISDN Telephone

We start with the algebraic specification *ISDN-Application* of the application. The specification of the ISDN telephone is a syntactical enrichment of the natural numbers (*NAT*). The sorts describe the connection with a participant (*Connection*), the internal state of the telephone (*State*) and the state of a connection (*CState*). The internal state is viewed in an abstract way, i.e. at most two connections can be achieved with the telephone (*mkState*). *mtConnection* states the empty connection. A (non-empty) connection consists of a telephone number and the status of the line (*mkConnection*). A line can either be *waiting* or *telephoning*. The function *call* describes the telephone call with a single participant, *secondCall* starts a telephone call with a second participant and the *conference* function enables a conference session between the user of the telephone and the two participants on the other lines. *call*, *secondCall* and *conference* have parameter restrictions denoted by a first order formulae after *pre*. All telephone calls are ended with *endCalls*. A telephone number is a natural number.

```
aspec ISDN-Application =
  semantics
    enrich NAT by
      sorts Connection, CState, State
      functions
        mkState: Connection, Connection → State,
        mtConnection: → Connection,
        mkConnection: Nat, CState → Connection,
        waiting, telephoning: → CState,
        call: Nat, s: State. pre s = mkState(mtConnection, mtConnection) → State,
        secondCall: Nat, s: State. pre ∃n: Nat.
          s = mkState(mkConnection(n, telephoning), mtConnection) → State,
        conference: s: State. pre ∃n, m: Nat.
          s = mkState(mkConnection(n, waiting), mkConnection(m, telephoning)) → State,
        endCalls: State → State
      axioms forall nr, nr2: Nat, s: State.
```

---

[1] The implementation of such an attribution would be a global variable (or set of global variables) describing the state of the application and at special nodes special application functions are called changing the global state variable

```
        call(nr, s) = mkState(mkConnection(nr, telephoning), mtConnection),
        secondCall(nr, call(nr2, s)) =
            mkState(mkConnection(nr2, waiting), mkConnection(nr, telephoning)),
        conference(secondCall(nr, call(nr2, s))) =
            mkState(mkConnection(nr, telephoning), mkConnection(nr2, telephoning)),
        endCalls(s) = mkState(mtConnection, mtConnection)
```
endaspec

As a next step we specify the dialogue of the telephone.

aspec ISDN-Dialogue =
  syntax
    enrich NAT **by**
      sorts Dialogue, Task, Call, SecondCall, Conference, EnterTNumber, CallMenu,
          SecondCallMenu, ConferenceMenu, EndMenu
      functions
        emptyDialogue: $\rightarrow$ Dialogue,
        mkDialogue: Task, Dialogue $\rightarrow$ Dialogue,
        mkCallTask: Call, EndMenu $\rightarrow$ Task,
        mkConferenceTask: Conference, EndMenu$\rightarrow$ Task,
        mkCall: CallMenu, EnterTNumber $\rightarrow$ Call,
        mkSecondCall: SecondCallMenu, EnterTNumber $\rightarrow$ SecondCall,
        mkConference: Call, SecondCall, ConferenceMenu $\rightarrow$ Conference,
        mkEnterTNumber: Nat $\rightarrow$ TNumber,
        CALL: $\rightarrow$ CallMenu,
        SECONDCALL: $\rightarrow$ SecondCallMenu,
        CONFERENCE: $\rightarrow$ ConferenceMenu,
        END: $\rightarrow$ EndMenu
  endaspec

A dialogue can be seen as a sequence of tasks. Therefore a dialogue is either an *emptyDialogue* or a *Task* followed by a *Dialogue*. The task of a telephone call consists of the telephone call and the ending of the call (*mkCallTask*). The task of the conference session consists of performing the conference call and then the ending of the calls (*mkConference*). To perform either a call or a call with a second participant an abstract menu-item[2] must be selected and afterwards the telephone number must be entered (*mkCall, mkSecondCall, mkEnterTNumber*). In the case of a conference the abstract *CONFERENCE*-menu must be selected after performing the first and second call. All calls are ended with *END*. The abstract menu-items are *CALL, SECONDCALL, CONFERENCE* and *END*.

The link between the application and the dialogue is defined by the attribution:

aspec ISDN-Attribution =
  attribution
    enrich NAT + ISDN-Application + ISDN-Dialogue **by**
      functions
        statebefore, stateafter: Dialogue $\rightarrow$ State
      with nodesorts Dialogue, Task, Call, SecondCall, Conference

      axioms forall d : Dialogue, t : Task, c : Call, sc : SecondCall, em : EndMenu,
          cm : ConferenceMenu, n : Nat.
      (1) statebefore(occ(d)) = mkState(mtConnection, mtConnection),

---

[2] By an „abstract menu-item" we mean a token which is delivered from the concrete representation, i.e. an abstract menu-item can therefore be e.g. a „concrete" menu-item, a pushbutton or in our direct manipulation user interface the clicking on the receiver.

(2) stateafter(sv[occ(emptyDialogue)]) = statebefore(sv[occ(emptyDialogue)]),

(3) stateafter(sv[occ(CONFERENCE)]) =
        conference(statebefore(sv[occ(CONFERENCE)])),
(4) stateafter(sv[occ(END)]) = endCalls(statebefore(sv[occ(END)])),

(5) statebefore(sv[mkDialogue(occ(t), d)]) = statebefore(sv[occ(mkDialogue(t, d))]),
(6) statebefore(sv[mkDialogue(t, occ(d))]) = stateafter(sv[mkDialogue(occ(t), d)]),
(7) stateafter(sv[occ(mkDialogue(t, d))]) = stateafter(mkDialogue(t, occ(d))]),

(8) statebefore(sv[mkCallTask(occ(c), em)]) =
        statebefore(sv[occ(mkCallTask(c, em))]),
(9) statebefore(sv[mkCallTask(c, occ(em))]) =
        stateafter(sv[mkCallTask(occ(c), em)]),
(10) stateafter(sv[occ(mkCallTask(c, em))]) = stateafter(sv[mkCallTask(c, occ(em))]),

(11) stateafter(sv[occ(mkCall(CALL, mkEnterTNumber(n)))]) =
        call(n, statebefore(sv[occ(mkCall(CALL, mkEnterTNumber(n)))])),

(12) statebefore(sv[mkConferenceTask(occ(c), em)]) =
        statebefore(sv[occ(mkConferenceTask(c, em))]),
(13) statebefore(sv[mkConferenceTask(c, occ(em))]) =
        stateafter(sv[mkConferenceTask(occ(c), em)]),
(14) stateafter(sv[occ(mkConferenceTask(c, em))]) =
        stateafter(sv[mkConferenceTask(c, occ(em))]),

(15) stateafter(sv[occ(mkSecondCall(SECONDCALL, mkEnterTNumber(n)))]) =
        secondCall(n, statebefore(sv[occ(mkSecondCall(SECONDCALL,
        mkEnterTNumber(n)))])),

(16) statebefore(sv[mkConference(occ(c), sç, cm)]) =
        statebefore(sv[occ(mkConference(c, sc, cm))]),
(17) statebefore(sv[mkConference(c, occ(sc), cm)]) =
        stateafter(sv[mkConference(occ(c), sc, cm)]),
(18) statebefore(sv[mkConference(c, sc, occ(cm))]) =
        stateafter(sv[mkConference(c, occ(sc), cm)]),
(19) stateafter(sv[mkConference(c, sc, occ(cm))]) =
        conference(statebefore(sv[mkConference(c, sc, occ(cm))])),
(20) stateafter(sv[occ(mkConference(c, sc, cm))]) =
        stateafter(sv[mkConference(c, sc, occ(cm))])

endaspec

We assume with every occurrence of sort *Dialogue, Task, Call, SecondCall* and *Conference* the attributes *statebefore* and *stateafter*. (1) states that the value of the attribute *statebefore* is *mkState(mtConnection, mtConnection)* at the root of every term of sort *Dialogue*. (2) specifies that *emptyDialogue* does not change the state. Selecting the abstract menu-items *CONFERENCE* and *END* change the state of the application (axiom (3) and (4)), such that the application functions *conference* and *endCalls* are called, respectively. (5)-(7) describe the attribute dependencies at nodes marked with *mkDialogue* and (8)-(10) for the syntax function *mkCallTask*. Axiom (11) calls the application *call* as described above. (12)-(14) defines the attribution rules for the function *mkConferenceTask* and (16)-(20) for the function *mkConference*. In (15) the attribute value of the attribute *stateafter* at nodes with an arbitrary superior tree and subordinate tree of the form *mkSecondCall(SECONDCALL, mkEnterTNumber(n))* is the result of the application function *secondCall* called with the second telephone number *n* and the value of the attribute *statebefore* at the same node as arguments.

In the same way the actual layout can be defined. Because of lack of space and since we are mainly interested in coupling the dialogue specification with the application, the attribution for the layout, namely two attributes describing the layout before and after a subdialogue, is omitted. Therefore changing the attribution for the layout changes the layout independent of the application and dialogue specification.

3 Proving Properties of User Interface Specifications

In this chapter we present an analyzing mechanism and a proof principle for the specification technique of attributed algebraic specifications.

3.1 Analyzing Specifications

First the analyzing technique for our specification formalism is outlined and afterwards the technique is applied to several problems of the ISDN example. It can be shown, e.g:
● is it possible to perform an action at all (section 3.1.2),
● does the dialogue description offer all (exported) application functions (section 3.1.3),
Moreover it could be show with this technique, e.g.:
● is an action reachable from another action.

3.1.1 Signature Flow Analysis

In the following section the considered problems are applications of the grammar flow analysis, or, since in our context „signatures" are used instead of „grammars", signature flow analysis. The following definition is an adaption and extension of [24] to our notions:

Definition (bottom-up signature flow analysis problem)

Given a signature $\Sigma = (S, F)$. A (*bottom-up*) *signature flow analysis problem* consists of
(1)   a set of domains $D = (D_s)_{s \in S}$,
(2)   a set of propagation functions
$$P = \left(p_f \colon D_{s_1}, D_{s_2}, \ldots, D_{s_n} \to D_s \right)_{(f \colon s_1, s_2, \ldots, s_n \to s) \in F},$$
(3)   a set of combination functions $\left(\nabla_s \colon \mathcal{P}(D_s) \to D_s \right)_{s \in S}$ and
(4)   a set of relations $(\subseteq_s \colon D_s, D_s \to Bool)_{s \in S}$.

A signature flow analysis problem defines a recursive equational system:
$$SFA\,[s] = \nabla_s \{ p_f (SFA\,[s_1], SFA\,[s_2], \ldots, SFA\,[s_n]) \mid (f \colon s_1, s_2, \ldots, s_n \to s) \in F \}$$
for all $s \in S$. The solution of the signature flow problem is the solution of the recursive equational system.

3.1.2 Conditional Reachability Problem for Menu-Items

As stated in the introduction an important property to consider is: do dialogues exist such that all menu-items can be selected and what is the condition for selecting a menu-item. To keep the specification of the ISDN telephone small it was assumed that each telephone call is realized, but in the real world it is possible that the called person is not at home or telephoning with somebody else. To maintain such situations it is necessary to introduce conditional syntactic functions to describe the allowed syntax terms. The precondition for the second call is that the first call would be realized. Thus the task description for the second call is partial, i.e. the following parameter restriction for the syntax function *mkSecondCall* is obtained, depending on the attribute *statebefore*:

mkSecondCall: SecondCallMenu, EnterTNumber.
pre $\exists n$: Nat. statebefore(sv[occ(mkSecondCall(SecondCallMenu, EnterTNumber)]) = mkState(mkConnection(n, telephoning), mtConnection) $\rightarrow$ SecondCall

The signature flow analysis problem of the conditional reachability problem for abstract menu-items is defined for the ISDN example as (under the assumption that the ISDN telephone has four abstract menu-items associated with the constants *CALL*, *SECOND-CALL*, *CONFERENCE* and *END*):
The signature is $\Sigma_{syn} = (S_{syn}, F_{syn})$ of the attributed algebraic specification *ISDN*.

(1) the set of domains is for all sorts $s \in S_{syn}$:

$$D = \{ (P_{CALL}, CALL), (P_{SECONDCALL}, SECONDCALL),$$
$$(P_{CONFERENCE}, CONFERENCE), (P_{END}, END)\},$$

for some preconditions P_{CALL}, $P_{SECONDCALL}$, $P_{CONFERENCE}$ and P_{END} being predicate formulae.

(2) the set of propagation functions is

$$p_f = (true, f) \quad \text{if } f \in \{CALL, SECONDCALL, CONFERENCE, END\}$$

$$p_{mkSecondCall}(SFA[SecondCallMenu], SFA[EnterTNumber]) =$$

$$\{ (pre_f \wedge pre_{mkSecondCall}, f) \mid (pre_p, f) \in SFA[SecondCallMenu] \cup SFA[EnterTNumber] \}$$

and

$$p_f(SFA[s_1], SFA[s_2], ..., SFA[s_n]) = \left(\bigcup_{1 \le i \le n} SFA[s_i] \right) \text{ otherwise}$$

with $(f:s_1, s_2, ..., s_n \rightarrow s) \in F_{syn}$ and pre_f the (computed) precondition of function f.

(3) the set of combination functions is for all sorts $s \in S_{syn}$:

$\bigcup: \mathcal{P}(D) \rightarrow D$ is the usual set union with the exception, that if $\left(pre_f^1, f \right)$ and $\left(pre_f^2, f \right)$ are elements in the obtained set then both elements are deleted. If $pre_f^1 \Rightarrow pre_f^2$ holds then $\left(pre_f^1, f \right)$ and if $pre_f^2 \Rightarrow pre_f^1$ holds then $\left(pre_f^2, f \right)$ is added to the obtained set, otherwise $\left(pre_f^1 \wedge pre_f^2, f \right)$ is added to the obtained set.

(4) a set of relations $\subseteq: D, D \rightarrow Bool$ such that $M_1 \subseteq_s M_2$ iff

$$\forall (pre_1, f) \in M_1 \exists (pre_2, f) \in M_2 \text{ such that } pre_1 \Rightarrow pre_2$$

Since the whole work is done in a logical framework the logical implication test (,,$\Rightarrow$") can be performed using a standard theorem prover.

A simple algorithm for our problem, if all abstract menu-items are reachable and under which conditions, is:

The initialization is done by assigning the information empty set to all sorts:

proc Init
  forall $s \in S$ **do** SFA[s] $:= \emptyset$ **od**
endproc

The true computation is done in the procedure SFA:

proc SFA
  change := true;
  while change **do**
    change := false;
    forall $s \in S$ **do**
      $SFA_s = \bigcup_{(f:s_1, s_2, \ldots, s_n \to s) \in F_{syn}} p_f$
      if SFA[s] $\subseteq SFA_s$ and $SFA_s \subseteq$ SFA[s]
      then nop
      else SFA[s] := $SFA_s \cup$ SFA[s];
          change := true **fi od od**
endproc

Calling the procedure *Init* for the initialization and then the procedure *SFA* results in computing the reachable menu-items for each sort. Especially for the sort *Dialogue* the reachable menu-items are the desired set of menus and the menu *SECONDCALL* is only reachable under the assumption that the first call was realized.

3.1.3 Application Problem for the Exported Application Functions

Another interesting property to check is whether there are dialogues such that all exported application functions, i.e. all functions which should be supported by the user interface, are called. In the ISDN example the exported application functions are the set {*call, secondCall, conference, endCalls*}. The problem is defined as follows:

The signature is $\Sigma_{syn} = (S_{syn}, F_{syn})$ of the attributed algebraic specification *ISDN*.

(1) the set of domains is for all sorts $s \in S_{syn}$:

  $D = \{call, secondCall, conference, endCalls\}$

(2) the set of propagation functions is

  $p_f(SFA[s_1], SFA[s_2], \ldots, SFA[s_n]) = used(f) \cup \bigcup_{1 \leq i \leq n} SFA[s_i]$ such that

  $used(f)$ computes the interesting application functions used in the attribution of the function f and $(f:s_1, s_2, \ldots, s_n \to s) \in F_{syn}$

(3) for all sorts $s \in S_{syn}$ the set of combination functions is:

  $\bigcup : \mathcal{P}(D) \to D$ the usual set union

(4) a set of relations $\subseteq : D, D \to Bool$ the usual set inclusion

The solution can be obtained by the algorithm of section 3.1.2 resulting in the set D for the rootsort *Dialogue*, i.e. dialogues exist such that all exported functions are called.

3.2 Proving Occurence Properties

The properties which can be shown by the following proof principle of attributed term induction are, e.g.:
● does the application have a given state before/after a special action is performed,
● does the dialogue description ensure the applicability of an application function,
● does the validity of local context conditions result in the validity of global context conditions,
● does a special property hold before performing an action.
For the telephone specification the first two items are shown by an example.

An *occurrence property* P for occurrence terms of sort s, i.e. of the form $c[occ_s(t)]$ for some context $c[z_s]$ and some term t of sort s, is a predicate formulae over the attributes for occurrences of sort s and the semantic functions of the attributed algebraic specification, describing dependencies between attribute values of that node. In the framework of user interface verification „dependencies between attribute values of that node" can be interpreted as „the application has a special state after/before a distinguished subdialogue". An occurrence property P is valid, iff $P(t)$ holds for all occurrence terms

$$t \in T^{occ_s}_{(S_{syn}, F_{syn})}.$$

The idea of the proof principle is to perform two kinds of induction for building the context $c[z_s]$ (a special kind of context induction using another ordering as in [18]) and for building the term t of sort s (a special kind of term induction), i.e. it must be shown that for all contexts $c[z_s]$ and for all terms t of sort s the property $P(c[occ_s(t)])$ is valid. The ordering used on contexts is the notion of an outer context and on terms the usual syntactical subterm ordering. $c_1[z_s]$ is an *outer context* of $c[z_s]$ if there exists a (non-trivial) context $c_2[z_s]$ such that $c[z_s] \equiv c_1[c_2[z_s]]$. The notion of outer context defines a Noetherian relation on contexts.

Attributed Term Induction:

Let $ASpec = (\Sigma_{syn}, Attr, Spec_{sem})$ be an attributed algebraic specification and P an occurrence property for occurrence terms of sort s_t.

To show that for all occurrence terms $t^{occ_{s_t}} \in \left(T_\Sigma^{occ_{s_t}} \right)_{rootsort(ASpec)}$ an occurrence property $P\left(t^{occ_{s_t}} \right)$ is valid, it is sufficient to show:

(1) For all minimal outer contexts $c_1[z_{s_t}]$ of sort $rootsort(ASpec)$ holds:

    (1.1) $P(c_1[occ(f)])$ is valid for all constants $f \in F_{syn}$ of sort s_t;

    (1.2) For all terms $f(t_1, t_2,..., t_n)$ with a function symbol $(f : s_1, s_2,..., s_n \rightarrow s_t)$

        $\in F_{syn}$ and terms $t_i \in \left(T_{\Sigma_{syn}} \right)_{s_i}$ $(1 \leq i \leq n)$ holds:

        Under the assumption that $P(c_1[occ(t')])$ is valid for all subterms t' of $f(t_1, t_2,..., t_n)$ of sort s_t, $P(c_1[occ(f(t_1, t_2,..., t_n))])$ must be valid;
        In particular, the validity of $P(c_1[occ(t')])$ can be assumed, if $sort(t') = s_t$;

(2) and

(2.1)   Under the assumption that $P(c_2[occ(t)])$ is valid for all outer contexts $c_2[z_s]$ of a context c_3 and all terms $t \in \left(T_{\Sigma_{syn}} \right)_s$, $P(c_3[occ(f)])$ must be valid for all constants $f \in F_{syn}$ of sort s_i;

In particular, the validity of $P(c_2[occ(t)])$ can be assumed if $t \in \left(T_{\Sigma_{syn}} \right)_{s_t}$;

(2.2)   For all terms $f(t_1, t_2,..., t_n)$ with a function symbol $(f : s_1, s_2,..., s_n \rightarrow s_t)$ $\in F_{syn}$ and terms $t_i \in \left(T_{\Sigma_{syn}} \right)_{s_i}$ ($1 \leq i \leq n$) holds:

Under the assumption that $P(c_2[occ(t)])$ is valid for all outer contexts $c_2[z_s]$ of a context c_3 and all terms $t \in \left(T_{\Sigma_{syn}} \right)_s$ and $P(c_4[occ(t')])$ is valid for all subterms t' of $f(t_1, t_2,..., t_n)$ of appropriate sort and all contexts c_4, $P(c_3[occ(f(t_1, t_2,..., t_n))])$ must be valid;

In particular, the validity of $P(c_2[occ(t)])$ can be assumed if $t \in \left(T_{\Sigma_{syn}} \right)_{s_t}$ and the validity of $P(c_4[occ(t')])$ can be assumed, if $sort(t') = s_i$;

The proof principle is a mixture of a kind of context induction [18] (implemented in ISAR [3]) and term induction. The correctness of the proof principle was shown in [1].

In our example of the ISDN telephone we want to show that at every node where the abstract conference menu-item is selected, i.e. at nodes of sort *ConferenceMenu*, the state of the application after selecting the *CONFERENCE*-menu is the telephoning of all three participants. Since the application function *conference* is applied only at nodes of sort *ConferenceMenu* in addition it can be shown that the parameter restriction of *conference* is satisfied.

Mathematically:

Theorem:

For all occurrence terms t of sort *ConferenceMenu* holds:

stateafter(t) =
    mkState(mkConnection(nr, telephoning), mkConnection(nr2, telephoning))

and

$\exists$ n, m. statebefore(t) = mkState(mkConnection(nr, waiting),
                    mkConnection(nr2, telephoning))
for some telephone numbers *nr* and *nr2*, being the dialogue property $P(t)$.

Proof:

In the *base of the context induction* all minimal outer contexts with context variable $z_{ConferenceMenu}$ and root sort *Dialogue* must be constructed. Therefore all functions with result sort *Dialogue* have to be considered being

   mkDialogue : Task, DialogueTask → DialogueTask

Now for all argument sorts, i.e. *Task* and *Dialogue*, a nested context induction must be

238

performed.

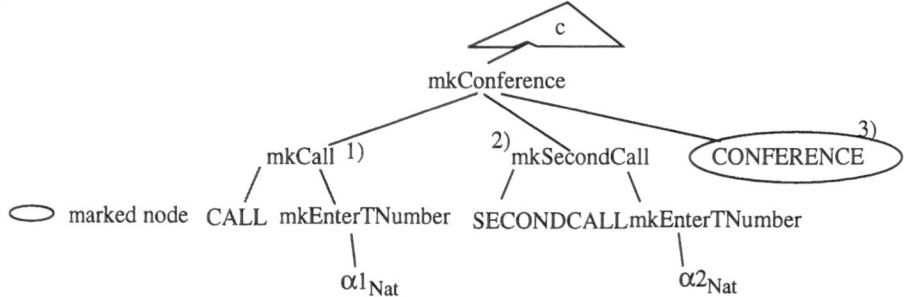

1) stateafter = mkState(mkConnection($\alpha 1_{Nat}$, telephoning))
2) statebefore = mkState(mkConnection($\alpha 1_{Nat}$, telephoning))
   stateafter = mkState(mkConnection($\alpha 1_{Nat}$, waiting), mkConnection($\alpha 2_{Nat}$, telephoning))
3) statebefore = mkState(mkConnection($\alpha 1_{Nat}$, waiting), mkConnection($\alpha 2_{Nat}$, telephoning))
   stateafter = mkState(mkConnection($\alpha 1_{Nat}$, telephoning), mkConnection($\alpha 2_{Nat}$, telephoning))

fig. 5 proof obligation

First argument of mkDialogue: Task

The actual context is $mkDialogue(z_{Task}, x_{Dialogue})$ with new variable $x_{Dialogue}$. In order to get a finite proof a more general context is used[3], namely $c[z_{Conference}]$ for an abstract context c (Because of lack of space no proof is given)[4].

The sort of the property *ConferenceMenu* does not agree with *Conference*, thus a nested context induction for the construction of the minimal outer context is done. All functions with result sort *Conference* have to be considered in the actual context being

$$mkConference: Call, SecondCall, ConferenceMenu \rightarrow Conference$$

For the first two argument sorts no contexts $c'[z_{ConferenceMenu}]$ of sort *Call* and *Second-Call*, respectively, exist (proof omitted)[5].

But with $c[mkConference(x_{Call}, x_{SecondCall}, z_{ConferenceMenu})]$ the minimal context is reached. Now a term induction on sort *ConferenceMenu* must be done. The only function to consider is *CONFERENCE* being a constant.

Thus we have to show

$$P(\sigma(c[mkConference(x_{Call}, x_{SecondCall}, occ(CONFERENCE)]))$$

holds for all ground substitutions σ, since we are only interested in ground occurrence terms resulting in the proof obligation:

[3.] As usual when doing induction proofs generalizations are necessary in order to get finite proofs or induction assertions which are general enough to finish the proof successfully. Here the problem of finding an appropriate induction assertion appears in choosing a suitable context before doing a nested context induction.

[4.] It is a kind of signature flow analysis problem presented in section 3.1. It must be shown that on every path from the root to a node of sort *ConferenceMenu* there is a node of sort *Conference*.

[5.] Again a kind of signature flow analysis (cf. section 3.1).

$P(c[mkConference(mkCall(CALL, mkEnterTNumber(\alpha 1_{Nat})),$

$\quad mkSecondCall(SECONDCALL, mkEnterTNumber(\alpha 2_{Nat})), occ(CONFERENCE))])$

for some constants $\alpha 1_{Nat}$ and $\alpha 2_{Nat}$ (being generalizations).

Visualizing the occurrence term the validity of the proof obligation P must hold at the marked node of the tree in fig. 5. Looking at the attribution shows the validity of the property P.

Second argument of mkDialogue: Dialogue

In this case again the context $c[z_{Conference}]$ is used for the nested context induction being a generalization of the context $mkDialogue(x_{Task}, z_{Dialogue})$. Therefore the same proof as for the first argument must be done.

In the *context induction step* we start with an arbitrary context $c2[z_{ConferenceMenu}]$. Since this context cannot be extended to a context $c3[z_{ConferenceMenu}]$ syntactically equal to $c2[c4[z_{ConferenceMenu}]]$ for some non-trivial context $c4[z_{ConferenceMenu}]$, in the context induction step no proof obligations have to be shown.

In our example of the ISDN telephone we have shown that after the conference menu-item is selected the state of the application is the telephoning of all three participants and the parameter restrictions of the application function *conference* is satisfied.

4 Concluding Remarks

We have pointed out how to specify user interfaces of interactive systems by attributed algebraic specifications and its verification by attributed term induction and signature flow analysis. The specification formalism allows the distinction between the application and dialogue description and it would also be possible to define the layout by attribution, thus the whole specification of an interactive application with a user interface can be described by the new approach, but the clean distinction between all the layers is preserved.

At the moment a system is under development for performing these proofs automatically. The system generates the proof obligations and then a theorem prover, called TIP [16, 17], is used for the verification of the obligations. The ISDN example could be proven by the actual prototype of the system. As seen in the example efficient heuristics can be obtained by using the technique of signature flow analysis. On the other side doing induction proofs often generalizations are necessary being in the usual case difficult to find but in the case of attributed term induction generalizations can often be automatically obtained by analyzing the signature.

[21] and [9] present another possibility for the verification of attribute grammars based on assertions analogous to the Hoare-calculus for the verification of imperative programs. But [9] states: „the practical usability of the proof method of Theorem (3.2.5) suffers from its theoretical simplicity" whereby this proof method is refined afterwards, but it remains difficult to find „good" assertions for each non-terminal. Moreover there are restrictions on the properties to prove and [9, 21] cannot be used for undirected attribute equations being very usuable for layout specifications.

Correctness aspects can only be considered in the framework of model based user interface tools [4, 5, 6, 14, 15, 20], since the layout oriented tools are too low-level. But there are model based tools which employ a specification technique with a missing logical framework, e.g. [4, 5, 6, 20]. Furthermore the dialogues are sometimes specified independent of the effects on the application. Working with pre- and postconditions as in [14, 15] makes the verification more difficult, since the property of the reachability test presented in this paper is a semantical problem and not a syntactical one. Specifying dialogues in the temporal logical framework makes proving properties more complicated than reasoning in the classical logic.

Up to now we have only considered some typical smaller examples, a next step is to consider several case studies in order to detect drawbacks of the actual system. But it seems that the specification and verification techniques can also be used for larger systems, since on the one side the specification technique allows modularisations and the proof can be handled by using efficent heuristics.

The specification technique presented here can be used as an input for the BOSS system [27, 28] by implementing the application functions in C++ and transforming the syntax and attribution part into the syntax of the system.

Acknowledgement. This work was partially sponsored by Siemens Corporate Research and Development, Department of System Ergonomics and Interaction (ZFE ST SN 51). I acknowledge Siegfried Schreiber and the referees for useful comments on draft versions of this paper.

References

1. B. Bauer: *Attributed Term Induction - A Proof Principle for Attribute Grammars*, technical report, Technische Universität München, TUM-I9403, February 1994
2. B. Bauer: *A Unifying Concept for Algebraic Specifications and Attribute Grammars: Attributed Algebraic Specifications*, technical report, to appear, 1995
3. B. Bauer, R. Hennicker: *Proving the Correctness of Algebraic Implementations by the ISAR System*, in: Proc. of the International Symposium on Design and Implementation of Symbolic Computation Systems 93, LNCS 722, Springer, Berlin, pp. 3-16, 1993
4. H. Balzert: *Der JANUS-Dialogexperte: Vom Fachkonzept zur Dialogstruktur*, Softwaretechnik, 93(13), 1993
5. H. Balzert: *Das JANUS-System*, Informatik Forschung und Entwicklung, 1994
6. F. Bodart, A.-M. Hennebert, J.-M. Leheureux, I. Provot, J. M. Vanderdonckt: *A Model-Based Approach to Presentation: A Continuum from Task Analysis to Prototype*, Proc. of the Eurographics Workshop „Design, Specification and Verification of Interactive Systems, pp. 25-39, 1994
7. L. M. Chirica, D. F. Martin: *An Algebraic Formulation of Knuthian Semantics*, 17th Annual Symposium on Foundations of Computer Science, IEEE, Houston, Texas, 1976
8. L. M. Chirica, D. F. Martin: *An Order-Algebraic Definition of Knuthian Semantics*, Math. Systems Theory, 13, pp. 1-27, 1979
9. B. Courcelle, P. Deransart: *Proofs of Partial Correctness for Attribute Grammars with Application to Recursive Procedures and Logic Programming*, Information and Computation, 78, pp. 1-55, 1988
10. J. Coutaz: *PAC, an implementation model for dialog design*, Proc. of the INTERACT 87, Elsevier, pp. 431-436, 1987.
11. P. Deransart, M. Jourdan, B. Lorho: *Attribute Grammars: Definitions, Systems and Bibliography*, LNCS 323, Springer, Berlin, 1988
12. H. Ehrig, B. Mahr: Fundamentals of algebraic specifications 1, EATCS Monographs on Theoretical Computer Science, 6, Springer, Berlin, 1985
13. J. Eickel: Logical and Layout Structures of Documents, Computer Physics Communication, 61, pp. 201-208, 1990
14. J. D. Foley, W. C. Kim, S. Kovacevic, K. Murray: UIDE - An Intelligent User Interface Design Environment, in: Intelligent User Interfaces, (eds.) J. W. Sullivan, S. W. Tyler, Addison

Wesley, ACM Press, pp. 339-384, 1991

15. J. D. Foley, P. N. Sukaviriya, T. Griffith: *A Second Generation User Interface Design Environment: The Model and the Runtime Architecture*, Proc. ACM INTERCHI 93, Conference on Human Factors in Computing Systems, Model-Based User Interface Development System 93, pp. 375-382, 1993

16. U. Fraus: *A Calculus for Conditional Inductive Theorem Proving*, Proc. of the CTRS '92, Nancy, LNCS 656, Springer, 1993

17. U. Fraus: *Mechanizing Inductive Theorem Proving in Conditional Theories*, Ph.D thesis, Universität Passau, 1994

18. R. Hennicker: *Context induction: a proof principle for behavioural abstractions and algebraic implementations*. Formal Aspects of Computing, 3(4), pp. 326-345, 1991.

19. H. U. Hoppe: *Task-Oriented Parsing - A Diagnostic Method to be Used by Adaptive Systems*, Proceedings of ACM CHI'88 Conference on Human Factors in Computing Systems, pp. 241-247, 1988

20. Ch. Janssen, A. Weisbecker, J. Ziegler: *Generating User Interfaces from Data Models and Dialogue Net Specifications*, Proc. ACM INTERCHI 93, Conference on Human Factors in Computing Systems, Automated User Interface Generation, pp. 418-423, 1993

21. T. Katayama, Y. Hoshino: *Verification of Attribute Grammars*, 8th POPL, Williamsburg, VA, pp. 177-186, January 1981

22. G. Krönert, G. Lauber, H.-G. Mannes: *Spezifikation, Prototyping und Implementierung von interaktiven Systemen und Verwendung von attributierten Grammatiken*, Software-Entwicklung, pp. 225-238, 1989

23. A. Limpouch: *Grammar-Based Formal Specification for the Object-Oriented User Interface Development*, Proc. of the Eurographics Workshop „Design, Specification and Verification of Interactive Systems, pp. 317-334, 1994

24. U. Möncke, R. Wilhelm: *Grammar Flow Analysis, in: Proceedings Attribute Grammars, Application and Systems*, International Summer School SAGA, LNCS 545, Springer, Berlin, 1991

25. S. J. Payne: *Task-Action-Grammars*, Proc. INTERACT 84 Human-Computer Interaction, North-Holland, pp. 527-532, 1985

26. P. Reisner: *Formal Grammar and Human Factors Design of an Interactive Graphics System*, IEEE Transactions on Software Engineering, 7(2), March 1981

27. S. Schreiber: *The BOSS System: Coupling Visual Programming with Model Based Interface Design*, Proc. of the Eurographics Workshop „Design, Specification and Verification of Interactive Systems, pp. 41-60, 1994

28. S. Schreiber: *Specification and Generation of User Interfaces with the BOSS System*, Proc. East-West International Conference on Human-Computer Interaction EWHCI'94, 1994

29. M. J. Tauber: *ETAG: Extended Task Action Grammars - A Language for the Description of the User's Task Language*, Proc. INTERACT 90 Human-Computer Interaction, North-Holland, pp. 163-168, 1990

30. J. A. Goguen, J. W. Thatcher, E. G. Wagner, J. B. Wright: *Initial Algebra Semantics and Continuous Algebras*, Journal of the Association of Computing Machinery, 24(1), pp. 68-95, January 1977

31. H. Qingyi: *User Interface Specification with Attribute Grammars: A New Approach*, Proc. 6th International Conference on Systems Research, Informatics and Cybernetics, Baden-Baden, 1992.

32. M. Wirsing: *Algebraic Specifications*, in: Handbook of Theoretical Computer Science, pp. 676-788, (ed.:) J. van Leeuwen, North Holland, 1990

A software demonstrator of modality theory

N.O. Bernsen and S. Lu

Centre for Cognitive Science, P.O. Box 260, Roskilde University,
DK-4000 Roskilde, Denmark

1 Introduction

For some years, the multimodal systems group at the Centre for Cognitive Science, Roskilde University, has been working on establishing and implementing the research agenda of modality theory. The research agenda for modality theory is the following [1]:

1. To establish sound conceptual and taxonomic foundations for describing and analysing any particular type of unimodal or multimodal output representation relevant to human-computer interaction (HCI);

2. to create a conceptual framework for describing and analysing interactive computer interfaces;

3. to develop a practical methodology for applying the results of steps (1) and (2) above to the problem of information mapping between work/task domains and human-computer interfaces in information systems design.

Modality theory thus aims to establish the theoretical and methodological basis for addressing the information mapping problem in its general form, i.e.:

Given any particular class of task domain information which needs to be exchanged between user and system during task performance, identify the set of input/output modalities which constitute an optimal solution to the representation and exchange of that information.

An ultimate objective is to use results in building computerised tools for the support of interface design.

We began work on the first part of this research agenda, i.e. the development of a taxonomy of output modalities in the media of graphics, acoustics and haptics. A (representational) *modality* is a way of representing information, e.g. at the human-computer interface. It was realised from early on that work progress might benefit from the support of a software tool in which we could represent large numbers of samples of output representations for the purposes of analysing their properties and testing possible taxonomy schemes. This lead to the development of Version 1 of the taxonomy workbench [16,17], which was demonstrated at INTERCHI '93. Version 1 is a database tool designed to assist research by (a) setting up a common multimedia/multimodal database of example output representations, (b) assisting the description and classification of these examples according to different assumptions about the modalities involved, and (c) enabling thought experiments such as, e.g., the testing of different hypotheses about features of the modalities and their interrelations.

When a robust, intuitively plausible and principled taxonomy of output modalities ([3,4,5], cf. below) had been established, the workbench in its current configuration had done its job of proving the usefulness of software support for modality theory development [2,12,13,14]. This gave rise to the idea of re-designing the software tool with four objectives in mind: (1) to create a software demonstrator of the taxonomy of output modalities; (2) to use the demonstrator to further explore the functional properties of different output modalities in order to map out which information a particular modality is suited for representing; (3) to support exploration of the information mapping methodology [7,9,19,20]; and (4) to move towards turning the demonstrator into a support tool for multimodal interface design.

The identification of functional properties of modalities is important to the achievement of the third part of the research agenda of modality theory (i.e. information mapping). We view representational modalities as having two broad kinds of property: declarative properties and functional properties. *Declarative properties* are the properties assigned to a particular modality in order to define or describe what it is. Thus, for instance, linguistic modalities share the property of being syntactic-semantic systems of meaning. The declarative properties of modalities explain how they represent information. *Functional properties* characterise which types of information a certain modality is good or bad, suitable or unsuitable at representing and sometimes also specify under which conditions this is the case. Arbitrary acoustics, for instance, may serve useful alert and alarm functions in low-acoustic environments but not in high-acoustic ditto. Successful information mapping must be informed by knowledge of functional properties. Whereas many functional properties can be analytically derived from the declarative properties of modalities, capture of other sets of functional properties requires an empirical, corpus-based approach in which different modality samples are analysed to identify their functional characteristics, often in conjunction with scenarios of use.

Based on the considerations just outlined, the original taxonomy workbench has now been completely redesigned. Its main objective still is to provide a computer-aided platform for analysing different modalities drawn from its large database in order to identify functional properties of unimodal modalities. The comprehensiveness of the functional properties identified will largely determine the applicability to interface design of modality theory.

The most important differences between Versions 1 and 2 of the system are the following:

1) *change of scope* from covering a variety of taxonomy ideas to concentrating on our current taxonomy of output modalities;

244

2) *change of focus* from a declarative taxonomy to a combined declarative/functional taxonomy (cf. above);

3) *upgraded functionality.* Version 2 incorporates revised versions of the analysis and classification facilities of Version 1 as well as a much improved search facility;

4) *two systems instead of one.* The system now has two distinct parts, namely a taxonomy workbench and a taxonomy demonstrator. Initially, the workbench and the demonstrator were both implemented on the OMNIS 7 platform [8]. The fact that frequent modification of hypermedia documents is a rather laborious endeavour in OMNIS 7, made us decide to port the taxonomy demonstrator into MOSAIC. This is currently being done.

This paper presents the taxonomy demonstrator. The focus is on demonstrating the scope and depth of a central part of modality theory, i.e. the theory of output modalities. Due to the limited space available, only a synoptic view of the theory can be provided. The usefulness of the demonstrator in furthering theory development will also become apparent, we hope. An outline of the taxonomy demonstrator and its underlying theory of output modalities is presented in Sect. 2. Sects. 3, 4, 5 and 6 focus on various dimensions of modality theory. Sect. 7 concludes and discusses future work.

2 Outline of the Taxonomy Demonstrator

The taxonomy of unimodal output modalities has been generated [4,5] from a set of (declarative) basic properties (see Fig. 1).

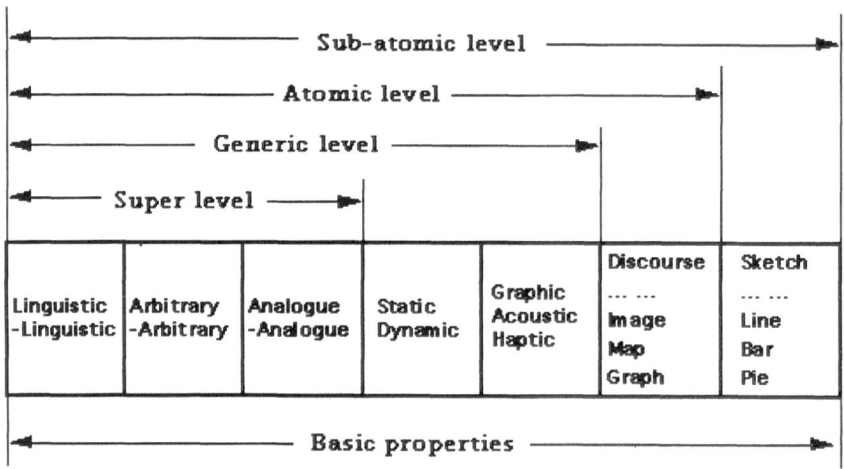

Figure 1. The underlying principles of the taxonomy of unimodal output modalities.

Unimodal modalities are representational modalities which, when combined together, constitute multimodal representations but which are not themselves multimodal. Unimodal modalities at the *super level* are defined by being either analogue or non-analogue, arbitrary or non-arbitrary, and either linguistic or non-linguistic. At the *generic level*, unimodal modalities are characterised, in addition, by being either static or dynamic, as well as being physically realised in one of the three media of graphics, acoustics and haptics. Additional basic properties are needed to distinguish between modalities at the *atomic level*. For instance, the basic properties of text, discourse, label/keyword, notation, gesture, writing and speech are used to distinguish between different atomic linguistic modalities. In one part of the taxonomy, i.e. analogue graphics, a *sub-atomic level* has been added at which even more fine-grained distinctions are needed for the taxonomy to properly serve its purpose. In this way, individual unimodal modalities are defined through their declarative *profile* as constituted by a set of basic properties.

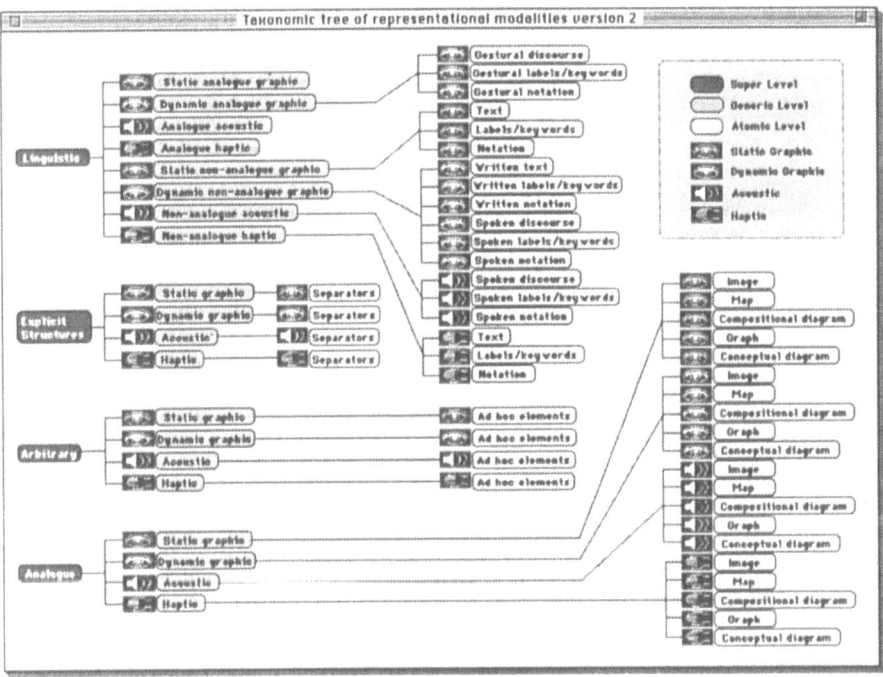

Figure 2. The taxonomy tree (OMNIS 7 implementation).

The hierarchical structure of the taxonomy is presented in Fig. 2 which shows the main screen of the taxonomy demonstrator. The taxonomy tree has 70 nodes, i.e. 4 at the super level, 20 at the generic level and 46 at the atomic level. In the tree structure, colour, being one of the information channels of graphics, is used to carry differential information. The super, generic and atomic levels are differentiated by their background colours, i.e. blue, blue/grey and light green, respectively. Different media are marked by different analogue icons, i.e. graphics by an eye, acoustics by a loudspeaker and haptics by a hand. Static and dynamic graphics are differentiated through the foreground colours of their icons, i.e. green and white, respectively. Property inheritance links are shown as lines connecting different unimodal modalities from left to right. Via these links, properties are inherited from the super level down to the atomic and sub-atomic levels, the latter of which is not shown in Fig. 2. The layout of the tree is mainly determined by spatial constraints. At the top right-hand corner, an explicit structure in a darker shade of grey contains the legend of the taxonomy tree.

The theory demonstrator consists of a series of hypertext/hypermedia documents which are of two categories, modality documents and lexicon documents. Accessed through the taxonomy tree and having a common document structure, *modality documents* define, explain and illustrate the unimodal modalities. Lexicon documents, accessed through modality documents and having free-style document structure, define, explain and illustrate additional key concepts of the theory of output modalities. The taxonomy tree provides the main structuring principle for these documents. The taxonomy tree is a graphic representation of the structure of the taxonomy of unimodal output modalities in a directly manipulatable form. Mouse-clicking on any node of the tree provides access to the relevant modality document.

The set of nodes in the taxonomy tree provides a pragmatically simplified version of the taxonomy of unimodal output modalities. For instance, the tree structure does not represent the theoretically valid distinctions between *static and dynamic acoustics* and between *static and dynamic haptics*. Instead, these distinctions are being applied internally in the documents on acoustics and haptics. Similarly, as a matter of theoretical principle some nodes in the tree do in fact have daughter nodes although these are not shown. For instance, the generic level modality *static analogue graphic language,* i.e. static graphic language using analogue signs, does have a set of atomic-level daughter nodes for representing hieroglyphic (or iconographic) writing in the modality types *text, labels/keywords* and *notation.* However, this information has been incorporated into the presentation of *static non-analogue graphic language,* i.e. static graphic language using non-analogue signs such as those which the reader is currently reading. The reason for these purely pragmatic reductions which have been made without loosing any important information, are (i) to reduce the number and nature of unimodal atoms to those which are expected to be important to interface design; and (ii) to avoid proliferation of - sometimes even useful - atoms in the acoustic and haptic media. More atoms can always be added within the theoretical boundaries of modality theory, when substantial information on them becomes important to HCI. In the absence of the pragmatic reductions just described, the number of nodes in the taxonomy tree (super, generic and atomic levels) would have been increased by 30 from 70 to 100 [5].

We now take a closer look at the different levels of the taxonomy, the media of graphics, acoustics and haptics, the distinction between static and dynamic modalities, and the modality and lexicon documents.

3 Levels of Representation

The levels of the taxonomy correspond to considering the world of representational modalities at different levels of abstraction. From the super level down to the atomic and sub-atomic levels, distinction is made between an increasing number of modalities as more and more basic properties are being introduced. The levels allow the study of unimodal modalities to be pursued in an orderly and step-by-step manner. They make it possible, for instance, to analyse a limited number of basic properties at a time. Starting from the super level, declarative as well as functional characteristics are passed on to the descendant modalities at the levels below. The characteristics of each basic property are analysed at the level at which it has been introduced. A core assumption is that the basic properties used to define a modality are all central to that modality's ability to represent information. For each basic property, its presence or absence in a modality has important effects on that modality's abilities to represent various kinds of information.

3.1 The Super Level

The super level represents the highest level of abstraction in the taxonomy. One step up from the super level is the root, i.e., all possible representational modalities in the media of graphics, acoustics and haptics. The modalities at the super level are defined by combinations of three sets of basic properties, such that these modalities are each either linguistic or non-linguistic, arbitrary or non-arbitrary, and either analogue or non-analogue. This yields four possible combinations of basic properties which each define a super level unimodal modality [4,5], namely, the linguistic, explicit structure, arbitrary and analogue modalities, respectively (see Fig. 2). Linguistic modalities, for instance, are defined from the following set of basic properties: linguistic, non-arbitrary and non-analogue. Linguistic modalities are non-arbitrary as they are based on an already existing system of meaning; they are non-analogue because language does not have a primarily analogue relationship to what it represents [4,6]. In a simple notation, the profile of linguistic modalities is <li,-ar,-an>. The profiles for explicit structure, arbitrary and analogue modalities are expressed as <-li,-ar,-an>, <-li,ar,-an> and <-li,-ar,an>, respectively. The super level does not have any deep theoretical significance as it simply reflects one among several possible, all incomplete, classifications of the generic-level modalities.

3.2 The Generic Level

From the super level to the generic level, the taxonomy is further differentiated through distinctions between different media and states of representation. The *medium* determines how a modality is being instantiated physically while the *state of representation* specifies whether or not a modality affords freedom of perceptual inspection. The taxonomy covers the media of graphics, acoustics and haptics and distinguishes between static and dynamic states of representation. The former is elaborated in Sect. 4, the latter in Sect. 5 below. Taking into account the pragmatic reductions noted in Sect. 2 above, the taxonomy includes twenty generic level unimodal modalities as presented in Fig. 2. There are eight linguistic generic unimodal modalities, i.e., static graphic language using analogue signs, dynamic graphic language using analogue signs, acoustic language using analogue signs, haptic language using analogue signs, static non-analogue graphic language, dynamic non-analogue graphic language, non-analogue acoustic language, non-analogue haptic language. There are four generic unimodal modalities under each of the super level categories explicit structure, arbitrary and analogue modalities, respectively. The profiles of, e.g., the four analogue generic unimodal modalities are <-li,-ar,an,st,gr>, <-li,-ar,an,dyn,gr>, <-li,-ar,an,st/dyn,ac> and <-li,-ar,an,st/dyn,ha>, respectively. This shows how the first three basic properties in each profile have been inherited from the super level. The reader may have noticed the seemingly contradictory notion of 'analogue' in first four linguistic generic level modalities. These refer to languages using analogue *signs* rather than languages which are, as such, analogue. The latter would be self-contradictory according to the theory. The point is that languages are primarily syntactic-semantic systems of meaning and, as such, essentially non-analogue modalities. Only secondarily, through the use of analogue signs in some languages (such as hieroglyphs), may a language possess an analogue aspect.

3.3 The Atomic Level

Generally speaking, the atomic level is the lowest level in the taxonomy so far. The unimodal modalities at this level are intended to be used as 'basic building blocks' by interface designers. Basic properties introduced at the atomic level, unlike those introduced at the generic and super levels, do not manifest themselves across all branches of the taxonomy. Rather they are specific to the descendants of a certain super level modality. In the linguistic family, the basic properties are: gestural, written, spoken, text, discourse, label/keyword and notation. The basic properties of image, map, compositional diagram, graph and conceptual diagram are introduced in the analogue branch of the taxonomy, whereas the basic properties separator and ad hoc element are the grandchildren of the explicit structure and arbitrary modalities, respectively. Atomic modalities inherit both declarative and functional properties from their parental super and generic level modalities. The profile of, e.g., static graphic conceptual diagrams is <-li,-ar,an,st,gr,con.dia>.

3.4 The Sub-Atomic Level

Unimodal modalities at the sub-atomic level are not visible on the main screen of the theory demonstrator but must be accessed via their parental atomic level documents. As said above, the unimodal modalities at the atomic level are normally the lowest-level modalities in the taxonomy. However, in some parts of the taxonomy, notably the analogue modalities, information representations have been so richly developed that more fine-grained distinctions are necessary for the sakes of both sophistication of the theory and its potential practical use in interface design. One such analogue atomic modality is the static graphic graph which in our analysis has three sub-atomic descendants: the line graph, bar graph and pie graph, respectively. These graph types show functionally related quantities, independent quantities and percentages of wholes, respectively. In the corresponding modality documents, these notions have been appropriately generalised. For instance, bar graphs are in fact graphs in which any geometrical shape in 1D, 2D, or 3D can be used whose length, area, or volume represents the quantities in question. It follows that Figs. 3 (a) and (b) are as much instances of bar graphs as is Fig. 9 further below. In Fig. 3 (a), area is being used for showing size in square miles of states relative to the size of their overseas empires whereas in Fig. 3 (b) volume is used to show coal and oil-gas reserves in various regions.

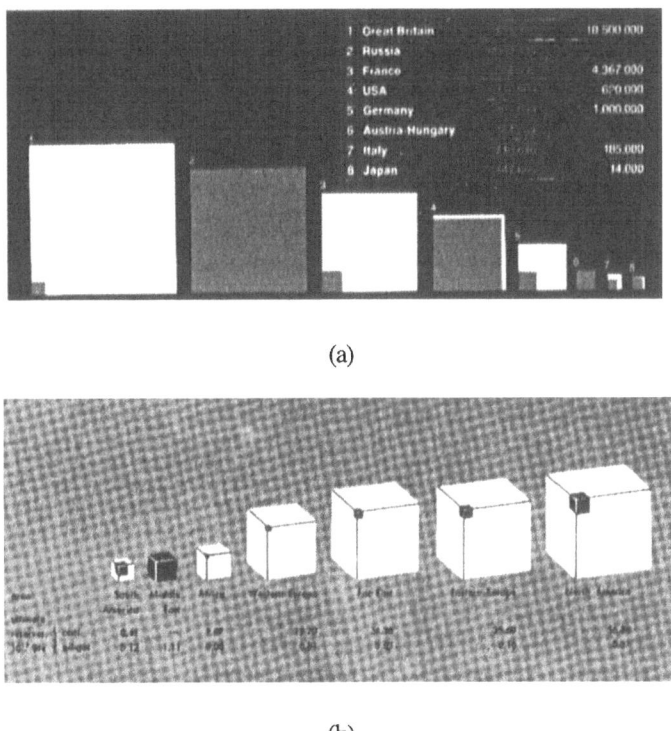

(a)

(b)

Figure 3. Variety of bar graphs [11].

4 Media of Representation

The medium of a representational modality is the physical substrate in which it is realised and perceived. Among all possible media, the media of graphics, acoustics and haptics are considered the most relevant for interface design purposes. The medium of a certain unimodal modality is of fundamental importance to that modality's suitability for representing information in a specific interface design context. The fact that different media have different information channels at their disposal similarly has important implications for their usability for different design purposes. Each output medium is uniquely characterised by a set of information channels [10]. An *information channel* is a humanly perceivable aspect of a medium which may be used to carry information.

4.1 The Graphic Modalities

Throughout human civilisation, the medium of graphics or the visual medium has been a central vehicle for the representation of information. It is therefore not surprising that certain graphic modalities, such as static typed language, graphs and images, have been more extensively studied than any type of acoustic or haptic representation. Yet, a full appreciation of all graphic modalities still remains to be made. Graphics have at least the following information channels: shape, size (length, width, height), texture, resolution, contrast, value (grey scales), colour (brightness, hue and saturation), position, orientation, viewing perspective, spatial arrangement, short-duration repetitive change of properties, non-repetitive change of properties, movement, displacement (relative to the observer), and temporal order.

4.2 The Acoustic Modalities

Until recently, acoustic modalities have had a rather limited role in HCI. This contrast sharply with human-human interaction, in which acoustic modalities are of central importance. However, this disparity is gradually being removed by advances in technology.

Figure 4. A multimodal representation composed of a dynamic graphic image and a dynamic acoustic image.

In many cases, acoustic modalities may provide an alternative or supplement to graphic modalities. For instance, acoustic images strongly augment the (virtual) realism of events, processes or situations rendered in dynamic graphic images. Fig. 4, using dynamic graphic and acoustic images, shows the demolition of a building. Furthermore, acoustic modalities generally have two primary advantages over graphic and haptic modalities: (1) they allow users to simultaneously monitor and identify sources of information in all possible directions, not just in the direction of the gaze or body surface; (2) they enable users to distinguish, monitor, and switch attention among simultaneous sources of sound or among sounds with disparate sound parameters. However, the potential of acoustic modalities is still largely waiting to be explored. Dynamic acoustic language (speech) is likely to become a powerful rival of typed graphical user interfaces, and the power of acoustic graphs for the exploration of high-dimensional data is going to be heard.

Acoustics have at least the information channels loudness, pitch, timbre, rhythm, duration, temporal order and source location. Acoustic linguistics has the following additional information channels: voice quality, stress, intonation, dialect, accent, personality.

4.3 The Haptic Modalities

Haptics are currently an impoverished medium in interface design, partly because of technological limitations and partly because, under normal circumstances, haptic representations are inferior to graphic representations in terms of information density and speed of acquisition. This situation is likely to change as the technology for haptic representation improves. Haptic representations comprise much more than representations for the visually handicapped and have important potential roles in representing information to normal users. They increase the (virtual) realism of representations and may convey information through bypassing overloaded visual and acoustic sensors.

Haptics have at least the following information channels: shape, size (length, width, height), texture (surface quality), position, orientation, temperature, pressure, voltage, spatial arrangement, movement, repetitive change of properties, non-repetitive change of properties, and temporal order.

The taxonomy demonstrator includes scanned images of real haptic representations rather than the haptic representations themselves. Two haptic representations are presented here. Fig. 5 is taken from the modality document on haptic compositional diagrams and shows the internal structure of the earth. Fig. 6 is from the haptic map modality document.

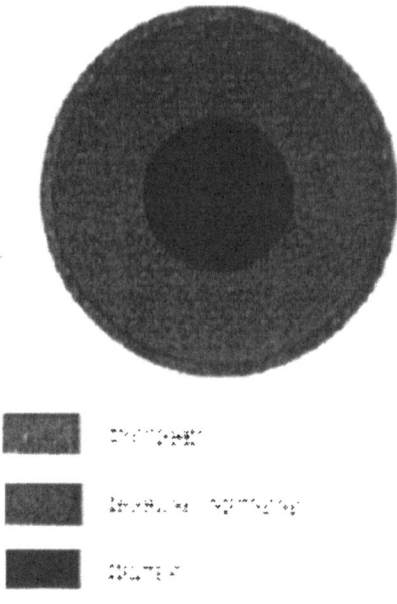

Figure 5. Scanned image of a unimodal haptic compositional diagram with bimodal legend using texture and haptic keywords, respectively. The diagram shows the geological composition of the Earth. Differently coloured surfaces have different texture.

Figure 6. A unimodal haptic map of the world.

5 States of Representation

Any unimodal modality is either static or dynamic. The distinction between static and dynamic modalities is, however, defined in terms of whether or not *freedom of perceptual inspection* is possible of the information represented by the modality rather than in terms of, say, the absence or presence of perceptible physical change. Freedom of perceptual inspection means that the user is allowed time to inspect, in random order and as long as desired, the information presented. Freedom of perceptual inspection is compatible with some amount of perceptible change as long as the change is repetitive and the cycle of repetitions is of relatively short duration as in, e.g., acoustic alarm signals or blinking graphics (cf. Fig. 7).

Figure 7. The blinking mail icon in this window is a static multimodal representation consisting of a static graphic image and a static graphic typed label (keyword).

As remarked in Sect. 2 above, the taxonomy tree does not incorporate distinctions between static and dynamic modalities in the haptic and acoustic media. These distinctions are made in the underlying modality documents, however.

6 Document Structure

The theory demonstrator currently includes 134 hypermedia documents comprising some 150 Kb of (non-illustrated) text. Structured in terms of the taxonomy tree (Fig. 2), these documents are of two types, modality documents and lexicon documents.

6.1 Modality Documents

Modality documents define, explain, analyse and illustrate the unimodal modalities from the point of view of interface design support. These documents share the same document structure which includes the following entries:

• Profile

- Inherited declarative and functional properties
- Specific declarative and functional properties
- Information mapping rules
- Combinatorial analysis
- Relevant operations
- Identified types-of

Each modality document is illustrated by some 5-10 illustrations selected such as to show both prototypical examples, important non-prototypical and marginal cases, interesting multimodal combinations, etc. What follows is a walkthrough of the modality document structure exemplified by illustrations from various modality documents.

1) *Profile.* A notation is used to express the profile of the modality, i.e. the combination of basic properties which defines the modality as being distinct in kind from other modalities at the same level. This was illustrated in Sect. 3.1 above.

2) *Inherited declarative and functional properties.* These are the properties, basic or otherwise, which the modality inherits from higher levels of the taxonomy. Except for the super level modalities, all modalities inherit an important part of their properties from higher levels. Thus, generic level modalities inherit the categorical and functional properties of their parent node at the super level, atomic modalities inherit the properties of their parent nodes at the super and generic levels, etc. To keep individual modality documents short, these properties must be retrieved through the hypertext links. The following example shows the list of links to inherited properties in the gestural notation modality document (hypertext links are underlined):

- linguistic modalities

- dynamic modalities

- graphic modalities

- notation

Dynamic graphics have the following information channels: (a) those of static graphics: shape, size (length, width, height), texture, resolution, contrast, value (grey scales), colour, brightness, hue, saturation, position, orientation, viewing perspective, spatial arrangement, short-duration repetitive change of properties; (b) in addition to those of static graphics: non-repetitive change of properties, movement, displacement (relative to the observer), and temporal order.

The dimensionality of dynamic graphics is: 1-D, 2-D and 3-D spatial, time.

Gestural notation thus inherits the properties of the linguistic, dynamic, graphic and notational modalities. As the information channel and dimensionality information is important to have close-at-hand, it is repeated in the document rather than having to be retrieved through hypertext links. Because of the pragmatic node-reduction policy

(Sect. 2), the gestural notation document presents both static and dynamic gestural notation. Fig. 8 shows an example of static gestural notation.

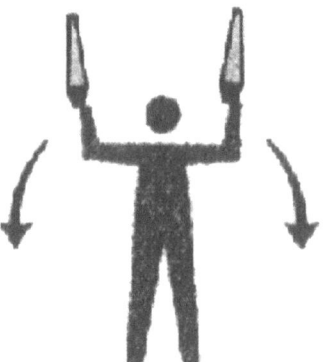

Figure 8. Static gestural notation: a marshalling signal which means 'move ahead' [18].

3) *Specific declarative and functional properties.* These are the properties which characterise the modality as being specifically different from its sister modalities with which it may share a common ancestry. For instance, in the arbitrary modality document (super level), the entry on 'Specific declarative and functional properties' includes the point that "Arbitrary modalities and aspects of modalities express information through having been defined ad hoc at their introduction." This implies that information represented in arbitrary modalities, whether graphic, acoustic or haptic, in order to be properly decoded by users, requires to be introduced in some non-arbitrary modality, such as some linguistic modality or other.

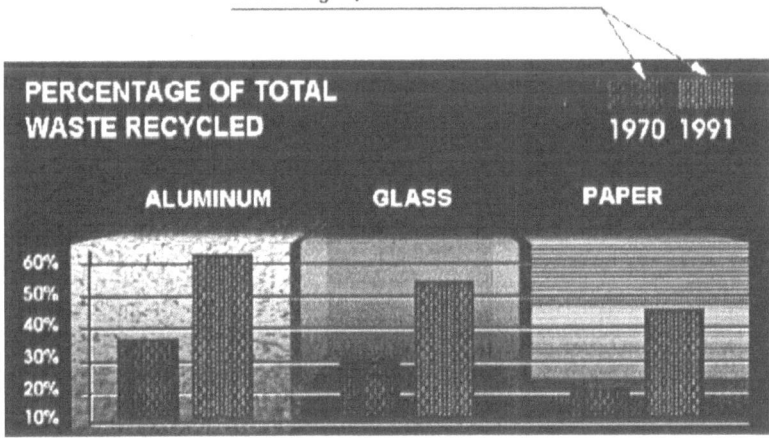

Figure 9. Dependence on linguistic modalities of an information channel used ad hoc.

This is demonstrated in Fig. 9 in which ad hoc use of the graphic information channel colour (blue for the left-hand bar and green for the right-hand bar in a pair) has been defined in static graphic typed language labels/keywords in the graph legend. Without this linguistic annotation, nobody would be able to interpret the graph. The graph compares waste recycling of aluminium, glass and paper in the years 1970 and 1991 in the USA.

4) *Information mapping rules* are similar in many respects to production rules. They express aspects of information which a particular unimodal modality is good at, or unsuited for, representing and sometimes under which conditions this is the case. Information mapping rules are crucial to, and their use for interface design support is being investigated as part of, the development of the information mapping methodology (cf. Sect. 1 above).

One of the information mapping rules in the static graphic image document is:

Facilitate the visual identification of objects, processes, or events <->
Consider including high specificity static graphic images in as high dimensionality and resolution as possible.

This rule effectively states that static graphic images are good tools for identifying objects, and that identification is further enhanced through high specificity (a large amount of detail in as many information channels as possible), high dimensionality (2 1/2D or 3D better that 2D), and high image resolution. The rule is read from left to right as an if-then rule. From right to left, the rule says that "Modality X is good at representing Y". An illustration of this rule, and hence of one of the advantages of the static graphic image modality, is the use of photographs in criminal investigation. It is virtually impossible to linguistically describe what a person looks like in such a way that the person may be uniquely identified from the linguistic description [6]. Use of static graphic images, such as the one shown in Fig. 10, makes this an effortless undertaking. Indeed, a picture can sometimes be worth more than a thousand words. Or, rather, this proverbial classic not only applies to pictures but to analogue representations in general, irrespective of whether they are embodied in graphics, acoustics or haptics.

5) *Combinatorial analysis.* This form of analysis addresses compatibilities and incompatibilities between the modality presented in a particular modality document and other unimodal modalities. For instance, in the modality document on explicit static graphic structures, it is stated under 'combinatorial analysis' that "explicit static graphic structures combine well with any static or dynamic graphic modalities, whether linguistic, analogue or arbitrary". This may be illustrated by Figs. 7 and 11. In Fig. 11, a Macintosh window is represented as a layered series of unimodal explicit static graphic structures. In Fig. 7, these unimodal explicit static graphic structures form part of the multimodal representation. Speaking more generally, combinatorial analysis is highly important to the discovery of patterns of compatibility and

incompatibility between unimodal modalities. Such patterns would begin to constitute a (unimodal) modality combination 'syntax'.

Figure 10. A unimodal static graphic image of high specificity.

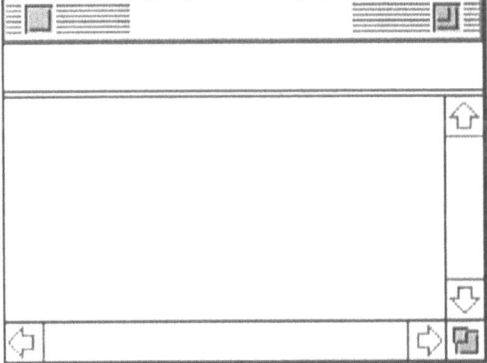

Figure 11. Nested unimodal explicit static graphic structures: the Macintosh window.

6) *Relevant operations.* These are operations which may be applied to the current unimodal modality. An operation may be defined as a meaningful addition, reduction, or other change of information channels or dimensionality in a representation

instantiating some modality. The purpose of an operation is always to bring out more clearly particular aspects of the information to be presented. Dimensionality reduction, as in reducing common road maps from 3-D to 2-D without any loss of relevant information; specificity reduction, as in replacing an image with a sketch; saliency enhancement, as in selective colouring; and zooming are some of the operations applicable to analogue graphic modalities. Similarly, **boldfacing**, *italicizing* and underlining are common operations in graphic typed languages (see 6).

7) *Identified types-of.* These are the specific types of a unimodal modality, which are found one level down in the taxonomy hierarchy. For instance, dynamic non-analogue graphic language (generic level) has six atomic types:

- Dynamic written text
- Dynamic written labels/keywords
- Dynamic written notation
- Graphic spoken discourse
- Graphic spoken labels/keywords
- Graphic spoken notation

The three dynamic graphic spoken language modalities are graphic representations of someone speaking and may be used for lip reading and acoustic language disambiguation.

6.2 Lexicon Documents

Lexicon documents define, explain and illustrate the key concepts of modality theory. There are currently 68 such documents or concepts. To mention but a few, dimensionality, information channel, interpretational scope, modality structures (icons, lists, tables, etc.), saliency, metaphor, and specificity are all lexicon document entries. Due to the heterogeneous nature of their topics, no rigid document structure has been enforced on lexicon documents. Most lexicon documents include a definition and a number of illustrations but are otherwise tailored to their specific contents. Lexicon documents are not directly accessible from the taxonomy tree (or main screen), but are reached through hypertext links from modality documents and other lexicon documents.

7 Discussion and Future Work

As remarked in the introduction, it remains an open question to what extent the current version of the workbench will need to be further re-designed in order to function as a design support tool. A key question concerns automation. The information mapping methodology assumes that practical information mapping is done in two broad iterative phases [3]. In the first phase, information is collected and succinctly represented concerning the information to be represented and exchanged between user and system during task performance on the artifact to be designed. In the second phase, this information is 'put through' a design tool based on modality theory, which will map the collected domain and task information onto a set of input/output modalities which could optimise the interface to the artifact. The question is whether the workbench might be developed into such a tool. One possibility might be to fully automate the workbench by developing its current set of information mapping rules into the rule set of a knowledge-based system which could support interface design at any level of detail. However, a recent case study of a realistic design process [20] strongly indicates that this is not feasible. The real world of IT artifacts and their various work domains, tasks to be supported, user types, etc. is quite simply too complex and unmanageable to make such an endeavour a realistic one. At the opposite extreme, the workbench might not be automated at all but would make its information easily accessible to interface designers who would use their 'natural intelligence' to let the information constrain their design decisions. Furthermore, the workbench information should be developed down to a certain level of detail only, leaving the lower levels of interface design detail to designer craft skill, guidelines, standards, etc. The latest case study [9] suggests the existence of a natural division of labour between rule-based information mapping on the one hand, and the subsequent design of lower-level interface details on the other. In addition, this study investigates a first extension of modality theory from being solely a theory of output representational modalities to being a theory of the interaction between input and output modalities. Our most recent work demonstrates the feasibility of building a theory of input modalities along the principles of the theory of output modalities presented in this paper.

References

1. N.O. Bernsen: A research agenda for modality theory. In Cox, R., Petre, M., Brna, P. and Lee, J. (Eds.): Proceedings of the Workshop on Graphical Representations, Reasoning and Communication. World Conference on Artificial Intelligence in Education, Edinburgh, 43-46, August 1993

2. N.O. Bernsen: Matching information and interface modalities. An example study. Esprit Basic Research project GRACE Deliverable 2.1.1. (1993)

3. N.O. Bernsen: Modality theory in support of multimodal interface design. In Proceedings of the AAAI Spring Symposium on Intelligent Multi-Media Multi-Modal Systems, Stanford, March 1994, 37-44

4. N.O. Bernsen: Foundations of multimodal representations. A taxonomy of representational modalities. Interacting with Computers Vol. 6, 4, 347-71. (1994)

5. N.O. Bernsen: A revised generation of the taxonomy of output modalities. Esprit Basic Research project AMODEUS-2 Working Paper RP5-TM-WP11, (1994)

6.   N.O. Bernsen: Why are analogue graphics and natural language both needed in HCI? In Paterno, F. (Ed.): Design, Specification and Verification of Interactive Systems. Proceedings of the Eurographics Workshop, Carrara, Italy, June, 165-179. Forthcoming in the Focus on Computer Graphics Series, Springer Verlag 1995

7.   N.O. Bernsen and A. Bertels: A methodology for mapping information from task domains to interactive modalities. Esprit Basic Research project GRACE Deliverable 10.1.3. (1993)

8.   N.O. Bernsen, S. Lu and M. May: Towards a design support tool for multimodal interface design. The taxonomy workbench and theory demonstrator. Esprit Basic Research project AMODEUS-2 Working Paper RP5-TM-WP5. (1994)

9.   N.O. Bernsen and S. Verjans: Designing interfaces by information mapping. A case study of the CERD design. Esprit Basic Research project AMODEUS-2 Working Paper (forthcoming). (1995)

10. E. Hovy and Y. Arens: When is a picture worth a thousand words ? Allocation of modalities in multimedia communication. Paper presented at the AAAI Symposium on Human-Computer Interfaces, Stanford (1990)

11. A. Lockwood: Diagrams. A visual survey of graphs, maps, charts and diagrams for the graphic designer. London: Studio Vista (1969)

12. M. May: Representations and homomorphisms. A taxonomy of representations for HCI, part 1. Esprit Basic Research project GRACE Deliverable 2.1.5 (1993)

13. M. May: Levels of representations and mappings. A taxonomy of representations for HCI, part 2. Esprit Basic Research project GRACE Deliverable 2.1.6. (1993)

14. M. May: From semantic types to multimodal presentations: Case studies. A taxonomy of representations for HCI, part 3. Esprit Basic Research project GRACE Deliverable 2.1.7. (1993)

15. M. May: Taxonomy and levels of mappings in the construction of multimodal interfaces. Workshop Notes from AI-ED '93: World Conference on Artificial Intelligence in Education, Edinburgh, August. Workshop on Graphical Representations, Reasoning and Communication. (1993)

16. M. May and N.O. Bernsen: The taxonomy workbench. Esprit Basic Research project GRACE Deliverable 2.1.8. (1993)

17. M. May and R. Tobin: The taxonomy workbench. Purpose, functionality and layout. Esprit Basic Research project GRACE Deliverable 2.1.9. (1993)

18. E.R. Tufte: Envisioning information. Cheshire: Graphics Press 1990

19.   S. Verjans: EuroCODE: Preliminary information mapping analysis of an AMODEUS common exemplar. Esprit Basic Research project AMODEUS-2 Internal Report RP5-TM-IR1. (1994)

20.   S. Verjans and N.O. Bernsen: PaTerm: A case study in information mapping. Esprit Basic Research project AMODEUS-2 Working Paper RP5-TM-WP6. (1994)

Acknowledgements. The work reported in this paper was done on grants from the Esprit Basic Research project AMODEUS-2 and the Danish Research Council for the Natural Sciences whose support is gratefully acknowledged.

Towards a Systematic Building of Software Architecture: the TRIDENT Methodological Guide

François Bodart, Anne-Marie Hennebert, Jean-Marie Leheureux,
Isabelle Provot, Benoît Sacré, Jean Vanderdonckt

Facultés Universitaires Notre-Dame de la Paix, Institut d'Informatique
Rue Grandgagnage, 21, B-5000 Namur (Belgium)
Tel : + 32- (0)81- 72 50 06 - Fax : + 32- (0)81- 72 49 67 - Telex : 59.222 Fac. Nam.B
E-mail : fbodart@info.fundp.ac.be

Abstract. When designers are facing the question how to build an application architecture practically, they often have to consider various arguments and factors coming from different perspectives: decomposition criteria in architecture design, dialog independence in user interface (UI) design, methodology to follow in a development team. These factors are not easy to conciliate, forcing designers to make trade offs or unbalanced choices. In this paper, we discuss an architecture model, which is part of TRIDENT project, that addresses these issues. It consists of a generic architecture model for highly interactive business oriented applications. It is accompanied with a practical task-based methodology for building an architecture that automatically preserves desired criteria. Assumptions made for the architecture model, its content and the semantics of relationships are explained. The systematic approach is exemplified by a complete architecture case throughout the paper. Software Architecture Analysis Method (SAAM) is finally applied to prove the benefits of this architecture and to evaluate it with respect to relevant criteria. This paper suggest first steps towards a systematic building of a software architecture.

1 Introduction

Several architecture models which are convenient for an interactive application have already been introduced [1,6,7,14,15]. Though they can be examined according to a generic metamodel [16], it is not always clear to judge the appropriateness and the quality of these models [8,9]. Up to now, gained experience shows that a multiplicity of factors is to be considered :

- traditional architectures coming from software engineering do not support UI design easily : architectures should provide relevant abstractions needed for configurable UI components, particularly when UI is adaptable [4];
- application architectures should satisfy usual decomposition criteria : e.g., high internal cohesion, weak coupling degree, easy component reusability [1];
- application architectures should meet more advanced criteria needed by interactive application development : e.g., conceptual simplicity, reuse of code, quality of resulting UI, easy maintenance [16];

- separating UI functionality from application semantics is one of the most important goals of architecture design [16];
- particular architectures should adhere to a generic model that supports this separation and respects mentioned criteria [6,7,14,15,16].

These opposed considerations are not effortless to manage simultaneously so that the quality of resulting architectures are not easy to judge. SAAM has been introduced for this purpose [8,9]. Whereas existing architecture models can be described, understood and evaluated through SAAM, such models do not suggest any methodology to follow for reaching an architecture

- that is intrinsically compatible with the architecture model,
- that automatically preserves expected criteria,
- that rests on task analysis rather than simply technical considerations,
- that guarantees compatibility with task model rather than application model,
- that allows systematic generation and easy change of interaction techniques.

However, several works already consider task aspects in their approach [11,12]. In this paper, we report on TRIDENT (Tools foR an Interactive Development ENvironmenT) which utilizes an architecture model and promotes a systematic methodology that addresses these issues.

2 Background on TRIDENT

The main goal of TRIDENT is to allow interface designers to generate as automatically as possible a user interface to a highly interactive business oriented application from specifications describing different models (e.g., task model, object oriented entity/relationship model) [2,3]. Multiple aspects such as selection of presentation units, choice of appropriate interaction objects, computer-aided placement of interaction objects, computer-aided window sequencing, basic conversation generation are covered [3].

This generation also encompasses a code skeleton of the application containing the required abstractions for a practical and effective architecture. This paper is dedicated to the methodological steps required for building practically such an architecture in this context. This methodology supposes that task analysis and presentation design have already been performed. We show now the contents of these pre-requisite. More details are found in [3].

2.1 Task Analysis

One of the results of task analysis is a model describing the interactive task the user has to carry out. This task behavior model can be graphically represented with an *activity chaining graph* (ACG). An ACG depicts an information flow between functions chained to define a business logic in order to reach the goal(s) assigned to the interactive task.

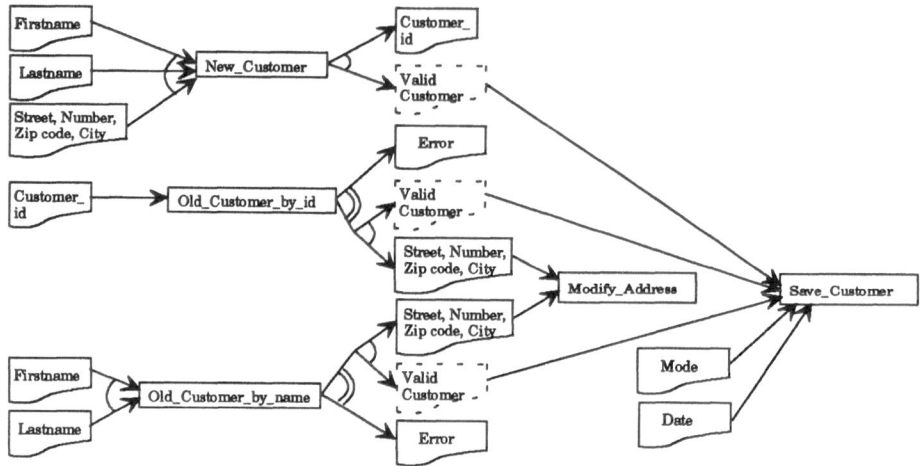

Fig. 1 The ACG of the task "Recording a customer"

The ACG for interactive task "Recording a customer" is reproduced in fig. 1. Each function receives input informations, representing data required for the good execution of the function : for instance, informations Firstname, Lastname, Address should be provided in order to execute New Customer function. Each function produces output informations which are either external to the user (e.g., Customer_id) or internal to another function (e.g., Valid_Customer). Termination of a function execution enables the function chaining to progress one step further in the ACG. The input of input informations, the display of output informations and the function chaining are compatible with OR links (no arc of a circle), AND links (simple arc), XOR links (double arc). For instance, the AND link between Firstname, Lastname, and Address means that all informations are needed ; the XOR link between Error and the set of informations Valid_Customer, Address means that either the error message will be produced or the combination of the informations will be sent and displayed.

2.2 Presentation Design

UI presentation is designed with the following concepts :

- *concrete interaction object* (CIO) : this is a real object belonging to the UI world that any user can manipulate such as a push button, a list box, a check box. A CIO is composite if it can be decomposed into smaller units and is simple if it cannot;
- *abstract interaction object* (AIO) : this consists of an abstraction of all CIOs from both presentation and behavior points of view, independently of target environments;
- *window* : this is a root window that could be considered as a logical window for AIO and a physical window, a dialog box or a panel for CIO. Every window is

itself a composite CIO, composed of other simple or composite CIOs. All windows are geographically delimited on the user's screen;

- *presentation unit* (PU) : this consists of an input/display world required for carrying out any sub-task of a particular interactive task. Each presentation unit can be decomposed into one or many windows which may not be all displayed on the screen simultaneously. Each PU is composed by at least one window called *base window* from which other windows are chained.

Presentation design, explained in details in [3], roughly consists of identifying appropriate PUs, composed of windows, themselves composed of AIOs at design time transformed into CIOs at run time. According to the ACG introduced in fig. 1, the user can either add a new customer or modify a previously existing one. For this purpose, such a customer can be searched through a database by identification number or by both firstname and lastname. Consequently, two PUs might be identified: one PU1 covering functions `New_Customer`, `Old_Custo-mer_by_id`, `Old_Customer_by_name`, and `Modify_address` ; another PU2 covering only the function `Save_Customer`.

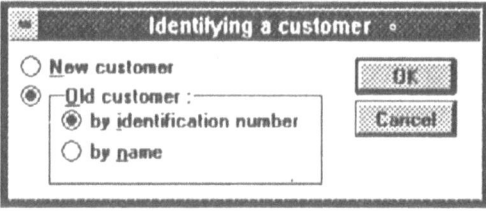

Fig. 2 Presentation of window W11

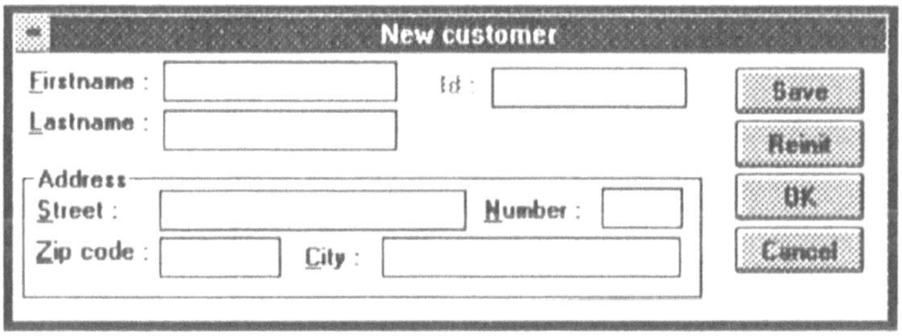

Fig. 3 Presentation of window W12

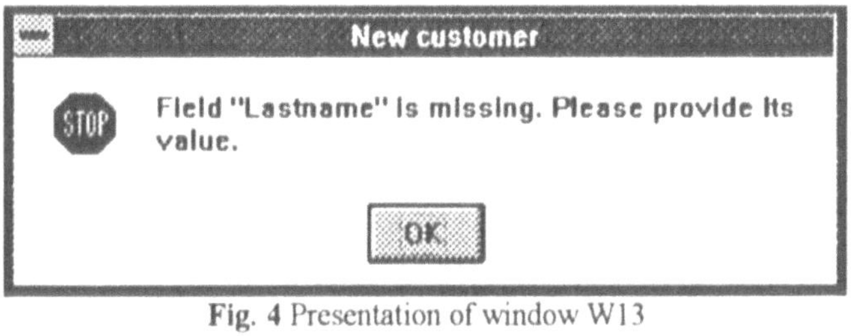

Fig. 4 Presentation of window W13

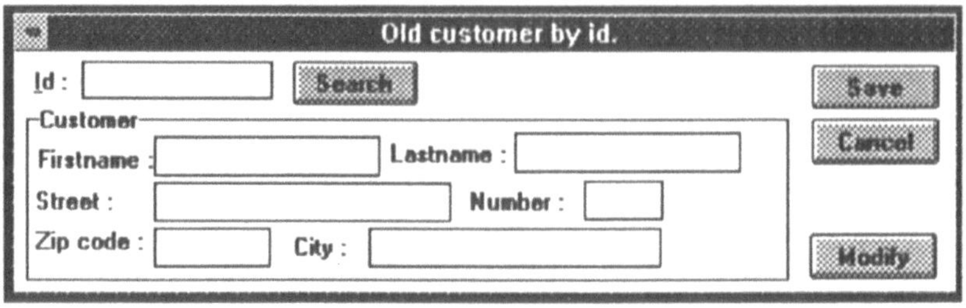

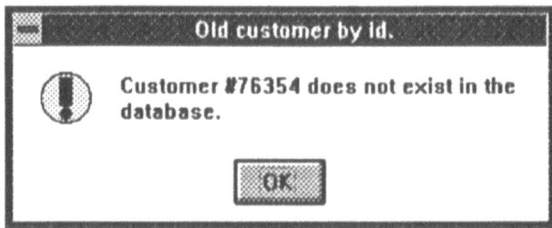

Fig. 5 Presentation of window W14

Fig. 6 Presentation of window W15

With respect to the ACG, PU1 can be divided into seven windows :

1. a dialog box W11 enabling the user to select a dialog from the three alternatives (new customer, old customer by id or old customer by name) (fig. 2);
2. a window W12 enabling the user to add a new customer by providing all informations (fig. 3);
3. an error message W13 for warning the user if some information is missing in W12 (fig. 4);
4. a window W14 enabling the user to search a customer by identification number, and then to modify it when needed (fig. 5);
5. a message W15 warning the user if provided customer id. does not lead to a customer existing in a database (fig. 6);
6. a window W16 enabling the user to search a customer by both firstname and lastname, and then to modify it when needed (similar to W14);
7. a message W17 warning the user if provided firstname and lastname do not lead to a customer existing in a database (similar to W15).

Similarly, the presentation unit PU2 can be composed of one window W21 in order to input Mode and Date before finally recording the customer (fig. 1). This approach defines a presentation by iterative refinement starting from global objects to end up with terminal objects according to the structure shown in fig. 7.

Such a presentation structure consists of a hierarchy of CIOs for each interactive task (IT). Summarized outline of presentation structure of our exemple is given in fig. 8 with the CIO name in brackets (see fig. 2 to 6).

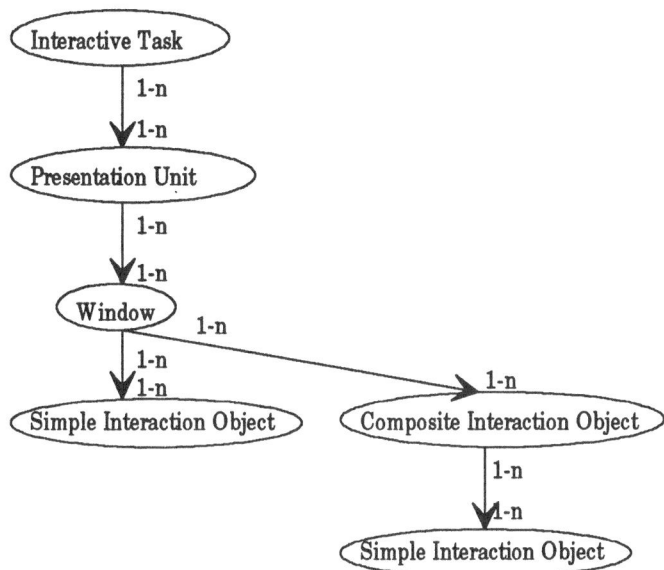

Fig. 7. Structure of presentation

IT_Recording_a_Customer
    PU1_Identifying_a_Customer
        W11_Customer_Identification (dialog box)
            Customer_Type (radio button)
            Old_Customer_Search (radio button)
            Ok (push button)
            Cancel (push button)
        W12_New_Customer (window)
            Firstname (edit box)
            Lastname (edit box)
            Address (group box)
                Street (edit box) ...
            Save, Reinit, Ok, Cancel (push buttons)
        W13_Field_Missing (error message)
        W14_Search_by_id (window)
            ...
        W15_Id_nonexistent (warning message)
        W16_Search_by_name (window)
            ...
        W17_Name_nonexistent (warning message)
    PU2_Storing_a_Customer
        W21_Final_input (dialog box)
            Mode (edit box)
            Date (edit box)

Fig. 8. Presentation structure

3 TRIDENT **architecture model**

The two required pre-requisites, i.e., the writing of ACG from task analysis and presentation design, have been introduced. Before detailing a systematic approach for deriving an application architecture, it is necessary to define the architecture model to be respected.

3.1 Assumptions

The proposed architecture model consists of a hierarchy verifying the following methodological assumptions :
- each hierarchy element should be derived - directly or indirectly - from task analysis;
- autonomy - as perfect as possible -, which is similar to separation, should coexist between elements representing application components and UI components. At the level of UI components, this autonomy is prolonged between components realizing the conversation (the dynamic behavior) and components realizing presentation (static appearance) [2]. We are able to afford these autonomy assumptions since, in the area of business oriented applications, the disposition of CIOs is not necessarily synonym of semantic.

3.2 Content of the model

The proposed architecture model [2,3] consists of a hierarchy of generic elements illustrated in fig. 9.

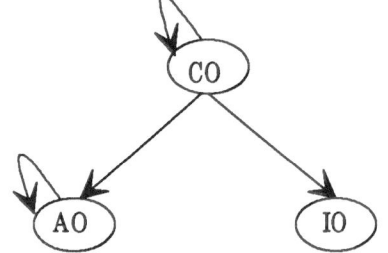

Fig. 9 Generic scheme of the architecture model

This architecture model is composed of three object classes for which identification, behavior rules and relationships can be described as follows :

1. a class of *Control Objects* (CO) is a generic class decomposed into COs of different types for managing the dialogue and insuring a mapping between data structures of the application and those of the presentation. Each CO holds its own behavior which consists of a portion of this dialogue management and this mapping. This behavior takes the form of a *script* written with a rule language [2,3]. This script can be partially represented graphically with a state-transition diagram;

2. a class of *Application Objects* (AO) is a class which cannot be decomposed since its elements represent the application functions; it is important to ensure that the necessary functions are included in the architecture since functional requirements [1] play a vital role in assigning semantic meaning to the interactive task and its sub-tasks;

3. a class of *Interaction Objects* (IO) is a generic class containing two kinds of CIOs : CIOs issued from input/output informations and CIOs strictly implied by the dialogue (e.g., the push buttons enabling the function triggering).

The rules that govern the behavior of these three object classes are identical as well as the authorized relationships between any pair of two objects in this hierarchy : each object is an *agent* [1,6]. If an arrows links a father object to any child object, then a relationship is established between them meaning that the father object "uses" a child object. More precisely,

- a child object send to a father object events related to the significant behavior states;
- a father object calls the primitives offered by a child object in order to obtain informations required to proceed with the steps of the behavior.

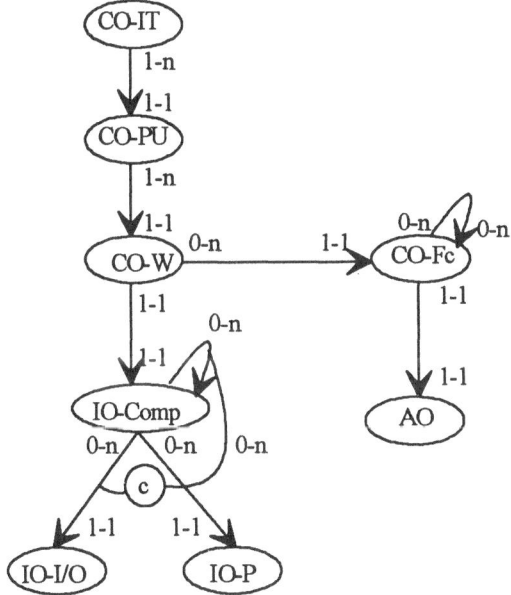

Fig. 10. Structure of Control Objects

3.3 Application Objects (AO)

They represent a particular application component in the sense that, for each function appearing in the ACG, there is a corresponding AO in the hierarchy. If the current application already exists and is written with a non object oriented language to be reused, then each function will be encapsulated in a new AO for which the function code will make one the object's methods. If the current application is a new one, it will be immediately written according to any object-oriented language and a new AO will be inserted for each application function.

The set of all AOs forms the *functional machine*, whatever the case. The function triggering belonging to this functional machine determines a functional business logic represented by the ACG. Each AO in the proposed hierarchy is always a child object of one and only one control object, the one which is responsible for the common function.

3.4 Control Objects (CO)

They are responsible for managing another interface component in the sense that, for each step for composing the presentation, there is a corresponding CO in the hierarchy. The composition of presentation invites us to isolate windows which are dynamically sequenced in presentation units. The various presentation units therefore materialize the context required for carrying out the interactive task. Moreover, the hierarchy of COs can be built on the same schema (fig. 7) so that the following COs are useful:

- CO-IT : the only control object corresponding to the interactive task;
- CO-PU : the control objects corresponding to the presentation units;
- CO-W : the control objects corresponding to the windows;
- CO-Fc : the control objects corresponding to the application functions.

This structure is detailed in fig. 10. Every CO corresponding to an application function (CO-Fc) is a child object of a window control object (CO-W), the one which holds all CIOs required to trigger the function from the functional machine.

3.5 Interaction Objects (IO)

They create the UI presentation in the sense that they represent on one hand input/display data (e.g., edit box, radio button, check box) - these are the *input/output interaction objects* (IO-I/O) -, and, on the other hand, the control elements (e.g., push buttons, icons) - these are the *presentation interaction objects* (IO-P).

These objects have been selected by the expert system and are finally equivalent to CIOs belonging to physical environments like Ms-Windows, OSF/Motif, etc.

Every IO, whether IO-I/O or IO-P, is a child object of a CO-F control object to which it send events representing significant state changes. It holds primitives providing to the father object the values to be transmitted. Most of the time, these primitives are the native methods provided by the tool kit.

3.6 Semantic of relationships in the architecture

The main semantics of relationships involved in the architecture are enumerated below:

- Semantic of CO-IT→CO-PU relationship : the CO corresponding to the interactive task (CO-IT) manages the dynamic chaining of PUs, that is loads and unloads - sequentially or concurrently - a particular PUi according to events received from a PUj.
- Semantic of CO-PU→CO-W relationship : the CO corresponding to a PU (CO-PU) manages the dynamic chaining of windows, that is displays and undisplays - with tiling or overlapping - a particular window Wi according to events received from another window Wj.
- Semantic of CO-W→CO-Fc relationship : the CO corresponding to a window (CO-W) calls the CO corresponding to the application function when all conditions required by this call are fulfilled, that is when all data required by the function to be performed are available in the child objects of the CO-W. The CO corresponding to the application function (CO-Fc) send to the CO-W an event warning the process termination.
- Semantic of recursive relationships between CO-Fc : the COs corresponding to the application functions are exchanging events between themselves to maintain the ACG dynamic consistent and call mutually services one from each other in order to exchange these informations.
- Semantic of relationships between IO... and CO-W : the IOs - whether IO-I/O or IO-P - are those objects which are directly in touch with the user reaction ; the father objects calls their services to know which entries have already been performed by the user and send themselves events reflecting their contents to their father objects.

4 Systematic Approach for Architecture Building

We assumed that task analysis with writing of ACG and definition of presentation have already been performed, as indicated previously.

4.1 List of architecture objects

The list composed of objects of the three kinds includes:

- a control object corresponding to the interactive task (CO-IT);
- a control object corresponding to each presentation unit (CO-PU$_1$,...,CO-PU$_n$);
- a control object corresponding to each window of each presentation unit (CO-PU$_1$F$_1$,...,CO-PU$_1$F$_m$,..., CO-PU$_n$F$_1$,..., CO-PU$_n$F$_p$);
- a control object for each function in the ACG (CO-Fc);
- an interaction object for each input/output information for all functions (IO-I/O);
- an interaction object for each presentation induced object (IO-P).

4.2 Procedure

The systematic approach for deriving the architecture consists of a four steps procedure:

1. writing the *primary hierarchy of presentation COs* from presentation design : each entry in the presentation structure outlined in fig. 8. is mapped onto a presentation CO (fig. 11) with "uses" relationships (depicted as arrows in fig. 11) between them according to the same hierarchical structure.
2. writing the *primary hierarchy of functional COs* from the ACG : each function in the ACG is mapped onto a functional CO with "uses" relationships between them according to the special property : the primary hierarchy of function COs is quite the inverse hierarchy of the ACG (fig. 12).
3. encapsulating of functions into AOs and linking to the functional COs : each function in the ACG is encapsulated in a corresponding AO to be linked with a "uses" relationship to the related functional CO highlighted in step 2.
4. integrating both hierarchies with special "uses" relationships to obtain the final architecture which is summarized in fig. 13.

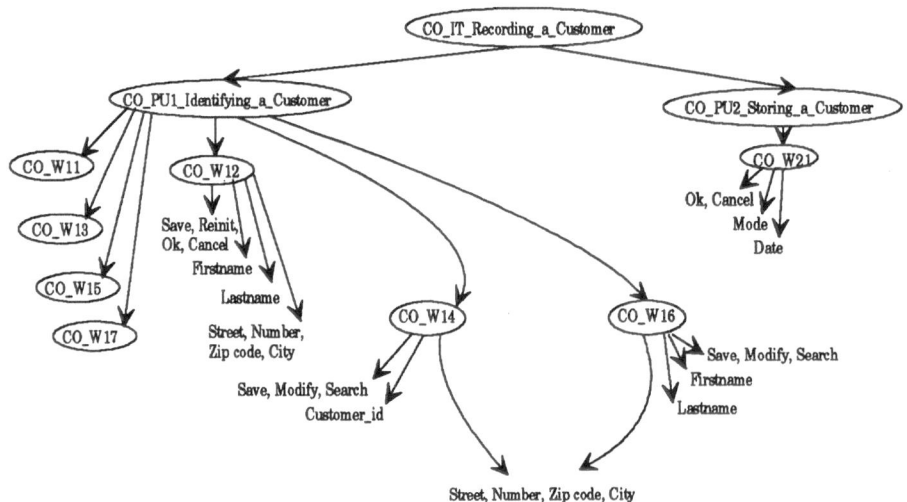

Fig. 11 Hierarchy of presentation COs

4.3 Relationships between architecture objects

"Uses" relationships linking different objects can be systematically created as follows:

- connect any control object corresponding to a presentation unit to the control object corresponding to the interactive task from which it depends (CO-IT→CO-PU);

- connect any control object corresponding to a window to the control object corresponding to the presentation unit which contains this window (CO-PU→ CO-W);
- connect any interaction object corresponding to an input/output information to the window in which the function having this information as parameter is located (CO-W→IO-I/O);
- connect any interaction object corresponding to an information induced by the presentation to the window where it appears (CO-W→IO-P);
- connect any object control corresponding to an application function to the control object corresponding to the window in which this function is performed (CO-W→CO-Fc).

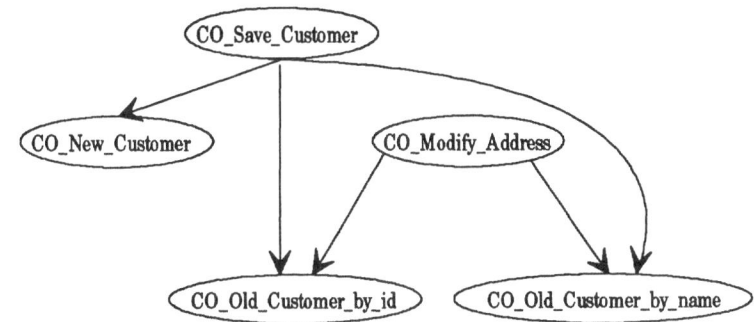

Fig. 12 Hierarchy of functional Cos

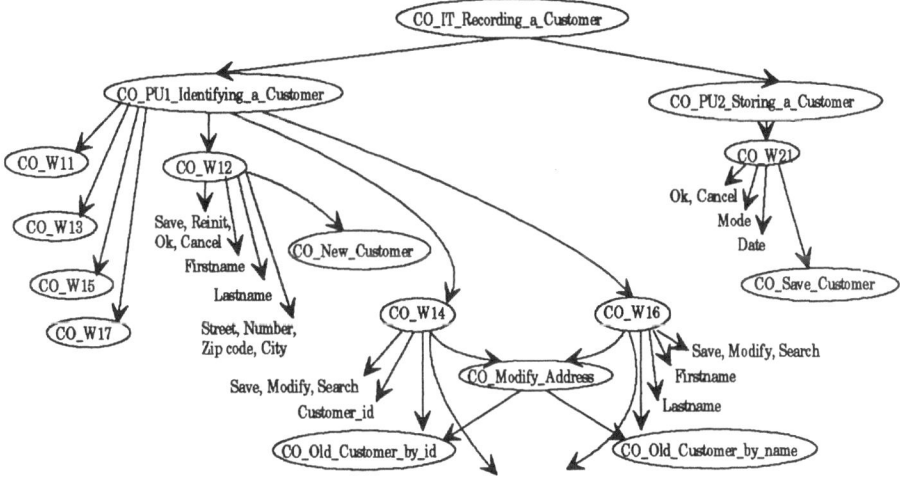

Fig. 13 Final architecture after integration

5 Related Work

Numerous existing architecture models, such as PAC [6], Chiron-1 [15], UIDE [14], are extensively reported [1,7,8,16]. Hence, we will only compare TRIDENT architecture with two significant architecture models. In order to achieve separation, PAC objects [6] are structured into three perspectives:

1. *abstraction* where system concepts and functions are located,
2. *presentation* containing interaction behavior or system image,
3. *control* that maintain consistency between abstraction and presentation.

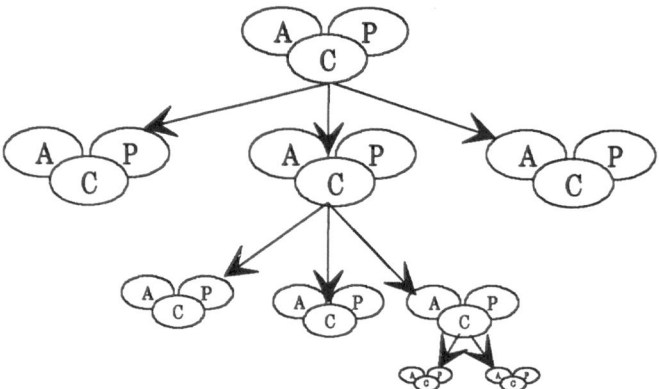

Fig. 14 PAC architecture as a hierarchy of objects

TRIDENT's objects are structured in the same way : application objects are equivalent to abstraction, interaction objects are equivalent to presentation, and control objects are equivalent to control. Moreover, PAC and TRIDENT's objects are agents since they exchange events related to abstract state memory (abstraction), graphical state memory (presentation), and control memory (control).

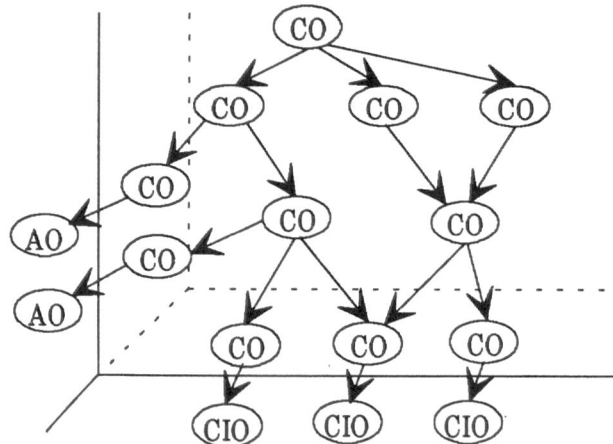

Fig 15. TRIDENT architecture as a graph of COs, AOs and CIOs

But the largest difference comes from the point that, according to PAC, an entire interactive application is globally viewed as a hierarchy of PAC agents. Therefore, abstraction, presentation and control are completely distributed at all levels in this hierarchy (fig. 14). This is not the case with TRIDENT's objects : first, the whole control is a graph (no longer a hierarchy) made up of COs ; second, the presentation is made up of CIOs which are linked to the final presentation COs (in the bottom dotted part of fig. 15); third, the whole abstraction is made up of AOs which are linked to the final functional COs (in the left dotted part of fig. 15). The proverb "divide to conquer" is applied globally to the three aspects separately.

From a methodological point of view, PAC provides rules for deducing, defining and decomposing objects. Despite this fact, the applicability of these rules is left to the designer's expertise and are subject to interpretation : this might not guarantee to reach univocally to the same architecture for a same application. It is not always obvious to recognize which solution supports evaluation criteria and offers the most numerous advantages.

Conversely, TRIDENT's systematic approach tries to provide guidance for deriving an architecture from an activity chaining graph and presentation design. But, on the other hand, PAC objects support interruptible manipulation, parallelism of inputs and outputs, dynamic inter-referential behavior. This last feature is not supported by TRIDENT's objects since they are completely statically defined during design time.

UIDE objects are also structured into general object, composed of application objects (on which application functions are performed) and interface objects (with which the user interacts) [14]. The comparison is still more straightforward since interface objects are subsequently refined into presentation objects (corresponding to IO-P in TRIDENT) and system interface objects (corresponding to IO-I/O in TRIDENT).

UIDE emphasizes especially the ability to express application objects in terms of action, parameter, parameter constraint, pre-condition and post-condition and the ability to automatically generate the run time architecture from application model. In TRIDENT, pre-condition and post-condition of each function appearing in the ACG automatically consists of a first-order predicate formula which is a conjunction and/or disjunction of input informations (for pre-condition) and output informations (for post-condition). Automatically generated source code is sometimes believed to be unmaintainable by human programmers. We think that reliance on the ACG may provide better understanding and follow-up of a generated architecture.

6 Architecture Description and Conclusion

TRIDENT architecture satisfies a particular set of desirable criteria according to the Arch model [14] since functionalities of the proposed architecture do not have components that cross the boundaries of Arch's components.

276

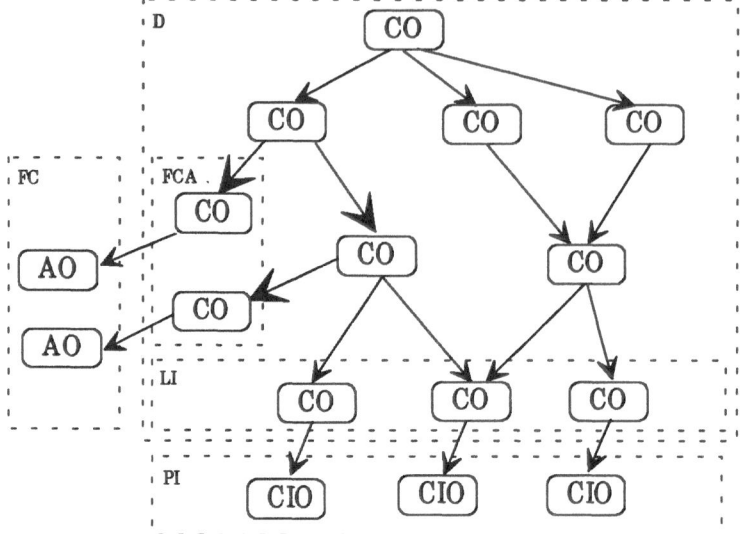

Fig. 16 TRIDENT architecture with functional roles

SAAM method [8,9] is therefore applied to evaluate TRIDENT architecture. Our interpretation is given in fig. 16 where functional roles of each object type are represented according to the Arch model [16]. We see that there is a structural separation between the Physical Interaction (PI) and Logical Interaction (LI) roles in the presentation. Another structural separation appears between Functional Core (FC) and Functional Core Adapter (FCA). LI and FAC both belong to the Dialogue (D).

That analysis, based on the Arch model, is motivated by modifiability/portability and, indeed, these characteristics are succesfully supported. But non-functional characteristics should also be of concern : this architecture model, although highlighting many qualities and being prescriptive, may not fit all types of interactive applications because this is impossible to define [16]. Experience shows that it is mostly appropriate for moderately complex business applications with no real-time capabilities, but with reasonable system response time. Productivity of development tools can be maximized and conceptual simplicity ranges from low to high. This is especially important when physical toolkit and hardware platforms independences are required.

Acknowledgments

SAAM and the DSV-IS'95 anonymous referees for helpful comments on a previous version of this manuscript. This work was supported by the "Informatique du Futur" project of "Service de la Politique et de la Programmation Scientifique" under contract N°IT/IF/1. Any opinions, findings, conclusions or recommendations expressed in this paper are those of the authors, and do not necessarily reflect the view of the Belgian Authorities.

References

1. L. Bass, J. Coutaz: Developing Software for the User Interface. Reading: Addison-Wesley 1991
2. F. Bodart, A.-M. Hennebert, J.-M. Leheureux, I. Sacré, J. Vanderdonckt: Architecture Elements for Highly-Interactive Business-Oriented Applications. In L. Bass, J. Gornostaev, C. Unger (eds.). Lecture Notes in Computer Science. 753. Berlin: Springer-Verlag 1993, pp. 83-104
3. F. Bodart, A.-M. Hennebert, J.-M. Leheureux, I. Provot, J. Vanderdonckt: A Model-based Approach to Presentation: A Continuum from Task Analysis to Prototype. In F. Paterno (ed.): Proceedings of 1st Eurographics Workshop on Design, Specification, Verification of Interactive Systems DSV-IS'94 (Carrara, June 8-10, 1994). Eurographics Series 1994, pp. 25-39
4. G. Cockton: Spaces and Distances: Software Architecture and Abstraction and their Relation to Adaptation. In M. Schneider-Hufschmidt, T. Kühme, U. Malinowski (eds.): Adaptive User Interfaces. Amsterdam: Elsevier Science Pub. 1990, pp. 79-108
5. G. Cockton: The Architectural Bases of Design Re-use. In D.A. Duce, M.R. Gomes, F.R.A. Hopgood, J.R. Lee (eds.): User Interface Management and Design. Berlin: Springer-Verlag 1991, pp. 15-34
6. J. Coutaz: PAC, An Implementation Model for Dialog Design. In Proc. of Interact'87 (Stuttgart, September 1-4, 1987). Amsterdam: Elsevier Science Pub. 1987, pp. 431-436
7. D.A. Duce, M.R. Gomes, F.R.A. Hopgood, J.R. Lee: User Interface Management and Design. In Proc. of the Workshop on User Interface Management Systems and Environments (Lisbon, June 4-6, 1990). Berlin: Springer-Verlag 1990
8. R. Kazman, G. Abowd, L. Bass, M. Webb: Analyzing the Properties of user Interface Software Architectures. Carnegie Mellon University, School of Computer Science, Technical Report CMU-CS-93-201, 1993
9. R. Kazman, L. Bass, G. Abowd, M. Webb: SAAM: A Method for Analyzing the Properties of Software Architectures. In Proc. of 16th International Conference on Software Engineering (Sorrento, May 1994), pp. 81-90
10. A.-M. Hennebert: La hiérarchie des Objets de Contrôle : Règles de construction. Internal TRIDENT report, Institut d'Informatique, Namur, April 6, 1994
11. T. Moher, V. Dirda, R. Bastide, Ph. Palanque: A Bridging Framework for the Modeling of Devices, Users, and Interfaces. Technical Report UIC-EECS-ICE-94-13, University of Illinois, 1994
12. L. Nigay, J. Coutaz: A Design Space For Multimodal Systems: Concurrent Processing and Data Fusion. In S. Ashlund, K. Mullet, A. Henderson, E. Hollnagel, T. White (eds.): Proceedings of the Conference on Human Factors in Computing Systems INTERCHI'93 (Amsterdam, 24-29 April 1993). New York: ACM Press 1993, pp. 172-178
13. I. Provot: L'enregistrement d'une commande téléphonée. Internal TRIDENT report, Institut d'Informatique, Namur, December 17, 1993
14. P. Sukaviriya, J.D. Foley, T. Griffith: A Second Generation User Interface Design Environment: The Model and The Runtime Architecture. In S.

Ashlund, K. Mullet, A. Henderson, E. Hollnagel, T. White (eds.): Proceedings of the Conference on Human Factors in Computing Systems INTERCHI'93 (Amsterdam, 24-29 April 1993). New York: ACM Press 1993, pp. 375-382

15. R. Taylor, G. Johnson: Separations of Concerns in the Chiron-1 User Interface Development and Management System In S. Ashlund, K. Mullet, A. Henderson, E. Hollnagel, T. White (eds.): Proceedings of the Conference on Human Factors in Computing Systems INTERCHI'93 (Amsterdam, 24-29 April 1993). New York: ACM Press 1993, pp. 367-374

16. UIMS Tool Developers Workshop: A Metamodel for the Runtime Architecture of an Interactive System. SIGCHI Bulletin 24, 1, pp. 32-37 (1992)

The Design of Narrative Virtual Environments

Mark Green

Department of Computing Science
University of Alberta
Edmonton, Alberta, Canada

Abstract. The hardware technology for the production of virtual environments (VE) has been available for at least five years, but very few software tools have been developed for this new technology. Existing software tools are very low level, forcing the application developer to use programming to produce most of the application code. Many VE applications will be developed by non-programmers, who don't have the skill or time to use today's low level tools. The development of high level tools has been hindered by the lack of models and specification techniques for these user interfaces. Since this interaction style is quite new, its not surprising that these models and techniques haven't been developed. Now that we have some experience with the development of VE applications, its time to start considering the formal basis of this interaction style.

This paper presents our initial attempt at developing a formal model for narrative virtual environments, and the specification techniques that go along with this model. The model and specification techniques that we have developed form the basis for a set of software tools that can be used by non-programmers to produce narrative virtual environments.

1. Introduction

The production of virtual environments is a very time consuming process. At the present time there are few high level tools to assist with this process, therefore, virtual environment development relies heavily on programming. Since 1989 we have been working with the Banff Centre for the Arts on the production of artistic virtual environments, and this collaboration has resulted in a number of significant environments [Laurel1994]. All of these virtual environments were produced by teams consisting of both programmers and artists. This process is too expensive, due to its reliance on a team of programmers, and too frustrating for the artists, since they can't directly take part in the environment construction process. These problems can be partially solved by producing a set of software tools that support non-programmers in the production of virtual environments.

High level tools for user interface design and implementation must be based on a formal model of the user interfaces to be produced, and specification techniques for describing them. Thus, in order to produce high level tools for virtual environment development, there must first be a formal model of this user interface style, and specification techniques that can be used to describe them. Without a good formal model, high level tools will be little more than ad hoc collections of tricks, that will behave in an inconsistent manner and be difficult to use. Since this is a new user interface style, little work has been done on developing formal models for it. We are now just beginning to have enough experience with the development of virtual environments to consider developing formal models for them. This paper presents our initial attempt at producing such a model for virtual environments, and specification techniques for different aspects of these user interfaces. This work has mainly concentrated on identifying the requirements for a formal model and specification techniques, rather than on the development of definitive models or specification techniques. Thus, this paper is short on formal details, and concentrates more on what needs to be done.

The next section of this paper describes the types of virtual environments that we are interested in. The third section covers the formal model of virtual environments that we are developing. The remaining sections describe the tools we are developing and the specification techniques they employ. The work described here is still in progress, so the results are still incomplete.

2. Narrative Virtual Environments

The state of the art in virtual environment design is still quite primitive. At the present time very few successful VEs have been designed, so there is very little experience to draw upon in the design of new environments. One thing that is becoming apparent is that there are different types of virtual environments, and these different types of environments require different design methodologies and tools. In our work we have identified three types of virtual environments:

1) Exploratory Environments - This type of environment is characterized by an exploration of a 3D space. This exploration mainly involves navigating through the space, with little or no interaction between the user and the objects in the space. Architectural walkthroughs and some scientific applications are examples of this type of application.

2) Design Environments - The main purpose of this type of environment is to produce some type of 3D object. The environment consists of a collection of primitive parts and tools for producing objects, and the user's main goal is to manipulate these tools in order to produce some type of object. Most computer aided design (CAD) applications are examples of this type of environment.

3) Narrative Environments - The main purpose of a narrative environment is to provide the user with some experience that is entertaining, develops some skill, or conveys some information to the user. These environments typically consist of collections of objects the user can interact with, and a number of scenarios that the user can explore. The designer provides the overall structure for the scenarios, but the the choice of path through the environment is largely up to the user. Most simulation, education and game applications are examples of this type of environment.

This paper mainly deals with narrative virtual environments, though some of the techniques discussed here are also applicable to the design and implementation of other types of environments. The main reasons for concentrating on this type of environment is our experience in designing these environments, and a readily available source of feedback on the tools that we develop.

A narrative VE can be viewed as a collection of *scenes*. Where each scene has its own set of objects and interactions with the user. A scene can be viewed as a subenvironment, in the sense that the user can only interact with (and see) the objects in the current scene. The user typically spends a significant amount of time in each scene, and the transitions between scenes requires some action on the part of the user.

A *narrative* is used to structure the scenes in an environment. The narrative determines the set of scenes that can be reached from the current scene, the user actions causing transitions between scenes, and how these transitions occur. Each scene in the environment typically has more than one scene that can follow it. The next scene is determined by the user, through the actions that he or she performs. Each path through the environment (the sequence of scenes visited) is called a *scenario*, and each of these scenarios presents the user with a different view of the environment.

The division of an environment into a number of scenes has several advantages. From the authoring point of view, it divides the design problem into smaller chunks that are easier to handle. At any point in time the designer concentrates on a small part of the environment, with a smaller object set and significantly fewer interactions between objects. By introducing the narrative component, the designer can view the environment as telling a story (or multiple stories). This allows the designer to structure the information or experience they present to the user. This makes environment design easier. Second, the division of the environment into scenes makes it possible to produce more efficient implementations of the environment. Only the objects in the current scene need to be displayed to the user, and they are the only objects that we need to compute the behaviors for. For large environments, this can significantly effect the amount of computing resources required to run the environment. Culling techniques can be used to reduce the number of objects that must be displayed, but if the designer has already partitioned the environment for us, we can save a considerable amount of computation in the culling process. Third, the division of the environment into scenes encourages the reuse of environment components. The more modular the environment is, the easier it is to modify or reuse parts of. This could save a considerable amount of design time for future environments.

The design of a narrative VE can be divided into three tasks:

1) Object Design - This task deals with the design of object geometry and behavior. The designer identifies the objects that will appear in the environment, produces the geometry for each of these objects, and then defines their behaviors.

2) Composition - This task deals with selecting the objects appearing in each scene, and then positioning and orienting them within the scene. At this stage the designer also determines the interactions between the objects in the scene, and between the user and these objects.

3) Narrative - In this task the designer interconnects the scenes in the environment.

The designer determines the events that will cause transitions between scenes, and how these transitions will occur.

3. A Formal Model for Narrative VEs

This section starts with a discussion of two types of applications that illustrates the basic requirements for our formal model and the resulting software architecture. This is followed by a concise statement of the requirements and an outline of the formal model.

3.1. Application Types

The two application types presented in this section illustrate two aspects of narrative VE's. In the first application type, the environment is divided into a number of separate spatial domains, with the transitions between these domains forming the main structure of the narrative. In the second example there is only one spatial domain, but there are many temporal domains. The main structure of the narrative is the transition between the different temporal domains.

The first application type is typical of many artistic/entertainment applications and some educational environments. In these applications the environment is divided into a number of mutually exclusive spatial domains. When the user is in one domain, he or she is unaware of the other domains, and can only move between the domains by triggering a transition in the narrative. Each spatial domain has its own message or set of skills to be learned. In the case of game applications, the spatial domains can be viewed as the levels of the game, and in educational applications, each domain has its own set of concepts or skills that are to be transferred to the user. In the game application, the transition between domains will occur when the level is complete, and in educational applications the transition will occur when the user has demonstrated mastery of the concepts. In the case of artistic environments, each domain has its own message, or tells part of the story, and transitions between domains are triggered when the user has performed some action or a time limit has been reached.

The first type of application is illustrated by many artistic virtual environments. In these environments each scene tells part of the story, and typically lasts for several minutes. These scenes can have complex geometry, with some of them having on the order of a million polygons. This amount of geometry can't be displayed in real-time without a considerable amount of tuning and special purpose display techniques. In addition, the objects in these environments can have quite sophisticated behaviors. It can take a considerable amount of time to design these behaviors, and they can consume a significant amount of execution time while the environment is running. Due to the complexity of each scene, most workstations can only keep a few scenes in memory at any time. Thus, the application must page in scenes as the user moves through the environment.

Once a scene is complete, the application must move to a new scene. This action is represented by a transition from the current scene to the next scene. There are two constraints on these transitions:

1) Artistic. The user can't move instantly from one scene to another, since the transition will be too sharp, causing the user to lose the flow of the piece. In other forms of media, devices have been developed that smooth the transitions from one scene to the next, reducing the shock to the user. Similar techniques must be developed for virtual environments, and our specification techniques must support their development.

2) Technical. With current hardware, the transition from one scene to the next requires a consider amount of disk activity as the new scene information is swapped in. This usually requires several seconds, and the user must be entertained while this is occurring. The environment can't freeze while the new scene information is read.

Existing artistic environments use a range of narrative devices to smooth the transitions between scenes. One device is fading out the current scene over several seconds, and then fading in the new scene over several seconds. Another device is to provide a simple scene that forms a bridge between the two scenes. This bridge has a small number of objects with limited interactions, requiring a small amount of execution time while the new scene is read. Both of these narrative devices require some programming, and are hand-crafted for each environment.

The first type of application has the following characteristics that are important for our formal model. First, there are very few common objects that appear in all or most of the domains. Second, each domain has its own set of objects that have their own unique behaviors. This object and behavior set will change as the user moves from one domain to another. Third, the transitions between domains are identifiable events. When the transitions occur, the set of objects the user is interacting with changes. The old objects disappear and the new ones appear. This transition must be carefully managed so it doesn't seem to be totally chaotic. The transition itself takes a certain time period, which is at least several seconds, and while it is occurring something must happen to occupy the user. The environment designer must carefully design these transition, and our software must provide support for their design.

In the second type of application, the environment is divided into a number of temporal domains, which are mutually exclusive. At any point in time, the user is in one of these domains and his actions will be governed by the objects that are active at that time. A typical example of this type of application is a simulator or training program. For example, consider a driving simulator where the user is learning how to handle different driving situations, such as being cut-off by another driver, or a child running out in front of his vehicle. Each driving situation can be viewed as a separate temporal domain, having its own set of objects used for that particular driving situation. The user will always be in the same spatial domain, inside a car or truck driving along a road. When a scene transition occurs, this spatial domain won't change, instead several new objects will be added to the environment.

For example, a new temporal domain could add a car to the environment, at some distance behind the user. This car then passes the user, and in the process cuts him off. There is no obvious transition between these domains, otherwise the student will know that something is about to happen, and most of the objects in the environment are common across all the temporal domains. The transition between domains are largely under the control of the designer, though the user's reactions might be one input to the transition decision. The environment designer has a set of situations that he or she wants to present to the user, and these situations shouldn't be presented in a totally deterministic manner. The main activity in environment design is producing the individual situations, plus a decision process that will control the transitions between the different situations.

The nature of transitions is different in the two types of applications. In spatial domain environments, the transitions form an important part of the story, and they are quite visible to the user. The designer carefully designs the transitions so they make a positive contribution to the environment, and carry part of the story. In temporal domain environments, the transitions are invisible and happen instantaneously. The transition itself isn't important, the main concern is with the state that it leads to. The transition is viewed as a decision mechanism, and not part of the environment itself.

3.2. Requirements

Based on the above discussion, the main requirements for our formal model of narrative environments are:

1) The object is the basic unit of geometry and behavior. Our concern isn't with the details of object geometry and behavior, since this is not relevant to narrative design. Object geometry and behavior is produced by a separate set of tools and this information is imported into the environment at run-time. By factoring out geometry and behavior, the model and tools developed for narrative design address a wider range of applications, since they make no assumptions about how the environment is presented.

2) Support for a global object set. In time domain environments, most of the objects are active for the duration of the simulation, and in spatial domain environments there are usually a few objects that appear in most of the scenes, thus the architecture most support a global object set that is always active.

3) Dynamic grouping of objects to produce scenes. In spatial domain environments, there can be a large number of scenes, with each scene having a different set of objects. These object sets will be constructed dynamically as the user moves from one scene to another, instead of creating the complete set of objects for all scenes at the start of the run. In time domain applications, the set of active objects can change over time, due to time transitions. In this type of environment, the model must provide a way of introducing new objects when required.

4) Dynamic mapping (scene based) of triggers to object behavior. Object behaviors are triggered by events that occur in the environment. These events could be the result of user actions, or the actions of other objects. The mapping between events and the behaviors executed in response to them must be under the control of the environment designer. For each scene the designer must be able to specify the actions that trigger each object behavior, and these actions can change from one scene to another.

5)   Transitions as a separate entity with a similar structure to scenes. In the case of spatial domain environments, there can be a sharp transition between scenes, where most of the object in the current scene disappear and the objects for the next scene appear. Environment designers must have the ability to control these transitions, since it may not be possible to switch the object set instantaneously, and and an instantaneous switch my be confusing to the user or spoil the mood of the environment. The designer must be able to specify transitions, that act like scenes, in the sense that they have an object set and behaviors.

6)   Transition management mechanisms that determine when transitions occur and support both spatial domain and time domain environments. The designer must be able to specify the actions that cause the transition, the scene they lead to, and the duration of the transition.

3.3. A Sketch of the Formal Model

This section presents a sketch of the formal model that we are developing for narrative virtual environments. At this point the model is still incomplete, and there are details that still need to be filled in.

This model assumes the existence of a set of objects, O, and a set of events E. Each object is capable of displaying itself in the environment, and has a set of behaviors that are executed in response to events. At this level, how the object displays itself or executes its behaviors isn't important, we only assume the existence of these object attributes. Section 4 briefly describes some of the techniques that we have used to describe object geometry and behavior. The model also assumes a set of events used to trigger object behaviors and transitions between scenes. Again, we aren't concerned with the format of these events, only that they exist and can be used to trigger different actions. Section 5 describes the techniques that we use for event specification.

At first it might appear that state machines are a good model for narrative virtual environments. In the case of spatial domain environments this model is a pretty good match, but it must be augmented for time domain environments, since the notion of state isn't as strong here. Our model consists of the current object set, o, the current event mapping, em, and a transition network or state machine. The current object set, o, is a subset of O, and contains all the objects that are displayed at the current time. The initial state of the environment defines the initial value for o, and its value changes as the environment moves from one state to the next. The event mapping em, is a mapping from events in E, to objects in o and their behaviors. Each entry in em can be viewed as a 3-tuple, with one component of this tuple being the event, and the other two components being an object and one of its behaviors. When the event occurs, the corresponding behavior in the tuple's object is executed. Again, the initial value of em is determined by the initial state of the environment, and changes as the environment moves from one state to the next.

The state machine is used to modify the contents of o and em. The states correspond to the scenes and transitions in the virtual environment, and the state transitions correspond to the events triggering transitions between scenes. Each state transition is triggered by an event from E. There are several way in which o and em can be modified by a state transition. One approach is to have each state contain the new values for o and em, which works quite well for spatial domain environments, where there is little global information that needs to be carried from state to another. In the case of time domain environments, each state only makes a small change to o and em, since most of the objects are global. This suggests that the states should encode the changes in o and em, and not their new contents. Each state contains a list of objects, o_r, to be removed from o, a list of objects o_a to be added to o, and similar sets em_r and em_a of tuples to be removed from and added to em. Note, that o_r could specify that all the objects should be removed from o, facilitating the description of spatial domain environments. In order to maintain consistency, any tuples in em that mention an object in o_r are also removed from em.

We considered adding the modifications to o and em to the state transitions, instead of the states, as is typically done with transition diagrams when they are used to describe 2D user interfaces. This approach wasn't used for two reasons. First, it doesn't match our intuitive notion of how these environments are designed. Since we are using this model as the basis for our design tools we want a model that is as intuitive as possible. Second, it was too easy to produce inconsistencies in the environments. Some states must have the same values of o and em, no matter which path is used to reach them. If the transitions contain the modifications to o and em, then all the transitions leading to one of these states must produce the same result, which may be hard to guarantee. When we have more experience with this model, we will know whether we have made the correct decisions.

There are two types of states in this model. Regular states represent the scenes in the environment, and transition states represent the transitions between scenes. The first state of a scenario is a regular state, and the environment then alternates between transition and regular states. In terms of a state diagram, every regular state has arcs leading to transitions states, and every transition state has arcs leading to regular states. Using states to represent transitions gives the designer more flexibility in transition design.

A transition state has four attributes. First, an object set, o_t, that contains the objects that are displayed during the transition. Second, an event mapping, em_t, describing how events are mapped to object behaviors during the transition. Third, the duration of the transition, that is a non-negative real value. Four, a decision procedure that is used to determine the arc to be followed after the transition. In spatial domain environments the first three attributes are used. During the transition, the user interacts with the objects in o_t, using the event mapping em_t. The third attribute specifies the duration of the transition, the time in which o_t is displayed and the event mapping em_t is active. In the case of temporal domain environments the duration is zero, and the decision procedure is used to determine the next state in the environment. For these environments, o_t and em_t aren't used.

The following two short examples illustrate how this model can be used to described the two types of virtual environments. Both of these examples have been simplified to illustrate the basic techniques, and don't represent realistic environments. The first example is based on a spatial domain environment that has two scenes and one transition. The first scene has object set o_1, and event mapping em_1. The second scene has object set o_2, and event mapping em_2. There is also a common object set o_c, with event mapping em_c. The transition consists of a tunnel that leads from scene one to scene two, and the user can perform some navigation actions while being pulled through the tunnel. The object set an event mapping for the transition state are:

$$o_t = \{tunnel\}$$

$$em_t = \{navigation\ actions\}$$

The duration of the transition is 10 seconds, the time required to traverse the tunnel. The state diagram for this environment is shown in figure 1.

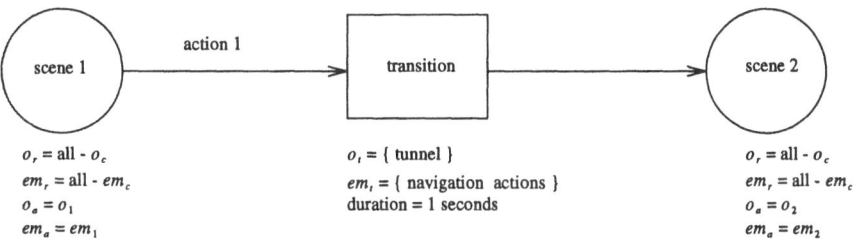

$o_r = \text{all} - o_c$
$em_r = \text{all} - em_c$
$o_a = o_1$
$em_a = em_1$

$o_t = \{ tunnel \}$
$em_t = \{ navigation\ actions \}$
$duration = 1$ seconds

$o_r = \text{all} - o_c$
$em_r = \text{all} - em_c$
$o_a = o_2$
$em_a = em_2$

Figure 1 State diagram for spatial domain example

The second example is a simple temporal domain environment based on a driving simulator. The main scene in the driving simulator represents driving without any problems. This state is called the neutral state, and has object set o_n, and event mapping em_n. There are three problem states in this environment:

1) cut-off state: object set o_c, and event mapping em_c

2) drunk driver state: object set o_d, and event mapping em_d

3) pedestrian state: object set o_p, and event mapping em_p

There is a transition state that controls which of the problem states is selected, and each problem state is followed by a null transition back to the neutral state. There are numerous decision procedures that could be used for the transition state. The simplest is to assign a constant probability to each problem state, and base the decision on this probability. More complex decision procedures will vary these probabilities based on the success or failure of previous trials. The state diagram for this example is shown in figure 2. A more realistic simulation will have sequences of problem states, with each state having two arcs leaving it, one for success and one for failure.

Since the same basic model is used for both spatial and temporal domain environments, it is possible to combine them to produce a mixed environment. For

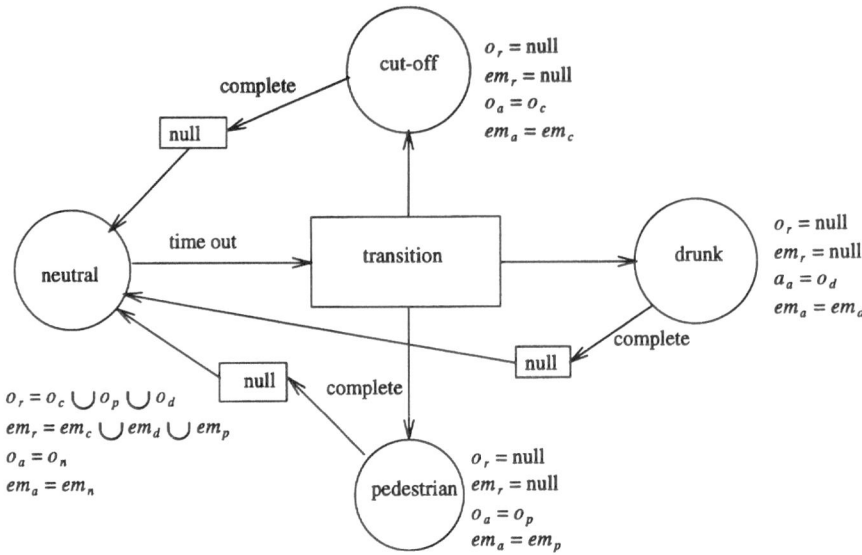

Figure 2 State diagram for the simple driving simulator

example, a driving simulator could have several spatial domains corresponding to different driving conditions. Each of these spatial domains can then be viewed as a temporal domain environment. This type of environment could be described by a single state diagram.

This model addresses single user environments, and doesn't deal with the possibility of multiple users sharing the same environment. It isn't clear that this will cause a problem, but it is an area of concern.

4. Object Design Tools

We have developed several tools for designing object geometry and behavior. The basis for these tools is the OML (Object Modeling Language) programming language, a interpretive language for describing object geometry and behavior. Object descriptions in OML are similar to objects in most object oriented programming languages. OML supports most standard geometrical modeling primitives and operations, such as polygons, NURBS curves and surfaces, transformations, hierarchical modeling, lighting models and texture mapping.

The interesting part of this language is behavior specification, which is based on the relational model developed by Hanqiu Sun [Sun1993]. In this model a unit of behavior is described by a relation that has three parts; a source object, a responder object and an action. The source object is the object or event causing the motion. The responder object is the object that performs the motion, and the action describes how the responder reacts to the source's action. The OML code for an object doesn't specify the events that the object responds to, just the responses themselves. The event specification, and the mapping from events to object behaviors is part of the input to the environment manager described in the next section.

An explosion behavior could be triggered by a collision event between two instances. The specification of this event and the mapping to the explosion behavior is part of the specification used by the environment manager, while the change in object geometry caused by the explosion is part of the OML code for the object. In this model designers doesn't specify the time when actions occur, instead they concentrate on how the object responds to events in the environment. There are mechanisms for triggering events at either fixed points in time, or relative to the occurrence of another events, so traditional time based animation techniques can still be used.

Behaviors can influence each other. Once a behavior has been triggered, it can suspend the actions of other behaviors, or trigger other behaviors. For example, an animal may have a walking behavior that is always active, except when it it about to collide with another object. When a possible collision is detected, the collision avoidance behavior is triggered, and this behavior suspends the walking behavior until collision avoidance has terminated. This allows the programmer to develop standard behaviors, such as walking, without concern for exceptional conditions, such as collisions. In this way the motion specification can be modularized, and the development process simplified. High level control over relations allows for the integration of traditional animation techniques, such as keyframing, with more reactive motion specifications. In the above example, the walking behavior could be keyframed, and the animal will still be able to respond to collisions, since the collision response interrupts the keyframed walking behavior. Thus, even though keyframing is used to define the behaviors, they are still capable of responding to events occurring in the environment. This model has been formalized, and the formal description of it can be found in [Sun1991-Sun1993].

An interactive program, called JDCAD+, has been developed for specifying object geometry and behavior [Halliday1994]. This program can be used by non-programmers, and produces an OML program as its output, allowing objects developed in JDCAD+ to be easily integrated with the other tools we are developing.

5. Environment Composition and Narrative Tools

Our approach to scene composition and narrative design is based on the idea of an environment manager. This program manages or controls the execution of a virtual environment. Its input is a description of the environment to be executed, and its assembles the objects required by the environment, manages their responses to events, control object display, and provides performance monitoring and debugging facilities. There are several advantages to using an environment manager. First, it allows environment designers to work at a higher level than program code, and thus avoids a number of device and machine dependencies. Second, it provides a range of debugging and performance monitoring tools that assist the designer with the development and tuning of the environment. Third, it provides a degree of portability that isn't possible with other environment design tools.

Our current environment manager, described in [Wang1995], supports single scene environments with multiple users. We are currently extending this environment manager to handle environments with multiple scenes using the model presented in section 3. One of the major problems encountered in our current environment manager is specifying events in a portable way. Since virtual reality is an immature technology, there isn't a standard configuration of 3D devices that is universally available. The equivalent of the combination of a keyboard and mouse, that is assumed by all 2D user interfaces, doesn't exist for virtual reality. Thus, virtual environment designers are faced with the problem of specifying user interaction without knowing the devices that will be used for this interaction.

To assist with this portability problem, we have been developing a model and notation for describing the events that trigger object behaviors. This model is based on a rather simple view of logical input devices. In this model a logical input device can either generate a trigger or a value. A *trigger* is an event or action that occurs at a particular instant in time. A trigger could be mapped to a button press or a glove gesture, depending upon the physical realization of the user interface. A *value* is a continuous reading of an input device and is assumed to consist of a 3D position and orientation. A value could be generated by any one of a wide range of 3D tracking devices. The specification of the environment consists of a list of trigger names and value names. The environment specification assumes that these name will be mapped to physical devices when the environment is executed, and this mapping will be site specific. For example, there could be table that maps trigger names to buttons or glove gestures, and values to different 3D trackers. In many ways this mapping is similar to translations in X.

One approach to solving this problem is the device mapping used in the MR Toolkit. In the MR Toolkit each input device is handled be a separate server, and each server has a unique server name. A system wide table, called servertab, is used to map the server name to the workstation where the server is located, and provide any device dependent information. For values only the name of the sever, plus an optional minor code, is required to identify the device. The minor code is used for trackers that have multiple sensors that are all processed by the same server. In this case the minor code identifies the particular sensor to be used. The syntax that is used to specify values is:

value value_name server_name(minor)

In the case of triggers there are two possibilities. First, the device could be a collection of buttons. Most of our trackers have a set of buttons mounted on them, that are used to indicate events. A button is specified using basically the same syntax as a value; the name of the button server followed by a minor code identifying the particular button, or buttons, that are pressed. Second, the device could be a glove and the trigger is the recognition of a particular gesture made with the glove. For this type of trigger there are three pieces of information that are required, the server for the glove device, the file containing the gesture information, and the name of the gesture. The following syntax is used to specify this information:

trigger trigger_name gesture(server_name(minor), gesture_file, gesture)

As an example consider the device mapping for a simple application. This application requires the head and hand positions as values, and three triggers called move, grab, and release. The device mapping that is used for this application is:

```
value head eyephoned
value hand datagloved
trigger move glovebutton(1)
trigger grab glovebutton(2)
trigger release glovebutton(4)
```

Given the set of triggers and values that are available, the events used in the environment can be specified using an event language. An *event* has a boolean value that is evaluated on each update of the virtual environment. If the event value is true in the current update, the object behaviors mapped to it are executed in the current update. The primitives that can be used in event expressions are shown in figure 3. Obviously, triggers are primitives in this notation. Each object can export one or more condition procedures that also serve as primitives. These procedures are executed in each update, and return a boolean value. One of the important things occurring in an environment are collisions between objects, thus they form another type of primitive in our language. The designer can specify a collision with a particular object, a class of objects, or any object. Every object in the environment has a bounding box associated with it. Another language primitive is whether a value is located inside or outside of an object's bounding box.

```
tick
trigger
condition_procedure(parameter values)
collision(instance)
collision(object)
collision(ANY)
in(value,instance)
out(value,instance)
```

Figure 3 Primitive event expressions

Our event language has the standard boolean operators, allowing the designer to combine primitives or events to produce more complex conditions. In addition, it has operators that examine the history of event expressions. The start operator is true, if the event expression is true in the current update, but false in the previous one. Similarly, the stop operator is true, if the event expression is false in the current update, but true in the previous one. The middle operator has the value true if the event expression is true in both the current and previous updates. The syntax for these expressions is shown in figure 4.

event | event
event & event
~ event
start (event)
stop (event)
middle (event)

Figure 4 Event expression syntax

For example, the following event expression is used to generate an event in the first update that the grab trigger occurs with the hand in the object box:

start(grab) & in(hand,box)

Once an event has been defined it can be used to control one or more object behaviors. Each object instance has a mapping that specifies the behaviors to be executed when particular events occur. This mapping is specified when the instance is created. The syntax for instance creation is:

instance object_name instance_name (parameters)
    actions
            mappings
    end

The actions part is optional and consists of one or more mappings, where each mapping has one of the following forms:

1) event_expression behavior_specification
2) event_expression { behavior_specifications }

In the first form there is a single behavior specification, and in the second form there are several behavior specifications enclosed in { and }. When the event expression is true, the behavior specifications are executed. The individual behavior specifications have the following format:

behavior_name
suspend(behavior_name)
activate(behavior_name)
trigger(behavior_name,dt)

The first form of behavior specification is a behavior procedure that is executed when the event expression is true. The next two forms control the state of a behavior procedure. The suspend form suspends the behavior so it can't respond to any events, and the activate form returns the behavior to a state where it can respond to events.

The last form of behavior specification triggers a behavior at some point in the future. The parameter, dt, is added to the current time to produce the time when the behavior will be executed.

6. Conclusions

This paper has examined the problem of developing formal models and specification techniques for virtual environments. The requirements for these models and techniques have been outlined, along with a quick sketch of our current research in this area. This work is still quite primitive, and there is considerable amount work that still needs to be done.

None of the techniques mentioned in this paper have dealt with the issue of real-time, which is one of the most important problems in virtual environments. A virtual environment must maintain a minimum update rate, which is at least 10 updates per second. For most applications, the computations required exceed the 100 msec that are available for each update. There needs way of specifying the importance of various aspects of the user interface, so the limited amount of computation time can be allocated to the most important parts of the virtual environment.

References

Halliday1994.S. Halliday and M. Green, A Geometric Modeling and Animation System for Virtual Reality, *VRST'94 Proceedings*, 1994, 71-84.

Laurel1994.B. Laurel, R. Strickland and R. Tow, Placeholder: Landscape and Narrative in Virtual Environments, *Computer Graphics 28*, 2 (1994), 118-126.

Sun1991.H. Sun and M. Green, A Technique for Animating Natural Behavior in Complex Scenes, *Proceedings 1991 International Conference on Systems, Man, and Cybernetics*, 1991, 1271-1277.

Sun1992.H. Sun, A Relation Model for Animating Adaptive Behavior in Dynamic Environments, *Ph.D. Thesis, University of Alberta*, 1992.

Sun1993.H. Sun and M. Green, The Use of Relations for Motion Control in an Environment with Multiple Moving Objects, *Graphics Interface'93 Proceedings*, 1993, 209-218.

Wang1995.Q. Wang, M. Green and C. Shaw, EM - An Environment Manager for Building Networked Virtual Environments, *VRAIS'95 Proceedings*, 1995.

On The Expression Of Interaction Properties Within An Interactor Model

Panos Markopoulos

Dpt. of Computer Science, QMW College, University of London
Mile End Road, London E1 4NS

Abstract. This paper introduces a formal model for the description of interactive systems based on the interactor model of [15, 17]. Similarly to that model, it is intended to be used constructively for building specifications of interfaces as compositions of interactors. Changes are brought about to two aspects of the model: firstly, a modularised representation of control information is achieved which supports the independent description of the data transforming behaviour of the interactor and of the temporal constraints imposed on that behaviour. Secondly, distinct representations of 'result' and 'display' data handled by an interactor are related within a process algebraic framework, allowing the expression of usability related properties of interaction.

1 Introduction

This paper presents an approach to modelling interactive systems based on the concept of the interactor. The model introduced is a variation of the interactor model of Paterno' and Faconti [15, 17] which is referred to below as the Pisa interactor. The changes introduced allow for the separation of the interactor specification into two components: one implements the data operations performed by the interactor and the other embodies the dialogue control elements of its specification. This separation is preserved when forming compositions of interactors. The modeller may choose between two different views of the interface specification: an architectural view where the interface is specified as a composition graph of simple interactors and a 'design oriented' view where a 'centralised' dialogue control component may be inspected and modified. Another consideration in forming the model has been to reproduce, at this more 'concrete' level, descriptions of the properties of interactive systems introduced in [1, 9, 19]. To this end, it is essential to distinguish between those aspects of the state of the interactor which are relevant to the application and those which are shown to the user.

The meaning and some of the different uses of the interactor concept are introduced in section 2. An informal description of the proposed model, in section 3, brings out the motivations and concerns which led to variations from the Pisa model. A detailed account and formal description of the interactor model is given in sections 4 and 5. Comparisons are also drawn with the Abstract Interaction Objects model by Duke and Harrison [6], which will be referred to below as the York interaction model.

The LOTOS formal specification language [2] is used to describe interactors. LOTOS has a process algebra component and a data typing component, a duality which renders it a powerful notation for the specification of interactive graphics systems. A brief example is presented in section 6. In section 7, properties of interactive systems are described in terms of the observable behaviour of interactors. In section 8, the contribution of this research is summarised and its relationship to current and future research activities is outlined.

2 Interactors

Interactors are primitive abstractions used in the description of interactive systems. They can be thought of as software architecture abstractions similar to objects in object oriented programming. Definitions vary with their intended use. Faconti defines an interactor as an entity of an interactive system capable of reacting to external stimuli; it is capable of both input and output by translating data from a higher level of abstraction to a lower level of abstraction and vice versa [7]. Input and output functionalities and events are distinct and the display is simply modelled by the display events offered by the interactor. The Pisa model proposes the use of interactors as a design construct by modelling the interface software as a graph of communicating interactors [17]. At the lowest level they interact with the user and at the highest levels they communicate with the application.

Duke and Harrison view the interactor as a component in the description of an interactive system that encapsulates a state, the events that manipulate the state and the means by which the state is made perceivable to the user of the system [6]. The York interactor extends the software engineering notion of the object in that it maintains distinct representations of the object's internal state and its display. The York interactor does not distinguish between layers of abstraction of data or the source of events. Its intended use is primarily analytical.

Structuring interface software in terms of interactors is similar to conceptual architecture models for interactive software like PAC [3] and implementation architectures like MVC [10]. Interactors have been used also as an implementation construct for the input model of the GARNET [13] user interface development environment, encapsulating device and application independent behaviours of interactive components.

3 Informal introduction of the ADC interactor

The Abstraction Display Controller (ADC) model distinguishes two aspects of the interactor description: the data behaviour i.e. the data operation it supports and the control information, pertaining to the temporal ordering of its behaviour. The former is modelled by the Abstraction and Display Unit (ADU) whose function is that of translating data in two directions between levels of abstraction and the latter is modelled by the Controller component (C). The ADU maintains a state representation which will be called the *abstraction* and a representation of its output status the *display*. Conceptually, the abstraction is similar to the model of the MVC architecture [10] and the abstraction of the PAC model [3]. The display is similar to the MVC notion of a view.

Data from the user or the application side may be input to the ADU which will update its status information accordingly. The ADU may output its display status towards the user side or an interpretation of the abstraction status, the *result*, to the application side. Communication of data is modelled as LOTOS events offered over 'gates' of the ADU, each of which is dedicated to a particular direction of communication.

296

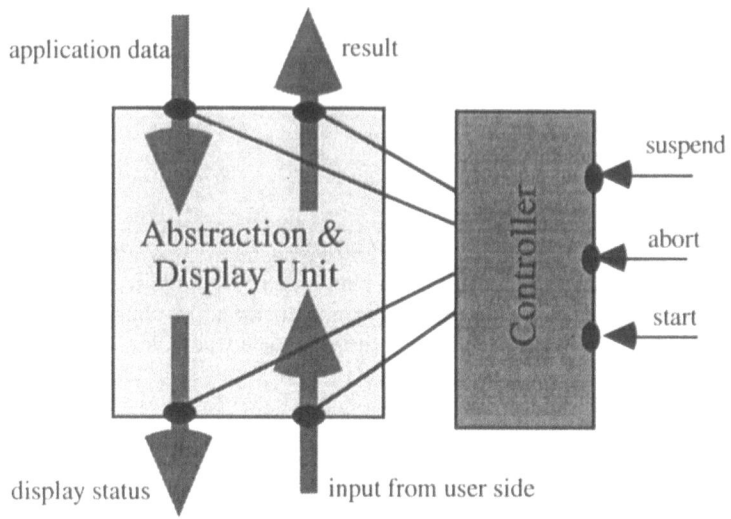

application data   result

Abstraction & Display Unit

Controller

suspend

abort

start

display status   input from user side

user side (level n)

Fig. 1. A schematic view of the ADC interactor

The ADU does not impose constraints on the temporal behaviour of the interactor: it always offers events on all its gates. At any instance during the course of interaction, the ADU offers to 'buffer' information that flows between user and application, converting the data to the appropriate representation in each direction. What may or may not be an allowable sequence of events is defined by the *controller* component in terms of constraints on the behaviour of the ADU. The composition of the ADU and the controller forms the ADC interactor, shown in figure 1. Thick arrows represent the input and output of data to the ADU. Control events, represented with single lines, will enable or disable the communication of data over the gates of the ADU. The controller also describes suspension and termination of the interactor operation.

This modular description of control information aims to make the ADC interactor more usable as a design oriented representation. Temporal ordering constraints on the behaviour of the interactor are represented independently of the data handling behaviour of the interactor, as a set of constraints applied to its externally observable behaviour. This is in contrast to the Pisa interactor where the specification of the temporal ordering of events is by the composition of lower level entities. The difference is that between a resource oriented specification and a constraint oriented specification [20]. One advantage is that it allows for the easy inspection and customisation of the interactor by applying constraints on its observable behaviour.

Interactors are derived as instantiations of the ADC model by defining the operations on the data in the fashion introduced in [15]. Interfaces are modelled as compositions of interactors, using the composition operators of LOTOS. Definition of the start, suspend and abort behaviours of the interactors allows interfaces to be configured dynamically.

The composition of two (or more) interactors has two facets: the composition of their effect on the data transmitted, which is achieved in practice by 'piping' the data from one to the other, and the composition of their control specifications. The advantage of

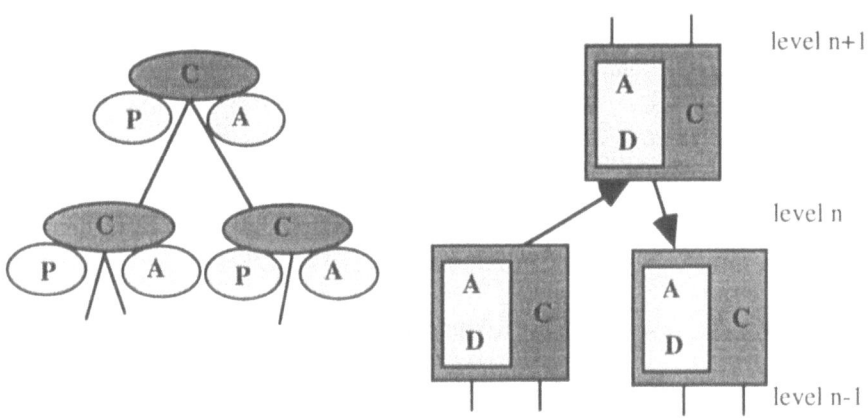

Fig. 2. Although similar to PAC, the controller has a different role in the ADC model.

the modularity introduced with the ADC model should become more evident when compositions of interactors are associated with a single separable control component. In other words, the effect of the composition operators on the controller component can be abstracted in a new controller component.

The components of the interactor identified above (abstraction, display and controller) are reminiscent in purpose and naming to those identified by the conceptual software architecture PAC [3]. PAC is mentioned because it supports a distinct control component (although the model did not prescribe how the control information was to be represented in this component). There is an important difference between the ADC and PAC interactors: the PAC controller handles all communication between the presentation and abstraction components and translates data between the two formalisms. Such communication is 'hidden' from the ADC controller which simply imposes external 'dialogue' constraints on their operation (figure 2).

4 The Abstraction and Display Unit (ADU)

The ADU mediates between a higher level of abstraction and a lower level of abstraction. It can receive information from either side, process the information and pass it on to the other side. It maintains the local state of the interactor which consists of the *abstraction* and the *display*. The ADU offers the following operations on these state components:

- *input*: it constructs a new abstraction status by interpreting data input from the user side with respect to the display status and the abstraction status.
- *echo*: it constructs a new display status by interpreting data input from the user side with respect to the display status and the abstraction status.
- *result*: an interpretation of the abstraction status is constructed; this may be sent to the application side.
- *render*: the display status is updated with respect to data received from the application side. Thus the application (or higher level interactors) may impose constraints on the graphical appearance of the interactor in question.
- *receive*: the abstraction status is updated with respect to data received from the application side.

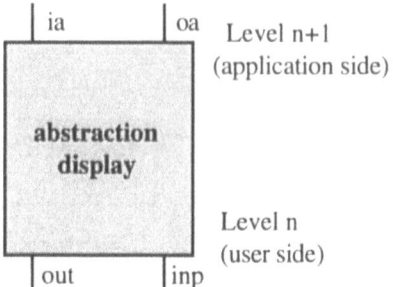

Fig. 3. The ADU process, its gates and state parameters

The input function defines the syntactic as well as semantic dependence of user input to the current output. Also we note that an interactor may receive from higher levels of abstraction, both data that will modify the abstraction information it holds and data that will modify the description of its display.

The overall concept is similar to the Pisa model with two important exceptions:

(a) Trigger events, which signal when the data held by the interactor should be input towards the application or output towards the user, are not distinguished from other input events from the user or the application side. For the ADU a trigger event is just another input event; the trigger behaviour is seen as a control structure so it is described in the controller component (which is discussed in the next section).

(b) In the Pisa model, state information which in the ADC model is held by the *abstraction* parameter is divided between the collection and measure processes. The Pisa interactor communicates user input to higher levels of abstraction and display information in the opposite direction, but does not capture the same notion of local state as is desired in this study.

Contrasted to the York interactor, we note the constructive, rather than analytic, nature of the ADC model and the different perspective offered by a process algebraic framework for the definition of the model. The York model represents explicitly the relationship between the state internal to the interactor and the part of the state that is displayed to the user. The York interactor does not differentiate trigger events either; in fact it does not distinguish between events for input, output etc.; this kind of control information is captured indirectly by the effect of events on the local state of the interactor.

Having described the functionality of the ADU, its operational description can be given. In the process algebraic framework of LOTOS, the ADU is considered as a recursive process that continuously offers events over four gates. The ADU may:

- receive data from the application side via gate *ia*. The data is interpreted using functions *receive* and *render*.
- output to the lower level its display status via gate *out*.
- receive data from the user side via gate *inp*. This data may modify the currently held display and abstraction status, using functions *echo* and *input* respectively.
- send an interpretation of the currently held state information to higher levels of abstraction via gate *oa*, using function *result*.

Notably there is an asymmetry in handling the abstraction and the display data. The display is transmitted as it is, while an interpretation of the abstraction is transmitted. Regarding the display status which is observable via the gate *out*, it is important to distinguish between what is actually displayed and information that has not been displayed yet. For example, consider a sequence of consecutive input events that have not been echoed (given that there is no built in constraint for immediate echo of the input). These input events are interpreted with the last display status offered on the gate *out*. Thus, two variables are needed to describe the display: one holds the last data offered on the output gate (held below by formal parameter *ds*) and the other, the data that will be displayed with the next output event (formal parameter *dc*). This is a necessary complication since there is no constraint that output will occur immediately after an input or an output trigger.

A formal specification of this model in LOTOS is presented below. The data type *ad* defines the generic to interactors operations on the data, as described above.

```
type ad is
sorts
    inp_data, abs, disp, ia_data, oa_data
opns
    input   :    inp_data, disp, abs       ->    abs
    echo    :    inp_data, disp, abs       ->    disp
    render  :    disp, ia_data             ->    disp
    receive :    abs, ia_data              ->    abs
    result  :    abs                       ->    oa_data
endtype
```

The behaviour of the ADU can be described in LOTOS as follows:

```
process adu[inp, out, ia, oa](a: abs, dc, ds: disp) : noexit :=
    oa!result(a);      adu[inp, out, ia, oa](a, dc, ds) []
    out!dc;            adu [inp, out, ia, oa](a, dc, dc) []
    ia?x:ia_data;      adu[inp, out, ia, oa](receive(a,x), render(dc,x), ds) []
    inp?x:inp_data;    adu[inp, out, ia, oa](input(x,ds,a), echo(x,ds,a), ds)
endproc
```

5 Composition with the controller component

The controller applies temporal ordering constraints to the events offered at the gates of the ADU. Constraints are expressed concisely using the multi-way synchronisation of LOTOS, which allows the incremental composition of constraints. This specification style has been termed constraint oriented [18]. The controller process synchronises with the ADU on all the gates of the latter. The interactor, which is the parallel composition of the two, may only engage in events in the order that the controller component allows. Their composition is as follows:

```
        adu [inp, out, ia, oa](initAbstraction, initDisplay, initDisplay)
                    |[inp, out, ia, oa]|
        controller [s, su, ab, inp, out, ia, oa]
```

The controller is started with a start event on gate *s*. This triggers process *run* which describes the run-time behaviour of the controller. Process *constraints* describes constraints on the order of the events offered on the gates of the ADU. Process *suspend* describes the suspension behaviour of the interactor: with the first *su* event interaction halts and with the second *su* event it resumes. The abort event *ab* terminates the operation of the interactor and the process exits. In the trivial case (below), *constraints* is a recursive process that allows all possible interaction sequences on the gates of the ADU.

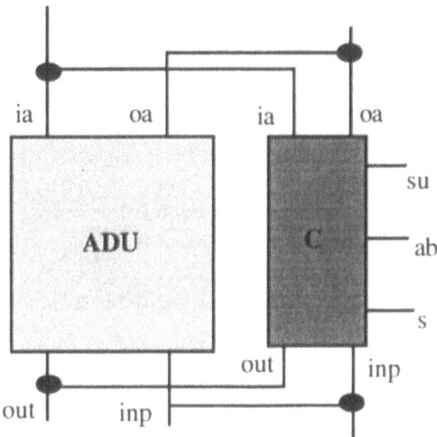

Fig. 4. Synchronisation of the ADU with the controller over all its gates

```
process controller [s, su, ab, inp, out, ia, oa] : exit :=
    s; run [su, ab, inp, out, ia, oa]
where

process run[su, ab, inp, out, ia, oa] : exit :=
    (constraints[inp, out, ia, oa]
            [>
    suspend [su, ab, inp, out, ia, oa])
where

process constraints[inp, out, ia, oa] : noexit :=
    ia?x:ia_data;              constraints[inp, out, ia, oa] []
    oa?x:oa_data;              constraints[inp, out, ia, oa] []
    out?x:disp;                constraints[inp, out, ia, oa] []
    inp?x:inp_data;            constraints[inp, out, ia, oa]
endproc

process suspend [su, ab, inp, out, ia, oa]: exit :=
    su;      (su; run[su, ab, inp, out, ia, oa]
              [] ab; exit)
    [] ab; exit
endproc
```

Alternative behaviours can be defined by modifying the *constraints* component of the controller. To put the constraint on the ADU that any data received from the application side is rendered instantly and that any input by the user is echoed instantly, the *constraints* process of the controller need only change as follows (changes are italicised):

```
process constraints[inp, out, ia, oa] : noexit :=
    ia?x:ia_data; out?y:disp;      constraints[inp, out, ia, oa] []
    oa?x:oa_data;                  constraints[inp, out, ia, oa] []
    out?x:disp;                    constraints[inp, out, ia, oa] []
    inp?x:inp_data;out?y:disp;     constraints[inp, out, ia, oa]
endproc
```

The interface designer may wish to distinguish the role of trigger events: output to the display or towards the application may be allowed only after a trigger event *out_t ,inp_t* respectively. For the ADU, the trigger event is simply treated as one more input gate from user or application. The process *constraints* is then written as follows:

```
process constraints[inp, out, ia, oa, inp_t, out_t] : noexit :=
    ia?x:ia_data;                        constraints[inp, out, ia, oa, inp_t, out_t] []
    out_t?x:ia_data; out?y:disp;         constraints[inp, out, ia, oa, inp_t, out_t] []
    inp?x:inp_data;                      constraints[inp, out, ia, oa, inp_t, out_t] []
    inp_t?x:inp_data; oa?y:oa_data;      constraints[inp, out, ia, oa, inp_t, out_t]
endproc
```

The advantages of this modular description of the controller are further illustrated, if, for example, one chooses to modify the role of triggering events, to demand that an input trigger does not affect the output behaviour and correspondingly the output trigger does not affect the input behaviour. Incidentally, this is the behaviour of the Pisa interactor which after an output trigger event may still receive data or an input trigger from the user.

```
process constraints[inp, out, ia, oa, inp_t, out_t] : noexit :=
    (ia?x:ia_data;                       constraints[inp, out, ia, oa, inp_t, out_t] []
    out_t?x:ia_data; out?y:disp;         constraints[inp, out, ia, oa, inp_t, out_t])|||
    (inp?x:inp_data; out?y:disp;         constraints[inp, out, ia, oa, inp_t, out_t] []
    inp_t?x:inp_data; oa?y:oa_data;      constraints[inp, out, ia, oa, inp_t, out_t])
endproc
```

This presentation has focused on the specification of single interactors. In fact, the modular controller component is expected to provide more benefits when forming compositions of interactors. The user interface can be modelled as a single interactor but also as a network of interactors. Compositions of interactors can be of two forms:

- the output from one interactor is directed to an input gate of the other. For such a composition to be possible, it is required that the intersection of the two domains of data offered over the connected gates is not empty. This type of connection works in almost the same way as has been demonstrated with the Pisa model [15,17].
- the behaviours of the interactors are composed into more complex ones e.g. their interleaving, their sequence etc. using the standard LOTOS process composition operators. Present work is investigating the conditions under which the ADC structure is preserved during these compositions.

6 A simple example

The example that follows demonstrates some of the ideas mentioned so far, namely, how interactor specifications are derived from the ADC model by instantiating the *ad* data type, how they are composed and, further, how the composition of two or more ADC interactors is an ADC interactor itself. The specification of a scrolling list which may contain any type of items e.g. icons, strings etc. is examined. The list is observed through a window whose contents depend on the window size and the position of the window relative to the displayed list, e.g. the index of the first displayed element. The user may scroll up and down the list by using a scrollbar.

The scrolling list is defined as the composition of a *scrollbar* interactor and a window display for the list, which will be referred to as a *list* interactor. Interactions are started,

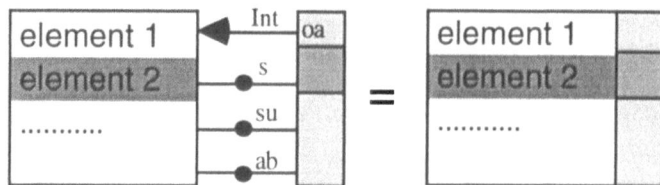

Fig. 5. A scrolling list as a composite interactor

suspended and terminated together, since they form part of the same interaction task, so the interactors synchronise on gates *s*, *su* and *ab*. The scrollbar receives input from the user as a cursor position, and converts this input to an integer value which is passed to the *list*. The integer value is passed via gate *oa* of the scrollbar interactor as an input to gate *inp* of *list* (figure 5). The latter interprets the integer value to produce a new starting position for the window thus achieving the effect of scrolling.

The data type *ls_ad* is the instantiation of the data type *ad* for the *list* interactor. It uses the data types *lstElements,* which models a list of elements, and *windowAndSelection,* which models the window display for the list. Their specifications include only those aspects of the operations that are necessary for the interactor specifications that follow.

```
type lstElements is Integer
sorts
    lstel, el
opns
    sel       :    lstel, Int      ->      lstel
    setstart  :    lstel, Int      ->      lstel
    which     :    lstel           ->      el
    wnstart   :    lstel           ->      Int
eqns
forall aList:lstel, N,M:Int
ofsort Int
    wnstart(setstart(aList, N)) = N;
    wnstart(sel(aList, N)) = wnstart(aList);
ofsort lstel
    sel(sel(aList,N),M) = sel(aList, M);
    sel(setstart(aList, N), M) = sel(aList,M);
ofsort el
    which(setstart(aList, M)) = which(aList);
endtype


type windowAndSelection is Integer, graphics
sorts
    window
opns
    mkWin        :    rectangle, Int      ->    window
    changeLne    :    window, Int         ->    window
    changeRect   :    window, rectangle   ->    window
    pick         :    window, pnt         ->    Int
    rect         :    window              ->    rectangle
    line         :    window              ->    Int
eqns
```

```
      forall index:Int, rct:rectangle, win:window, p:pnt
   ofsort rectangle
      rect(mkWin(rct,index)) = rct;
      rect(changeRect(win,rct)) = rct;
      rect(changeLne(win,index)) = rect(win);
   ofsort Int
      line(mkWin(rct,index)) = index;
      line(changeRect(win, rct)) = line(win);
      line(changeLne(win,index)) = index;
   endtype
```

The type *lstElements* defines an enquiry operator *which(aList)* that returns the selected element of a list. The selection of an element with index N for *lstElements* can be set by *sel(aList, N)*. Type *windowAndSelection* is associated with operation *pick(win, p)* which returns an index of the displayed window *win* (i.e. a line or icon number) given a mouse position *p*. Finally, the position of the window with respect to the list, can be set to N, by operation *setstart(aList, N)* which will use the integer value sent from the scroll bar.

```
   type ls_ad is lstElements, windowAndSelection
   opns
      inputPnt:        pnt, window, lstel      ->      lstel
      echoPnt:         pnt, window, lstel      ->      window
      inputNumber:     Int, window, lstel      ->      lstel
      echoNumber:      Int, window, lstel      ->      window
      render   :       window, lstel           ->      window
      receive :        lstel, lstel            ->      lstel
      scrListResult:   lstel                   ->      el
   eqns
   forall m: Int, p:pnt, w:window, aList,lstOld,lstNew:lstel
   ofsort  lstel
      inputPnt(p, w, aList) = sel(aList,pick(w,p));
      inputNumber(m, w, aList) = setstart(aList,m);
      receive(lstOld, lstNew) = lstNew;
   ofsort window
      echoPnt(p, w, aList) = changeLne(w, pick(w,p));
      render(render(w, lstOld), lstNew) = render(w,lstNew);
   ofsort el
      scrListResult(aList) = which(aList);
   endtype
```

Similarly, *scr_ad* defines the scrollbar functionality in terms of a graphical abstraction *scrBar* and a bounded value abstraction *boundedVal* (omitted for brevity). The enquiry operator *val(boundValue)* returns an integer result for the interactor.

```
   type scr_ad is  scrBar, boundedVal
   opns
      input   :     pnt, scrollbar, boundValue        ->      boundValue
      echo    :     pnt, scrollbar, boundValue        ->      scrollbar
      render  :     scrollbar, boundValue             ->      scrollbar
      render  :     scrollbar, rectangle              ->      scrollbar
      receive :     boundValue, boundValue            ->      boundValue
      result  :     boundValue                        ->      Int
```

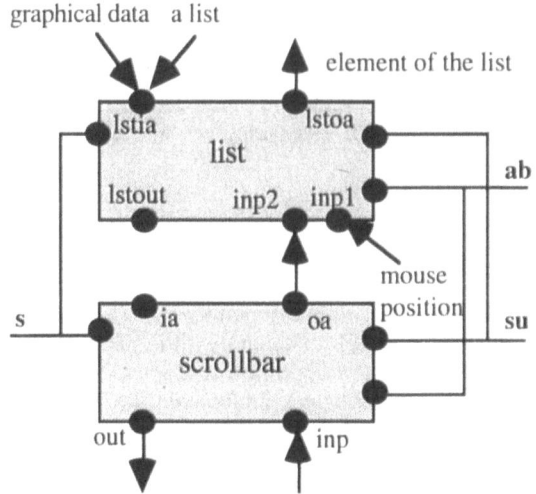

graphical data   a list

element of the list

mouse position

Fig. 6. The composition of the two interactors

```
eqns
forall r:rectangle, p:pnt, sb: scrollbar,  bv1,bv2: boundValue
ofsort boundValue
    receive(bv1, bv2) = bv2;
ofsort scrollbar
    echo(p,sb,bv1) = changePnt(sb, p);
    render(sb, r) = changeRect(sb, r);
    render(sb, input(p,sb, bv1))=changePnt(sb,p);
ofsort Int
    result(bv1)=val(bv1);
endtype
```

The ADU for the *list* interactor is as follows

```
process adu[inp1, inp2, out, ia, oa](a:lstel, dc, ds: window) : noexit :=
    oa!scrListResult(a); adu[inp1, inp2, out, ia, oa](a, dc, ds) []
    out!dc; adu[inp1, inp2, out, ia, oa](a, dc, dc) []
    ia?x:lstel; adu[inp1, inp2, out, ia, oa](receive(a,x),render(dc,x), ds)[]
    inp1?x:pnt; adu[inp1, inp2, out, ia, oa](inputPnt(x,ds,a),echoPnt(x,ds,a), ds) []
    inp2?x:Int; adu[inp1,inp2,out,ia,oa](inputNumber(x,ds,a),echoNumber(x,ds,a), ds)
endproc
```

The controller is the same as in the general case; only process *constraints* needs to be modified with the sort identifiers of data type *ls_ad*. The ADU and the controller for the scrollbar interactor are again straightforward instantiations of the general model and are omitted for brevity. The composition of the two interactors (figure 6), is written as follows (note the renaming to *oa* of gate *inp* in the instantiation of the interactor *lst*):

```
scr[s, su, ab, inp, out, a, oa] (initBV, initSB, initSB)
    |[s, su, ab, oa]|
list[s, su, ab, oa, lstout, lstia, lstoa] (initLst, initWindow, initWindow)
```

By its construction the ADC model is compositional: the result of the composition of two ADC interactors is an ADC interactor. For example, the composition of the previous section is equivalent to an ADC which is of the form:

> adu[inp, out, ia, oa, lstout, lstia, lstoa]
>> |[inp, out, ia, oa, lstout, lstia, lstoa]|
> controller [s, su, ab, inp, out, ia, oa, lstout, lstia, lstoa]

where *adu* is defined as

> scr_adu [inp, out, ia, oa](initBV, initSB, initSB)
>> |[oa]|
> lst_adu[oa, lstout, lstia, lstoa](initLst, initWindow, initWindow)

and *controller* is defined as

> scr_controller[s, su, ab, inp, out, ia, oa]
>> |[s, su, ab, oa]|
> lst_controller[s, su, ab, oa, lstout, lstia, lstoa]

7 Expression of interface properties within the ADC model

Analytic expressions of properties of interaction pertaining to the usability of interactive systems are presented below. Novel characterisations of interaction are not proposed; the presentation concentrates on expressions for properties of interaction introduced previously within other formal models. The intention is to suggest the analytic potential of the ADC model. Properties of interactive systems are examined below in two categories:

- logical properties of interactor behaviour. This category covers safety and liveness properties of the interface specification similar to those discussed in [14, 16, 18].
- properties of the correspondence between the information displayed and that sent to the application. These properties correspond to what has been termed 'result display properties' which have been discussed within various formal models e.g. the Interactive Processes model [19] the Agents model [1] and the red-PIE model [5]

First, a few concepts regarding LOTOS behaviour expressions and a generalised description of the gate sets of the ADC interactor are introduced.

7.1 A formal model for the study of interactors

Given a process B in LOTOS, a set of labelled transitions may be derived. These are denoted as $B - \alpha \rightarrow C$, where α is an action (label), and C is another behaviour expression. A LOTOS action declaration has the form g?x:t, where x is a variable and t is a sort identifier which indicates the domain of values over which x ranges. For example, g?x:integer specifies a set of actions $g<v>$ where $<v>$ is in the domain of the integers.

A sequence of unobservable internal actions, represented below by ε, may effect a transition from B to C denoted as $B = \varepsilon \Rightarrow C$. A second transition relation, needed to discuss the observed behaviour of transition systems, is defined as:

$$B = a \Rightarrow C \quad iff \quad B = \varepsilon \Rightarrow B_1 - a \rightarrow B_2 = \varepsilon \Rightarrow C$$

A trace is a sequence of observable actions in which the process may successfully participate starting from its initial state. The set of traces of a process B, denoted $Tr(B)$, is by its definition prefix closed, i.e. every prefix of a trace also belongs to the set of traces. A trace $\sigma \in \text{Tr(B)}$, defines a sequence of transitions as follows:

$$B = \sigma \Rightarrow C \text{ iff } \sigma = a_1..a_n \text{ and } B = a_1 \Rightarrow B_1 = a_2 \Rightarrow ... = a_n \Rightarrow C$$

For a given behaviour expression B, the set of outgoing transitions, i.e. all the actions for which a transition is possible will be denoted as $out(B)$.

A trace that cannot be extended because it is infinite or it has no outgoing transitions is called a *full trace*. Let $\mu Tr(B)$ denote the set of *full traces* of the process B. If a trace σ is finite then the last element of the trace is $last(\sigma)$, and b in σ will denote that an action b is in the trace.

Topology of interaction gates. The interaction model was introduced with only one gate for input from lower levels, one for display etc. For the more general discussion that follows it is more convenient to talk of sets of such gates as there could be more than one gates of each category.

The set of gates of the interactor can be partitioned into the set of input/output gates G_{io} and the control gates G_c.

$$G = G_c \cup G_{io} \text{ and } G_c \cap G_{io} = \emptyset, \ G_{io} \neq \emptyset$$

G_c consists of the subsets $G_{start}, G_{suspend}$ and G_{abort} where start, suspend and abort events respectively will be observed.

$$G_c = G_{start} \cup G_{suspend} \cup G_{abort}$$

G_{io} is the non-empty set of input and output gates of the interactor. It is further partitioned to two non-empty sets G_a and G_u, that communicate with higher and lower levels of abstraction respectively.

$$G_{io} = G_a \cup G_u \text{ and } G_a \cap G_u = \emptyset, \ G_a, G_u \neq \emptyset$$
$$G_a = G_{oa} \cup G_{ia} \text{ and } G_{oa} \cap G_{ia} = \emptyset$$
$$G_u = G_{inp} \cup G_{out} \text{ and } G_{inp} \cap G_{out} = \emptyset$$

7.2 Logical Properties

Input and output correctness, restartability, undo and properties of the connection of the interactors are examined under this heading. Some representative examples below demonstrate how such requirements can be expressed in terms of the ADC model. In the following UI denotes the initial state of the user interface described as an ADC interactor.

- Every input is echoed immediately
  If $UI = \sigma \Rightarrow UI' \wedge last(\sigma) = a?x: inp\_data \wedge a \in G_{inp}$ then

  $$\exists b \in G_{out}, D: disp, A: abs \mid out(hide \ G_{abort} \cup G_{suspend} \ in \ UI') = \{b!echo(x, D, A)\}$$

- Every user input is echoed eventually
  If $UI = \sigma \Rightarrow UI' \wedge last(\sigma) = a?x: inp\_data \wedge a \in G_{inp}$ then

  $$\forall \vartheta \in \mu Tr(UI') \bullet \exists b \in G_{out}, D: disp, A: abs \mid b!echo(x, D, A) \text{ in } \vartheta$$

- A command sequence is *restartable* if it is possible to extend it so that it returns to the initial state.

  $$\forall \mu \in Tr(UI) \mid UI = \mu \Rightarrow UI' \bullet \exists v \in Tr(UI') \mid UI' = v \Rightarrow UI$$

- Any command c followed by *undo* should leave the system in the same state as before the command (single step undo).

  $$\forall \sigma \in Tr(UI) \mid UI = \sigma \Rightarrow UI' \bullet \text{ if } UI' = c \Rightarrow UI'' \text{ then } UI'' = undo \Rightarrow UI'$$

Sufrin and He [19] noted that this definition for undo is unrealistically strict so they proposed the concepts of *weak* and *strong undo*. Their expression requires the

Display Predictability	$out(P_1) = out(P_2) \Rightarrow P_1 = P_2$
Result Predictability	$out(R_1) = out(R_2) \Rightarrow R_1 = R_2$
Honesty	$out(P_1) = out(P_2) \Rightarrow out(R_1) = out(R_2)$
Trustworthiness	$P_1 = P_2 \Rightarrow out(R_1) = out(R_2)$
WYSIWYG(weak)	$out(P_1) = out(P_2) \Rightarrow R_1 = R_2$
WYSIWYG(strong)	$P_1 = P_2 \Rightarrow R_1 = R_2$
Goal defines view	$out(R_1) = out(R_2) \Rightarrow P_1 = P_2$

Fig. 7. Expressions of some usability related properties

characterisation of application and user view of an interactor behaviour which is defined in the next section.

7.3 Result-Display Relationships

Sufrin and He [19] use the concepts of equivalence and indistinguishability of *results* and *views* to classify a set of usability related properties of interactive systems. In that context, *result* referred to the part of the application state that is relevant to the users' goals, and *view* to the part of the state that is made perceivable to the user. Such entities would be called equivalent if they were the same after a particular input sequence and indistinguishable if no further experimentation by the user, could betray any difference between them. Abowd [1] used the same classification adapting the definitions to his Agent model. He compared *results* and *displays* which were defined as restrictions on the internal state of an Agent. In general, they reflect the intuition that during interaction the user is only made aware of what is displayed and uses that to 'plan' her subsequent interactions. The user inputs have distinct effects on what is made perceivable and what is the effect of the interaction on the internal state of the system.

The same intuition, applied to this more architecture oriented model, requires the identification of two views of the interactor. One view of the interactor is from the system side and the other from the user side. The former consists in the behaviour of the interactor restricted to the output gates toward the system G_{oa} (the data that the system sends to the interactor is not of interest in this context, unless as a source of non-determinism). The user's view of the interactor can be defined as the interactor behaviour restricted over gates G_u, i.e. both input and output gates on the user side.

Consider the processes P and R defined with the pseudo-LOTOS expressions below.

$$P = hide \; G_c \cup G_a \; in \; UI \qquad R = hide \; (G - G_{oa}) \; in \; UI$$

The corresponding notions to those of equivalence and indistinguishability mentioned above, are quite intuitive within the process algebraic framework adopted. The observable behaviour of processes are compared with respect to two aspects: the events they offer to participate in, denoted by $out(Q)$ for a process Q and their behaviour as might be observed with subsequent experimentation. The latter concept has been formalised as the testing equivalence between processes [4] denoted by the equals sign (e.g. $P=Q$).

A summary classification of these properties similar to [1, pp.160] can now be written as in figure 7. Processes P and R are also useful in expressing refinements of restartability, undo properties and for expressing the predictability of a single command, as in [19]. Such expressions like those of figure 7, are useful intuitive aids for the designer, but in practice may prove impossible to verify automatically. For specifications like the scrolling list example, it is easy to see how the sets *out(P)* and *out(R)* may be infinitely large or that processes P and R may not be finite.

8 Conclusion - Future Work

The ADC interactor model introduced above is a development of the interactor model of Paterno' and Faconti [15, 17]. Its primary use is intended to be constructive for the formal specification of user interface designs. It may also be used analytically as is suggested by the exposition of a wide range of properties of interaction in section 7.

A formal description of the model was given in LOTOS. The use of a constraint based style of specification enabled the separation of the dialogue and the data transforming aspects of the interactor. This modularity was introduced to make the model more usable as a design notation. The ADC interactor can be used in a similar way to the Pisa model to describe particular interaction styles and to construct interface specifications as a composition of elementary interactors. Dialogue specification is localised within the control component; in fact a controller may be associated with a composition of interactors imposing constraints on their global externally observable behaviour. One of the aims of this research is to support the use of user task knowledge in the design of interactive systems. Current work is examining how such control information can be related to task knowledge. Previous research [11] has focused on representations of device independent task knowledge of users without reference to a particular system model and has attempted to prescribe relationships between task and system models [12]. The aim of this research is to provide a theoretical understanding of task based design and a practical way of embedding this into a design method.

The definition of properties of interaction in terms of the ADC interactor model is motivated by the goal of supporting automatic verification of interface designs. From a practical point of view it is interesting to examine the feasibility of supporting their automatic verification. To this end, a few research tools for the automated verification of LOTOS specifications are being experimented with. Two classes of verification techniques are of practical interest. One is the use of logical specifications of such properties as demonstrated in [17, 18]. The second approach is to construct behavioural specifications where the properties are described directly as higher level LOTOS specifications. Given appropriate abstraction criteria, the verification of a property amounts to verifying equivalence of an abstraction of the design specification with the property specification, using a verification tool such as [8]. This research is still in its early days; it is hoped that automatic verification of user interface properties will make research results from the application of formal methods to human computer interaction more usable within a design context.

Acknowledgements

Many thanks to Stephanie Wilson and to Jon Rowson for their comments and for proof reading this paper.

References

1.   Abowd G.D.:   Formal Aspects of Human Computer Interaction, PhD thesis, University of Oxford, Technical Report YCS 161, University of York (1992).

2. Bolognesi T., Brinksma E.: Introduction to the ISO specification language LOTOS. In: Van Eijk P., Vissers C., Diaz M. (eds.): The Formal Description Technique LOTOS, Elsevier Science Publishers BV (1989), 23-73.

3. Coutaz J.: PAC, an Object Oriented Model for Dialog Design. In: Bullinger H.J., Shakiel B. (eds.): Human Computer Interaction - INTERACT-'87, Elsevier Science Publishers BV (1987), 431-436.

4. De Nicola R. , Hennessy M.C.B.: Testing Equivalence for Processes. Theoretical Computer Science, North Holland, Vol. 34, 83-133 (1984).

5. Dix A.J.: Formal Methods for Interactive Systems, Academic Press (1991).

6. Duke D.J., Harisson M.D.: Abstract Interaction Objects. In: Hubbold R.J., Juan R. (eds.): Eurographics'93, Computer Graphics Forum, Vol. 12, No. 3, 26-36 (1993).

7. Faconti G.P.: Towards the Concept of Interactor. Amodeus Project Document: System Modelling/WP8 (1993).

8. Fernadez J.C., Garavel H., Mounier L., Rasse A., Rodriguez C., Sifakis J.: A toolbox for the verification of LOTOS Programs. In: 14th International Conference on Software Engineering, Melbourne, May (1992).

9. Harrison M.D., Dix A.J.: A state model of direct manipulation in interactive systems. In: Harisson M. D., Thimbleby H.W. (eds.): Formal Methods in Human Computer Interaction, Cambridge Univ. Press (1990), 129-151.

10. Krasner G.E., Pope S.T.: A Cookbook For Using the Model-View-Controller User Interface Paradigm in The Smalltalk-80 System, Journal of Object Oriented Programming, Vol.1, No.3, 26-49 (1988).

11. Markopoulos P., Wilson S., Johnson P.: Representation and Use of Task Knowledge in a User Interface Design Environment. IEE Proceedings~E, Computers and Digital Techniques, Vol.141, No.2, 79-84 (1994).

12. Markopoulos P., Gikas S.: Towards A Formal Model For Extant Task Knowledge Representation. In: Stary C (ed.): 1st Interdisciplinary Workshop on Cognitive Modelling and User Interface Development, Vienna (1994).

13. Myers B.A.: A New Model for Handling Input. ACM Transactions on Information Systems, Vol.8, No.3, 289-320 (1990).

14. Palanque P., Bastide R.: Petri net based design of user driven interfaces using the interactive cooperative objects formalism. In: Paterno' F. (ed.): Design Specification and Verification of Interactive Systems, Eurographics workshop, 215-228 (1994).

15. Paterno' F., Faconti G.: On the use of LOTOS to describe graphical interaction. In: Monk A., Diaper D., Harrison M.D., (eds.): People and Computers VII, Proc. HCI'92 Conference, Cambridge Univ. Press (1992), 155-173.

16. Paterno' F.: Definition of properties of user interfaces using action based temporal logic. In: Proceedings, 5th conference in Software Engineering and Knowledge Engineering (1993), 314-318.

17. Paterno' F.: A Theory of User Interaction Objects. Journal of Visual Languages and Computing, Academic Press Ltd, Vol. 5, 227-249 (1994).

18   Paterno' F., Mezzanotte M.:   Analysing Matis by Interactors and ACTL. Amodeus Project Document:. System Modelling/WP36 (1994).

19.   Sufrin B., He J.: Specification analysis and refinement of interactive processes. In: Harisson M.D., Thimbleby H.W. (eds.): Formal Methods in Human Computer Interaction, Cambridge Univ. Press (1990), 153-200.

20.   Vissers C.A., Scollo G., van Sinderen M., Brinksma E.: Specification styles in distributed systems design and verification.   Theoretical Computer Science Vol. 89, 179-206 (1991).

Applying A Structured Method For Usability Engineering To Recreational Facilities Booking User Requirements: A Successful Case Study

James Middlemass, Adam Stork, and John Long

Ergonomics & HCI Unit
University College London
26 Bedford Way
London WC1H OAP

Abstract

MUSE, a structured Method for Usability Engineering, was created to improve the practice of Human-Computer Interaction practitioners, a practice that is primarily one of designing artefacts that fulfil user requirements. This paper offers a case-study application of MUSE to a set of recreational facilities booking user requirements to produce an artefact. The paper presents: an overview of MUSE; the necessary features of an application; the user requirements; the details of the application; the resulting artefact; an assessment of the artefact with respect to the user requirements; and a comparison of the case-study's user requirements with those in Stork, Middlemass and Long (1995). Finally, it is argued that this case-study be considered 'successful', where a successful case-study extends the known frontiers of application of MUSE.

Keywords

Human-Computer Interaction; Human Factors; Structured Methods; Recreational Facilities Booking Systems; Transaction Support Systems; Software Engineering.

Introduction

Stork, Middlemass, and Long (1995), based on earlier work by Lim, Long, and Silcock (1990), propose that case-studies of methods can be considered 'successful' or 'unsuccessful'. Successful case-studies extend the known frontiers of the application of a method (i.e. they demonstrate that a method is applicable to a type of user requirements). Unsuccessful case-studies delimit those frontiers (i.e. they demonstrate that a method is not applicable to a type of user requirements), and so provide input to the development of further versions of a method. Successful case-studies are ones which produce interaction artefacts which fulfil their user requirements; while unsuccessful case-studies fail to do so. Stork et al. suggest that, to be testable, the known frontiers of application of a method can be expressed in terms of how well-defined, complex, and observable are the user requirements of successful and unsuccessful case-studies.

Stork et al. describe a successful case-study application of MUSE, a structured *M*ethod for *Us*ability *E*ngineering (Lim, Long, and Silcock, 1992 for an overview; and Lim and Long, 1994 for detail), to a set of domestic energy management user requirements to produce an interaction artefact. These domestic energy management user requirements are well-defined, simple, and observable. Stork et al. claim that the case-study is successful on the basis of evidence: that the interaction artefact fulfils the user requirements; and that MUSE was applied in the development of that artefact from the user requirements. The claim of a successful case-study extends the known frontiers of application of MUSE.

This paper also describes a successful case-study application of MUSE, but to a different set of user requirements – those for recreational facilities booking. The claim for success is based on evidence: that the resulting interaction artefact fulfils the user requirements and that MUSE was applied in the development of that artefact from the user requirements. Since the user requirements are less well-defined and more complex than the domestic energy management user requirements in Stork et al., but equally observable, it is claimed that the case-study presented here further extends the known frontiers of application of MUSE.

The paper describes: an overview of MUSE; the necessary features of a MUSE application; the case-study's user requirements; an appropriately detailed (to highlight those features) application of MUSE to the user requirements to produce an artefact; the resulting artefact; an assessment of whether the artefact fulfils the user requirements; and a comparison of the case-study's user requirements with those of Stork et al. Finally, some conclusions are suggested.

Overview of MUSE

MUSE is a structured analysis and design method for human factors engineers. The method is configurable for use with software engineering structured methods, such as Yourdon, JSD, SSADM, etc. The product of MUSE is the specification of an interaction artefact, the software engineering method producing a specification of an implementable artefact incorporating the interaction artefact.

MUSE approaches design in a 'top-down' manner based on information derived 'bottom-up' and progresses from the specification of general features of the tasks to be performed by the user, derived from analysis of the user requirements and from existing systems, to the specification of the details of the interaction artefact. The application of MUSE is considered to be an iterative process, both overall and internally, supporting the production of the best first-attempt artefact following the initial complete application.

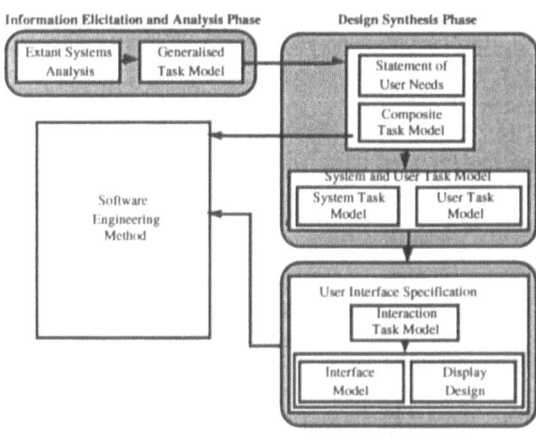

Figure 1: A schematic representation of the MUSE method

Figure 1 shows a schematic diagram of the MUSE method together with an (unspecified) software engineering method. There follows an outline of the three phases of the method and a description of its main products.

The first phase is that of Information Elicitation and Analysis which involves identification of features of extant systems that are problematic for users and so are to be excluded from the target system, and desirable features that are to be included. The phase also involves the creation of a general model of the target artefact following the users' requirements.

The second phase, that of Design Synthesis, establishes: the human factors perspective on the design; the semantics of the application domain; and a conceptual design of the target artefact. The conceptual design is checked with that of the software engineering method, to ensure that a correct implementation is possible. Allocation of function between the user(s) and computer(s) is performed towards the end of this phase.

The final phase is that of Design Specification in which the conceptual design is decomposed to a detailed device-specific implementable specification of the interaction artefact.

Features of a MUSE application

The following necessary features of a MUSE application were identified by Stork et al. (1995):

1. the artefact be considered completely and appropriately at all levels of design, from conceptual to detailed;

2. the artefact be consistent across all levels of design (including the user requirements);

3. domain knowledge be assessed and applied to the artefact at appropriate levels of design;

4. human factors knowledge (as well as software engineering knowledge) be assessed and applied to the artefact at appropriate levels of design;

5. desirable qualities of extant systems be assessed and integrated into the artefact at appropriate levels of design;

6. the design rationale implicated in the previous three concerns be made explicit with respect to the artefact;

7. the above concerns be addressed by MUSE products, with appropriate scope and notation, using MUSE procedures.

The User Requirements

The user requirements for this application of MUSE resulted from the observation by two sports players using the sports centre of University College London ('A' and 'J') that the recreational booking facilities (for squash and pool) were less than satisfactory. The sports centre had installed a computerised recreational booking system with a single 'terminal' (a small liquid crystal display and keyboard) located in the same building as the sports facilities. Both players were dissatisfied by the booking of their desired usage of the recreational facilities, even when the desired facilities were available. This dissatisfaction was generally felt to be associated with: the user interface and functionality of the installed system; and its location in a different building, at some distance from that in which the two players worked. The sports centre had some rules concerning the booking of the recreational facilities which were considered acceptable by the two players. For example, members: only may make a booking; must not book more than seven days in advance; must pay the appropriate booking fee at the time of booking; must book sessions in units of one hour; and must not change a booking.

The sports centre recognised that the computerised booking system raised some difficulties for users generally, since it replaced the system by another (which in turn was replaced by a manual system which used a reservation book). However, since the relacements were located in the same place as the original computer terminal had been, the two players remained dissatisfied.

A requirement for an example application of MUSE for dissemination purposes[*] led to the application of MUSE to the user requirements of 'A' and 'J' for a bespoke artefact to address the above dissatisfaction. An assumed appropriate cost for a new recreational booking system was considered to be £10,000. The users were expected to be the two players who expressed the dissatisfaction, 'A' and 'J'; both of whom were regular users of Apple Macintosh computers.

Application of MUSE to the User Requirements

The features of a MUSE application (above) embodied in the case history are highlighted by placing the number of the feature in superscript at the end of the sentence containing the feature.

Information Elicitation and Analysis Phase

A list of extant systems which promised to inform subsequent design was produced. The list included the existing computerised booking system and several related systems, such as: 'client' software for remote access across computer networks; on-line diary systems; multiple-selection configuration screens of applications software; and teleshopping systems [5]. Three extant systems were selected for analysis. They were considered sufficient to inform the first iteration of MUSE [5]:

---

[*] The ESSI (1995) project at University College London required an example application of MUSE to support the teaching of MUSE to the industrial partners on the project.

i) The existing system was selected to examine the extant tasks of booking squash and pool facilities. Analysis identified user problems resulting from design features of the system. Such features were to be excluded from the target artefact [4,5];

ii) A related system, an Apple Macintosh based network terminal emulator, Telnet 2.5, was selected to examine the tasks of accessing remote computers across networks [3,4,5];

iii) A related system, an Apple Macintosh based network information retrieval program, TurboGopher, was selected to analyse tasks involving partially-automated host selection and control. It does not require users to select the host or enter details of their user identifier (ID) and password, features of Telnet found problematic by some users [3,5].

Appropriate human factors techniques (observational studies, task analysis, etc.) were applied to construct MUSE extant Task Descriptions containing structured diagrams and supporting tables; see extracts in Figures 2,3, and 4 [6,7]. These analyses identified information likely to inform later design and support novel design speculations [1,4,5].

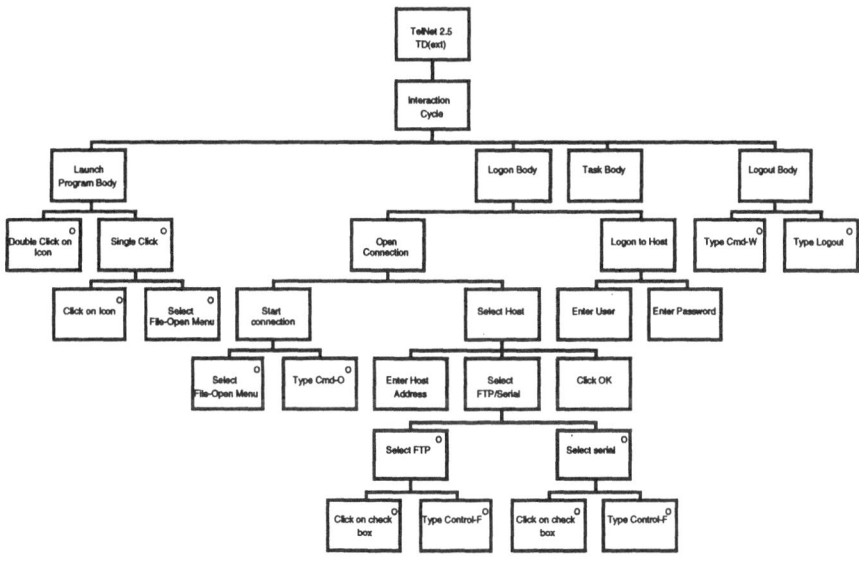

Name	Description	Observation	Design Implication	Speculation
Open Connection		Users reported difficulty with remembering the address of their host, and frequently made errors whilst entering it.		Automatic Connection to Host
Logon to Host		Macintosh users did not like using command line interfaces such as UNIX.		GUI Interface

Figure 2: Telnet: Extract from extant Task Description

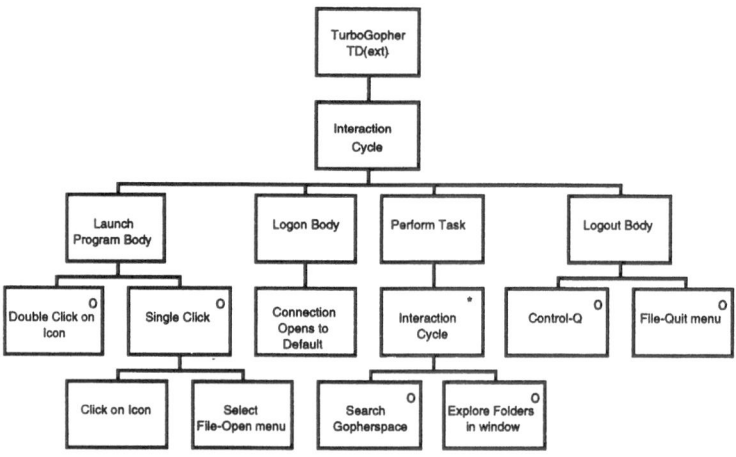

Name	Description	Observation	Design Implication	Speculation
Perform Task	The user can perform as many iterations as they like before quitting	The users of the RFBS will be restricted as to the total number of bookings they may make, but there would be no restriction on the number of 'check booking' or 'buy credit' iterations		
Logout Body	There is a choice of methods available to terminate the session	This is a common feature of Macintosh applications	The users of the RFBS should have a choice of methods for ending the session, compatible with the standard Macintosh interface	

Figure 3: TurboGopher: Extract from extant Task Description

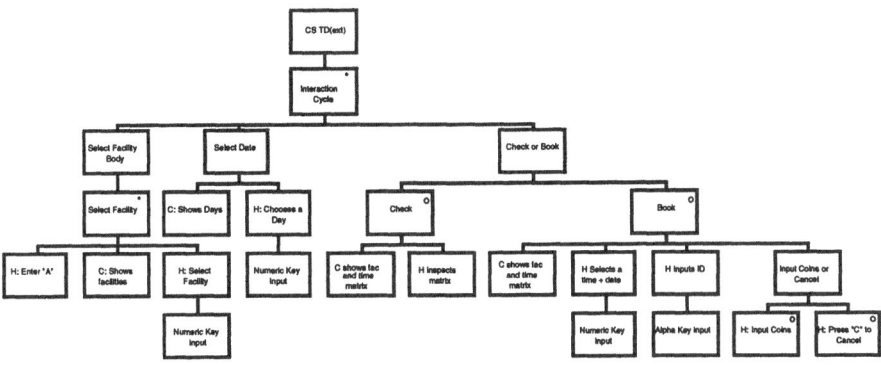

Name	Description	Observation	Design Implication	Speculation
Select Facility	The user must first choose which facility they are interested in	This appears to assume that the user has a specific desire to play a certain sport rather that to just do do something at a certain time, which is probably true of most users	It will probably be appropriate to get users to choose the facility first	
Select Date	The user must select the day on which they wish to play	The user selects from a list of days	The user will still have to select a day in the new system, and it will probably be appropriate to select from a list	
Check or Book	The two activities are similar, apart from in booking the user may select a time and identify themselves to book it		Checking and Booking could use a similar screen layout	
C shows fac and time matrix	The computer displays a matrix showing the IDs of those who have booked slots and the times and facilities booked by them	It is probably unnecessary to disclose the identities of the owners of the booked slots, apart from for the bookings that belong to the user	The user will have to be identified earlier in the booking cycle	
Inputs coins or cancel	The user inputs coins to pay for the booking, or else can cancel the booking	This is to ensure that users do not book a court and fail to pay for it if they do not use it.	It will probably still be necessary to extract payment at the time of booking,	There must be some provision for payment over the network at the time of booking

Figure 4: Current System: Extract from extant Task Description

The high-level tasks represented in these MUSE products were based on different systems combined into a Generalised Task Model of existing systems, see Figure 5 [5,6,7].

318

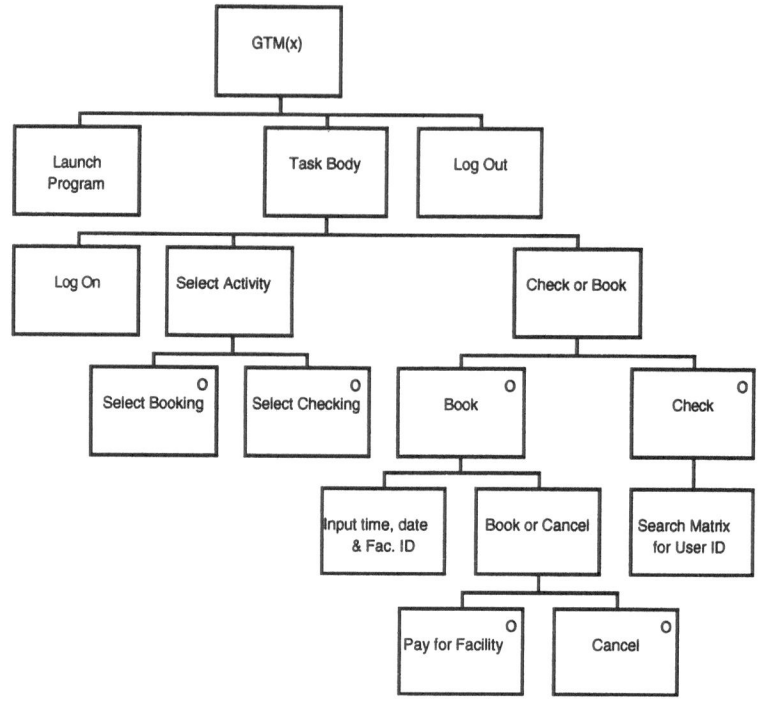

Name	Description	Observation	Design Implication	Speculation
Log on	This consists of the user providing some identifier, such as a password; casual users did not like providing the user id and password separately	This is for security purposes, either to safeguard data or computer processing resources	The user will have to identify themselves to the booking computer to stop people from using each others accounts	
Book	Users specify the time and facility they want to use, and can either pay for it or cancel		This will probably be an appropriate model to use for the RFBS	

Figure 5: Existing Systems: Generalised Task Model structured diagram and extract from supporting table

The user requirements form the basis of a General Task Model of the target artefact, shown in Figure 6 [2,7]. Comparison with the Generalised Task Model of existing systems shows that the high level structure of the task remains the same, but the lower level activity has been modified consistent with the user requirements [2,5]. The purchase of credit units has been included in the target artefact, as suggested by analysis of the existing system (Figure 4) [5].

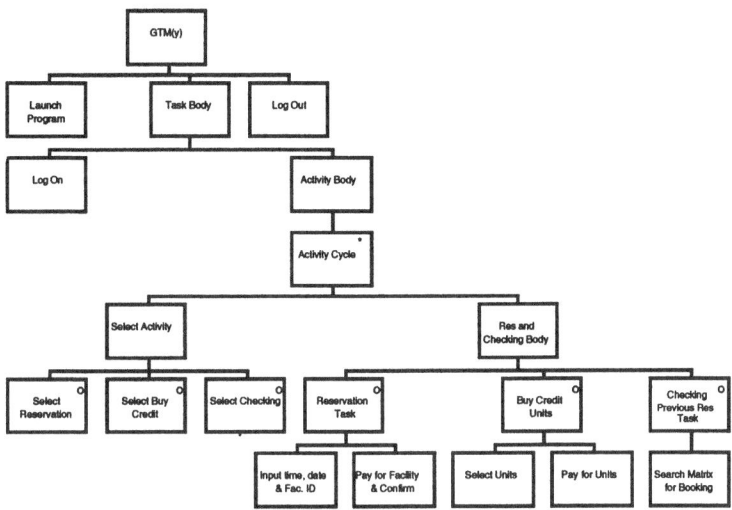

Name	Description	Observation	Design Implication	Speculation
Input time & Facility ID	Users select the day and time of recreation, and what facility they want to book	The user would be best supported by having all of this information on screen simultaneously		
Pay for Facility and confirm	The user finalises the booking			There will also be an option not to book
Activity cycle	The iteration has been changed from that shown in CS TD(ext)	The user is not required to re-enter the facility and date if they want to change the time		

Figure 6: RFBS: Generalised Task Model of target artefact structured diagram and extract from supporting table

Design Synthesis Phase

The first activity of the Design Synthesis Phase summarises the information from the extant systems analysis to produce a human factors perspective on the user requirements [4,5,6]. This Statement of User Needs for the target artefact is presented below. The statement exposes both specific design issues arising from analysis of the exising system, and general issues arising from the application of human factors knowledge [6].

RFBS: Statement of User Needs

Specific design issues:

- The system does not allow correction of input errors during the interaction cycle. The only choice open to the user is to restart the cycle.
- The system does not allow users to confirm their input.
- Machine-enforced sequential search is onerous, and tabular matrix search would preferable.
- The system does not indicate the current state of availability of recreational facilities and time-slots, unless these are entirely booked for the particular day. As such, the current design forces the user to adopt a 'trial and error' approach for the location of available and/or suitable time-slots.

General design issues:

- The target artefact should follow the conventions of the standard Macintosh User Interface; Smith and Mosier 3.0/6: Consistent User Actions.
- The target artefact should facilitate network access by users who are familiar with the standard Macintosh user interface, and should not require knowledge of network usage.
- The target artefact should provide feedback at each stage concerning input selections and error messages; Smith and Mosier (1986) 3.0/14: Feedback for Control Entries, 1.0/3 Feedback during Data Entry.
- It should allow users to confirm selections before acting on the inputs; Smith and Mosier (1986) 1.0/14: Feedback when Changing Data
- It should provide on-screen instructions for progressing the interaction; Smith and Mosier (1986) 4.4/1: Guidance Information always Available
- There should be some facility for enabling the user to make payment for use of the facility at the time of booking, possibly either by having paid for a number of credits previously, or perhaps by use of a credit card or Switch transaction.
- After entering the personal identification number, the artefact should allow more than one booking to be made after the number has been verified.

A further product generated at this time is the Domain of Design Discourse description[1,7]. It summarises the information collected during the analysis of existing systems, concerning relationships between entities in the task domain [3]. It is shown in Figure 7, with the table detailing the nature of the relationships assumed between domain entities [6]. The description records such details as the fact that the system should restrict access to 'legal' users (i.e. those who have a valid identity), and that these users will demand rights to a particular facility at a particular time [3,6]. These rights are transferred by allocation of a specific 'slot', on a 'first come first served' basis (i.e. there are no users who receive preferential treatment) in return for a payment of 'rent' [3]. Notice that the Domain of Design Discourse description is only concerned with details of the task domain and does not specify device-specific details, such as how payment for the use of the facility is to be made [3].

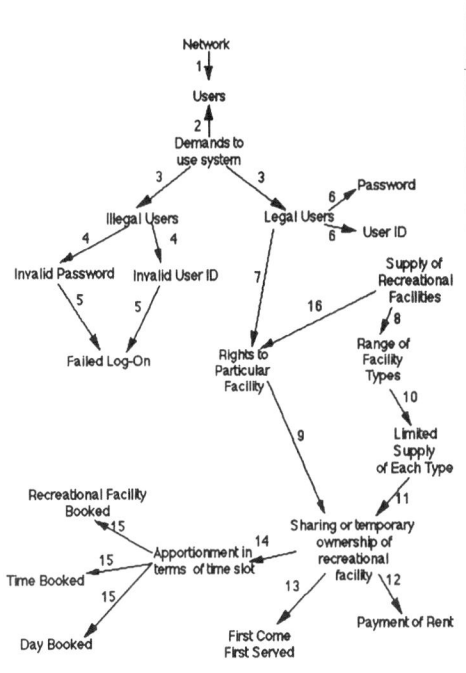

Node	Description	Number	Relation
Network		1	has a number of
Demands to use system		2	from
Demands to use system	Demands for booking the facilities may come from legal or illegal users	3	there are 2 types of user
Illegal Users	May be legal users who do not identify themselves correctly, or hackers	4	are identified by
Failed log-on	There are two conditions that should lead to a failed log-on	5	leads to
Legal users	Legal users will have a valid identity	6	have a
Legal users	Legal users are entitled to demand rights to facilities	7	demand
Supply of Recreational facilities	There are Squash Courts and Pool Tables	8	there are a
Rights to particular facility		9	given by the process of
Range of Facility types	There is a finite quantity of each facility	10	with a
Limited Supply of Each Type	The supply of facilities is limited by the opening hours of the sports centre	11	requires
Sharing or Temporary Ownership of Recreational Facility	Customers require the exclusive use of the facility for some period	12	temporary ownership requires
Sharing or Temporary Ownership of Recreational Facility		13	on the basis of
Sharing or Temporary Ownership of Recreational Facility		14	organised by
Apportionment in terms of time slot	Customers will book the facility for a definite period of time	15	booking has attributes of
Supply of Recreational Facilities	The availability of rights to a facility is determined by the supply of those facilities	16	provides

Figure 7: RFBS: Domain of Design Discourse Description

The Composite Task Model Stage produces a conceptual design for the target artefact based on the associated artefact Generalised Task Model and the Generalised Task Model derived from information elicited concerning existing systems [1,2,5,7].

An extract from the Composite Task Model is presented in Figure 10, showing the part of the interaction in which the user has opted to make a booking [6]. The user checks their free time (an off-line task, i.e. one not supported by the target artefact) and their funds are checked (an on-line task, i.e. one supported by the target artefact). If they have insufficient funds, they are notified, and prevented from booking facilities for which they cannot pay [3]. If their funds are sufficient, they enter details of the facility, day, and time that they wish to book [3]. They then have the opportunity to confirm or cancel the booking (in accordance with the Statement of User Needs) [2,4,5]. As the Composite Task Model is device independent (and error free), no assumptions have yet been made concerning the details of implementation [1].

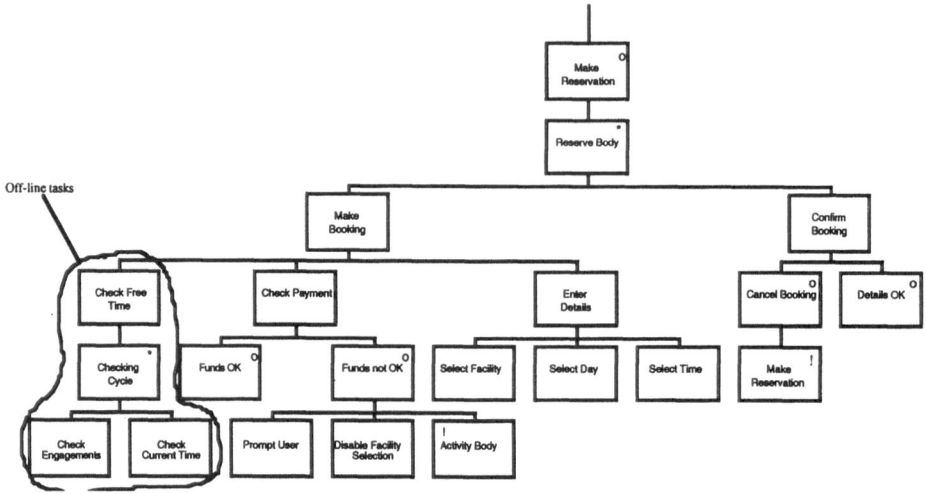

Figure 8: RFBS: Extract from Composite Task Model

Production of the System Task Model involves further decomposition of the Composite Task Model's on-line tasks to specify the structure of the dialogue between the user and the computer by attribution of actions to the computer ('C') or to the user ('H') [1,2,4,7]. Figure 9 shows an extract of the System Task Model structured diagram, the decomposition of the 'make reservation' body of the Composite Task Model.

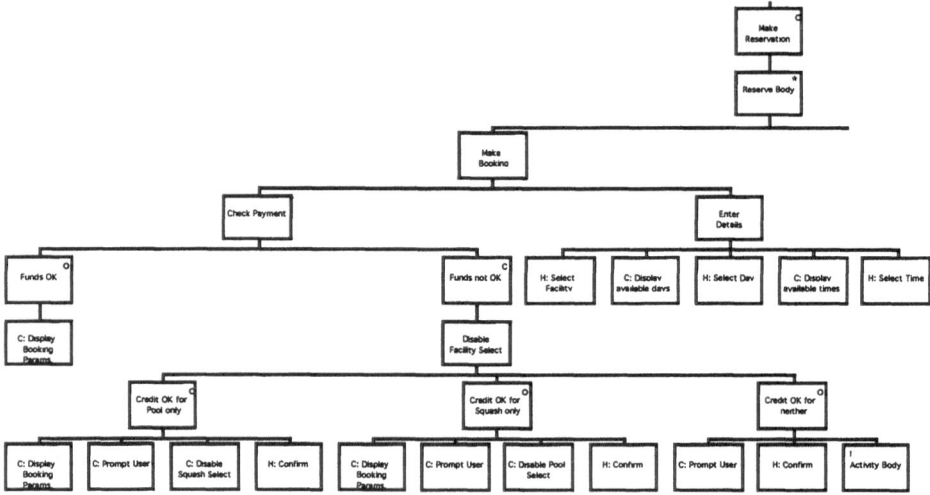

Figure 9: RFBS: Extract from System Task Model structured diagram

Additionally, a User Task Model of the target artefact is produced, containing details of off-line tasks [1,7]. In this case, the off-line tasks involve the user comparing their existing plans for the period available for booking to establish suitable times for recreation [1]. It was considered that these plans were likely either to be represented mentally or in a diary. The supporting table for the User Task Model records that the representation of the booking period in the target system should be compatible with the user's representations in order to provide the most effective support for the booking task [4,6,7]. Human factors guidelines inform this design feature [4,6].

Design Specification Phase

The first activity of the Design Specification Phase involves producing an Interaction Task Model of the target artefact, based on the System Task Model [2,7]. The Interaction Task Model is a device dependent, but error-free, model of the interaction [1]. It shows user actions required to progress the task as well as the interaction, and indicates where screens are to be consumed and new screens are to be presented [1,2]. An extract from the Interaction Task Model is shown in Figure 10 [6].

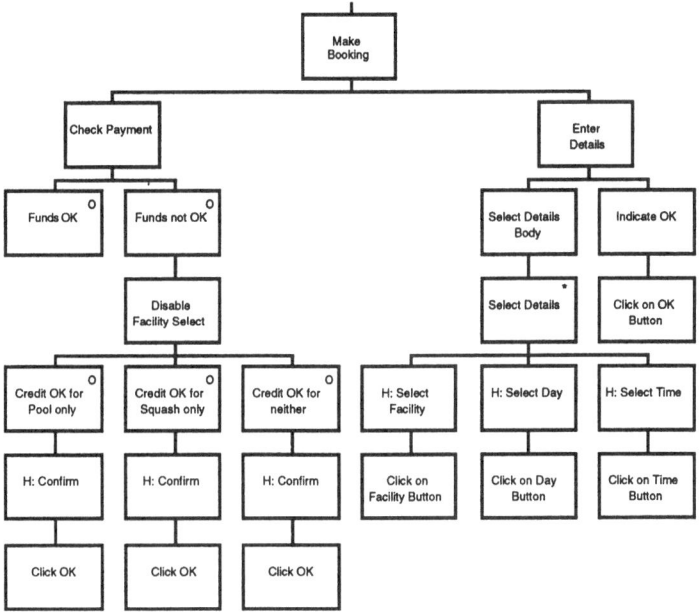

Figure 10: RFBS: Extract from Interaction Task Model structured diagram

In accordance with the Statement of User Needs, the Interaction Task Model conforms to the conventions of the Apple Macintosh system [2,4]. References to specific details of the Macintosh User Interface Guidelines (Apple Computer, Inc., (1985)) are recorded in the supporting table [2,4]. The booking part of the task is shown in Figure 10. If insufficient funds are available, the user is notified of the fact [3]. In line with Macintosh conventions, notification is by a modal dialogue, with the user clicking an 'OK' button to continue the dialogue [4]. If sufficient funds are available, no acknowledgement is required, and the user selects the booking details before clicking an 'OK' button to indicate that they have finished making selections [3,4].

The Interaction Task Model and the Domain of Design Discourse description are used to inform the design of Pictorial Screen Layouts, which show the layout of interface objects on the screens comprising the user interface [1,2,3,7]. An example Pictorial Screen Layout is shown in Figure 11; the screen illustrated corresponds to the 'make booking' part of the Interaction Task Model shown in Figure 10 [2,6]. Although 'payment checking' is

324

allocated to the computer, a human factors guideline suggests that the amount of credit should be visible to the user (Smith and Mosier (1986); 6.3/16: Displaying Data to be Changed) [4]. In line with the guideline listed in the Statement of User Needs (Smith and Mosier, 1986; 4.4/1: Guidance Information Always Available), on-screen instructions are specified to provide the user with additional support for the task [4].

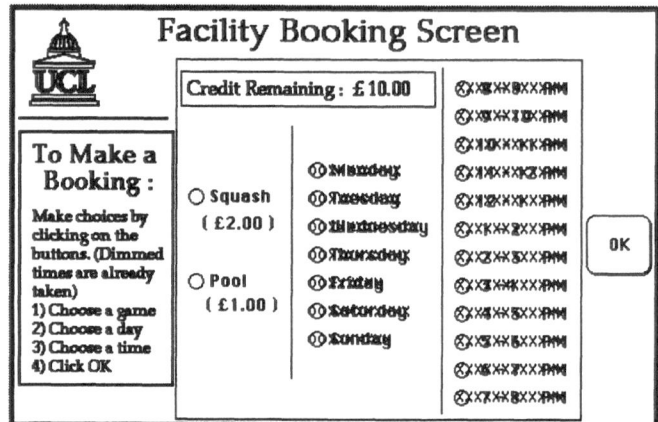

Figure 11: RFBS: Pictorial Screen Layout of Booking Screen

The behaviours of the objects included in the screens are described using a set of Interface Model products [1,2,7]. An extract from the Interface Model is shown in Figure 12 [6].

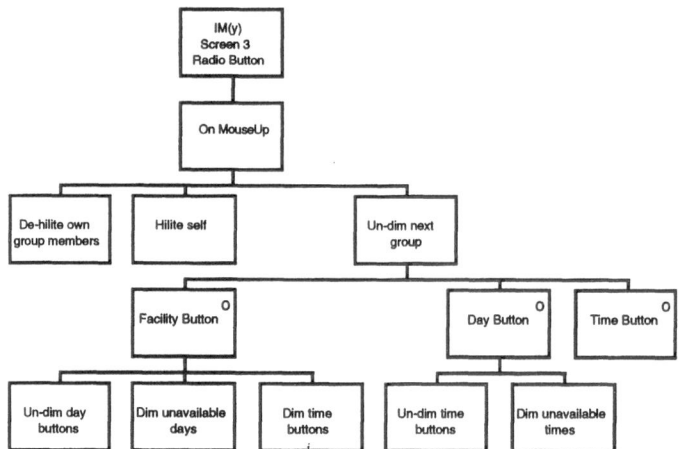

Figure 12: RFBS: Extract from the Interface Model structured diagram

The extract shows the behaviour of the radio buttons used to select the facility, day, and time desired by the user. Following Macintosh conventions, selection of one radio button de-hilights other members of the same group, and those unavailable for selection remain dimmed [4]. Hence, until a button from the 'facility' group has been selected, the 'day' buttons remain dimmed, and until a 'day' button has been selected, the 'time' buttons remain dimmed. Days or times which are already booked or unavailable, are indicated by the corresponding button remaining dimmed [2]. The objects comprising the user interface are further described in the Dictionary of Screen Objects [1,7]. The entries corresponding to the radio buttons described above are shown in Figure 13 [6].

Screen Object	Description	Design Attributes
Sc 3 Facility Buttons	Allow selection of squash or snooker bookings	Radio buttons; remain hilited when selected, remain dimmed if insufficient credit. Only one of the 2 buttons may be selected at one time
Sc 3 Day Buttons	Allow selection of day for booking	Radio Buttons; remain hilited when selected. Remain dimmed until a facility is selected; unavailable days remain dimmed.
Sc 3 Time Buttons	Allow selection of timeslot for booking	Radio Buttons; remain hilited when selected. Remain dimmed until a day is selected; times already booked by others remain dimmed
Sc 3 OK Button	User confirms booking; triggers transition to Booking Confirmation Screen	

Figure 13: RFBS: Dictionary of Screen Object entries for radio buttons

The specification of the User Interface for the case-study artefact is completed by a Dialogue and Error Message Table, which lists all the error messages that could be presented during the interaction, and a Dialogue and Inter-Task Screen Actuation Description which details the points in the interaction at which screens are consumed and the conditions that trigger the presentation of an error message [1,2,7]. An extract from the Dialogue and Inter-Task Screen Actuation Description corresponding to the part of the interface, described in detail above, is shown in Figure 14 [6]. The part of the Dialogue and Error Message Table corresponding to the error messages specified in Figure 14 is shown in Figure 15 [6].

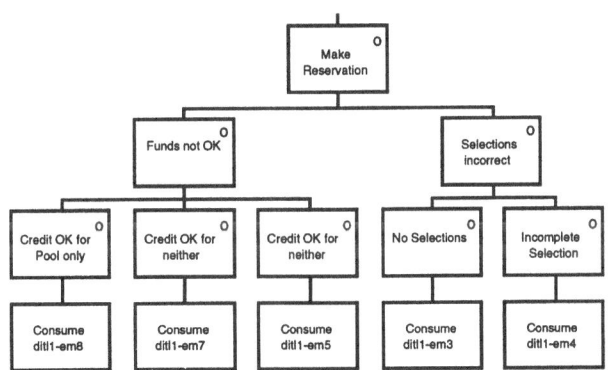

Figure 14: RFBS: Extract from the Dialogue and Inter-Task Screen Actuation Description

Message No.	Message
em 3	Click on the buttons to book, or press 'Go Back' to cancel
em 4	Sorry, you must choose a day and a time
em 5	Insufficient Credit. Buy more units?
em 7	Insufficient credit for Pool - Squash only
em 8	Insufficient credit for Squash - Pool only

Figure 15: RFBS: Extract from the Dialogue and Error Message Table

Taken together, the products of the Design Specification phase constitute the specification of the RFBS interaction artefact.

Assessment of the Artefact

Assessment of the artefact was conducted by asking the target users ('A' and 'J') whether the artefact corresponded to the requirements that they had expressed. Both were surprised by some aspects of the design. In addition, some (detailed) aspects did not meet their (detailed) requirements. However, the users agreed that the artefact satisfied their requirements as they had been originally and generally expressed (as stated at the beginning of this paper). Thus, the application of MUSE was considered to be successful in this respect.

Further assessment of the artefact was obtained by means of an expert walkthrough conducted by an experienced human factors engineer. The conclusions of the report are that overall the artefact successfully addresses the user requirements, is easy to use, and easy to learn. However, some reservations were expressed concerning incompatibility between the instructions given to the user and the apparent representation of the task domain at the start of the booking transaction. Before a facility has been selected, all 'day' and 'time' buttons are dimmed (to indicate that they cannot be selected at that stage of the interaction). The on-screen instructions state that 'dimmed times are already taken', and it was considered that a naive user may conclude that there are no available slots and attempt to terminate the booking at that stage. A further reservation concerned incompatibility between booking pool facilities by the hour and the conventional process for establishing rights to a pool table, which is on a 'payment per game' basis. Finally, it was felt that when a user cancels a potential booking they may expect to be returned to the booking screen rather than to the main menu, since such a return would be more consistent with the notion of 'quitting' an operation, rather than cancelling it. These reservations violate none of the necessary features for a MUSE application indicated above. They may merely indicate that more than one artefact is able to satisfy the same set of user requirements; that experts differ in their designs; and that empirical assessment may be needed to decide between such differences. Thus, the application of MUSE was again considered to be successful in that the RFBS was considered to fulfil the user requirements.

Comparison with the Requirements of Stork et al (1995)

The user requirements from Stork et al. involve the specification of a bespoke artefact to solve the following problem (at a reasonable cost for the benefits): 'A's domestic routine occasionally requires him to remain at home to work in the mornings, after the central heating normally switches off. On these days, he finds it difficult to estimate when he will leave, which can result in him being too cold, if he is at home for longer than expected. The specified artefact involved the heating remaining on, until 'A' switched it off as he left the house, using a button located beside the front door.

Superficially, the user requirements in this case-study would seem defined to the same extent as those of the case-study in Stork et al.: crudely, their text descriptions are of approximately the same length (in the originals). However, the user requirements here need more extensive definition than for those of Stork et al.: they are based on two players, rather than on one occupant; the domain involves transactions (between the player(s) and the sports centre) with rules of engagement, rather than no transactions; the domain involves multiple planning and control (between the players), rather than individual planning and control; the maximum and minimum cognitive and physical effort of two users must be specified, rather than of one user (including details of locations in the University rather than locations in a home); and the maximum and minimum capabilities of more than one computer must be specified, rather than those of one embedded device. Since there is less to define for the user requirements in Stork et al. than the user requirements here, and they are both currently defined to approximately the same extent, the user requirements here can be informally said to be less well-defined than those in Stork et al.. The lack of definition might derive from a more general definition, a less complete definition, or both.

The complexity of the user requirements can be directly related to the difficulty of satisfying the user requirements: the more difficult, the more complex. Satisfying the user requirements in this case-study is more difficult than fulfilling the user requirements in Stork et al. because: designing for domains which involve multiple transactions is assumed to be more difficult than designing for domains which involve no such transactions; designing for domains which involve multiple planning and control is assumed to be more difficult than designing for domains which involve individual planning and control; designing for the reduction in movement between multiple locations is assumed to be more difficult than designing for the reduction in movement between two locations; designing interfaces for network software is assumed to be more difficult than designing interfaces for non-networked software; designing full-screen multiple-dialogue mouse-driven interfaces is assumed to be more difficult than designing embedded devices; designing for two users is assumed to be more difficult than designing for one; and designing networked multi-user database systems is assumed to be more difficult than designing non-networked single-user flat-file single-record database systems. The user requirements in this case-study can be said, therefore, informally to be more complex than the user requirements in Stork et al..

The user requirements in this case-study and in Stork et al. can be considered equally observable: in this case-study they were observed by 'A' and 'J'; and in Stork et al. they were observed by 'A'.

Conclusions

It has been shown above: that the artefact was developed by the application of MUSE to the user requirements; that the artefact fulfils the user requirements; and that the user requirements are less well-defined and more complex than those of Stork et al. (1995), but equally observable. The known frontiers of application of MUSE can be said, therefore, to have been extended by this successful case-study.

Acknowledgements

This research was supported by the European System and Software Initiative as part of application experiment 10290 (Benefits of Integrating Usability and Software Engineering Methods).

References

APPLE COMPUTER INC., 1985, *Inside Macintosh® Volume 1*. Addison-Wesley Publishing Company, Inc., Reading, MA.

ESSI, 1994, *MUSE Generic Training Manual.* Unpublished Report, Ergonomics and HCI Unit, University College London.

LIM, K.Y., LONG, J.B., and SILCOCK, N., 1990, Requirements, Research and Strategy for Integrating Human Factors with Structured Analysis and Design Methods: The Case of the Jackson System Development Method. In E.J. Lovesey (Ed.) *Contemporary Ergonomics, Proceedings of the Ergonomics Society's 1990 Conference, Leeds, April 1990.* Taylor and Francis, London, pp. 32-38.

LIM, K.Y., LONG, J.B., and SILCOCK, N., 1992, Integrating Human Factors with System Development: An Illustrated Overview. *Ergonomics*, 33, 12, pp. 1135-1161.

LIM, K.Y., LONG, J.B., 1994, *The MUSE Method for Usability Engineering.* Cambridge University Press, Cambridge.

SMITH, S.L. and MOSIER, J.N., 1986, *Guidelines for Designing User Interface Software.* The MITRE Corporation, Bedford, MA.

STORK, A., MIDDLEMASS, J., and LONG, J.B., 1995, Applying a Structured Method for Usability Engineeering to Domestic Energy Management User Requirements: a Successful Case-Study. Submitted to *Human Computer Interaction 1995 (HCI '95).*

A Formal Design for Mutually Composed Multiple Media in Presentations

Roger Took

Human Computer Interaction Group,
Computer Science Department,
University of York,
York YO1 5DD, UK
email: roger@minster.york.ac.uk
tel: 0904-432741

ABSTRACT

The motivation for this paper is to design a simple but expressive representation for the arbitrary organisation and nesting of text and images in presentations like user interfaces and document browsers. The design defined here achieves this with a single generic hierarchical structure, called a *TANGLE*, instantiated with two node types, *BLOCK*s and *SPACE*s, to carry text and images respectively, and two mappings which represent how text may be *framed* in graphical spaces, and images may be *embedded* in text blocks. In addition, a *projection* function is defined by which visualisations from the structure can be generated. The inclusion of other media types is also discussed.

1 Introduction

In existing interactive environments that allow the construction and composition of text, graphics and other media, it is often the case that there are *inconsistencies* in interaction with media at different levels in the presentation structure, be this a window manager or a WYSIWYG document processor. For example, not all visible text may be editable (even if the application designer requires it), and interaction with editable text may vary depending on whether the text is presented within a terminal emulator, a text editor, a type-in field, or an icon caption. The inconsistencies are even wider in the presentation of graphics, video or sound.

Beyond the basic theories of text and graphics as sequences of characters and sets of images respectively, with associated constructor and destructor operations, there are clear requirements to support the *logical* and *physical* organisation of these media, and their mutual *composition*. Both documents and interactive user interfaces may consist of a logical organisation of sections and subsections etc., physically arranged on the page or screen. These logical and physical structures may be quite orthogonal. Ideally also text may be arbitrarily nested within graphics and vice versa. It is also of benefit to be able to *share* or *replicate* a textual or graphical component over multiple structures.

This organisation requires a powerful structural design without bias towards either text or graphics. Graphics standards have increased their support for structure: GKS [1] has only a two level structure (primitives and segments), while PHIGS [3] allows a general hierarchy. However, in both of these text is treated simply as a content type with no structure of its own. The converse is the case in the emerging text standards. In ODA [4] graphics is a content type, while SGML [2] does not cover graphics at all. Also, text models rarely support the sharing of structures – [7] is an exception.

At the same time a number of commercial presentation systems and protocols are being developed that are likely to have more impact in practice. The World Wide Web already has several browsers, and its basic html markup language, which allows the insertion of images and sound in text, will inevitably sprout local extensions. The danger but liklihood, however, is that these extensions will simply exacerbate any original design limitations. On the other hand, Microsoft's *Object Linking and Embedding* and Apple/IBM's *OpenDoc* [5] are basic infrastructures for *compound* documents in which media-intensive applications are accessible via their *products*. This trend is a major shift away from monolithic application-oriented computing towards structured *object*-oriented computing, and the intuitiveness and flexibility of the structural design is critical to its success.

While the design presented here is formal (and the author recognises the limitations of such descriptions [9]), it is driven by the experience of implementing similar but less general designs as interactive user interface managers [13, 11], and in particular in a screen operating system called *Presenter* [10, 12]. Interactive editing or manipulation of documents and user interfaces requires at least that their structure persist along with their visualisation, otherwise user selections cannot be made. Thus we expect the present design too to be implemented as a dynamic abstract data type with state (i.e. an *object*) rather than in a static markup language [6].

Below we first present (Section 2) the generic structure as an extended ordered graph with as yet undefined nodes. We show in Section 2 how this structure can in general be *projected* onto a display surface. We then (Section 4) instantiate the structure with particular node types, especially nodes to contain text and graphics. We finally show in Section 5 how these different media types are composed in the display projection.

2 The Generic Structure

We wish the fundamental structure to be as general and powerful as possible. We start with an ordered graph structure which is generic in its *NODE* type:

$$ORDERED\_GRAPH[NODE] == NODE \nrightarrow \text{seq } NODE$$

This structure maps parent *NODE*s to (possibly empty) sequences of child *NODE*s. Note that child *NODE*s may themselves parent sequences of children, and any *NODE* can be a member of the child sequences of a number of parent

*NODE*s. However, this structure is too free for our purposes in that it allows *cyclic* mappings between parents and children. That is, there is nothing to stop a *NODE* on an *ORDERED_GRAPH* from being its own ancestor via some sequence of parent-child mappings. Cyclic structures are not finitely evaluable into visual presentations. We therefore define the generic *tangle* structure we use for our design as an *ORDERED_GRAPH* with an *acyclic* constraint. This is expressed in a Z [8] schema, again parameterised by *NODE*:

$$\begin{array}{|l}
\underline{\quad TANGLE\,[NODE]\quad\rule{9cm}{0pt}} \\
\quad tangle : ORDERED\_GRAPH[NODE] \\
\quad parents : NODE \leftrightarrow NODE \\
\quad leaves : \mathbb{P}\,NODE \\
\hline
\quad parents = \{parent : NODE;\ child : \mathrm{ran}(tangle\ parent) \bullet child \mapsto parent\} \\
\quad leaves = \{n : NODE \bullet tangle\ n = \langle\rangle\} \\
\quad acyclic(parents) \\
\quad \mathrm{dom}\ parents \subset \mathrm{dom}\ tangle \\
\end{array}$$

Z schemas are divided into a *signature*, which declares variables and their types, followed by a *predicate*, which expresses constraints on the variables. The schema is understood to represent the set of instances of the variables for which the predicate holds true. Z's mathematical language is fairly standard.

The essential design structure is thus represented by a *tangle*, which is an *acyclic ORDERED_GRAPH*. The acyclic constraint is expressed via a derived relation *parents* which maps all child *NODE*s on the *tangle* to their parent *NODE*s. *parents* is a relation since we still allow *NODE*s to have a number of parents. The predicate *acyclic* is defined in the appendix. *tangle* captures all the information needed to define the structure of particular instances of the design.

The last constraint imposed by the schema is less concerned with conceptual issues as with preserving the integrity of the representation. There are two ways of representing leaf *NODE*s in *ORDERED_GRAPH*. A leaf may either be present in some child sequence but *not* present in the domain of the graph, or it may be present in the domain but map to an *empty* child sequence. We would have to interpret either of these representations as leafness, but for the sake of consistency and simplicity we choose only one of these for *tangles*. Since we wish also to be able to represent *isolated NODE*s, i.e. *NODE*s with neither children nor parents, only the second representation is appropriate. This is because an isolated *NODE*, not being a child, could not be represented on *tangle* at all using the first representation. We therefore need a constraint that forces all leaf *NODE*s to map to empty child sequences. This we do by requiring that at least all child *NODE*s (i.e. the domain of *parents*) be present in the domain of *tangle*, and so at least map to the empty sequence ($\langle\rangle$). Now, for example, the *tangle* consisting just of the single (isolated) *NODE* n is represented $\{(n \mapsto \langle\rangle)\}$, and the *parents* relation is empty. As a useful consequence of this constraint, the domain of *tangle* contains only and all the *NODE*s of the structure.

This representation constraint also means that we have a simple test for leafness: a *NODE* n is a leaf if *tangle* $n = \langle\,\rangle$. Using this test the schema *TANGLE* also defines a derived set *leaves* of *NODE*s. These are all the *NODE*s which have no children. We could similarly derive the set of *root NODE*s as all *NODE*s (in the domain of *tangle*) which have no *parents* (i.e. dom *tangle* − dom *parents*). However we have no immediate need for this set in the paper.

This structural design does not force the child *NODE* sequences to be injective. Thus we can represent *tangles* such as $\{p \mapsto \langle c, c\rangle\}$, in which notionally there are *two* arcs from p to c. However, the design provides no way to distinguish these arcs. This is no loss of expressive power, since it is always possible to insert different intermediate *NODE*s between p and c if we wish to give these arcs different properties.

With these constraints, the *tangle* can represent a general directed acyclic ordered graph (which may consist of disjoint hierarchies or isolated *NODE*s). Note, however, that if a *tangle* has more than one root, then these roots are not mutually ordered. If an order is required for roots, it is a simple matter to add a parent *NODE* which orders them as its children. *NODE*s may be shared by more than one parent, but the position of a *NODE* in the child sequence of one parent is independent of its position in the children of any of its other parents. Hence the name tangle!

As an example, the *tangle*:

$$t = \{a \mapsto \langle b, c\rangle, b \mapsto \langle d, e\rangle, c \mapsto \langle e\rangle, d \mapsto \langle\,\rangle, e \mapsto \langle\,\rangle\}$$

can be illustrated (the left-to-right layout reflects the ordering of the child *NODE*s):

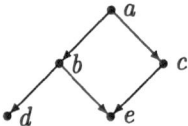

3 Projection

An essential capability of any presentation design is that its *projection* into a visualisation be well defined. We do this here to the extent of extracting sequences of *paths* of *NODE*s from the *tangle*. As detailed in the next section, each path can then be visualised depending on further properties of its *NODE*s.

Starting from any *NODE*, a sequence of paths, themselves sequences of *NODE*s whose head is the original *NODE* and whose last element is a leaf *NODE*, can unambiguously be generated from a *tangle* using a function *untangle*:

$$\underline{\quad untangle : \text{seq } NODE \rightarrow \text{seq seq } NODE \quad}$$

$$untangle = paths \; \langle \rangle$$
$$WHERE$$
$$paths = \lambda \; p, \langle h \rangle \frown t : \text{seq } NODE \bullet$$
$$\quad paths \; p \; \langle \rangle = \langle \rangle$$
$$\quad paths \; p \; \langle h \rangle \frown t = \langle p \frown \langle h \rangle \rangle \frown paths \; p \; t \qquad \qquad [\text{If } h \in leaves]$$
$$\quad paths \; p \; \langle h \rangle \frown t = (paths \; p \frown \langle h \rangle \; (tangle \; h)) \frown paths \; p \; t$$
$$\qquad \qquad \qquad \qquad \qquad \qquad \qquad \qquad \qquad \qquad \quad [\text{If } h \notin leaves]$$

We assume that the *untangle* function is defined *within the scope* of the *TANGLE* schema (we have not defined it there simply for clarity of exposition), so that the particular *tangle* structure is an implicit parameter. *untangle* is defined over *sequences* of *NODE*S for later convenience. The definition uses the auxiliary function *paths*, which is specified in a pattern-matching style for concision. *paths* accumulates the sequence of paths in its first parameter p, and for *untangle* this is initially empty. The second parameter to *paths* is a sequence of *NODE*s in which h is the head *NODE* and t the tail sequence. This parameter carries the current sequence of (sub)root *NODE*s each of whose paths the function is accumulating.

For example, three paths can be derived from the root *NODE* a of the *tangle* t above:

$$untangle \; \langle a \rangle = paths \; \langle \rangle \; \langle a \rangle$$
$$= (paths \; \langle \rangle \frown \langle a \rangle \; (tangle \; a)) \frown paths \; \langle \rangle \; \langle \rangle \qquad \qquad [a \notin leaves]$$
$$= (paths \; \langle \rangle \frown \langle a \rangle \; (tangle \; a)) \frown \langle \rangle$$
$$= paths \; \langle a \rangle \; (tangle \; a)$$
$$= paths \; \langle a \rangle \; \langle b, c \rangle$$
$$= (paths \; \langle a \rangle \frown \langle b \rangle \; (tangle \; b)) \frown paths \; \langle a \rangle \; \langle c \rangle \qquad \qquad [b \notin leaves]$$
$$= (paths \; \langle a, b \rangle \; \langle d, e \rangle) \frown paths \; \langle a \rangle \; \langle c \rangle$$
$$= (paths \; \langle a, b \rangle \; \langle d, e \rangle) \frown (paths \; \langle a \rangle \frown \langle c \rangle \; (tangle \; c)) \frown paths \; \langle a \rangle \; \langle \rangle$$
$$\qquad \qquad \qquad \qquad \qquad \qquad \qquad \qquad \qquad \qquad \qquad [c \notin leaves]$$
$$= (paths \; \langle a, b \rangle \; \langle d, e \rangle) \frown (paths \; \langle a \rangle \frown \langle c \rangle \; (tangle \; c)) \frown \langle \rangle$$
$$= (paths \; \langle a, b \rangle \; \langle d, e \rangle) \frown (paths \; \langle a, c \rangle \; (tangle \; c))$$
$$= (paths \; \langle a, b \rangle \; \langle d, e \rangle) \frown (paths \; \langle a, c \rangle \; \langle e \rangle)$$
$$= (paths \; \langle a, b \rangle \; \langle d, e \rangle) \frown \langle \langle a, c \rangle \frown \langle e \rangle \rangle \frown paths \; \langle a, c \rangle \; \langle \rangle$$
$$\qquad \qquad \qquad \qquad \qquad \qquad \qquad \qquad \qquad \qquad \qquad [e \in leaves]$$
$$= (paths \; \langle a, b \rangle \; \langle d, e \rangle) \frown \langle \langle a, c, e \rangle \rangle$$

$$= (\langle\langle\langle a, b\rangle \frown \langle d\rangle\rangle \frown paths\ \langle a, b\rangle\ \langle e\rangle\rangle \frown \langle\langle a, c, e\rangle\rangle \qquad [d \in leaves]$$

$$= (\langle\langle a, b, d\rangle\rangle \frown paths\ \langle a, b\rangle\ \langle e\rangle\rangle \frown \langle\langle a, c, e\rangle\rangle$$

$$= (\langle\langle a, b, d\rangle\rangle \frown \langle\langle a, b\rangle \frown \langle e\rangle\rangle \frown paths\ \langle a, b\rangle\ \langle\rangle\rangle \frown \langle\langle a, c, e\rangle\rangle$$
$$\qquad\qquad [e \in leaves]$$

$$= \langle\langle a, b, d\rangle\rangle \frown \langle\langle a, b, e\rangle\rangle \frown \langle\langle a, c, e\rangle\rangle$$

$$= \langle\langle a, b, d\rangle, \langle a, b, e\rangle, \langle a, c, e\rangle\rangle$$

Each path in this sequence starts with the specified root *NODE* (a), and ends with a leaf *NODE*. This also demonstrates how the same leaf *NODE* (in this case e) can be projected down several different paths.

4 Specific Structures

In this section we show how the generic *TANGLE* can be specialised to a textual or graphical structure, and loaded with specific content and properties. In this way a path on a *textual* tangle may contain a character at its leaf, and properties like font or point size at any *NODE*. On the other hand, a path on a *graphical* tangle may contain an image at its leaf, and properties like geometric transformations at any *NODE*. Thus, if need be, the visualisaton properties of characters or images can be specified individually, locally, or globally, depending on proximity to the projection root. [12, 11] detail how such properties can be *inherited* and *composed* down textual or graphical paths.

4.1 Basic Elements

In order to accommodate both text and graphics in the design in as representation-independent a manner as possible, we simply declare two basic node types:

$$[SPACE, BLOCK]$$

We will give no further formal definition of these, but only note, informally, that *SPACE*s are intended to represent groupings of graphical coordinate spaces, and *BLOCK*s are intended to represent textual character groupings. We assume that there are unbounded numbers of both types of node.

The design itself we wish at least to contain both structured text and structured graphics. This is expressed simply by instantiating the generic *TANGLE* structure with the node types *SPACE* and *BLOCK*:

$$\begin{array}{|l}
T : TANGLE[BLOCK] \\
G : TANGLE[SPACE]
\end{array}$$

This is a Z *axiomatic* schema, whose scope is global. We thus avoid having to give it a name, but we intend this to be the central formulation of the design in this paper. Thus any particular instance of the design will contain a text *TANGLE T* and a graphics *TANGLE G*. This dual instantiation carries perfectly adequately the observation that while text and graphics may have the same generic structure, particular graphics and text structures will necessarily be distinct and will co-exist.

4.2   Content

We have said nothing formally so far about the *content* of these structures, although we have assumed that text structures contain characters and graphics structures contain images. Content can simply be expressed by mappings between *SPACE*s and *BLOCK*s and appropriate content types (we assume basic types *CHAR* and *IMAGE*):

$$
\begin{array}{|l}
\text{\textit{text} : \textit{BLOCK} $\nrightarrow$ \textit{CHAR}} \\
\text{\textit{image} : \textit{SPACE} $\nrightarrow$ \textit{IMAGE}} \\
\hline
\text{dom \textit{text} $\subseteq$ \textit{T.leaves}} \\
\text{dom \textit{image} $\subseteq$ \textit{G.leaves}}
\end{array}
$$

Each of the *content* mappings is restricted to the *leaves* of its particular *tangle* structure. This allows the super-structure in each *tangle* to be a *logical* organisation of either its textual or graphical content. Thus *BLOCK*s can represent paragraphs or other sections of text, while *SPACE*s can represent sub-parts of a graphical composition. On the other hand, the *ordering* of the *tangle*s is interpreted differently in the two domains. In the textual *T.tangle* the ordering of the *BLOCK*s clearly represents the order of characters contained in the leaf *BLOCK*s (via *text*), while in the graphical *G.tangle* we take the ordering of *SPACE*s to represent the *layering* in the z-axis of their *IMAGE* content (via *image*).

For example, consider the following illustration of a *T*, in which the *text* mapping is illustrated by the appearance of a character inside the leaf *BLOCK*s, and the *tangle* structure is illustrated by arrows from (solid) non-leaf *BLOCK*s to the first child in their sequence of children. The non-leaf *BLOCK*s are also labelled for the purpose of explanation:

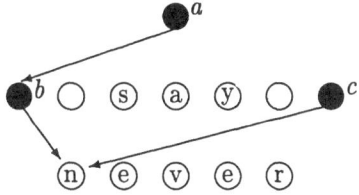

Assuming that *last* returns the last elements of the *untangle*d paths, the result of:

text ○ *last* ○ *T.untangle*⟨a⟩

is the text sequence:

never say never

If the *BLOCK*s *b* and *c* possessed different property mappings, for example different point sizes or fonts, then the text sequence could be visualised with the *never*s of different sizes or fonts. We only have space to mention this informally.

The application to graphics is similar, except that we assume *SPACE* properties such as geometric transformation and transparency which are composed down the path, and map the ordering of different paths to display layering, as noted above. The following is a *G tangle* (in which the *image* mapping is again illustrated by the appearance of the *IMAGE* inside a leaf *SPACE*):

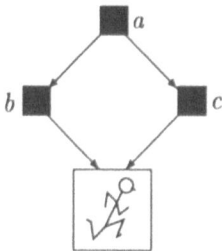

This *tangle* might be visualised by the same mechanism (assuming *SPACE*s *b* and *c* possess different geometric transformation and transparency properties):

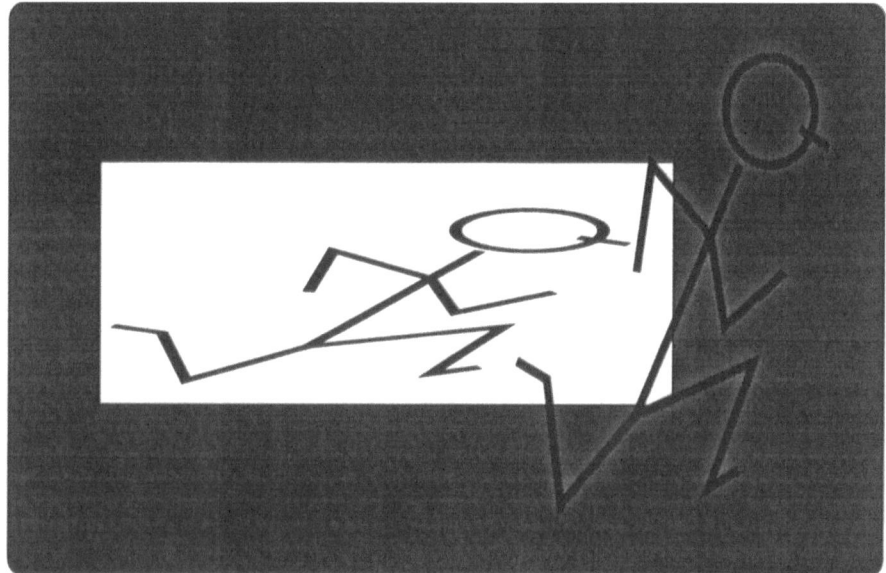

Note how the order of *tangle paths* is rendered here as display overlapping priority.

5 Composing Text and Graphics

Although we have defined the text and graphics structures T and G separately, one major requirement of the design is that it *compose* text and graphics. In addition, we especially do not want to place any restrictions on the depth or order of the nesting of text and graphics, for example that text is only ever contained in graphics or vice versa, such as are imposed by existing standards.

However, it is at this point that certain asymmetries emerge in the design as an unavoidable consequence of the differences between textual and graphical geometries. When graphics is embedded in text, for example, it is projected within the textual geometry, and is thus subject to formatting constraints along with its surrounding characters. Thus we expect embedded graphics to be affected by text insertions or deletions:

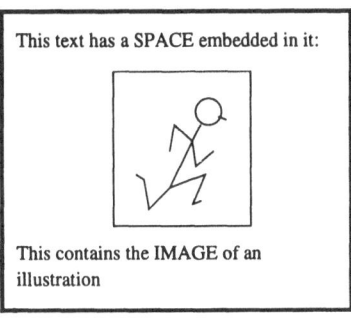 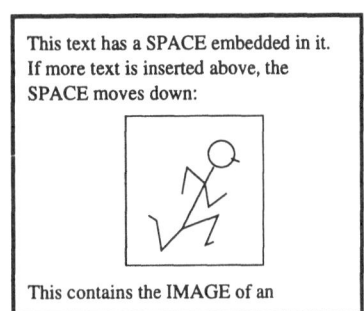

The structural constraints on graphics embedded in text can be expressed:

$$embed : BLOCK \twoheadrightarrow SPACE$$

dom *embed* $\subseteq$ *T.leaves*
ran *embed* $\subseteq$ dom *G.tangle*
dom *embed* $\cap$ dom *text* $= \varnothing$

That is, the function *embed* maps leaf *BLOCK*s to *SPACE*s. The *BLOCK*s so mapped must not already have content via *text*, and the *SPACE*s mapped to must already be on the graphics structure G.

On the other hand, when text is framed in graphics we must allow for the possibility that the text sequence is too long to be framed in a single *SPACE*. We need therefore to specify a *sequence* of *SPACE*s into which the text represented by a *BLOCK* can be poured [6], such that as text overflows from one, it runs on into the next:

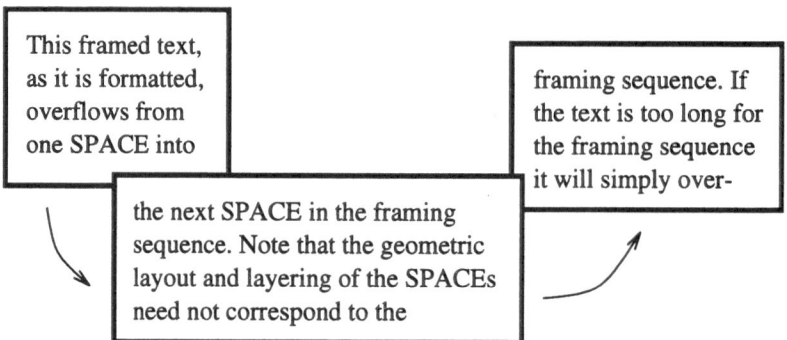

Thus the structural constraints on framed text are slightly different from those on embedded graphics, in that a function *frame* maps *sequences* of leaf *SPACE*s to *BLOCK*s:

$$frame : \text{iseq}\, SPACE \nrightarrow BLOCK$$

$s \subseteq G.leaves$
$s \cap \text{dom}\, image = \varnothing$
$\text{ran}\, frame \subseteq \text{dom}\, T.tangle$
$\bigcap ss = \varnothing$
WHERE
$\quad ss = \{f : \text{dom}\, frame \bullet \text{ran}\, f\}$
$\quad s = \bigcup ss$

Again, however, the *SPACE*s so mapped must not already have content, and the *BLOCK*s they are mapped to must also be part of the text structure T. In addition, the *SPACE*s in the domain of *frame* must be unique. It would not make sense to have the same *SPACE* framing two different text *BLOCK*s. However, we do not exclude one *BLOCK* being framed by a number of different viewing *SPACE*s.

While the illustrations here show rectangular *SPACE*s, theoretically they may be arbitrarily shaped. This is an issue for further realisation of the design.

Finally, we must ensure that no cycles can develop through embedding and framing when the structures T and G are combined:

$acyclic[BLOCK]\ (framed \,\underset{9}{\circ}\, embedded)$
$acyclic[SPACE]\ (embedded \,\underset{9}{\circ}\, framed)$
WHERE
$\quad framed = \{f : \text{dom}\, frame;\ s : G.parents^* (\!|\ \text{ran}\, f\ |\!) \bullet frame\, f \mapsto s\}$
$\quad embedded = \{e : \text{dom}\, embed;\ b : T.parents^* (\!|\ \{e\}\ |\!) \bullet embed\, e \mapsto b\}$

The $SPACE \leftrightarrow BLOCK$ relation *embedded* maps embedded *SPACE*s to the *BLOCK*s, and all their ancestors (*parents**) which *embed* them. Similarly, the $BLOCK \leftrightarrow SPACE$ relation *framed* maps framed *BLOCK*s to all the *SPACE*s which *frame* them. The two acyclic constraints expressed in the schema are equivalent, and either would be sufficient: no *BLOCK* or *SPACE* can reach itself along any closed composition of *embedded* and *framed*, i.e. along any path of this combined structure.

6 Conclusions

We have presented a very general design for combining text and graphics in a presentation structure. The design has been constructed from a simple generic structure (*TANGLE*), instantiated with only two node types, *BLOCK* and *SPACE*. Two further mappings, *frame* and *embed*, are necessary to link these two instances of the structure.

We have been able to give only a very informal impression of the possible content and properties of the two types of node, and the mechanisms by which these would be visualised on a display. In particular, we have not specified the mappings from *NODE*s to properties such as geometric transformation or visualisation attributes. These details, however are at a lower level of abstraction than the basic structure of the design which we concentrate on here. A further interesting prospect is the use of the *tangle* structure to represent the organisation and ordering of other media types, in particular those which are ordered temporally such as sound and video. The mutual composition of *tangles* of these types with the text and graphics structures, and their projection to the user, is a rich design area.

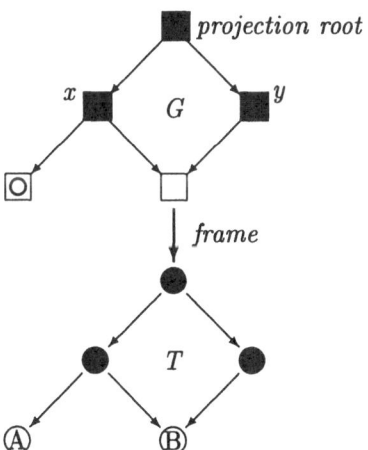

Fig. 1. A Composed Text and Graphics *tangle* Structure

As a final illustration, Figure 1 shows a possible *SPACE* structure *G* with a *framed BLOCK* structure *T* (we assume that *SPACE*s *x* and *y* have different

340

geometric transformation properties). The T and G *tangles* here happen to have the same shape. In general, of course, this is not necessary. Figure 2 shows a possible surface projection of this structure.

There is not space in this paper to show how such structures are *constructed*. Clearly, clean intuitive operations must be provided to create, paste and cut nodes and load them with properties. These operations are relatively easy to define directly on the logical structures. The far more interesting question is the means by which the *end user* might update and access such structures. This is much less straightforward because the end user perceives not the structure, but its projection.

ȦBB

Fig. 2. A Surface Projection

In Figure 2, for example, if the end user selects the middle character B from the left string in the surface projection, how should we construe this action in terms of the structure? In the structure there is only one prototype for the character B, and so selecting this in effect would select *all* of the projected instances of B. If the user also expects to be able to select projected instances individually, then the *paths* in the design must be made identifiable to the user. We leave this for further realisation of the design.

Appendix

We define *acyclic* as a generic *single-place* predicate. Its parameter is a relation on the generic type:

$$
\begin{array}{l}
[X] \\
\hline
acyclic : \mathbb{P}(X \leftrightarrow X) \\
\hline
\forall R : X \leftrightarrow X \bullet acyclic(R) \Leftrightarrow \forall x : X \bullet (x \mapsto x) \notin R^{+}
\end{array}
$$

In other words, a relation is *acyclic* if no element x maps to itself in the (non-reflexive) transitive closure ($^{+}$) of the relation.

References

1. *Information Processing Systems - Computer Graphics - Graphics Kernel System (GKS) functional description (ISO 7942)*. ISO Central Secretariat, Geneva, 1985.

2. *Standard Generalised Markup Language (SGML)(ISO DIS 8879)*. Geneva, 1986.

3. *Information Processing - Computer Graphics - Programmers Hierarchical Interactive Graphics System (PHIGS) (DIS 9592-1:1987(E))*. Geneva, October 1987.

4. *Information Processing - Text and Office Systems: Office Document Architecture (ODA) and Interchange Format (ISO DIS 8613 part 1-8)*. Geneva, July 1987.

5. The OpenDoc Design Team etc. Opendoc required reading packet. Technical report, Apple Computer Inc., April 1994.

6. V. Joloboff. Trends and standards in document representation. In *Proc. Conf. Text Processsing and Document Manipulation*, pages 107–124, Nottingham, 1986. Cambridge University Press.

7. G. D. Kimura. A structure editor for abstract document objects. *IEEE Trans. Software Engineering*, SE-12:417–435, March 1986.

8. J. M. Spivey. *The Z Notation - A Reference Manual*. Prentice Hall International, 1989.

9. R. K. Took. Putting design into practice: Formal specification and the user interface. In M. Harrison and H. Thimbleby, editors, *Formal Methods in Human-Computer Interaction*, pages 63–96. Cambridge University Press, 1990.

10. R. K. Took. Surface interaction: A paradigm and model for separating application and interface. In *Proc CHI '90*, pages 35–42. ACM, April 1990.

11. R. K. Took. Integrating inheritance and composition in an objective presentation model for multiple media. In F. H. Post and W. Barth, editors, *Proc. Eurographics '91*, pages 291–303. North-Holland, September 1991.

12. R. K. Took. *Surface Interaction: Separating Direct Manipulation Interfaces from their Applications*. PhD thesis, Computer Science Department, University of York, 1991.

13. R. K. Took. The active medium: A conceptual and practical architecture for direct manipulation. In P. Gray and R. K. Took, editors, *Building Interactive Systems: Architectures and Tools*, Workshops in Computing Series, pages 6–22. Springer-Verlag, May 1992.

This article was processed using the LaTeX macro package with LLNCS style

Role of Verification

M.D. Harrison

Human-Computer Interaction Group,
. Department of Computer Science,
University of York, York, YO1 5DD, U.K.
Email: mdh@minster.york.ac.uk.

1 Participants

Bernard Bauer
Chris Bramwell
Peter Bumbulis
David Duke
Michael Harrison (Rapporteur)
Fabio Paternò (Chair)
Steve Reeves
Pierre Roche

2 Basis for Discussion

All members of the working group had an interest in formal verification and, at some level, were concerned with the formal specification of interactive systems. During the early stages of discussion, a number of topics were briefly identified. An initial suggestion was that the group should produce a "design space" for verification techniques. This idea was discarded. It was felt that work on a design space would be premature; the dimensions were, as yet, unclear. However, it was agreed that this would be a relevant topic for future work. The group concerned itself with two issues. It was agreed that the two key topics in verification were: checking that specifications satisfy requirements, and verifying that implementations were correct with respect to specifications. The key issue for discussion was agreed to be the nature of the distinctiveness of interactive systems in the context of verification. A further initial discussion topic was the problem of developing an interface for a verifier. The problem here was that of making verification tools accessible to appropriate people, for example human factors designers. Although this was believed to be an important topic, it was initially discarded as outside the scope of the discussion though picked up again briefly later.

3 What is different about interactive systems?

A number of issues are significant in verifying interactive systems as opposed to systems in general.

Requirements specifications are based on claims, either explicit or implicit, about *user* performance. Here a description or model of the user's knowledge and capabilities must be reconciled with the specification of the system. Similarly user's views of different modalities (speech, sound, display, gesture etc.) must be integrated in the requirements that are checked against specifications.

The specification itself must emphasise the interactive behaviour of the system. It will be necessary therefore to make salient the system's presentation, as well as the actions that may be carried out by the user as part of the specification, in more detail than is usual in software specification.

It is also the case that the interface provides a different perspective on the refinement process. In moving from an abstract view of characteristics of the interface to concrete interface objects properties may be lost. For example, some aspects of the determinism of the system may not be inherited through the interface refinement process although, in general, total or partial correctness must be preserved.

4   Approaches to proving

A number of distinctions are important when it comes to checking properties. The first is the form in which the requirements are expressed. The options are to use more complex logics (for example, modal or real time) in which the proof theory is more elaborate, or propositional logic with explicit time variables to capture elements of state change and time. It is also likely that some of the requirements that express usability characteristics may be most easily expressible in terms of deontic or other normative operators. The second is whether to use theorem proving techniques to verify the requirements or to move from the theory provided by the specification to an underlying model in which the properties can be checked. The difficulty with theorem proving is the essential undecideability of the process; the difficulty with model checking is that the model limits the possible systems that can be expressed.

We discussed different methods of proof checking, in particular natural deduction, tableau methods, resolution, and rewriting techniques, and discussed their pros and cons. We further discussed issues related to an interface with a theorem proving assistant. In this context, theory stores and proof plans were considered. While theorem proving for interactive systems is dependant upon the result of general work in the verification community, we hope that interest and applications from a new community and perspective might spur on further development.

5   Model checking versus theorem proving

We discussed what types of property could not be proved by model checking. We considered a simple description of cut and paste in a text editor. Our concern was to prove that cut followed by paste had no effect on the state of the document. A theorem proving approach based on an axiomatic model of the editor was contrasted with a model checking approach based on a description of the editor in terms of a LOTOS behaviour and properties expressed in ACTL. There was some discussion as to whether the properties could be adequately captured in terms of the second model.

6 Validity and Challenges

We then discussed whether there are situations, in the context of interactive systems, where verification techniques are currently deemed necessary and where they are being used in practice. In the necessary and used categories we discussed the aviation example of flightdeck moding where failure could be disastrous. Here a company, of which members of the working group were aware, used statecharts and statemate, a model checking solution. Verification here consisted in simulation of the paths that were potentially problematical.

In an Esprit project, on the other hand, Amodeus 2, axiomatisations of the mental recognition of modalities have been used as a basis for verification.

The group agreed that a specific challenge to the community was required to highlight the particular problems of interactive systems. It was therefore suggested that the different groups interested in verification specify the MATIS system (a multi modal airline information system). The specification should then be used to demonstrate the range of properties that could be expressed and verified within each approach. Examples of desired MATIS properties include repair properties (for example, it is always impossible to undo the effect of an action) as well as requirements on the interleaving of modalities.

The Challenge Of Time *

Chris Johnson

Department of Computing Science, University of Glasgow,
Glasgow, G12 8QQ

Abstract. In the past, temporal problems have not played a central role in the development of human-machine interfaces. The timing of individual commands seldom affects single users interacting with stand-alone applications, such as text-editors and spreadsheets. This situation is changing. The increasing use of mutlimedia applications, distributed systems, computer supported cooperative work tools and process control environments is forcing designers to consider temporal aspects of usability. It is a non-trivial task to synchronise the activities of multiple operators working through several different modalities on many different machines. Unfortunately, traditional techniques that rely upon rapid prototyping or iterative development cannot easily be used to address the many different timing issues that arise during the design of this new generation of interactive systems. In contrast, formal specification techniques provide concise and precise means of representing and reasoning about such interactive behaviour. This paper argues that existing notations are, however, poorly equipped to face the challenges posed by temporal aspects of usability.

1 Introduction

Designers are facing an increasing range of challenges when they attempt to synchronise human-machine interaction. For instance, users of the World Wide Web will recognise the frustration and error that can arise when information is delayed or cannot be retrieved from remote sites [9]. Similarly, users of multimedia and virtual reality systems will recognise that time plays a critical role in determining the quality of interaction [4]. Video images and audio output may be difficult to follow if they are delivered at an unacceptably slow rate. In computer supported cooperative work systems, delays in speech and text based communication can break established protocols and modes of working [7]. Automated control systems are increasingly providing information at a rate that exceeds the operators' ability to sample them [14]. Traditional techniques that rely upon rapid prototyping or iterative development cannot easily be used to address the range of temporal behaviours exhibited by such systems. The challenge of time is, therefore, to develop formalisms that are well equipped to represent and reason about the temporal properties of interaction.

---

* This document summarises the findings of a working group on temporal aspects of usability. The members of the group are listed at the end of the paper.

2 What Are The Problems?

Many of the problems that arise during the design of human-computer interfaces have temporal components. For instance, at a high level of abstraction developers must consider the time necessary to complete particular tasks. Frequently performed operations should not, wherever possible, take longer than infrequent tasks. Temporal problems also affect interaction at lower levels of granularity. The developers of window managers must determine the period that distinguishes double-click selections from two separate mouse-down events. The apparently ubiquitous nature of temporal problems is, however, an illusion. In many stand-alone applications, such as text-editors and spreadsheets, these issues are not as critical as the development of appropriate display formats or input sequences. In contrast, however, temporal aspects of usability are playing an increasingly important role in determining the quality of interaction with distributed systems and multimedia applications.

2.1 Distribution And The Pace Of Interaction

Figure 1 illustrates the sources of temporal usability problems in distributed systems. The physical properties of communications networks impose delays upon the transmission of information. This leads to frustration and error because it is difficult for operators to predict how long it will take before their commands are effective. For instance, attempts to retrieve remote information may be abandoned if an individual thinks that their request has failed. The new groups of users who are exploiting Internet resources cannot be expected to understand the mechanisms that support their communications with remote colleagues and information servers. This point is illustrated by the problems that arise when using browsers, such as Mosaic and Netscape. The temporal characteristics of these systems appear to be both bizarre and arbitrary for many of their users [6].

   Designers can adopt a number of techniques to support interaction with distributed systems. Unfortunately, many of these approaches are extremely complex. They frequently involve the integration of advanced communications facilities and novel interface design techniques. The complexity of such an integration makes this an important area for the application of formal methods. For example, the development of interlaced graphics and mirror sites enables information providers to alter the pace of interaction between users and their systems. Images may be gradually presented as they are retrieved rather than being displayed at the end of some unpredictable delay. Information may be cached at local sites so that users are not forced to repeat retrieval requests on distant machines. A problem with the current use of these techniques is that they introduce entirely new temporal usability problems. For instance, mirror sites can prevent users from predicting how long their requests will take. Some information can be retrieved from local sources whilst the rest must be requested from the original, remote, machine. These problems might be overcome by developing displays to provide more detailed feedback about the location of information and its rate

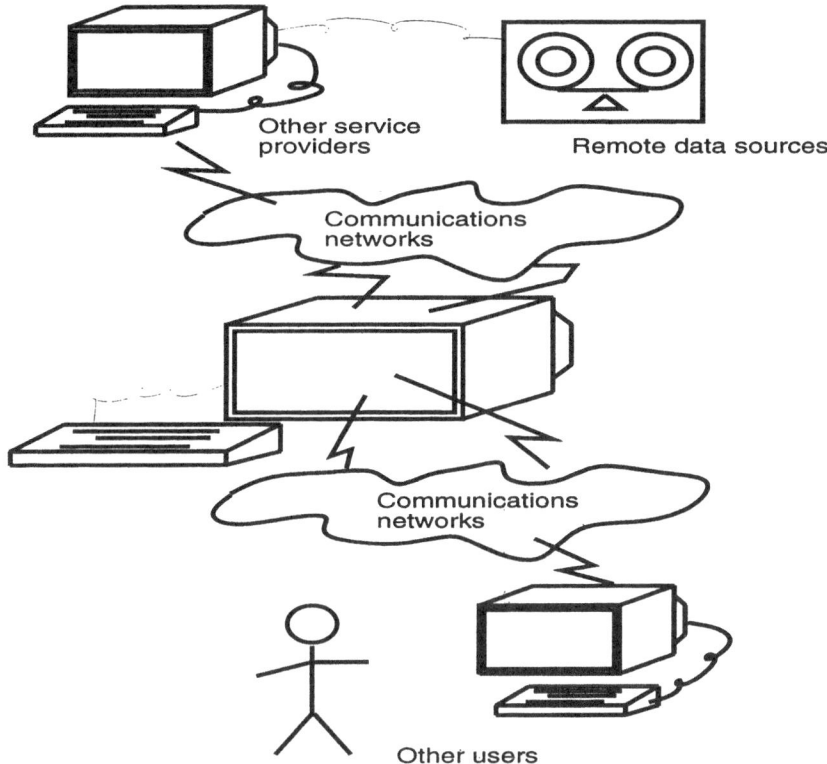

Fig. 1. The Problems Of Synchronising Distributed Interaction.

of transfer. Such presentation techniques create further temporal problems; designers must monitor and display the progress of information between various sites. The limited success of previous ad hoc solutions to these problems suggests that the precision and rigour of specification techniques might support interface development for distributed systems. However, if formal methods are to be of real benefit in this area then there are two temporal challenges that must be addressed:

- how can users be provided with an adequate representation of the flow of information from remote sites when the rate of transfer may have more to do with technological considerations rather than the geographical distances involved?
- how can users be provided with sufficient information about other users and systems so that they can make accurate predictions about the changing state of interaction over time.

2.2 Multimedia Bottlenecks

Time plays a critical role in determining the quality of interaction with multimedia applications. For instance, delays between frame updates can have a profound effect upon the use of video signals. If rates fall below 25Hz then users may perceive flicker, objects will appear to be blurred and motion will not be continuous. In such circumstances, users will frequently abandon video output in favour of more 'conventional' media. The causes of such temporal problems are illustrated by Figure 2. In one sense, the problems are similar to those cre-

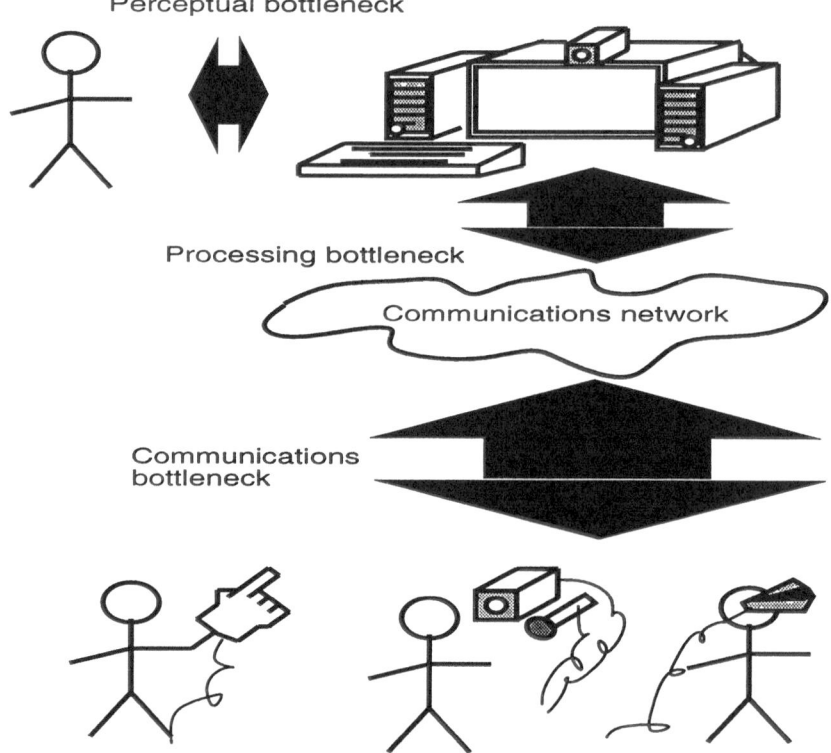

Fig. 2. The Problems Of Synchronising Multimedia Interaction.

ated by distributed systems. Limited communications facilities prevent designers from polling devices or providing updates as frequently as they would like. The delays caused by this bottleneck increase as the available bandwidth has to be shared amongst more and more devices. There are further problems. A second bottleneck arises from the limited processing resources that are currently provided by multimedia workstations. These limitations introduce delays into the continuous presentation of real-time media such as audio and video output. Finally, there is the perceptual bottleneck. The user's ability to sample and provide information would still create temporal usability problems even if the other two bottlenecks were solved. Designers must match the presentation of diverse information sources to the operators' finite perceptual resources.

A number of techniques can be used to reduce the problems caused by the various bottlenecks in multimedia systems. For instance, interlacing can be used to reduce the communications loading without seriously increasing screen flicker. Similarly, communications standards, such as the Asynchronous Transfer Mode (ATM), can be defined to improve the distribution of multi-media information [3]. None of the techniques, however, provides a panacea for the development of multimedia interfaces. For instance, ATM does not address the low level synchronisation issues that must be considered in order to guarantee a particular quality of service at the user interface. A more fundamental point is that quality does not simply relate to technological factors. It is closely tied to the user's tasks. This reflects a recent preoccupation with the communications and processing bottlenecks rather than the perceptual bottleneck in multimedia systems. For instance, if the loading on particular networks reduced the transfer rate of video images then users might be prepared to degrade that service in order to maintain good response times over the audio channel. This would maximise the utility obtained from one particular perceptual modality. Conversely, an audio link might be degraded in order to improve the transfer of graphical images or video information. At present, there are no convenient tools that designers can use to represent and reason about such strategies. The complexity of such synchronisation techniques makes this another important area for the exploitation of formal notations. Multimedia applications, therefore, provide further challenges for the specification and verification of interactive systems:

- how can designers represent the changing priorities that might be assigned to different modalities during the course of interaction?
- how can these priorities be adequately related to the changing demands of particular user tasks?

3 What's The Time?

In order to select an appropriate means of representing and reasoning about temporal properties of interaction, designers must first make certain decision about the nature of time. In particular, they must decide whether their model is based around real-time or intervals and whether their view of the future is linear or branching.

3.1 Models Of Time

Representing temporal properties of interaction is not as easy as it might first appear. The most obvious approach is to specify interface properties in terms of

350

minutes, hours and seconds. For example, designers might decide to present a warning if a retrieval request on a remote machine has not been answered within ten seconds. The first diagram in Figure 3 illustrates this approach. The timeline

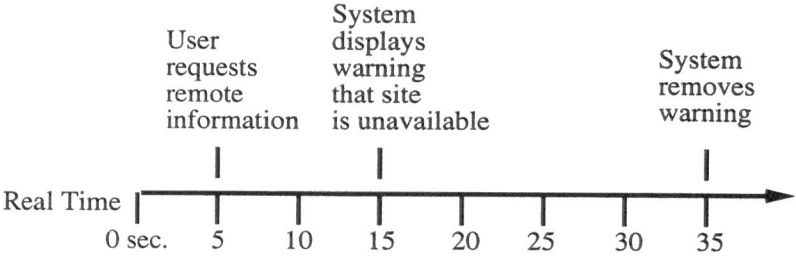

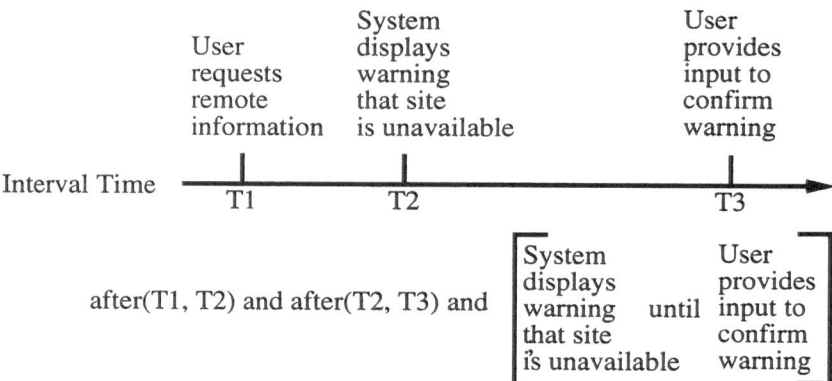

Fig. 3. Real And Interval Time.

shown in this picture can be formalised using various real-time extensions to first order logic:

$$retrieval\_failure(12:00:35) \Leftarrow user\_request(12:00:05) \wedge$$
$$failure\_warning(12:00:15) \wedge warning\_removed(12:00:35) \qquad (1)$$

There are a number of problems with real-time as a basis upon which to design distributed, multimedia applications. In particular, clauses such as (1) are extremely deterministic. The clause would not hold if the user requested the information at 12:00:06, 12:00:07, 12:00:08 and so on. This determinism has important consequences for the use of real-time notations as a means of satisfying the challenges mentioned in previous sections. For instance, a standard warning that is always presented after a ten second timeout hardly provides appropriate feedback about many different retrieval requests. Such a delay would be expected for retrieval tasks that involve low performance networks. Users would continually be presented with a failure warning even though their retrieval were taking the expected amount of time. Similarly, a ten second delay might be perfectly acceptable on heavily loaded machines, such as the National Centre for Supercomputing Applications' servers. In such circumstance, designers must either tailor the real-time requirement to particular retrieval tasks or seek alternative means of representing temporal properties that avoid such determinism.

The limitations associated with real-time notations can be avoided through the use of interval based formalisms. This approach is illustrated by the second diagram shown in Figure 3. A timeline is used to model the flow of events, interval requirements can then be constructed in terms of this underlying model. The example specifies that the user is informed about the failure of their command until they issue input to confirm that they have observed the warning. This is a temporal requirement in that it describes how interaction develops over time. It does not, however, specify the exact number of hours, minutes and seconds during which the display is presented. This approach avoids the temporal determinism of real-time notations. Interval formalisms can also be captured using textual notations, such as Manna and Pnueli's temporal logic [13]. In the following $\bigcirc$ can be read as 'in the next interval', $\mathcal{U}$ can be read as 'until':

$$retrieval\_failure \Leftarrow \bigcirc(user\_request \wedge$$
$$\bigcirc(failure\_warning \mathcal{U} user\_confirmation)) \tag{2}$$

Interval notations are appropriate for the early stages of development when the exact timings of interactive behaviour may not be known. Unfortunely, they lack the precision that is required during more detailed development. A more particular problem for the previous challenges is that interval based notations cannot easily be used to relate users' tasks in multimedia applications to the real-time properties of their underlying systems.

Designers must decide how they are to represent the future course of interaction with distributed or multimedia systems. For instance, interaction might be described in terms of a linear sequence of user inputs and system responses. This approach is illustrated in the first diagram of Figure 4. These linear models are captured in the textual forms of the interval (2) and real-time (1) clauses, shown above. Unfortunately, these approaches do not capture the uncertainty that frequently frustrates the operation of distributed and multimedia applications. Branching-time models avoid this problem by representing the future as a series of alternative paths. The second diagram in Figure 4 shows one future in which the user is presented with confirmation that their command is being dealt. In another 'parallel' future they are presented with a warning that the remote site has failed. As before, a range of textual notations have been developed to exploit these temporal models. For instance, Clarke and Emerson's Computation Tree Logic [2] might be used to require that users must confirm warnings that a retrieval request has failed. The AX quantifier is used to specify that the input

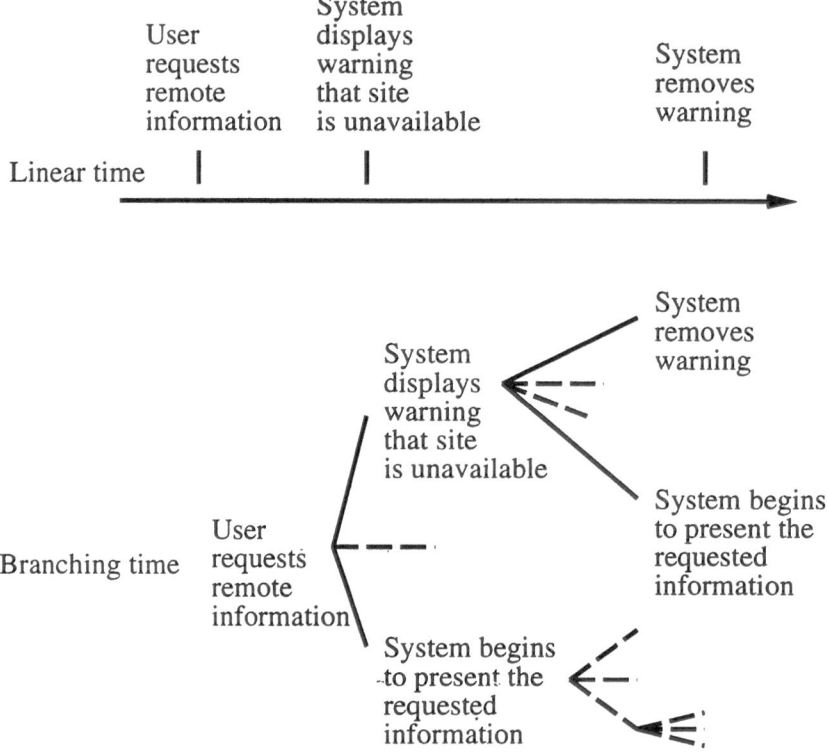

Fig. 4. Branching And Linear Time.

must be provided in all possible next intervals:

$$retrieval\_confirmation \Leftarrow$$
$$failure\_warning \wedge AX \quad user\_confirmation \qquad (3)$$

Clearly, the choice of real or interval time, linear or branching time will have an important impact upon the successful application of formal notations. This poses further challenges:

- what criteria can designers use to select an appropriate temporal model for their development tasks?
- is it possible to move between notation that support different temporal models as development progresses, possibly from imprecise temporal intervals to more precise real-time requirements?

3.2 Temporal Notations

Time can be represented by a number of different notationals. The major distinction here is between textual and graphical approaches. Petri Nets are, perhaps, the most widely applied graphical notation [1, 8]. The basic form provides means of capturing intervals and sequences of interaction. There also exist real-time and stochastic extensions that can be used to capture alternative future traces. Figure 5 shows how Petri Nets can be used to represent complex sequences of interaction in multi-user and distributed systems. This is the approach followed in [11]. They can also support user modelling [15]. A powerful attraction for the use of such graphical notations is that they have an intuitive appeal. The flow of event over time can be represented by the movement of tokens through the network. Token are shown as filled dots in Figure 5. Unfortunately, Petri Nets and similar graphical formalisms suffer from a number of limitations. They can quickly become intractable for large systems. Certain features, such as undo, are extremely difficult to capture using this approach to interface specification.

Tabular notations, such as the XUAN [5] shown in Figure 6, avoid some of the problems associated with the large-scale application of Petri Nets. The structuring mechanisms of the columns and rows provide some impression of the flow of time. XUAN also possesses a process algebra that can be used to describe additional temporal constraints. These provide a convenient means of composing large scale specifications in a manner that is, arguably, more tractable than the composition facilities provided by graphical notations. Unfortunately, tabular notations are less well developed than many of their textual and graphical counterparts. Whilst Petri Nets have 'established' real-time variants, the corresponding facilities in XUAN do not possess a clear semantics. There are no facilities for representing 'alternative' or branching futures in this tabular notation.

There are many different textual notations that designers might exploit to represent and reason about temporal properties of interaction. These range from higher order logics [2] to more established approaches such as Z, CSP and VDM [12]. For example, the following schema shows how Z can be extended to include temporal operators such as $\mathcal{U}$ (read as 'until') [10]:

$$
\begin{array}{l}
\underline{\quad Select\_Steam\_Circuit\_High\_Shut\_Down \quad\qquad\qquad} \\
Present\_Steam\_Circuit\_Display \\[4pt]
Multi\_User\_Events\_Display\_Attributes \\[4pt]
\hline
\forall\, user\_1, user\_2 : USERS \bullet \\
\quad user\_input\_event(user\_1, pump\_a\_icon) = on\_select \wedge \\
\qquad \neg\, (value(pump\_a\_press) = min(pump\_a\_press))\ \mathcal{U} \\
\qquad\quad user\_input\_event(user\_2, pump\_a\_icon) = on\_select
\end{array}
$$

The advantage of such textual approaches is that they have well-developed semantics and proof techniques. Tool support is available and many of these notations have been used in large-scale development tasks. It can, however, be

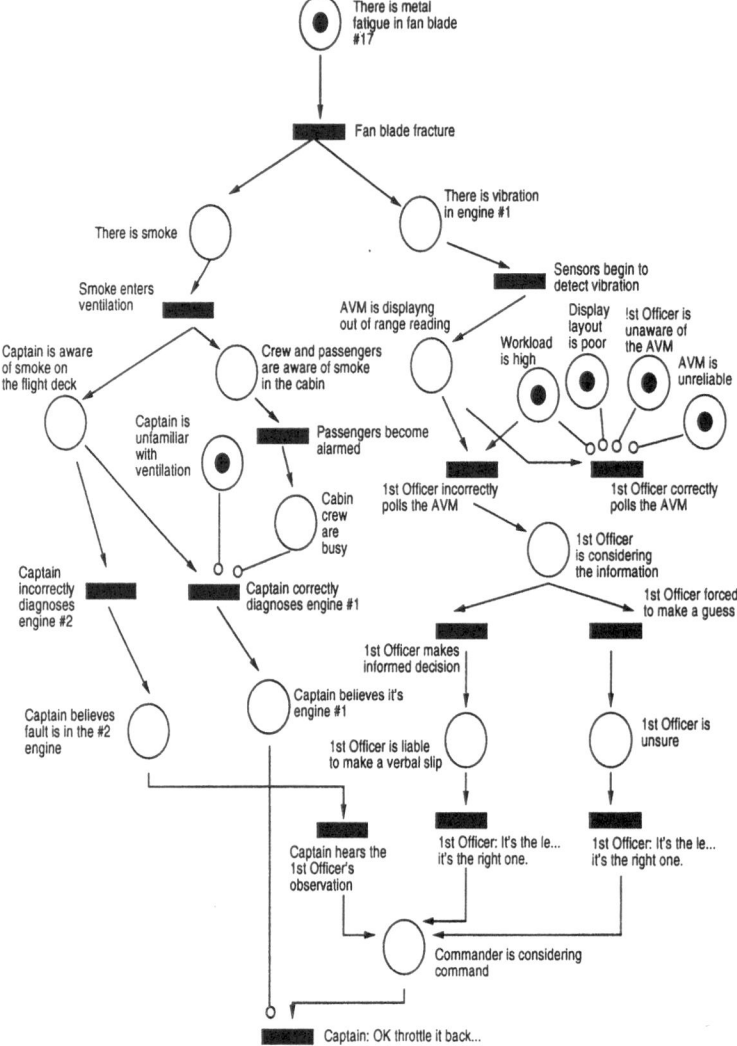

Fig. 5. A Petri Net Describing The Kegworth Air Accident

extremely difficult to visualise the interactive behaviour of an application from its textual description. This is significant because abstract notations should ease communication between and within design teams. If it is difficult for other design groups to identify the temporal properties within textual descriptions then this benefit may be lost.

It is not a simple matter to determine which of these different notational forms provides the greatest support for interface development. There are a num-

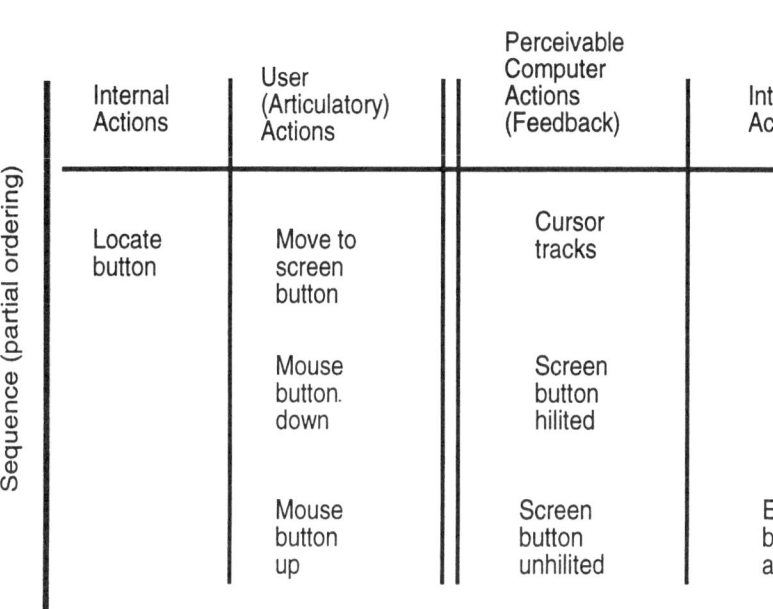

Fig. 6. An XUAN Task Description

ber of notational challenges that must be addressed before formal methods can be used to address temporal usability problems:

- how can a designer determine whether graphical, tabular or textual notations are more appropriate for their development task?
- how can the chosen notation be used most effectively to communicate temporal properties to the other designers, clients and users who will be affected by their observations?

4 Conclusions

In order to meet all of the challenges being posed by the temporal properties of modern interactive systems, we need an interval notation with real-time operators, a branching time approach that can also be used to express constraints over all possible futures, a graphical representation that is intuitive and easy to follow and yet has the power of textual notations for formal reasoning and proof.

Clearly, such a notation does not yet exist. This raises a number of important questions. For instance, should current research focus upon the development and extension of existing notations? In this way the particular weaknesses of Z, CSP etc might gradually be addressed so that they can more easily be applied to interface development. Alternatively, should research focus upon the development of novel methodologies that exploit more than one existing formalism? This could build upon the correspondence between Petri Nets and first order logics. Until these issues are addressed, interface designers are poorly equipped to face the challenges that time poses for the new generations of interactive systems.

Acknowledgements

This report is the product of discussions within the group that addressed temporal properties of interaction during the Bonas workshop. The members of the group were Stéphane Chatty, Alan Dix, David Duce, Phil Gray, Mark Green, Munos Jaime, Francis Jambon, Chris Johnson, Panos Markopoulos, Philippe Palanque, Graham Reynolds, Roger Took, Dick Van Schenk Brill and Kees Verhagel.

References

1. R. Bastide and P. Palanque. Petri Net objects for the design, validation and prototyping of user-driven interfaces. In D. Diaper, D. Gilmore, G. Cockton, and B. Shackel, editors, *Human-Computer Interaction—INTERACT'90*, pages 625–631. Elsevier Science Publications, North Holland, Netherlands, 1990.

2. E.M. Clarke and E.A. Emerson. Design and synthesis of synchronisation skeletons using branching time temporal logic. In D. Kozen, editor, *Logic of Programs 1981 - Proceedings*, LNCS 131, pages 52–71. Springer-Verlag, Berlin, FDR, 1982.

3. G. Coulouris, J. Dollimore, and T. Kindberg. *Distributed Systems: Concepts And Design*. Addison Wesley, Wokingham, United Kingdom, 1994.

4. S.J. Gibbs and D.C. Tsichritzis. *Multimedia Programming: Objects, Environments And Frameworks*. Addison Wesley, Reading, United Kingdom, 1994.

5. P. Gray, D. England, and S. McGowan. XUAN: Enhancing UAN to capture temporal relationships among actions. In G. Cockton, S.W. Draper, and G.R.S. Weir, editors, *People And Computers IX*, pages 301–312. Cambridge University Press, Cambridge, United Kingdom, 1994.

6. P. Gray and C.W. Johnson. Requirements for the next generation of user interface specification languages. In R. Bastide and P. Palanque, editors, *Proceedings Of The 2nd Eurographics Workshop On The Design, Specification And Verification Of Interactive Systems*. 1995.

7. C.W. Johnson. Applying temporal logic to support the specification and prototyping of concurrent multi-user interfaces. In D. Diaper and N. Hammond, editors, *People And Computers VI: Usability Now*, pages 145–156. Cambridge University Press, Cambridge, United Kingdom, 1991.

8. C.W. Johnson. The application of Petri Nets to represent and reason about human factors problems during accident analyses. In R. Bastide and P. Palanque, editors,

Proceedings Of The 2nd Eurographics Workshop On The Design, Specification And Verification Of Interactive Systems. 1995.

9. C.W. Johnson. Time and the web: Representing temporal properties of interaction with distributed systems. In *People And Computers X.* Cambridge University Press, Cambridge, United Kingdom, 1995.

10. C.W. Johnson. Using Z to support the design of interactive, safety-critical systems. *Software Engineering Journal*, 10(2):49–60, 1995.

11. C.W. Johnson, J.C. McCarthy, and P.C. Wright. Using a formal language to support natural language in accident reports. *Ergonomics*, 38(6):1265–1283, 1995.

12. M. Kooij. Interface specification with temporal logic. In S.J. Greenspan, editor, *The 5th International Workshop On Software Specification And Design*, pages 104–110. IEEE Computer Society Press, Washington, United States of America, 1989.

13. Z. Manna and A. Pnueli. Verification of concurrent programs: The temporal framework. In R.S. Boyer and J. Strother Moore, editors, *The Correctness Problem In Computer Science*, pages 215–273. Academic Press, London, United Kingdom, 1981.

14. V.C. Miles, C.W. Johnson, J.C. McCarthy, and M.D. Harrison. Supporting prediction in complex dynamic systems. In D. Diaper and N. Hammond, editors, *People And Computers VI: Usability Now*, pages 133–144. Cambridge University Press, Cambridge, United Kingdom, 1991.

15. T. Moher and V. Dirda. Revising mental models to accomodate expectation failures in human-computer dialogues. In R. Bastide and P. Palanque, editors, *Proceedings Of The 2nd Eurographics Workshop On The Design, Specification And Verification Of Interactive Systems.* 1995.

This article was processed using the LaTeX macro package with LLNCS style

Working group report: user and task modeling

Thomas G. Moher

Department of Electrical Engineering and Computer Science
University of Illinois at Chicago, Chicago, IL 60607, U.S.A.

Abstract. Ten workshop attendees participated in a working group discussion of user and task modeling. An overarching theme to the discussion concerned the problem of the impact of formal modeling on software development in practice, and what might be done to facilitate that transfer. The discussion resulted in the identification of potential research questions and some specific challenges for formal modeling proponents.

1 Formal modeling vs. "real" software development

There was some sense of frustration among the group concerning the limited integration to date of formal user and task modeling in "regular" software development. On the one hand, there is now a significant body of research demonstrating the practicality and benefit of formal user modeling in real applications. On the other hand, it is quite clear that the "killer applications" which have changed the face of computing were created without the benefit of (and, in fact, often in total ignorance of the existence of) formal modeling techniques.

One reason cited was the widespread and persistent perception of the "difficulty" of creating and understanding formal specifications, and indeed this theme was subsequently discussed in Marie-Claude Gaudel's keynote talk later in the day. It was agreed that this remains an important and difficult problem, and one which would benefit from increased interaction between the formal modeling community and researchers in programming and cognition.

Some members of the group felt that this perception issue was even more serious, that in fact there was a feeling among some developers that the use of formal methods stifled creativity. There was a consensus in the group that our collective experience was quite the opposite, that the use of formalism provided insights which our intuition did not always offer. It remains a challenge to the HCI formal modeling community to demonstrate that formal methods spur creativity rather than suppress it.

Another factor in the failure to adopt formal user modeling lies in the perceived cost/benefit ratio. Modeling and empirical validation are, if not so conceptually difficult as some would believe, still quite expensive, and unlikely to be adopted if the software developer does not see a clear advantage to their use.

The challenge for the formal modeling community, then, is to more clearly demonstrate those benefits, and to identify classes of applications for which formal modeling may be most appropriate. Participants identified a number roles for formal user and task modeling, including the ability verify properties of a model, to check the model against application and user requirements, to obtain quantitative characterizations of system usage (including timing), and the validations of tasks with respect to the systems that support them.

A second observation was that we need to do a better job of focusing our efforts on those classes of applications' with the greatest need for formal modeling, so as to develop a body of proofs-by-demonstration of the effectiveness of formal techniques.

The group identified three classes of applications as meeting these criteria. The first are safety-critical applications; examples discussed included air-traffic control and medical life-maintenance systems. The second class of applications are those for which the cost of development is especially high; such systems represent a major risk on the part of their developers. The third class are those in which cost of use is high, either because an application's users are themselves a scarce resource (e.g., CEOs, physicians), or because the application has a large user base (e.g., word processors, WWW browsers).

2 Formal modeling in practice

Device models and task models share certain components: their interaction affordances. Each model may be defined separately, but in order to model global (user-device) system behavior, the associations must be reconciled. Component sharing motivates the concurrent development of device and user/task models; this is the driving principle of user-centered development methodologies. James Middlemass discussed how the MUSE methodology employs hierarchical task modeling to identify the objects comprising a system.

In practice, concurrent development may not be practical. In many software development projects, the application domain is already fairly mature, and there may be a large base of user experience and "canonical tasks" from which to draw. In cases like this, task models developed for other projects might be reusable (at least in part), raising the possibility of constructing task/user models prior to software design. In other cases, the purpose of developing task/user models is to assess the usability of pre-existing software.

The discussion group agreed that there is no such thing as software without user/task models; the only issue is whether or not they have been made explicit. As the claims analysis folks have long argued, software designed without reference to explicit user and task models nonetheless reflects implicit theories of the way that it will be used and the capabilities of its users.

3 The nature of tasks

There was an extended discussion of the nature of tasks and the modeling formalisms which might be appropriate for different task types.

One interesting classification dimension was offered by Rémi Bastide, who led a discussion on just what kinds of tasks should be modeled. Rémi distinguished between *nominal tasks* (descriptions obtained from manuals, or spontaneously expressed by users in response to "how-to" questions), *effective tasks* (observed procedures from actual users, including errors, unnecessary steps, shortcuts, etc.), and *minimal tasks* (optimal task plans afforded by the software). The group discussed the issue of which of these models are most appropriate to use for different modeling goals.

An orthogonal task dimension based on temporal classification of tasks was presented by Bob Fields. Bob contrasted among *continuous tasks* (background tasks designed to maintain system invariants), *periodic tasks* (requiring user interaction at fixed intervals), and *intermittent tasks* (non-scheduled tasks, often with high priority for user attention.)

The group identified other task classification dimensions, including domain-based classification, classifications based on human processing constraints and capabilities, and classifications based on the intensity of interaction, among others. The general consensus was that the classification of tasks along various dimensions might help researchers to characterize more clearly the intended domain of their task modeling formalisms, and there is every reason to believe that a rich set of complementary formalisms with well-defined domains of applicability—rather than a single "solution"—is the desirable goal.

4 Task models

Users construct task plans in response to supplied or constructed goals. The actions specified in the task plan include a combination of interactions with device affordances and user reasoning. For many simple tasks, the plans are "compiled" and represent skilled, deterministic behavior.

Dan Olson emphasized the importance of thinking about the information first, rather than the tool which works on the data. Among users skilled with particular application affordances, the real challenge of task planning derives from decisions based on the underlying data. A simple example is a program which allows linear traversal with quantized "jumps" through a list of items. The goal of retrieving a particular record is almost wholly related to the users' knowledge of the relative density (and distribution) of records; a simple plan based solely on the characteristics of the (software) device would not address this reality.

There was some discussion of the effort involved in developing task models. Thomas Elwert argued for the importance of reuse, if not of task models themselves, then of the knowledge obtained in the process of constructing task models. The group discussed the notion of preserving task modeling information in a hierarchical structure, so that new tasks could be described in terms of inheritance and specialization; we also discussed the potential danger of overgeneralization in task model reuse. Stéphane Sire and Jean Vanderdonkt offered some views on the granularity of task modeling.

5 Modeling web surfing

During our discussion of fruitful application domains for formal user/task modeling, Tom Moher posed a challenge to the group to consider how (or whether) formal task modeling had anything to add to the design of WWW browsers, arguably the fastest-growing interactive application class (and with the largest potential user base) in existence.

What are the goals of a browser user? Sometimes the goal is to find something specific; at other times, however, the user is simply "surfing" the WWW, in what appears to be undirected activity.

This issue prompted a lively debate. Some members held that this was not goal-directed activity, and that lacking a goal, task planning in the usual sense was not possible. Others held that in fact there was an identifiable goal, even for "random browsing," that goal being to "find something which keeps me entertained or interested."

While at first glance "something interesting to me" did not appear to be a formalizable goal, several advocates argued strongly that this goal could be refined to provide evaluable criteria for plan formulation. A knowledge of the user's general job responsibilities, areas of interest, time available for browsing, etc., could lead to formal task models which might well characterize user behavior.

The discussion of the Web brought home Dan Olson's earlier observations on the importance of the underlying data; a task model for Web usage is likely to be much more dependent on the topology and content of the Web than on the browser. In fact, there is an interesting source of tension between browser designers and Web content designers; the former is interested in making it easy to leave, while the latter is interested in getting the user to stay.

6 Participants and research interests

Participant	Research Interest
Stéphane Sire	CSCW, telepresence
Olivier Esteban	Visual construction of Interfaces
Thomas Elwert	Reuse of task modeling knowledge
Renaut Zorolla	Evaluation of multi-user interfaces
Jean Vanderdonkt	Interactive business applications (TRIDENT)
Tom Moher	Integrated HCI models
James Middlemass	Usability engineering (MUSE)
Bob Fields	Design of psycho-physical systems; errors
Dan Olsen	Architectures for interactive systems
Rémi Bastide	Task models/system model integration

Towards a taxonomy for interactive graphics systems

G. Pierra

LISI/ ENSMA
B.P. 109 - 86960 FUTUROSCOPE Cédex
e-mail : pierra@ensma.univ-poitiers.fr

Abstract. It has often been pointed out that the different architecture models proposed for interactive computer graphics were too much imprecise. Global architecture models intended to define the macro-modules that constitute such systems do not precise the functional description nor the interface of these modules. Multi-agent models, intended to define the micro-structure of the building blocks of such systems, do not precise the criteria to be used for agent identification and structurization, nor the complete set of relationships that exists between these agents and the domain-specific component that represents the semantic part of the system.

In this report we propose a taxonomy for interactive graphics systems through seven orthogonal criteria. These criteria enable to classify every systems during the analysis phase. The possible uses of this taxonomy include the following:

   - facilitating the selection process of a suitable architecture model for a system under design,

   - enabling the architecture model designers to precise the classes of systems that constitute the target application domain of their models,

   - promoting the emergence of precise architecture models that address the requirements of the different categories of interactive graphics systems.

1 Introduction

The goal of architecture models for interactive graphics systems is, or should be, to provide guidelines to system designers, both for modular decomposition of their system, and for selection of the suitable software tools. In fact, a lot of models have been proposed. Therefore, the first designer's choice is to select the suitable architecture model for the system under design.

The UIMS Tool developers Workshop [22] already pointed out that the suitable architecture of the application may depend on the designer's goals (e.g., maximising runtime performance vs. buffering the remainder of the system from the effects of evolving Interaction Toolkits). In this report we suggest that such an architecture is heavily dependent on the specific requirements of the target application and we propose seven orthogonal criteria that enable to classify systems during their analysis phases.

This paper results from the discussions that took place during the Eurographics Workshop on Design, Validation and Specification of Interactive Systems (DVS-IS'95) in the Working Group on Taxonomy. The members of this working group were the following: B. David (ECL, Fr), P. Girard (LISI/ENSMA, Fr), F. Jensayer (Roskilde Univ., Dk), J. Munoz (LIS/Toulouse 1 Univ., Fr), G. Pierra (LISI/ENSMA, Fr), M. Rautenberg (ETHZ, Ch), J. Vanderdonckt (FUNDP/Namur, Be). The starting point of these discussion was a position paper [19].

The content of this report is as follows. In the first section, we recall the content of the Arch model [22] that provides a useful framework for describing the runtime architecture of interactive systems. In the second section, we discuss the goal of the taxonomy and the meta-criteria used to select the relevant criteria. In section three we present the criteria that define the proposed taxonomy.

2 Architecture models for interactive graphics system

A lot of models exist for the design of interactive systems. Each model focuses on a different point and is intended to solve a different problem. Static architecture models mainly address the modular structure of the system. Some of them, such that the Seeheim model [12], or the Computer Graphics Reference Model [2, 7] suggest a top-down approach. They define the macro-modules that should constitute the system. Some others, like MVC [11] or PAC [4], suggest a bottom-up approach. They define the structure of the building blocks that should constitute the complete system. Dynamic architecture models are intended to capture the behaviour of interactive systems. Once again some of them are more top-down oriented, such that the models based on the linguistic approach [9, 23], some others, often called multi-agent models, define the fine-grain reactive units that should be used to model this behaviour [6, 8, 13, 17, 21]. It is not clear how the top-down-oriented and the bottom-up-oriented models fit together. And it does not exist any consensus about when, and even how, the different models should be used [5, 20].

In order to get a common understanding and terminology about the runtime architecture of these systems, a series of workshops took place in 1990 and 1991. The result of these workshops, known as the Arch model, was published in 1992 [22]. The Arch model defines five components (sub-systems) for the architecture of interactive systems. The two ends of this architecture are the *Domain-Specific Component* and the *Interaction Toolkit Component* that may be considered, for some applications, as pre-existent (see fig 1)

The *Interaction Toolkit Component* implements the physical interaction with the end-user (via hardware and software). The *Domain-Specific Component* controls, manipulates and retrieves domain data, and performs other domain-related functions. Between these two ends, the *Dialogue Component* has responsibility for task level sequencing and for mapping back and forth between domain-specific formalisms and user-interface-specific formalisms. Two more components are defined for buffering an operational system from changes in technology. The *Presentation Component* buffers from changes in user interface toolkit by providing an abstract view of user Interaction Objects. The *Domain-Adaptor Component* is a mediation between the Dialogue and the Domain-Specific Components. In this report, the Interaction Toolkit Component and the Presentation Component will sometimes be referred to as the *user-side components*, the Domain-Specific Component and the Domain-Adaptor Component as the *domain-side components*.

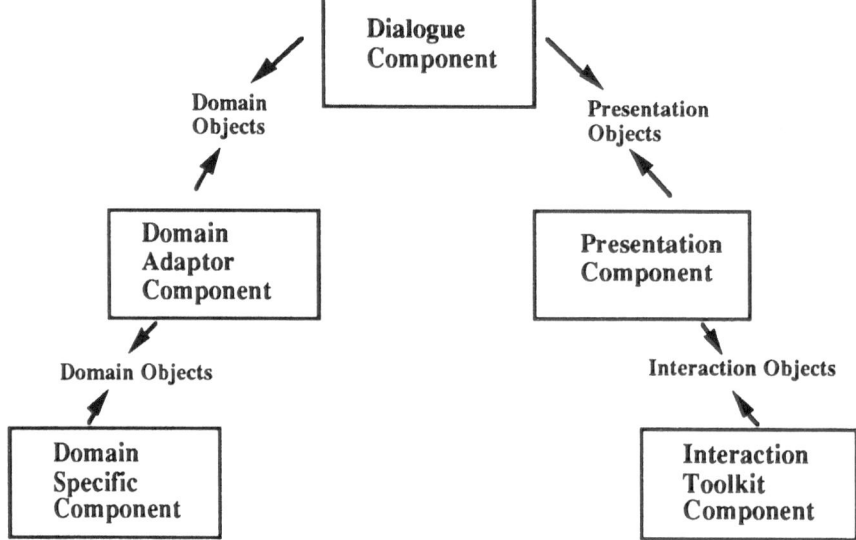

Fig. 1. The Arch model

To acknowledge the diversity of real-world applications, the Arch report points out that the same functionality may be shifted from one component to another one of the architecture. It uses the term "Slinky" to emphasise that the Arch model is in fact a meta-model that may be differently tailored both regarding the component to which is assigned some particular functionality (functional specification), and regarding the data flow between the various components (interface specification). Besides, the Arch model does not consider, but implicitly for the Interaction Toolkit Component, the internal structure of each component.

It shall be noticed that, unlike most of the other proposed models, the Arch model is not intended to be a prescriptive model. In particular, the model itself does not specify neither how to separate an interactive system into the different identified subsystems, nor the internal structure of each subsystem. The main interest of this model is to substantially define a framework within which any interactive system or prescriptive model for such systems may be described and/or compared. This framework may thus be used to discuss the criteria that significantly affect the software architecture of interactive systems.

3 Goals of the taxonomy

The goal of the proposed taxonomy is to identify the characteristics of interactive graphics systems that have a major impact on the design of these systems. The intended uses of such a taxonomy include the following
- facilitating the selection process of a suitable architecture model for a system under design,
- enabling architecture model designers to precise the classes of systems that constitute the target application domain of their models,
- promoting the emergence of precise architecture models that address the requirements of the different categories of interactive graphic systems.

In order to support the first usage, the values of the characteristics used as taxonomy criteria shall be known before the beginning of the design process, i.e., during the analysis phase.

Regarding the criteria that should be used in the taxonomy, the Arch (meta-) model enables to assess the impact of given characteristics on the system architecture. Every characteristics may be considered as relevant criteria for the taxonomy if their values:
- affects the functionalities which are assigned to some Arch component (functional specification) and/or,
- affects the data flow between the different Arch components (interface specification), and/or
- affects the internal structure of some Arch component (detailed design).

4 The proposed taxonomy

We assume that the system analysis is done using some object oriented analysis (OOA) method, (e. g., the COAD&YOURDON OOA method [3]).

The result of such an analysis is twofold. First, the Domain Objects are modelled. In our proposed taxonomy, two criteria address the Domain Objects structure. Second, the system's responsibilities are defined. In interactive systems the fundamental system responsibility is to support the user tasks [1]. Two criteria address the task structure. In order to cover a large spectrum of applications, two other criteria address the actor model and characterise the control source (the user, the Domain-Specific Component, both) and the number of simultaneous users. The last criteria address an operational constraint on the system that results from multi-modal interactions.

All the criteria, but the control source criteria, identify orthogonal degrees of complexity for the system under design. For each criterion, only two values are discussed: the simplest case and the most complex case. Actual systems are often in between, and ad-hoc practices are sometimes used to remove some degrees of complexity.

The proposed criteria are the following.

4.1. Tasks arity

An application supports mono-object tasks if each user task involves only one (simple or structured) Domain Object. It supports multi-object task if a task involves several Domain Objects. Mono-object tasks may be encapsulated into Domain Object representation. They may be supported by direct manipulation techniques. In the simplest case, the dialogue component may not exist on its own. Multi-object tasks shall be represented independently from the Domain Objects. Direct manipulation techniques are not possible. Some dialogue component, of which the structure is independent from the object structure, shall exist. A typical ad-hoc solution to avoid this degree of complexity consists in providing multi-object selection (e.g., rubber rectangle) and enabling the user to do the same task on the set of objects (set traversal [14]). As an example, Mac Draw™ only supports mono-object tasks. Example of multi-object tasks are provided by the drafting systems that enable to create lines as , e. g., tangential to two circles.

4.2. Tasks structuring

An application supports atomic task if the user must specify each of its tasks independently, the result of this task being recorded in the state of the Domain-Specific Component. An application supports structured tasks if the user may input in pre-order its task/sub-task hierarchy [16], the result of the overall tasks being only recorded in the application domain component when the whole task hierarchy has been input. The support of structured tasks needs to record the state of the dialogue independently from the state of the Domain-Specific and of the Interaction Toolkit components. Atomic tasks may be encapsulated either in Domain Object or in Interaction Objects. Typical ad-hoc solutions to avoid this degree of complexity consists in providing modal dialogue variables that may be recorded in the Interaction Toolkit Component and in designing some predefined structured task patterns associated with a specific set of interaction objects (e.g., structured sets of dialogue boxes).

An example of structured task is provided by graphic expressions such expressions enable to specify an operand of some high level task by means of a function which the domain are other objects (e.g., to define the centre of a circle as the middle-point of some line).

4.3. Domain Objects autonomy

The Domain Objects are autonomous if the presentation of each Domain Object is only (or mainly) dependent on the state of the corresponding Domain Object. The Domain Object are relational if the presentation of each Domain Object is dependent on the state of other Domain Objects. If the Domain Objects are autonomous, each Domain Object may be mapped onto one Interaction Object that supports its rendering function [6]. If the Domain Objects are relational, the Interaction Toolkit Component shall provide rendering spaces that are used by a global rendering feature of the domain-side components. Graphics Standards, such that GKS [10], PHIGS [18] or CGRM [7] provide high-level mechanisms for rendering (geometric) related objects. Models like MVC [11] or PAC [4] are straightforward for rendering autonomous objects. Moreover, when Domain Objects are autonomous, high level semantic feedback may be shifted from the domain-side components to the user-side components. It is not possible when objects are relational.

4.4. Domain Objects structuring

Domain Objects are structured when several levels of objects, structured by aggregation, may be accessed by the user. They are simple when one Domain Object is not part of another Domain Object. When Domain Objects are (highly) structured, the designation of one Domain Object may only be interpreted by the domain-side components. It requires a complete traversal of the system by the user-defined events. When Domain Objects are simple enough, the pick identifier may be interpreted, and echoed, by the user-side components. A typical ad-hoc solution to avoid this degree of complexity consists in providing some "association" function that enables gathering several objects in an aggregate object, the internal object being no longer pickable. This is done, for instance, in Mac Draw™.

4.5. Control source

The fifth criterion characterises the source of the events of which the type changes the dialogue component state. It may be either the user (interactive application) or the Domain (conversational application) or both (dialogue application). The dialogue component should offer asymmetric functionalities in the two first cases. It offers symmetric functionalities in the last one.

4.6. Mono/Multi user interactive system

A mono-user interactive system correspond to a system where only one user dialogues with a Domain Specific Component. This category of systems belongs to the scope of the Arch model. Multi user systems enable several users to interact with the same Domain-Specific Component. Multi-user interactive systems require an "Y" runtime architecture where several instances (with possible links) exist for some Arch components.

4.7. Sequential Vs Real Time interactive system

An interactive system is sequential if the behaviour of the system is only dependant on the order of the sequences of events and values input by the user-side and the domain-side components. It is a Real Time interactive system when the behaviour is also dependent on the time where an event or a value occurs. A Real Time system needs to have a timer within its Dialogue Component. It has been proved that multi-modal Interactive systems were Real Time Systems [15]. The following table summarises the proposed taxonomy.

criteria			
tasks arity	**mono-object tasks** • Task representation may be encapsulated in object representation. *Example:* Mac Draw™		**multi-object tasks** • Tasks shall be represented independently from objects. *Example: Database graphical interface*
tasks structuring	**atomic tasks** • no (or few) dialogue context. *Example:* Mac Draw™		**structural tasks** • A structured dialogue context shall be explicitly modelled. *Example: use of a display calculator to input some real value to a current task*
objects autonomy	**autonomous objects** (the presentation of Domain Object depends only on the state of the corresponding Domain Object) • One object in the user-side components reflects each Domain Object *Example:* Mac Draw™		**relational objects** (the presentation of a Domain Object depends on the state of the other Domain Objects). • No one-to-one relationship between Domain Objects and presentation objects *Example: process control interface*
objects structuring	**simple objects** • object designation may be done in the presentation component *Example:* Mac Draw™, *GKS*		**(highly) structured objects** • only Domain-side components are able to identify the Domain Object selected by a pointing device *Example: solid modelers*
control source	**user: interactive application** • **asymmetric dialogue** - control events come from the user - Domain reports to the Dialogue component (e.g., semantic error) - Domain reports by rendering to the user *Example: graphic editor*	**Domain: conversational application** • **asymmetric dialogue** - control events come from the Domain - data flow from and to the user *Example: login process*	**user + Domain: dialogue application** • **symmetric dialogue** - control events come from both the user and Domain - data flow from and to both the user and Domain the user *Example: process control interface*
mono/multi user	**mono user** • The run time architecture corresponds to the Arch model		**multi user: Y model** • The designer shall decide which components are shared and which ones are not *Example: CSCW systems*
sequential/Real Time	**sequential** • no timer *Example: usual Business applications*		**Real Time** • A timer shall exist in the Dialogue Component *Example: multi-modal systems*

Table 1: Taxonomy of interactive graphic system

Conclusion

In this report we have proposed a taxonomy of interactive graphics systems that is based on seven orthogonal criteria. We have shown that each of these criteria has a significant impact on the suitable architecture of the system to be designed. The values of these criteria are known during the analysis phase of a system. Therefore, they may be used to evaluate the suitability of a particular prescriptive architecture model for a system under design.

In this report, we have not discussed the suitability of any existing prescriptive architecture model for the various categories defined by the taxonomy. Nevertheless, it is hoped that reference to this taxonomy will contribute to the emergence of new and more precise prescriptive architecture models for the different categories of interactive systems we have identified.

References

1. Bass, L., Coutaz, J.: Developing software for the user interface, Addison-Wesley (1991).

2. Carson, G.: Introduction to the Computer Graphics Reference Model, Computer Graphics, 27, 2, 108-118, (1993).

3. Coad, P., Yourdon, E.: Object Oriented Analysis, Prentice Hall (1991)

4. Coutaz, J.: Interface homme-machine : un regard critique. Journées d'étude AFCET: Interface Homme-Machine, Paris, 21 oct. 1992,1-24 (1992)

5. Coutaz, J.: PAC: an implementation Model for Dialog Design. Proc. Interact'87, North Holland Publ., 431-436 (1987).

6. Duke, D., Harrison, M.: Abstract Interaction Objects. Computer Graphics Forum, 12, 3, 25-36 (1993).

7. Faconti, G.: The Reference Model of Computer Graphics. in: D.A. Duce *et al.* (eds): User Interface Management Design. New York, Berlin Heidelberg New York Tokyo: Springer-Verlag 1990, 7-14 (1990).

8. Faconti, G., Paterno, F.: An Approach to the Formal Specification of the Components of an Interaction, EUROGRAPHICS'90, 481-494 (1990).

9. Foley, J., Wallace, V.L.: The Art of Natural Graphic Man-Machine Conversation. Proc. of IEEE G2, (1974).

10. ISO/IS 7942, Information Processing Systems, Computer Graphics, Graphical Kernel System - Functional Description (1985).

11. Goldberg, A.: Smalltalk-80: The Interactive Programming Environment, Addison-Wesley (1984).

12. Green, M.: Report on on Dialogue-Specification Tools. In: G.E Pfaff (eds.): User Interface Management Systems. New York, Berlin Heidelberg New York Tokyo: Springer-Verlag 1985, 9-20 (1985).

13. Green, M.: A survey of three dialogue models, ACM Trans Graph. 5, 3, 244-275 (1986).

14. Halbert, D.: Programming by example, PhD. Thesis, Berkeley, California (1984).

15. Nigay, L.: Conception et modélisation logicielle des systèmes interactifs : application aux interfaces multimodales, PhD. Thesis, Université Grenoble 1 (1994).

16. Norman, D.: User Centered System Design, Lawrence Erlbaum Associates (1986).

17 Paterno', F.: A Theory of User-Interaction Objects, Journal of visual languages and computing, 5, 3, 227-249, (1994).

18 ISO/IS 9592:1989, Information Processing Systems, Programmers Hierarchical Interactive Graphics System - Functional Descritpion (1989).

19. Pierra, G., Girard, P., Guittet, L.: Towards precise architecture models for computer graphics: The H^4 architecture, position paper, in: Pre-Proceeding of Eurographics Workshop on Design, Validation and Specification of Interactive System, Bonas, France, June (1995).

20. Ten Hagen, P.: Critique of the Seeheim Model. in: D.A. Duce *et al.* (eds): User Interface Management Design. New York, Berlin Heidelberg New York Tokyo: Springer-Verlag 1990, 3-6 (1990).

21. Ten Hagen, P., Derksen, J.: Parallel input and feedback in dialogue cells. In: G.E Pfaff (eds.): User Interface Management Systems. New York, Berlin Heidelberg New York Tokyo: Springer-Verlag 1985, 109-124 (1985).

22. The UIMS Developers Workshop - A Metamodel for the run time Architecture of An Interactive System; SIGCHI Bulletin, 24, 1, 32-37 (1992).

23. Woods, W.: Transition network grammars for natural langage analysis. Comm. ACM,13, 10, 591-606 (1970).

Martin Göbel (ed.)

Virtual Environments '95

Selected papers of the Eurographics Workshops
in Barcelona, Spain, 1993, and Monte Carlo, Monaco, 1995

1995. 134 partly coloured figures. VII, 307 pages. ISBN 3-211-82737-4
Soft cover DM 108,–, öS 756,–. (Eurographics)

The book contains 22 selected and revised papers that have been presented in EG workshops in Barcelona and Monte Carlo. The areas covered are visual presentation aspects, gesture and speech interaction issues, applications and VE system, demonstrating very clearly the emphasis and the results of various research activities in the field.

Demetri Terzopoulos, Daniel Thalmann (eds.)

Computer Animation and Simulation '95

Proceedings of the Eurographics Workshop
in Maastricht, The Netherlands, September 2–3, 1995

1995. 156 partly coloured figures. VIII, 235 pages. ISBN 3-211-82738-2
Soft cover DM 89,–, öS 625,–. (Eurographics)

The sixteen papers in this volume present novel animation techniques and animation systems that simulate the dynamics and interactions of physical objects (solid, fluid, and gaseous) as well as the behaviors of living systems such as plants, lower animals, and humans (growth and metamorphosis, motion control, locomotion, etc.). The book vividly demonstrates the confluence of animation and simulation, a leading edge of computer graphics research that is providing animators with sophisticated new algorithms for synthesizing dynamic scenes.

Prices are subject to change without notice

Springer-Verlag Wien New York

Sachsenplatz 4–6, P.O.Box 89, A-1201 Wien · 175 Fifth Avenue, New York, NY 10010, USA
Heidelberger Platz 3, D-14197 Berlin · 3-13, Hongo 3-chome, Bunkyo-ku, Tokyo 113, Japan

Riccardo Scateni, Jarke J. van Wijk, Pietro Zanarini (eds.)

Visualization in Scientific Computing '95

Proceedings of the Eurographics Workshop
in Chia, Italy, May 3–5, 1995

1995. 110 partly coloured figures. VII, 161 pages. ISBN 3-211-82729-3
Soft cover DM 85,–, öS 595,–. (Eurographics)

13 contributions cover a wide range of topics, ranging from detailed algorithmic
studies to searches for new metaphors. The reader will find state-of-the-art results and
techniques in this discipline, which he can use to find solutions for his visualization
problems.

Patrick M. Hanrahan, Werner Purgathofer (eds.)

Rendering Techniques '95

Proceedings of the Eurographics Workshop
in Dublin, Ireland, June 12–14, 1995

1995. 198 partly coloured figures. XI, 372 pages. ISBN 3-211-82733-1
Soft cover DM 118,–, öS 826,–. (Eurographics)

31 contributions give an overview on hierarchical radiosity, Monte Carlo radiosity,
wavelet radiosity, nondiffuse radiosity, radiosity performance improvements, ray
tracing, reconstruction techniques, volume rendering, illumination, use interface
aspects, and importance sampling. Also included are two invited papers by James Arvo
and Alain Fournier.

Prices are subject to change without notice

Springer-Verlag Wien New York

Sachsenplatz 4–6, P.O.Box 89, A-1201 Wien · 175 Fifth Avenue, New York, NY 10010, USA
Heidelberger Platz 3, D-14197 Berlin · 3-13, Hongo 3-chome, Bunkyo-ku, Tokyo 113, Japan

Martin Göbel, Heinrich Müller, Bodo Urban (eds.)

Visualization in Scientific Computing

1995. 150 figures. VIII, 238 pages. ISBN 3-211-82633-5
Soft cover DM 118,–, öS 826,–. (Eurographics)

Visualization is the most important approach to understand the huge amount of data produced in today's computational and experimental sciences. Selected contributions treat topics of particular interest in current research, for example visualization of multidimensional data and flows, time control, interaction, and volume visualization. Readers may profit in getting insight in state-of-the-art techniques which might help to solve their visualization problems.

Wolfgang Herzner, Frank Kappe (eds.)

Multimedia/Hypermedia
in Open Distributed Environments

Proceedings of the Eurographics Symposium
in Graz, Austria, June 6–9, 1994

1994. 105 figures. VIII, 330 pages. ISBN 3-211-82587-8
Soft cover DM 118,–, öS 826,–. (Eurographics)

This book represents the results from the Eurographics symposium on "Multimedia/Hypermedia in Open Distributed Environments", June 6–9, 1994, Graz, Austria. Its six sessions "Standards and Standards Exploitation", "Demonstrations" "Tools", "Hypermedia and Authoring", "Architectures", and "CSCW and Information Services" give a comprehensive overview about current research arvo development, including the future mm/hm standards MHEG and PREMO. This reader will profit in getting up-to-date information about the current trends in (the development of) mm/hm services and applications in open, distributed environme ray

Prices are subject to change without notice

Springer-Verlag Wien New York

Sachsenplatz 4–6, P.O.Box 89, A-1201 Wien · 175 Fifth Avenue, New York, NY 10010, USA
Heidelberger Platz 3, D-14197 Berlin · 3-13, Hongo 3-chome, Bunkyo-ku, Tokyo 113, Japan

Springer-Verlag
and the Environment